ADOPTION, MEMORY, AND COLD WAR GREECE

ADOPTION, MEMORY, AND COLD WAR GREECE

Kid pro quo?

Gonda Van Steen

University of Michigan Press
Ann Arbor

Published in the United States of America by the University of Michigan Press

Manufactured in the United States of America

Printed on acid-free paper

First published December 2019

A CIP catalog record for this book is available from the British Library.

ISBN 978-0-472-13158-7 (hardcover : alk. paper)
ISBN 978-0-472-12606-4 (ebook)

A book for the abandoned . . .
with every admiration for what they have made of themselves

CONTENTS

Digital materials related to this title can be found on the Fulcrum platform via the following citable URL https://doi.org/10.3998/mpub.11333937

AUTHOR'S NOTE

All translations from the original modern Greek and Dutch sources are mine, unless otherwise noted. The transliteration of Greek names is a vexed problem. In practice, it generates doublet forms depending on personal and publishers' preferences, hence Argiriadis and Argyriadis (Argi/yriadi[s] or Argi/yriadou for women), Beloy(i)annis and Belogiannis, etc. Doublets such as Dalla and Dala, Frederica and Frederika, Vassilis and Vasilis, and Metera and Mitera are common as well. Also, the official forms of Greek first names, used in formal writing such as on birth and death certificates, alternate with their informal versions, hence E/Aikaterina and Katerina referring to the same person.

I thank the members of the Argyriadis family who let me listen in on their story and trace published interviews they gave to the *Eleftherotypia* newspaper in 1980. With their help, I could also piece together anew the snippets of information that they have allowed to enter into the public record and into the Wikipedia entry on Elias Argyriadis (in Greek, based on the contributions and corrections made by various authors). I have meticulously scrutinized the writing and revision history of this Wikipedia entry, and I conclude that it does not contain any details that the Argyriadis family members have not already made public. I myself, however, have thus far refrained from contributing to this online record. For reasons of confidentiality, the adoption dossier of the Argyriadis girls is still closed, but plenty of information has been published via newspaper reports and interviews, which I have used judiciously. I have remained mindful of my responsibility to the family as I have written (and illustrated) this book, and I have therefore resorted to pseudonyms and a few fictitious details to cover the American side of the story. I have changed the names of many more adoptees, adoptive parents, and intermediaries, to protect my informants' anonymity, unless the adoptees or adoptive parents themselves have already published their personal information (De Boer, Dionou, Giangardella, Heckinger, Johnson, Kelmis, Moessinger, Rijnsdorp, Touwen, van Dongen, van Haren). I have also adhered to any other restrictions that my informants have set, but I appreciate that they have allowed me to keep the complete interviews in my personal archive. I have further secured key informants' formal consent as required by US federal regulations on the protection of human subjects in research. The stories of my informants, however, are all true. I have read and listened to them with both respect and humility, all the more so since I myself do not (technically) hold a place in the famous "adoption triad" of birth parent, adopted child, and prospective parent.

I have conducted this research and writing project with a diverse readership in mind, including those who feel that my subject matter strikes (too) close to home. Therefore, I have not disguised the speaker's "I" or some of the toolmarks of this study's research and writing process. I have made all reasonable efforts to contact the copyright holders of this book's cover photograph and of two more figures, but to no avail. Any omissions will be rectified in future printings if notice is given to the publisher or to me. I see this project as a work in progress, to which I may have to add subsequent notes. I remain open to revising in light of other Greek adoption narratives and experiences, about which I am eager to learn from readers who are willing to grant interviews or share archival materials.

FOREWORD

John O. Iatrides

Under the best of circumstances, the adoption of an orphaned, abandoned, or unwanted child can be the purest form of philanthropy: the outpouring of selfless love for a fellow human being. Rather than the prospect of years in dreary institutions and an uncertain future, the homeless youngster is provided with a secure, caring, and reasonably affluent environment in which to grow into adulthood and a productive life. For their part, the adopting adults are rewarded with the opportunity to embrace a stranger's offspring and guide the child as their own toward self-discovery and fulfillment. But adoptions rarely occur under ideal circumstances. As Gonda Van Steen demonstrates in this remarkably revealing study, adoptions can be the cause of lifelong suffering for all involved, but especially for the children who are helpless to shape their future. In real life, the handling of adoptions and their ultimate outcomes are determined by countless and often chaotic factors. They include a country's politics, resources, culture, traditions and laws, its religious practices and social prejudices, and, lastly, the competence, priorities, and ethical standards of those in a position to decide what is to be done in each adoption case.

The focus of Van Steen's investigation is narrow and well defined; her sources include an impressive variety of published and archival materials, legal records, and numerous interviews and recollections. She has chosen to explore the historical setting and the sociopolitical, legal, bureaucratic, and cultural framework that determined the selection of Greek children for adoption by foreigners, among them many Greek American couples, in the aftermath of World War II and the communist insurgency of 1946–49. Official Greek and United Nations estimates reveal the country's devastation and deaths caused by the war and enemy occupation: between 340,000 and 375,000 children lost one or both parents. Thus, one of every eight Greek children was orphaned. The Civil War, in which a total of approximately 46,200 adults were killed, added considerably to the number of children orphaned or abandoned.

According to official records, during the years 1950–62 some 3200 children were adopted by American families. This is the period in which, driven by the dynamics of the emerging Cold War, American intervention in Greece became profound and pervasive, resulting in a so-called patron-client relationship. Adoption policies in the two countries were a natural by-product of that asymmetric relationship in which, beyond providing massive economic and military assistance, American officials burnished the image of Washington's generosity and compassion by endorsing the much-publicized "saving" of homeless children. Among civilian initiatives, the American Hellenic Educational Progressive Association (AHEPA) played an important if not unblemished role. For the Greek authorities, the "export" of orphans and unwanted children to foreign countries, especially America, helped cement bilateral cultural ties and offered significant relief for the country's crippled economy and totally inadequate welfare services and humanitarian institutions. Assisting the government's agencies were church parishes, civic organizations, and various enterprising agents, for whom fees and other payments collected from adopting foreigners provided opportunities to exploit the system for personal gain. Queen Frederica's Royal Welfare Fund focused much of its attention on children of families stigmatized as leftist and exerted powerful if indirect influence over adoption issues.

During 1950–62, fear of communism, domestic and international, manifested itself in every aspect of Greek politics and civil society. Inflamed by a sharp ideological divide and the brutality of civil conflict, it led state authorities and armed paramilitary bands to persecute not only known communists but their sympathizers, real or suspected. Among the victims of virulent anticommunism were children whose families were suspected of having supported the insurgents. Most were from rural areas where, in the absence of adequate government protection, villagers had little choice but to submit to the dictates of armed leftist gangs. After the defeat of the insurgency, conservative governments treated such villagers as "anti-national" and discriminated against them in countless ways.

The pursuit of prominent members of the outlawed communist party (KKE) was particularly intense in urban centers where the KKE continued to maintain an active underground network. An important thread running through Van Steen's captivating narrative—and the principal impetus behind her research project—is the case of Elias Argyriadis, a forty-four-year-old communist in whose home outside Athens the authorities discovered in November 1951 hidden wireless transmitters with which the KKE communicated with authorities in Bulgaria and Romania. He and three others were found guilty of espionage by a military tribunal, sentenced to death, and executed. Katerina Dalla, the mother of two of his three teen-age daughters, committed suicide. The couple's tragic deaths condemned the entire family to endless persecution, blatant injustice, and despair. The authorities took custody of the two younger girls and arbitrarily arranged for their adoption by an American family without the possibility of contact with their siblings and their relatives in Greece. In 2013, the adult son of one of the two adopted women, who grew up in America knowing nothing about his mother's roots, persuaded her to tell him the little she could—or wished to—remember about her past. After an internet search led him to discover Van Steen's scholarly pursuits and special interests, he solicited her help in investigating his mother's early years. Van Steen's willing response, and her ever-expanding research efforts over several years, are meticulously chronicled in this outstanding book.

The study of adoption practices in Greece is a complicated, tedious, and sensitive task. In addition to assuming fluency in the formalistic (*katharevousa*) and vernacular (*dimotiki*) variants of the Greek language, it involves the utilization of social science theory, memory studies, and meticulous methodology. It presupposes a sound understanding of contemporary Greece and especially of the poisonous impact of the Civil War on every aspect of society; it also requires a good grasp of the depth of American "penetration" of postwar Greece. And while displaying a social worker's professional skills and compassion in dealing with traumatized children and despairing adults, the researcher must seek to maintain scholarly objectivity and detachment. *Adoption, Memory, and Cold War Greece: Kid pro quo?* leaves no doubt that Van Steen has met all such attributes and was uniquely qualified to carry out this complex and sensitive project. A classical scholar and linguist, she holds the prestigious Koraes Chair of Modern Greek and Byzantine History, Language and Literature, and is Director of the Centre for Hellenic Studies, King's College London.

Van Steen has examined all categories of Greek children, including orphans, abandoned and "illegitimate," selected for foreign adoption during 1950–62. In doing so, she has opened a revealing window into the politics, culture, and social practices that predominated in postwar Greece. She portrays a highly centralized and clientelist state driven by fierce anti-communism and lacking the resources and capabilities to provide adequate relief and a rudimentary safety net for the destitute among its people. She concludes that for many officials and private agencies, foreign adoptions were not only desirable but necessary. This was particularly true in cases of children whose families were stigmatized as "anti-national." The bulk of Van Steen's research and resulting narrative deals with her interactions with

adoptees—including the very young—and with multigenerational families on issues that are highly personal, emotional, and tragic. Few readers
familiar with the period will fail to agree with the author's assertion that in
the violence, dislocation, and misery that engulfed Greece in the 1940s and
1950s, the heaviest burden of suffering fell on women and children. Aware of
the continuing controversy on the causes and consequences of the turmoil,
Van Steen leaves no doubt about where she stands: "It is extremely hard for
any student of the Greek events to come to an objective reading of the Civil
War, in which no party remained innocent and no family remained unaffected. If I need to, or if I am seen to, take sides with the Left or the Right, I
side with the children who were too young to know what side they were on."

Having explored one of the darkest periods in Greek history, the author
contributes to the nation's collective memory valuable insights into the
impact of the Civil War upon its most innocent victims. Combining meticulous scholarship with empathy, this seminal study of the selection of children for foreign adoption during the 1950s and 1960s has earned Gonda Van
Steen the lasting gratitude of all students of contemporary Greece.

PREFACE

"Is this a career change?" my colleague asks. "No," I state firmly. "Each new research project has taken me on a new journey to and through Greece, but this journey may well be the most interesting and adventurous one. I am in it for life." This is not a book that I, as a nonadopted academic, ever expected to write, not after twenty-five years of applying myself to ancient Greek theater and reception studies. Dare I say that the topic of the Cold War Greek adoptions found me? I knew nothing about the hundreds of Greek children who left their home country as orphans and adoptees from the 1950s through the mid-1960s, until, one day in 2013, a total stranger sent me an email. Mike is the young man's name, and he was looking for a scholar of modern Greece who would be willing to answer a few questions. Mike prefers that I not use his last name, but he was in his late twenties and he himself did not read any Greek. He is the son of a woman who was adopted from Greece but who had no answers to share. So Mike googled "Modern Greek Studies" and my name popped up. I could have ignored his initial question, but it just grabbed me:

> Dear Dr. Van Steen,
>
> My mother was born in the mountainous terrain of Northern Greece, and she and her younger sister came to the States in 1955, as orphans adopted by a Greek American family. My mother recently revealed to me that her father was Elias Argiriadis, who was captured and executed by the [Greek] government for being a communist. I know almost nothing about this man except for my mother's hesitant testimony. . . .
>
> Mike

Full of confidence, I started answering Mike's emails. I even boldly promised that I would find some sources written in English that he could consult to try to solve the family puzzle. That turned out to be an overconfident promise. I discovered only hyped newspaper reports and online posts on the subject of the "missing" Greek adoptees who had been dispatched "illegally" to the United States in the postwar era. I looked and looked but could not find a single rigorous analysis, let alone a comprehensive study. My interest now piqued, I decided to write a short article on the subject, using Mike's lost family history as a catalyst. That short article never materialized. Instead, the project morphed into the book that you are holding. I had so many questions that I needed to answer for myself and for the Greek adoptees (and I make every attempt to do so in this volume): How come those two siblings left Greece to be adopted? Was this a double adoption facilitated by the Greek state or by the Greek American parents? What happened to the rest of the sisters' family? What about their parents? Did one have to be of Greek descent to adopt Greek children and bring them over to the United States? Was it easy to do? Were the children of Greek communist parents more likely to be placed on the international adoption track? What did communism entail in post–Civil War, "pacified" Greece? Were these adoptions rooted in the Greek Civil War (nominally 1946–1949), or were they more closely impacted by the Cold War climate? Did Greek and Cold War anticommunism "expedite" the political adoptions? What part did social mores and economic hardships play? I had my work cut out for me. This book, then, offers up as much analysis and documentation as I can provide at this time. It does so in a format that reconstructs the quest for knowledge, which is, after all, the common drive among "my adoptees," my readers, and myself, as I keep looking into the many Greek adoptions and keep making new discoveries. Significantly, Greece's history intertwines here with American history, and the personal stories merge into the bigger picture of more than 3,000 postwar adoptions of Greek children by American parents.

Thus the project has long transcended Mike's inquiries and has gained relevance for adoptees and interlocutors of various backgrounds. It has become the social history and critique of a formerly unexplored phenomenon, a mass phenomenon that caught me by surprise, as it will the readers and even adoption-studies specialists. Along the way, I sought to interview more Greek adoptees and/or their children. Word-of-mouth and Facebook served as my initial channels for connecting with Greek adoptees. Over time, bonds of goodwill and trust were forged that deepened my contacts with many more adoptees. These relationships eventually led to other adoptees seeking me out for assistance with their specific queries. Generally speaking, I could not and cannot lead them to their birth families, but I have been able to answer many of their most urgent questions about Greek postwar adoption practice, how it operated, who facilitated it, who kept records, and where these records can be found. I claim no extraordinary expertise, only quiet commitment. It is a commitment inspired by the devotion that the Greek adoptees themselves have brought to their lifelong endeavor to complete their stories. It is a persistent quest that I hope to continue to support. Occasionally, the journey does lead to unexpected destinations. No, I will not become a professional search expert, and I do not anticipate a career change. But let me still share with you the joy captured in the following true story:

"Now that you have found my daughter, I can die in peace," the eighty-year-old mother says in Greek. "No," I respond, "*na sas zisei*," "may she live for you," "may you have many more years together." "I had given up hope that I'd ever see her again," the mother whispers, "I never even had a picture of her. I can hardly believe anyone would care enough to bring us together after fifty-nine long years." "I care," I affirm, but I do not say much more. Emotions are catching up with me as well. "Now how exactly is your current research relevant?" colleagues and friends ask me in the subtlest way possible. "It's pretty specialized," I admit, "but I did reconnect a biological mother with her adult daughter, who was taken from her as a forty-day-old child some fifty-nine years ago." "Oh," they respond, "now that's the kind of stuff that changes lives." Linda knew she was Greek-born, but she grew up in Texas without any exposure to things Greek. She approached me in March of 2017. I promised that I would help her retrieve some documents from the Greek institution that had hosted her as a baby for a few months. "Don't expect to receive more than half a page from the orphanage's logbook," I warned. "At best you'll learn about your condition when you were first entered into the institution as a baby of unknown origins." Six weeks later, no less than eight pages arrived in the mail at Linda's home address. Linda got in touch immediately. "Help! All this stuff is in Greek! What am I supposed to make of this?" "I'll help out," I promised. Easier said than done. The documents revealed the name of a biological mother, but the name appeared in three different spellings. They also disclosed the name of a remote mountain village on mainland Greece, but its name appeared in four different versions. I wracked my brain. My lifelong study of ancient Greek and historical linguistics should be good for something! I finally decided on one name for each, the mother and the village, and made a good guess that relatives might still be living in the same region. After that, the discovery process unfolded over a mere three days. The biological mother still lived on the outskirts of the village where she had given birth to her only child, a child born "out of wedlock" and therefore undesired by any of her older relatives. The family patriarch left instructions (and a small bribe) for the child's judgmental god-mother: "Get rid of it!" The godmother abducted the baby and delivered it to an orphanage in Athens. She also declared that the mother had abandoned her child and would probably do so again if she were obliged to take the baby back. A few months later, Linda was adopted by a childless, loving Texas couple, who were—conveniently—told that the baby's mother had died in childbirth. Fifty-nine years passed. Linda saw the documents but did not judge, she only kept hoping. I just helped out. How can one possibly remain a distant researcher when given the opportunity to touch lives?

INTRODUCTION

Quests, Questions, and Answers

Email message of 28 August 2013, from an unknown sender:

Dear Dr. Van Steen,

My mother was born in the mountainous terrain of Northern Greece, and she and her younger sister came to the States in 1955, as orphans adopted by a Greek American family. My mother recently revealed to me that her father was Elias Argiriadis, who was captured and executed by the [Greek] government for being a communist. I know almost nothing about this man except for my mother's hesitant testimony . . . .

   Mike X.

28 August 2013
Dear Mike,

Thank you for contacting me. I am intrigued by your story, which opens up a black page from Greece's mid-twentieth-century history. I'd love to learn more and may be able to answer a few of your most urgent questions. The context to your mother's adoption will be key here. . . . Please do ask your mother if her father left a diary, letters, etc.

   Gonda

29 August 2013
Gonda,

Regretfully, retrieving information from my mother about her father or Greece in general is difficult. She was severely traumatized from her early childhood. After the execution of her father, my mother also witnessed the suicide of her mother.

   Mike

When War Strikes Home

The challenge of accounting for the disparate strands of the sociohistory of the Greek Civil War (nominally 1946–1949) looms large. The history of the mass adoptions of Greek children by couples in the United States extends the painful war's aftermath well into the 1950s and through the early 1960s. Early instances of these postwar and Cold War adoptions may be called "political" adoptions, and they are exemplified by the infamous case alluded to above. After approximately 1955, however, a new and larger wave of US-bound adoptions from Greece acquired different characteristics. The post-1955 adoptions were far more grounded in social and economic restrictions, and many of their subjects were "illegitimate" children or the offspring of severely distressed families. This book weaves the little-known but extensive Greek adoption movement into the broader narrative of Cold War political and social history. It also links US-bound adoptions to Greece's postwar reconstruction and to its varying levels of civic participation during the early Cold War. This study further attempts to let many voices speak to the contested phenomenon of Greece's adoption circuit, whether by way of an extended, cross-generational case study, or through the multivocality of adoption stories, testimonies, and quotations. Meanwhile, it answers the important questions of how and how many. How did these adoptions from Greece happen? How many adoptees are we talking about?

First, World War II (1940–1944) brought to Greece deadly famine, political violence, and widespread devastation under three different Axis occupation forces, the Nazi Germans, the Italians, and the Bulgarians. Greece joined the Allied cause early on, engaging in active resistance, but it paid a high price for its sacrifice (at the very least) through the end of the decade, when the external and defensive war turned into an aggressive civil war. For one, the British helped to re-install the Greek royal house in September 1946, against the will of large segments of the Greek population. The Greek monarchs had fled the country during World War II, and a rehabilitated royal dynasty was as insecure as it was unwelcome. The Greek Civil War exacerbated long-festering ideological rifts and inflicted its own deprivations and massacres. A full decade of dislocation and human suffering saw entire Greek villages and families uprooted, if not fiercely divided. The Greek communist-led resistance of World War II, especially, had been insisting on social and political reform. But its rise to popular power and its openness to Soviet communism alienated the conservative establishment, which also feared that the Greek communist leaders would be willing to sacrifice Greek Macedonia to Slav and Soviet expansionist designs.

Even though the destructive turmoil nominally ended in the late summer of 1949, the Greek Left and the Right never genuinely reconciled in the standoff over reform and plain political power, which marred subsequent decades. The broader ideological spectrum of complex mid-twentieth-century Greek politics included, among others, inveterate communists, mere leftist sympathizers, socialists, centrists, liberal republicans, right-wing conservatives, Greek palace supporters and reactionary monarchists, and staunch believers in the power of the military. The Right, the royalists, and the military tended to be pro-American and had, in turn, most to gain from US backing and aid. With many groups in the middle of the spectrum, they joined in an uneasy nationalist and anticommunist coalition during the Civil War and the Cold War years. It took at least through the mid-1970s (and the collapse of the reactionary Greek military dictatorship of 1967–1974) for genuine political and social reform to catch up with the global cultural transformation.

The war decade left the Greek communist resistance fighters tainted, through the 1970s, with the stigma of betrayal, no matter what their involvement had been. It also left the Greek Right tainted into the twenty-first century with the stigma of brutal and random oppression. The wars' public memory, let alone its imprint on history-writing or school instruction, has been at the center of much debate, which is still-ongoing.[1] The controversies tend to be politically and ideologically charged, but the public memory and testimony that feed into social history may well be more important.

---

1.   Many aspects of the Greek Civil War and of the Cold War in Greece remain disputed, and the debates are likely to continue. Koulouris (2000) has compiled the bibliographical record on the Greek Civil War up through 1999, which includes accessible collective volumes in English such as Iatrides and Wrigley (1995). He notes the absence of leftist written testimonies (2000: 72), which has been partly remedied since. From 2000 on, scholarly debate about the Greek Civil War has flourished to the point of perhaps detracting from other domains of history(-writing). Recent studies in English on the Greek Civil War and its aftermath include Carabott and Sfikas (2004); Gerolymatos (2004 and 2016); Hatzivassiliou (2006, with focus on the Cold War); Kalyvas (2006: 246–329, on the Argolid); Mazower (2000); Panourgia (2009: 81–116, or her ch. 5); and Voglis (2002). Also noteworthy is Kalyvas's "firebrand" chapter of 2000, titled "Red Terror: Leftist Violence during the Occupation," which generated vocal Greek reactions as well. Important sources in Greek include Gardika et al. (2015); Kalyvas and Marantzidis (2015); Lymberatos (2015); Marantzidis (2010); Margaritis (2000–2001); Sfikas (2007); and Van Boeschoten et al. (2008). Sfikas and Mahera (2011) offer an example of the ongoing sharp critique of the "new wave" represented by Kalyvas and Marantzidis. Paschaloudi (2010) discusses the shaping of the Greek collective memory and political speech of the 1950s through mid-1960s. A new addition to the scholarly study of the Civil War as a historical episode and movement is Voglis's book of 2014, characterizing the war as a "weak revolution." The topic of Cold War Greece is nearly completely absent from Immerman and Goedde (2013).

The war decade of the 1940s cast a long shadow over Greece's social and communal structures. Under the dire circumstances of both wars, mothers and children were the worst-afflicted victims. The late 1940s "pro"-children's evacuation campaigns enacted by the Greek communists, on the one hand, and by the Greek Queen Frederica, on the other, have now been insightfully studied.[2] In contrast, the mass movement of orphans and adoptees sent to the capitalist West by the Greek Right of the postwar and Cold War years has remained unexplored. This book, informed by archival research and inspired by the testimonies of many US-based but Greek-born adoptees who recall 1950s childhood experiences, is a first attempt to remedy this lacuna, to provide the human missing link.

Before the Civil War, the total number of Greek war orphans (who had lost one or both parents) was estimated to be 340,000 to 375,000.[3] The outbreak of the war caused the number to rise again (but it was offset by the many children who aged out of the "child" category). By 1950, one of every eight Greek children was orphaned, for a total of 339,913 orphans, according to statistics provided by the Greek Ministry of Social Welfare. The count of children who had lost a father was nearly three times as high as the number who had lost a mother. Some 36,000 children had lost both parents.[4] Anne Wood-Ritsatakis cites the number of 7,632,801 for the Greek population of 1951, according to the census of the time. About one-fifth of the Greek population lived in "Greater Athens" in 1951, but, a decade later, that proportion had risen to about one-fourth.[5] The Greek population total of 1940 was 7,462,064, of whom 37.5 percent, or 2,800,000, were children.[6] The small difference between the population counts of 1951 and 1940 strikes home the devastating impact of the war decade. During wartime, Greek widows and families, themselves reconfigured in many forms, struggled under untold hardships, which, along with draining waves of (internal and external) migration, lasted through the late 1950s.

This study is, however, less about the historical facts of 1950s Greece than about what these forgotten data have come to mean in the lives of indi-

---

2.   See below, pp. 49–51.
3.   Anon., *The Ahepan* (Sept.-Oct. 1946, 15–16), referring to surveys carried out by the Greek government and also by UNRRA, the United Nations Relief and Rehabilitation Administration. See Kliafa (2016: 70); Vervenioti (2009: 84); and also Margaret Thompson (1947: 19, 20), speaking as field director for the Greek War Relief Association.
4.   The official numbers are quoted in several news reports, as in Anon., *I Thessalia*, 11 January 1950, and also by Parmenas (1949: 402, 405).
5.   Wood-Ritsatakis (1970: 193, her table A.2).
6.   Anon., *I Thessalia*, 11 January 1950, citing statistics provided by the Greek Ministry of Social Welfare.

viduals both closer to and far removed from those events. My objective has been to enrich a field of historical inquiry, that of the controversial Greek Civil War and its transformation into the Cold War, with the "lived" experience of that transformation in later decades and in new geographical and ideological locales. Our notion of "deep Civil War" must capture precisely this temporal, spatial, and psychological extension of the Greek Civil War beyond the actual victims, the first generation of child victims, and into the second generation of survivors, or "postsurvivors" (to use a term established in Holocaust studies). The deep Greek Civil War, like most civil wars, did not begin with the armed struggle, and it did not end with a decisive victory-versus-defeat scenario. The Civil War's depth reached far into the future, to affect how subsequent generations have interpreted it, ignored it, used it, exploited it, and so on. Thus, our concept of the deep Civil War centers on the more subjective poses by which the present has read and construed the troubled past, acknowledging, too, that these (re)constructions are constantly intruded on by modern exigencies.

The horrific conditions of war in Greece throughout the 1940s led to autocratic governmental structures. With the Greek Right and the monarchy in charge through most of the postwar years, even the few existing humanitarian organizations and philanthropic institutions became highly centralized and, by sheer necessity, unimaginative in their search for practical and inexpensive solutions. Mass overseas adoptions of Greek-born children became not only possible but, according to many, necessary and even inevitable. By the onset of the 1950s, many more children were deemed or made "adoptable" than would have been the case under normal circumstances. The leap from uncontested domestic to (often) unchecked US-bound adoptions was not a big one, especially when it coincided with a growing interest among American parents to adopt foreign children and with the appropriate US legislation to make the first mass intercountry adoptions feasible.[7] Thus, Greece's predicament of the post–Civil War years, as well as Greek-American relations and Cold War dependencies, started to exert a greater impact than the facts and fictions of the 1940s.[8] Admittedly, the end of the

---

7. "Intercountry adoption" was the term primarily used in the 1950s for international or transnational adoption. My use of the term "American" in this book is confined to people in the United States. Similarly, I employ "America" and "the States" as informal synonyms for the United States. The Greek word for adoption is υιοθεσία (*yiothesía*), with the first part of the compound referring to the placement of a *son* in a new family. The word has been used in a gender-neutral sense, and the placement of girls has actually been slightly more common in postwar Greek adoption practice. Nonetheless, a better term would be τεκνοθεσία (*teknothesía*), "child placement."

8. I am indebted to Alexander Kazamias, who kindly shared a full copy of his unpublished

Civil War did not finally resolve the problems and conflicts that had dominated the war decade: successive Greek administrations remained inexperienced in welfare work and continued to face the absence of resources. An effective safety net, capable of providing basic and fair assistance to the socially stigmatized and the defenseless (unwed mothers and "illegitimate" children), did not come about until—arguably—the mid-1960s or mid-1970s. With this painfully slow move toward betterment, my narrative and analysis follow the progression from the early politically driven adoptions to the socially motivated adoptions and the Cold War placements of the later 1950s through early 1960s, with the development of "push factors" being surpassed by "pull factors" (in adoption parlance).

Even the case of the political adoptions associated with the 1952 execution of communist "spies" (among them Nikos Beloyannis and Elias Argyriadis) is less about endings than it is about twilight zones and eventual new beginnings. It is less about the aftermath of the Greek Civil War than it is about the onset of the global Cold War. It is also less about lost parents than it is about their children's future through adoption, whose consequences extended into the next generation. How did the adoptions of the young daughters of Elias Argyriadis mesh with the political circumstances of the early 1950s? How did they affect the adoptees themselves and the family members left behind in Greece? My opening study of this prominent case also answers the legitimate question, "Why should anyone care about overseas adoptions that happened more than half a century ago?" But let me first deliver a few answers to Mike and also further historical details, to help the reader unfamiliar with postwar Greece contextualize the story.

The 1952 execution of the communist figurehead Nikos Beloyannis has marked and marred twentieth-century Greek history as a sad reminder of the divide between the communist-dominated Left and a powerful, royalist, and pro-US Right, which was symptomatic of the global Cold War crisis. What is less often remembered, however, is that the three comrades put to death along with Beloyannis also had lives, families, and children. Moreover, some of these children ended up bearing the full weight of the political conflict in which their parents had become embroiled. The story of the Argyriadis siblings, at once a Greek and an American tale, highlights some of the injustices resulting from the US's campaign to save Greece from communism in the 1950s. The younger Argyriadis sisters were dispatched as

---

book manuscript with me. He has pointed to the pitfalls of what he calls the "neo-Marxist/ *Marxisant* dependence narrative" in its antithetical relationship to the Greek ethnocentric or nationalist narrative (Kazamias, unpublished ms.: 11).

adoptees to small-town New England, where they started a (virtually) new life. For an older sister left behind in Greece, decades of harassment and limbo ensued. Their story strikes home the political meanings of the kind of family separations that were repeated frequently in the adoptions, many of them questionable or coerced, of Greek-born children to prospective parents abroad, most often to American couples. Therefore, the frequent dissolution of mother-child bonds or of more extensive birth-family ties, whether for political or for socioeconomic reasons, challenges the very notion of the reconstruction and democratization of postwar Greece under the auspices of the United States. Power imbalances most intimately played out in the America-bound adoptions of children from Greece.

Greece was one of the countries in which the superpowers of the Cold War, the United States and the Soviet Union, waged their "minor" proxy battles. Of course, there was nothing "cold" or "minor" about these battles for the victims, and especially for the children caught in the crossfire. These battles, including the Greek Civil War if it is seen as one of the Cold War's first episodes, operated on levels both formal and familial, but the familial one tends to be downplayed or overlooked. Against this backdrop, the "identity crisis," which is typically feared as a danger to which adopted children and dispersed families might be prone, mirrored Greece's own identity crisis. Through the discourse on Greek child welfare and intercountry adoption, identity questions surface that scrutinize both the adoptees' place of origin and their place of adoption; they force the question of Greece's own postwar identity, and they posit this identity as a process of discovery and disquietude.

Seldom are we reminded of the personal toll that political phobias and conspiracy plots take. The post–World War II Greek communist movement fell victim to perhaps the fiercest anticommunist campaign that the Cold War era saw. Yet the state-driven anticommunist scare was not the only site of plot and paranoia, given that the Greek Communist Party, too, tore itself apart through suspicion and mistrust within its ranks. The immediate fallout of such experiences was very traumatic to children, whose identities, like their parents', were unduly politicized. Moreover, these children of the deep Civil War, today's older adults, have unwittingly bestowed a legacy of memories on their descendants, a second generation of collateral victims whose existence is not easily freed from the so-called postmemory of the old political past. It is extremely hard for any student of the Greek events to come to an objective reading of the Civil War, in which no party remained innocent and no family remained unaffected. If I need to, or if I am seen to, take sides with the Left or the Right, I side with the children who were too young to know what side they were on.

Some themes and arguments in this book take priority over others that fulfill a more explanatory or auxiliary role. I aim to present the important story of the postwar Greek transnational adoption movement, but this story breaks down into stories and histories of Greek adoptions, each with its own thematic, temporal, and spatial complexities. Thus, this book situates the Greek adoption network in the context of the country's postwar politics and its domestic child welfare infrastructure. Conversely, this study delves into the postwar political and immigration history of the United States, shedding light on its child and orphan care. This book also draws on broader Cold War history and politics to connect not only ideologies but specific agendas and programs to the real lives lived by children and adults both in Greece and in the States. Direct exchanges with all possible parties of the Greek adoptee community have been important to me. This approach has encouraged me to probe well beyond the conventional framework of a Greek ethnography. I have aspired to make frank dialogue part not only of the fieldwork underpinning this book, but of its very composition. Therefore, the extensive human-interest story of part 1 must set up this (ongoing) study as an "interactive" conduit that takes the adoptee relative, the reader, and the researcher on a "source trip" to the roots of family, knowledge, history, and politics.

Part 1 of this book engages with the topics of adoption, trauma, and memory and, from a theoretical angle, speaks to issues raised by family disruption and postmemory. In particular, it aims to show how personal testimonies from memory may fruitfully be read, analyzed, and integrated into Greek history-writing. From a more practical historical perspective, part 1 transposes the aftermath of the Greek Civil War to the ground of the United States: it adds an unexpected American hook to a political adoption story, rooted in and characteristic of the fraught transition from Greece's reconstruction period to its age of development. It also contributes new, critical perspectives on different kinds of "genealogy," in addition to the obvious genealogy of the adoptees searching for their genetic ancestry: the genealogy of digging in the archives and uncovering the power relations of knowledge production (in the sense ascribed by Foucault); and the genealogy, or the lineage, of the panopticon-style institutions and top-down institutional care of postwar Greece. More specifically, it answers to the question of how Greek childcare could become so pervaded by the multiple and interrelated actions of a "mother" queen. Also, while the discourses on both the Greek Civil War and the Cold War have been thoroughly masculinized, this pairing of subjective story with objective analysis may bolster an emerging trend to finally devote more attention to women and children in times of conflict.

Children's testimonies show the ways in which individual memories affect narration, research, and art. This is a story, then, about the children first, which, nonetheless, writes the personal into the national and the national into the global.

Part 2 of this book broadens the case study of the postwar political adoptions to present a Greek-American adoption history, even more firmly set against the backdrop of the Cold War. It studies the deeper biopolitics of adoption from Greece to the United States in the 1950s and 1960s, and it thus counters the presentist notions in which Greek and wider public debates about adoption have been couched. My informants have been Americans, Greek Americans, and Jewish (Greek) Americans, who were adopted as infants or small children from Greek institutions between 1950 and 1962 (although prior and subsequent cases occur). Their testimonies inform my thinking about the "eligible alien orphans" (as per the US immigration terminology) who were selected from Greek state-run institutions with an entrenched bias against children of leftist origins and against those born to unwed mothers. These children were shepherded through an adoption system that worked by proxy, that is, through third-party intermediaries who appeared at the adoption hearings in Greek courts, so that the foreign adopters did not have to. The system was controlled by a small circle of state bureaucrats, orphanage directors, local mayors, doctors, lawyers, judges, Greek American community leaders, and even travel agents. The methods used ranged from legal and slow-moving to hasty, dubious, and plain illegal practices. By "illegal" practices, I mean to cover acts of coercion, bribery, lying and other forms of misrepresentation, whether orally or in written form, such as the faking of a new religious identity, of a child's foundling status, or even of a pregnancy itself. Thus part 2 charts the institutional landscape and the socioeconomic context that placed the Greek export of children for adoption on the fast track. It also depicts the Cold War societal background in which hopeful US couples turned to the (easy) solution of bringing over an "orphan" from Greece.

Part 3 of this book presents real-life Greek adoption stories with as much detail as my interviewees felt comfortable sharing (and after closely and repeatedly checking with them). This part closes by returning to Mike's story and that of the Argyriadis children in recent years. Thus this study's more psychologically oriented analysis of trauma, memory, and postmemory comes full circle. Thus, too, it affirms the power of personal experience and testimony to build the grounds-up structure of a research topic that is still in flux. It also helps to fill a gap in our knowledge of Greek-American relations. In part 3, international adoptees may recognize many of their private experiences, while those of Greek descent will find specific answers in the dates, places, names, and circumstances that steered adoption cases similar to their own.

All three parts of this book can be read in sequence but also separately. Readers who seek detailed historical and political background information to the Greek adoption movement of the 1950s and 1960s will benefit from following the book's logical sequence, delving first into the intricacies of an anticommunist persecution and adoption story. However, readers with knowledge of twentieth-century Greek history and adoptees themselves may want to postpone reading part 1 and proceed immediately to part 2, which confirms the ugly truth of children's commodification by adults for ideological and other self-serving purposes. All readers may want to consult this book's appendix 1, which presents a chronology of selected facts, juxtaposing family history with national, bilateral, and global history and adoption politics. Those turning immediately to part 3 and to the "Practical Information for Greek-Born Adoptees" in appendix 2, in the hope of recognizing their own story, may subsequently want to dig deeper and learn about the whole story. For those not directly involved, this appendix briefly reviews the historical trends and logistics of the postwar Greek-to-American adoption movement. It lays out the names of the intermediaries and the quick facts, all of which come into play in parts 1 through 3 of this book. It also suggests possibilities for further archival research, if significant new material were to become available. I have made a concerted effort to keep this book readable, to have it deliver clues, patterns, alternative voices, and background materials. As far as secondary sources are concerned, my preference has been for more-recent studies, which if they are in English will be more accessible to my readership of Greek-born adoptees and their descendants and communities, all seeking to contextualize their own lived realities.

Under the Sign of the Search

"How did this adoption traffic from Greece operate?" is the single most-urgent question that Greek adoptees keep asking me. "And just how many of us are there in the States?" The urgency behind these inquiries by the Greek-to-American adoptees is entirely valid, since they have been waiting for answers for some sixty long years. The approximate grand total of 3,200 Greek-to-American adoptions that took place between 1950 and 1962 gives us a much-needed ballpark figure (explained in part 2). Also, the question of "How could this happen?" is critical, and I deliver summarized answers in the outline of appendix 2.

The Greek adoptees' search is for reasons as well as roots. Somewhat unexpectedly, their search became mine when an odd email message dropped into my inbox in late August of 2013. This email was written by "Mike,"[9] a Greek adoptee's son, who soon found out how his personal story of family disruption fit into the Greek Left's symbolic repertoire of suffering through the post–World War II era. The 1955 adoptions of Mike's Greek-born mother and aunt mediated political and social relations at multiple levels, reaffirming the scholarly and public roles that family history may play. The trajectory of Mike's Greek family, traced in part 1, adds new and surprising depth to Greece's postwar orientation toward the West: it reclaims private life as a key battleground of sociopolitical ideas and practices in the looming Cold War. Mike's questions made me realize, too, that the search for answers affects multiple generations, and that it readily expands into a search for identity, for Greece, for a cultural connection or legacy, for a way to make up lost family time. The stories of Mike's Greek and American families and the searches initiated on either end resituate the complex but representative relationships between memory, genealogy, and nostalgic belonging. Adoptee lives are not independent, isolated entities; they are intertwined with other people's lives, and are often multigenerational and transnational in scope. The attempt at self-definition of the searching adoptee affects others, well beyond their own children. It cannot leave untouched anyone seeking to learn more about the United States's postwar engagement with Greece, whose sociopolitical history reveals the grievous practices of family disturbance and child removal. My analysis in parts 1 and 2 delves into the above topics but finds its anchor in the guiding structure as well as the concept of the search.

From the outset, the decades-long search of the Greek-born adoptees and their children has been a very interactive process, profoundly personal and public at once. It has covered the most diverse experiences, which are reflected in the multiple voices in which this book will continue to speak. My analysis lets many voices speak directly for themselves, often in an unedited format that testifies to the level of involvement of all the parties affected. The end result is a vocal analysis or discussion, based on the unadorned memory and testimony of the Greek adoptee community, which also explains the somewhat unusual structure of this book. This study's bolder composition, however, stays true to the diverse nature of an increasingly collective search

---

9. I have used pseudonyms to protect the anonymity of this family's informants who live in the United States. The facts about the Greek relatives are known, and many have been published by immediate family members in Greek newspapers and online opinion pieces.

and research project, which straddles macro and micro levels of analysis and the long as well as the short duration of historical time.

The multivocality of the testimonies cited drives, interrupts, and at times will shock the reader. These testimonies, each chosen for its psychological and analytical value, place private histories and national histories in a poignant dialectic relationship with each other, and together they spotlight the strange moral universe of the Cold War Greek adoption movement. The children adopted from Greece, even those who took a long time to internalize the rhetoric of opportunity in America, were often forced to negate their true feelings of loss, grief, or anger and to assimilate quickly to meet the desires and expectations of strangers. Many problems lay and lie in the long shadow of international adoption, in the conditions that enabled indiscriminate placements, and in the circumstances in which some of these random adoptions were carried out. Thus the stories of the Greek-born children adopted out to the States may shed valuable light on the convoluted Cold War period, the study of which remains dominated by historical misunderstandings and the perceptual filters of ideological constructs. The legitimacy of our historical quest must validate also the legitimacy of the adoptees' quests and questions and therefore the narratives of their life experiences.

My goal has been to blend profound sympathy and vivid evidence with painstaking research and writing. Nonetheless, the risk looms large that our research, writing, and discussion project will be one of and about educated adults: a history of what these adults have done or should have done for the children, based on sources produced by educated adults, who tell us about the work they themselves did on behalf of children. I acknowledge what several interviewees have expressed orally or in writing—different versions of, "It has always bothered me, as an adoptee, that others took off with my life story."[10] Admittedly, this restrictive situation, of outsiders telling stories and histories that speak for the children involved, may only change when the grown adoptees themselves and their descendants further engage in (post)memorial work. In the case of the children dispatched by postwar Greece, this work often takes the form of genealogical research on the adoptee's Greek ancestry or, more drastically, of the descendant revealing family secrets and breaking through reserves. Throughout the (long-silenced) Greek Civil War and the Cold War era, children were at the center of interests (and interest groups) in political and military developments, governmental authority, diplomacy, ideology, and religion. Therefore, too,

---

10. As per Greek-to-Dutch adoptee Marina van Dongen (2013b: 11): "Het heeft mij als geadopteerde altijd gestoord dat anderen . . . met mijn levensgeschiedenis aan de haal gingen."

the many testimonies incorporated in this book must reassert the voices of the young, unnamed, uneducated, or powerless. Speaking for themselves, these voices ease the reader into difficult ethical topics and emotionally charged subjects. Reading the narratives and files (however scant) of the Greek adoption history means reading a history of despair, poverty, and violence. Our search for the US-bound adoption traffic from Greece deepens our understanding of the human cost of political and economic dependencies on the United States, and of Western capitalist privilege. My quest to excavate and document this history of the young Greeks "enjoying Western privilege" offers a stark reminder of how long it took an exhausted country to start benefiting from postwar normalization.

On the American end, adoption policies and practices captured the ways in which the States wished to represent itself in the global theater of operations. Adoption became a metaphor for the national community, for the entire US nation as an open-minded family, ready to take in or "save" children who supposedly did not "belong" in the same close-knit, "American" fashion. The voices of birth parents, or the accounts of biological siblings, are typically missing from the Greek-to-American adoption stories that are still anchored in the lived realities of the Civil War. The birth mother, especially, tends to vanish from the histories of adoption, much as she disappears in the adoption arrangements. This absence is typical, perhaps, of many more adoption stories and histories that take on the perspective of the Western receiving countries and that are written by English-speaking representatives of those countries who do not master the languages of the sending nations. But this annihilation of the biological family and the country of origin is far from justified. Adoption scholars should therefore refrain from reiterating and deepening the erasure of the birth mother, especially, and should restore to her not only agency but also the capacity to make responsible decisions.[11]

This book tries to balance the American outlook with an ideological positioning grounded in the conditions of Greece itself. I hope to rehabilitate Greece as a sending country by detailing the texts as well as the contexts of its postwar adoption movement. But the Greek sources come with many limitations: they are scarce and remain subject to confidentiality clauses. Below, the reader may catch a rare glimpse of a birth father, observed through the eyes of yet another third party, a nurse working her shift at an orphanage in Thessaloniki:

---

11. Damousi (2017) places her helpful discussion of "responsible mothering" and the violence of erasure in the long span of the 1940s.

One afternoon . . . a man came to my ward and asked to see the baby. The man was about 50 years old and shabbily dressed. . . . He told me he was the baby's father. Because the baby was asleep, I opened the door for him, so he could just see it from afar. He cried, and he left two chocolates for me to give to the child later. . . . Then he left. Since then, he has not returned, neither before nor after the child's adoption.[12]

Pursuing the preadoption narrative threads (where possible) is a must, as in the case of the daughters of Elias Argyriadis. The elements of inevitable loss and rupture, vital components of many adoption stories as they are of these girls' experiences, would otherwise be absorbed into embellished accounts of unity and continuity, of the adoptive family and of the adopting nation alike. As much as adoption tales with happy endings may become national romances, adoptions gone awry, or even adoptions that "worked out," pose a collective challenge to the nation, its historical leadership, and its manifest ideology.

Not belonging myself to any "within-group" of adoptees, Greeks, or American-born citizens, my effort is about uncovering "routes" rather than idealizing roots. My descriptions are in no way meant to injure the feelings of the adoptees, their adoptive or birth families, or the representatives of agencies and other mediating parties, which could not escape entirely the biases of their own time. Terms such as "adoptee," "birth mother," "orphan," "choosing" and "matching" adoptees, children "special" enough to be "selected," "happy" adoptions, among several others, have been deemed inappropriate by some scholars and advocacy groups. But substitutes for these older, established terms have rarely been compelling. Driven by my desire to let the interviewees' testimonies resonate in their own words and thus ring true, I employ certain conventional terms without attaching any particular ideological or sociopolitical significance to them.

An Unexpected Introduction to a Traumatic Personal Past

Email message of 5 September 2013:

Dear Mike,

I found something that you can make sense of. A Google search brought up the following:

---

12. Nurse Katerina Tambakidou, a staff member at the Saint Stylianos Foundling Home, is quoted by Daravinga (1963: 6).

Χαρακτηριστική περίπτωση είναι αυτή της Έφης Αργυριάδη, της οποίας οι αδερφές χάθηκαν όταν υιοθετήθηκαν κρυφά και παράνομα από έναν Ελληνοαμερικανό. Η ίδια πιστεύει ότι η υιοθεσία ήταν εσκεμμένη καθώς πατέρας της ήταν ο Ηλίας Αργυριάδης, ο οποίος εκτελέστηκε μαζί με το Νίκο Μπελογιάννιj.

It essentially says that Effi Argyriadi lost her sisters when they were adopted secretly and illegally by a Greek American. She herself believes that the adoption was a calculated act since her father was Elias Argyriadis, who was executed along with Nikos Beloyannis.

The part with Beloyannis refers to a very public case of 1952, which is still remembered by many Greek leftists. You may recall that, in the aftermath of the Greek Civil War (1946–1949) and at the onset of the Cold War, there was plenty of paranoia about communists and "crypto-communists."

Gonda

5 September 2013
Gonda,

On my mother's birth certificate, her name is written as Ioanna Argiriadou. She has a younger sister, my aunt, who was two years old at the time of their father's execution. My mother was approximately seven at the time.

My aunt mentioned to me that someone from Greece tried to contact her in the 1980s claiming that he or she was a forgotten brother or sister. I forget the gender of the inquirer. Could there be another sibling?

Thanks, Gonda.

Mike

5 September 2013
Dear Mike,

Now you got me really puzzled, and that is a good thing. You have to tell me how much you can handle, and then you decide how much your mother can handle. Let me know what the next step is.

Gonda

6 September 2013
Gonda,

It's good to share this thinking with you. Please do tell me what more you find out.

    Mike

6 September 2013
Dear Mike,

Turns out you have not only an aunt Efterpi (Effi) but also a first cousin, Iliana (obviously named after her grandfather). Your mother Ioanna is mentioned on the web, and so is your youngest aunt Olympia, in this rather sharp statement (my translation follows the word order of the Greek text):

Τις άλλες δύο κόρες του Η. Αργυριάδη, Ιωάννα και Ολυμπία, η Ελλάς φρόντισε να τις στείλει στην Αμερική με τις αναίσχυντες επιχειρήσεις των υιοθεσιών, για να τις προστατέψει από το «μίασμα» του κομμουνισμού.

    The other two daughters of Elias Argyriadis, Ioanna and Olympia, "Hellas" took care to send them to America through the shameless business of the adoptions, to protect them from the "miasma" ["infection," "virus"] of communism.
    Also, a fellow Greek communist spent a lot of time teaching your grandfather and Efterpi how to use a wireless set:

Ο Βαβούδης προσπάθησε να εκπαιδεύσει αρκετούς στον ασύρματο (τον Αργυριάδη, την κόρη του Αργυριάδη, την Έφη κ.ά.).

    Vavoudis tried to teach the use of the wireless to quite a few people (Argyriadis, Argyriadis's daughter Effi, and others).
    This business with the wireless is important, as is the postwar anticommunist climate to which the first quotation refers. But I can explain those matters another time. For now, this tells me that Efterpi/Effi must have been older, and perhaps even by several years. Key question is now whether your mother remembers her older sister Effi. And most of all whether she is ready for the question.

I hope I haven't overwhelmed you with too much information. Keep me posted,

Gonda

24 September 2013
Gonda,

The information you sent me about a Greek sister named Effi is correct! I am shocked. I asked my aunt Helen (once named Olympia) about an estranged older sister. Helen is both able and willing to speak about this time. Apparently, Helen and Effi have been in contact for decades. I had no idea. Effi sent her a lot of photos through the years. My aunt is slowly sending me these documents via email. It's a lot to digest.

Mike

25 September 2013
Dear Mike,

I realize what a whirlwind the past few weeks must have been for you and for your aunt Helen. Effi's story is gripping. It is also interesting that, online, she firmly and repeatedly calls the American adoptions of her sisters illegal. That may be the next piece of information that is hard to deal with, and your aunt's and mother's perception of their adoptive family will, no doubt, inform that part of the story.

Gonda

Narrating Greek Civil War History in the Middle Voice

Mike's email set off an investigation into the 1950s circumstances that led from family separation to a political adoption story. This quest lets us recreate not only a family genealogy but also the symbolic genealogy of the Greek Left after its 1949 defeat and through the next decade, when the Left, the Center, and the Right of a dependent state failed to legitimately share political power. The family's experience helps us to unpack mid-twentieth-century Greek history and Greek-American relations through the specifics of its emblematic case, which have emotionally weighed down consecutive generations. Therefore, the story of the 1952 execution of the Greek communists charged with espionage must be framed by the story of how, when, where, and by whom these events came to be remembered and told. The very difficulties of discovering and telling the whole truth about a painful family history of the 1950s become an integral part of the narration that seeks to disclose the greater meaning of the events. They cannot be underplayed in the name of scientific objectivity. Mike's story personalizes the actors, agents, and agencies involved in a family trauma that is, at the same time, part of the nation's trauma.[13]

Thus far the story of the Argyriadis sisters has only ever been told in the passive voice. The last part of the title above draws on Hayden White's concept of writing history in the middle voice, which lets the activity recoil on itself, blurring the distinction between the subject-insider and the outsider and canceling out any temporal distance.[14] White distinguishes a kind of "intransitive writing" and refers to the subject that is presumed to be "interior" to the action.[15] Mike has been expressing his relationship to the Greek events in the middle voice, but it took him some time to discover that voice. The descendant's voice is crucial, nonetheless, because it inscribes the biography of a persecuted family into the "biography" of a troubled age. It does so through the linchpins of memory and adoption, of a double Greek-to-American placement, itself part of the larger phenomenon of Greece's postwar export of children for adoption. But, to strengthen my case, let me unpack the psychological, theoretical, historical, and political underpinnings to the above charged statement.

Mike's drive to grasp the family trauma raises issues regarding the limits of narration and representation—let alone of publication in an open forum. My initial (quoted) responses to Mike were driven by concern for my interlocutor. However, Theodor Adorno's aptly titled essay, "The Meaning of Working Through the Past" (1959), comes to mind. Adorno states, "A working through of the past understood as enlightenment is essentially such a turn toward the subject, the reinforcement of a person's self-consciousness

13. Recently, social historians of modern Greece have taken up the call for the uses of "global microhistory," realizing its potential for truly transnational studies that may "examine the concrete (un-)making of sociality in specific contexts." They hope to illuminate, especially, the "multidirectional flows between Greece and other countries," while exerting an "impact beyond academia" (Papadogiannis 2018: 119, in the published roundtable discussion of Avdela, Gallant, Papadogiannis, Papastefanaki, and Voglis 2018). Social history itself, as a distinct field, emerged in Greek history-writing only in the 1990s, as per the claims of Voglis and Gallant, interlocutors in the same roundtable discussion (2018: 110, 117, 120).

14. White (2010: 260).

15. White (1999: 38, 41).

and hence also of his self."[16] Adorno searched for a productive path toward meaningful remembrance for post–World War II Germany. He felt that "working through" the past could not deliver the same critical self-reflection as "working upon" the past, that is, processing the past more consciously in order to comprehend it more fully. Saul Friedlander has urged the researcher in turn to facilitate this "working through" trauma, in the psychoanalytical or Freudian sense. For him, aiding in this process of "working through" means *"confronting the individual voice* in a field dominated by political decisions and administrative decrees which neutralize the concreteness of despair and death."[17]

The process of "working upon" the past of the Greek Civil War has been an ongoing and intense project, but it still shows significant gaps pertaining to the study of families and children. Modern Greek historian Polymeris Voglis has observed that, while the collective history of Civil War communism has garnered ample scholarly attention in recent years, the same does not apply to the personal histories of Greek communists, and in particular, to those who held midlevel positions: for decades, the communist's subjectivity was suppressed and made subservient to the need for collective discipline and fortitude.[18] Intraparty friction, especially, took a huge toll on ordinary Communist Party members and their families, who were not to "indulge" in contemplating this human cost. Social anthropologist Penelope Papailias has noted that Greek fiction (mainly presented from the perspective of individual characters) has often stepped in for Greek history-writing and thus for the project of "working upon" the past. She makes important observations about the "reality-effect of Greek war literature," or Greek readers' openness to accept literature as history, when it considers aspects of the Civil War that have suffered from a lack of public debate or historiographical critique.[19] The validity of her statements extends to the post–Civil War adoptions of the children of Greek left-wingers. The trafficking in

---

16. Adorno (1998: 102).
17. Friedlander (1992: 53; italics his).
18. Voglis's remark (2013: 191–92) is part of his afterword to the published memoir of Communist Party member Kostas Paschaloudis, by the telling title of *From Now On, You'll Be Nikos* (2013; original Greek title: *Από δω και πέρα θα είσαι ο Νίκος*). Perhaps the most interesting juxtaposition of the (reluctantly shared) remembrances of a descendant-survivor and the personal account of an avowed communist parent has emerged in the joint publication by Electra Karankitsou of her own and her father's memoirs (Karankitsou, Electra, and Pantelis Simos Karankitsos 2013). In her afterword to this daughter-and-father book project (published more than a decade after the latter's death), Katerina Stefatou (2013) discusses the importance of repressed memory, second-generation curiosity and postmemory, and the therapeutic value of writing and sharing traumatic recollections.
19. Papailias (2005: 144–45).

Greek babies who are of leftist origins and become "available for adoption" is the topic of a 2005 novel by author, publisher, and investigative journalist Kostas Vaxevanis, entitled *The Lost Gene* (original Greek title: *Το χαμένο γονίδιο*). The novel stresses the critical involvement of Queen Frederica "of the Hellenes" and of the successive, palace-supported, reactionary governments of the postwar era. Thus Vaxevanis is one of the first few to have Greek literature depict members of the memory and postmemory generation of adoptees from the deep Civil War.

Postmemory in Greece takes on a particularly urgent dimension, covering for history and history-writing centered on individuals: in a 1989 move to seal a (temporary) pact of reconciliation between the Greek communists and the Right, both camps authorized the destruction of massive heaps of police and security files containing personal information dating back to the 1940s.[20] Given this void, social historians and those utilizing the methods and tools of multidisciplinary memory studies may shed light on the hidden folds of the deep Civil War, and may help build a cognitive model applicable to the study of other civil war conflicts and their long shadows as well. The term "postmemory," based on the concept of a memory that reaches back in the past beyond one's own birth, was first theorized by Marianne Hirsch in the context of Holocaust studies and media representations. It became established after appearing in the title of Hirsch's 1997 book, *Family Frames: Photography, Narrative, and Postmemory*. Hirsch denotes a second generation's relationships to the traumas of its parents, and her apt wording may help us better understand the experiences of the Argyriadis children and their descendants.[21]

Against the backdrop of the vast literature on trauma and memory studies and the "capacious analytic term" of "memory," Hirsch concentrates on the remembrance of the Holocaust and examines the role of the family as a space of transmission, thus building on Helen Epstein's moving work, *Children of the Holocaust* (1979).[22] Hirsch pays special attention to photogra-

---

20. Clogg (2013: 197–98); Close (2004: 272–74); Demertzis (2011: 148–49); and Samatas (2014: 60). See also the new, comprehensive study by Karamanolakis (2019).
21. Hirsch (1996, 1997, 2008, and 2012).
22. Hirsch (2008: 105). Joy Damousi structures her insightful 2015 study around the memories of war of the Greek immigrant families in Australia (2015: 146–72, 243–49, *passim*). Her chapter 8 (2015: 222–42) foregrounds second-generation Greek-Australian achievements in the arts, academe, and sports, which further express the diaspora experience and exorcize trauma (with extensive bibliographical references, 2015: 199–200, n4). A more popular article such as the one by Jean West entitled "Holocaust Survivors' Grandchildren Call for Action Over Inherited Trauma," in *The Guardian* of 3 August 2015, attests to the twenty-first-century currency of this topic. The concept of "epigenetic inheritance," the idea that traumatic environmental factors can affect the genes of offspring, again draws

phy as a "primary medium of transgenerational transmission of trauma."[23] Other scholars working at the intersection of oral history theory and memory studies have used different terms to capture the validity and intensity of the intergenerational transmission of memory.[24] Froma Zeitlin speaks of the postsurvivor as the "vicarious witness," who delivers "acquired testimony."[25] Rather than impede identification with the first generation, the sense of belatedness actually intensifies the subject's will to identify. Zeitlin also observes the common belated witnesses' involvement in mimetic reenactments of scripts over which they may only tenuously claim authorship, let alone author-ity.[26]

Postmemory suffers from an (understandable) misconception of its value as reliable testimony or proof. Some studies have even tried to scientifically capture the evidentiary contribution of postmemory, thus "quantifying" its presumed speculative nature.[27] I agree that empathic mimicry ensues from inherited wounds (whether spoken about, suppressed in silence, or situated at any stage in between), but also that these wounds can be cured with the quasihomeopathic treatment of remembering and reappropriating—

on studies of Holocaust descendants. See further Helen Thomson in *The Guardian* of 21 August 2015.

23. Hirsch (2008: 103). Efraim Sicher's edited volume first highlighted an afflicted second generation's imaginative modes of expression (1998). Aware of some of the criticisms that Hirsch's theory has attracted, Athanasios Anastasiadis applies her interpretive framework to the novel *The Jewish Bride* (original Greek title: *Η Εβραία νύφη*), published by Nikos Davvetas in 2009 and inspired by turbulent modern Greek history. Anastasiadis emphasizes that postmemory is not only an inherited but also an "investigated" form of memory (2012: 6). In the preface to their edited volume, *Tense Past: Cultural Essays in Trauma and Memory*, Antze and Lambek refer to "a forensics of memory" (1996: vii), which applies in our case as well. The memory of the subjects of this book, however, is less anchored in places, in sites or realms of memory or in the seminal *lieux de mémoire*, as defined by Nora (1989). Rogers, Leydesdorff, and Dawson (1999) place traumatic life stories in a broader, international perspective. The more recent collection of essays by Alexander et al. (2004) centers on cultural trauma, communal suffering, and collective identity. The 2013 volume edited by Demertzis, Paschaloudi, and Antoniou has brought the notion of "cultural trauma" to the forefront of the Greek debate. Demertzis defines memory, emotion, and identity as the fundamental elements of cultural trauma theory (2011: 146). Among the pioneering works in trauma studies remain, of course, Caruth (1996) and the volumes edited by Caruth (1995) and Felman and Laub (1992).

24. Danforth and Van Boeschoten have incisively deployed the broader categories of the politics of memory, war-related memory, and the memory war in the context of the Greek Civil War and its aftermath. They have stressed the complexities of the relationships between experience, memory, and narration (2012: 220, 221, 224). See also Van Boeschoten et al. (2008).

25. Zeitlin (2001: 128, 129).

26. Zeitlin (2001: 130).

27. See, for instance, Gangi, Talamo, and Ferracuti (2009).

indeed, of mimicking. The "limitations of verbal communication" can often be superseded by nonverbal, alternative forms of communication, such as self-expression through art.[28] The multifaceted relations between trauma and art have been the subject of a growing literature that, again, originated in Holocaust studies. However, Sophia Richman's recent book, *Mended by the Muse: Creative Transformations of Trauma* (2014), adds a Greek angle to the better-researched long view on Jewish history, experience, and memory.

The scholarly attention currently bestowed on the memory and post-memory generation and its childhood focus is encouraging: children were the theme of an April 2015 international conference in Slovenia, entitled "Hidden Children of the 2nd World War," held at the City Museum of Ljubljana. Tara Zahra centered her recent book, *The Lost Children: Reconstructing Europe's Families After World War II*, on the topic of the "lost identities of children" resulting from a war that has often been described as a "war against children."[29] Zahra also posits that the view of family separation as a form of trauma is relatively new, originating as it did in postwar campaigns to reunite and rehabilitate Europe's displaced families.[30] A 1994 psychological study by Mando Dalianis-Karambatzakis analyzed the effects of the ravages of the Civil War and postwar internments on Greek children's development.[31] In 1949–1950, the author was a political detainee herself at the Averof Prison in Athens, but she went on to pursue a career in child and adolescent psychiatry in Sweden. No study, however, has followed up on the children of the first generation of internees. All too often, children became the focal points of political and ideological rifts. Children of Greek left-wingers were not accorded any significant place in the postwar decades of Greece's reconstruction, let alone in international justice or humanitarian-

---

28. Kornetis (2014: 88). Kornetis focuses on the torture inflicted on activists of the 1968 generation and their children's patterns of anxieties to document the link between "transmittable trauma" in fiction and in reality (2014: 88). A novella by Elias Maglinis entitled *The Interrogation* (2013; original Greek title: *Η ανάκριση*) dramatizes how personal trauma and torture experienced by a father in the past of the Greek dictatorship affect his daughter's life and art in ways that are far from superficial. A recent crop of literature and art bespeaks the Greek side of a second-generation commitment to memorial literature and art in which imaginative work meets emotional labor. The 2015 movie *Sons of Greece: The Children of the Civil War* (original title: *Fils de Grèce: Τα παιδιά του Εμφυλίου*), directed by Dionysis Grigoratos, presents the interwoven memories and histories of the first through third generations of Greeks who experienced the Civil War. The movie further acknowledges the role of archiving, interpreting, and (re)performing the kind of deep trauma that is stirred up again by the current Greek economic and social crisis.
29. Zahra (2011: 3).
30. Zahra (2011: 18, 89).
31. The Greek edition of this doctoral dissertation was published in 2009. See also Dalianis and Mazower (2000).

ism. As Iosif Kovras has recently observed, the recovery of historical memory in Greece has, for far too long, been an academic debate from which the victims' relatives and civil society have been largely absent.[32] The child's human-interest story is, however, analytically vital to a better understanding not just of Greek political priorities, but of concerns of social justice and human rights that have lingered in obscurity. While the bibliography on the Greek Civil War continues to grow in volume and intensity, the era of 1949–1962 has remained one of the dark ages of modern Greek history, overlooking its human rights record in particular. Elias Nikolakopoulos has termed the unstable years of 1946–1967 the period of "weak" or "stunted democracy" (2001), which is certainly an understatement. The phrases "controlled democracy" and "guided democracy" are commonly used as well.[33]

Our opening study, a case study based on Mike's Greek family's personal history (with reference to many other relevant adoption narratives of Greek-born children), helps us construct a political and ideological "biography" of the dark era of 1949–1962. It uses methods of social science throughout, but its intellectual thrust remains humanistic in orientation. Our analysis strives to broaden the scope of what Greek social history and postmemory studies can tell us about Cold War Greece, and thus to contribute to intersecting sociopolitical and historical fields. I hope to enrich academic debate on the Cold War's human subjects by presenting not only new evidence, but also fresh critical perspectives. I investigate and document the postwar Greek adoption movement through family records, media representations, works of art, and other bold visual responses, aiming to bridge the textual and the sensory, the analytical and the subjective, to attain the socio-(con)textual. With Rachel Winslow, I advocate for a more historically oriented and interdisciplinary study of international adoption. Winslow has called this type of study "virtually absent before 2000."[34]

First, we learn that the implementation of Greek welfare and adoption policies has been steered by various anticommunist tendencies that spurred Greek government action for decades and that extended into the realm of emigration politics. Intercountry adoptions destabilize our reliance on analytical devices such as the notions of Cold War containment versus inter-

---

32. Kovras (2014: 130).

33. Close (2002: 88) and Mouzelis and Pagoulatos (2005: 88), respectively. Another standard reference is to the older volumes of papers presented at a 1993 conference on the period of 1945–1967, collected and published by the Sakis Karagiorgas Foundation (1994–1995, in Greek). The large majority of the papers included, however, foreground political and economic developments. More recent and more broadly conceived is the collection edited by Mazower (2000). See also Svolopoulos (1992–2001).

34. Winslow (2015: 332).

nationalization and transnationalism: they not only unveil what these foci might foreclose but also lay bare the fault lines of an (idealized) global and transracial integration. Forgotten policies, neglected ethical questions, and acts of "quiet migration" (to use the coinage of immigration specialist Richard Weil)[35] prove to have been inscribed in the creation of the global Cold War culture, of its perceived threats and its institutionalized "defenses." Thus, secondly, we deepen our understanding of Greece's relationship to war, reconstruction, and the phantom of reconciliation, alerting the reader to individual mentalities and cultural sensibilities of the period in question. With methodological insights gleaned from political sociology and social psychology, I seek to revise the tired notion of the "reconstruction"—and reconstruction only—of 1950s Greece. The details and results of my case study prove to have no place in the hyper-nationalist readings of Greek history from 1944 through 1974, but neither do they fit comfortably in the hyperleftist readings of the past forty years.

---

35. Weil (1984).

PART 1

THE PAST THAT HAS NOT PASSED

Memories from Another Greece

A Human-Interest Story from the "Stone Years" of Greece

Ποιός βλάκας ψέλλισε τη λέξη ελευθερία;
What fool uttered the word freedom?

   —Sophia Nikolaïdou, *The Elephants Are Dancing*, or *The Scapegoat*,
   2012: 135. Trans. Karen Emmerich, 2015: 93

At approximately 4:10 a.m. on Sunday, 30 March 1952, the Greek state had four men shot by a firing squad at the execution site of Goudi, near Athens. Nikos Beloyannis (born 1915) became the token communist martyr, but three of his collaborators died with him: Nikos Kaloumenos, Dimitris Batsis, and Elias Argyriadis.[1] Elias had been born in 1910, in Pergamon in Asia Minor, but, displaced as a child, he had grown up in a refugee settlement near Istiaia in northern Evia. By age forty-two, Elias had attained a long record of commitment to the Greek Communist Party (ΚΚΕ, Κομμουνιστικό Κόμμα Ελλάδας, founded in 1918). He had also served as a very competent technician and wireless operator. Some of his fellow detainees even called him "the man with the golden hands" or "Hephaestus," during the long months that they spent together in various political prisons and exile camps (Folegandros island, Akronafplia, Larisa).[2] Elias was a devoted father of four daughters.

The Greek right-wing state officially outlawed the Communist Party in December 1947 and engaged in years of anticommunist persecution of Party

---

1.   A document attesting to the execution order and death of the four men convicted was filed with the Athens Office of Vital Statistics on 2 June 1952. Because of its historical significance, it was featured in a publication on the subject of this recording office (Skiadas 2005: 96).
2.   Flountzis (1977: 99, 519); Lazaridis (1998: 208–10, part of a larger chapter on the "Beloyannis Affair," 205–30); and Vrachniaris (1983: 146).

members, many of whom continued to work clandestinely.[3] The four men executed by shooting belonged to the Greek communist underground of the late 1940s, and they took directives from the Party's Political Bureau. After its *de facto* loss of the Civil War in 1949, the Bureau had set up its headquarters in Bucharest. A communist radio station named "Free Greece" was broadcasting from Romania as well.[4] The Greek communist apparatus kept its male rank and file on a war footing, even though no further armed confrontations took place. However, this period of *paranomia* (παρανομία, literally "illegality") was typically harder on female than on male communists, who had to meet the demands not only of party conformity but of gender conformity.[5] Nikos Zachariadis, general secretary of the Greek Communist Party, represented the self-exiled leadership that oversaw the communists who had survived the debacle, whether they found themselves in Greece (in hiding or in prison), in the Soviet Union (mainly in Tashkent), or dispersed across Central and Eastern European countries. According to traditionalist interpretations of the Civil War, Zachariadis, who in 1931 had taken charge of the Greek Communist Party on instructions from Moscow, imposed the doctrinaire party line and rigid discipline of Soviet communism. By 1950, the KKE in exile had created an orbit of repression of its own, whose ramifications were felt in Greece.[6]

Out of touch with the situation on the ground in Greece, Zachariadis and other leaders stuck to a dogmatism that quelled internal dissent and punished failure, whether real or imagined.[7] They cast allegations of

---

3. Anastasia Mitsopoulou (2014) details the twentieth-century history of Greek anticommunism with special attention to rhetoric, educational practices, and literary receptions. For histories of the Greek Left, see Panourgia (2009) and Voglis (2002). The history of the Greek extreme Right has also been the focus of recent scholarly elaboration, as in the special section of *ArcheioTaxio* 16 (2014).

4. Tsekou (2013) documents the political refugees' life, work, organization, and education in Eastern Europe. Apostolidou (2010: chs. 2 and 3) discusses the literature produced by some of the refugees, which she qualifies as a "literature of trauma" (2010: 54).

5. Stefatos (2011: 112–13, 133–38).

6. Currently, historians tend to agree that the Greek Communist Party leadership acted on its own when, in 1946, it launched the Civil War; it did not heed Moscow's advice to delay resorting to an all-out armed insurrection. Once the Civil War was underway, however, and following Stalin's feud (and eventual split) with Yugoslavia's Tito in the spring of 1948, Moscow allowed the communist regimes of Eastern Europe to assist their Greek comrades by sending weapons and other supplies. Stalin himself, however, remained skeptical about the chances of the Greek communist insurgency winning, and he failed to meet Greek expectations of large-scale Russian interventions. See recently Steil (2018: 46–48).

7. Iatrides (2005) contextualizes Zachariadis's inability to adequately assess the political and military situation on the ground in embattled Greece and also the prospects of Soviet aid and/or intervention. Zachariadis had fled from Greece in December 1947, once the right-wing government had outlawed the Communist Party. The Party leaders feared an

betrayal on some of the men put to death, including Elias Argyriadis and his brother Vasilis.[8] By the early 1950s, the sense of threat ran very deep in the Greek Left. For this reason, the Communist Party Bureau had asked Beloyannis, a prominent member of its Central Committee, to reconstitute the various communist cells still operating in Greek urban centers.[9] The Party suspected that some of these cells had been infiltrated by right-wing agents or had been corrupted internally by "stool pigeons." The dreaded charge of being a *chafies* (χαφιές), a "snitch" or "informer," was enough to instantly ruin lives or to forever tarnish even the staunchest communist. Allegations of betrayal, therefore, were so common and at times so farfetched that they say less about the Argyriadis brothers than about the divisions that had started to tear apart the distrustful communist leadership.[10]

Over the next fifteen years, the Greek Marxist-communist movement fragmented; it still shielded itself by assigning culpability to specific indi-

---

escalation of the violence, which had started well before 1947 and had left many Greeks (and British officials) convinced that the Greek Communist Party planned to seize power by force. See further Iatrides (2018) and also the archival materials edited and published by Petropoulos, Zirganos, and Chatzidimitrakos (2016).

8. In his defense speech of February 1952, Beloyannis mentioned the "cowardliness" ("δειλία") of the Argyriadis brothers (quoted by Paraskevopoulos 1980: 157 and by Vournas 1981: 126). This attack seems to have been supported by Nikos Ploumbidis, who targeted mainly Vasilis Argyriadis (Ploumbidis, quoted by Vournas 1981: 147–48, 162). See also Paraskevopoulos (1980: 102–3). See further Karagiannis et al. (2011) and also the contemporary newspaper reporting on the extensive confessions made by Elias Argyriadis (starting with Anon. on the front page of the paper *Eleftheria* of 18 November 1951).

9. Petropoulos and Chatzidimitrakos (2015a: 19–23, 32).

10. Goaded on by conspiracy theories and plot psychosis, the Greek communist leadership engaged in extremes of recrimination and self-immolation. Zachariadis hurled some of his worst accusations at Nikos Ploumbidis, whom he called a traitor. On 12 March 1952, Ploumbidis had issued a public letter in which he claimed responsibility for the underground communist operation in Greece, in order to absolve Beloyannis of the gravest charges laid against him. Zachariadis declared the letter a falsification, thereby disowning Ploumbidis and "sacrificing" Beloyannis. Ploumbidis was later arrested, tried, and eventually executed by the Greek state on 14 August 1954. See further the voluminous collection of testimonies, documents, and historical analyses compiled by Kousidou and Stavropoulos (ca. 1998). The novel *Command* (1976; original Greek title: *Εντολή*), written by Dido Sotiriou, offers a literary and critical reflection on this sinister episode. Dimitris Ploumbidis, son of the victim of the Party as well as of the Right, found an outlet for his family trauma in the scholarly study of psychiatry and psychoanalysis (testimony of 16 June 2016). See, for example, Tzavaras, Ploumbidis, and Asser (2007–2008) and Dimitris Ploumbidis (1997; a foreword to a collection and contextualization of his father's letters and notes written from prison, published by Papachristou 1997). Because Nikos Ploumbidis's role has been controversial (despite his posthumous rehabilitation), formal memorial services tend to include fighters executed from the onset of World War II through 1952, not through 1954. The cutoff in 1952 adds to the common misperception that Beloyannis, Argyriadis, and the other two were victims of the very last executions.

viduals, but not to either theory or praxis. Some of its most vocal members and ideologues were dispossessed of their rights and voices under the guise of the Party's enforcement of strict discipline and its semblance of unity. When the reactionary Greek military dictators staged their coup on 21 April 1967, the old myth of happy Communist Party members marching unstoppably toward revolution and eventual victory had long been debunked. Any communist resistance against the military regime was a long time coming. Festering tensions, aggravated by the routine suppression of differences and occasional smear campaigns and purges, led to the Greek Communist Party split in 1968, into the Communist Party of Greece of the Interior and a second camp that stayed loyal to the Soviet Union.[11] Also, through the late 1970s and 1980s, the Left made concerted efforts to mediate the past through redemptive narratives harkening back to the "glory days" of World War II resistance, but not of the Civil War.

Post–Civil War Greece saw a fierce power struggle in which the only politician to champion leniency toward the defeated Left lost out against the hard-line right wing, which benefited from vital support donated by the United States. This lone voice was center-right prime minister Nikolaos Plastiras, whose initiatives for reconciliation and amnesty were doomed to failure. After the November 1952 election, the reactionary Right managed to hold on to power until 1963 (or, with a brief interruption, until 1974). The Right's hatred of communists and "cryptocommunists" built on long-standing fears of Bulgarian or Slav "agents" and "infiltrators," to whom it ascribed the evil intent of trying to dissolve the traditional Greek state. Greece of the 1950s through early 1960s may be characterized as a police state that virulently persecuted communists, but made a show of going after communist leaders in particular. American Realpolitik, backed by the Marshall Plan (officially known as the European Recovery Program), let successive Greek right-wing governments, the military, and police forces discriminate against leftist citizens with impunity. The Truman Doctrine as well as the Marshall Plan placed Greece on the very front line in the battle against international communism and prioritized political stability internally. They also placed the new policy of dispatching unprecedented aid in the very service of foreign policy.[12]

---

11. Panourgia (2009: 265–66) and Voglis (2002: 230).

12. For new perspectives on the Marshall Plan and its effects in Greece, see the October 2009 special issue of the *Journal of Modern Greek Studies*. The 1948 Marshall Plan implemented strategic aspects of the Truman Doctrine, which the United States issued in March through May of 1947 and which pertained to Turkey as well (Gallant 2016: 254–56; Panourgia 2009: 244–49). See also the volumes edited by Eichengreen (1995) and Sfikas (2011), for broader

US President Harry Truman, who espoused a more muscular containment policy as part of his Cold War strategy, created the Central Intelligence Agency (CIA) in 1947. In 1950, he initiated the Campaign of Truth
to combat the "Big Lie" of Soviet communism.[13] Thus Truman was among
the first to develop (Manichean) propaganda as an "official *peacetime* institution,"[14] contrasting the American "way of life free from coercion" with
that of countries resorting to "terror and oppression" to "impose their will,
and their way of life, upon other nations" (Truman, 12 March 1947). To preserve international peace and security, the United States had to assist free
peoples in maintaining "their free institutions and their national integrity
against aggressive movements that s[ought] to impose upon them totalitarian regimes" (Truman, 12 March 1947). By early 1952, the United States had
secured full membership for Greece in the NATO alliance (founded in April
1949). In 1953, Greece granted the States the right to use military bases and
facilities on its sovereign territory, along with the (much-maligned) privilege that American personnel violating the law would not be subjected to
the Greek judicial system. American defendants were tried in the United
States for crimes committed in Greece under the "extraterritoriality agreement," which the Greeks deemed offensive and humiliating.[15]

To retrace the intricate Greek political history of the years and months
leading up to the March 1952 executions, let me provide a basic outline in
the following few paragraphs. The international outcry about the Greek
government's executions of communists had peaked in May 1948, mainly in
Britain. It only abated when the leniency legislation of 30 September 1949
passed and reprieves began to be granted, bringing executions to a temporary halt.[16] After the turbulent late 1940s, several political parties had

---

European and transnational perspectives, and the comprehensive studies by Jeffery (2000),
Stathakis (2004), and Steil (2018). Buchanan (2014: 256–65) and Crandall (2014: 165–73)
have recently discussed the rise of American power in Greece and the Eastern Mediterranean during and after World War II, acknowledging Greece's importance as a prime
setting for a test of strength. The 1982 book by Lawrence Wittner is still useful as well. A
short but paternalistic film such as *The Story of Koula*, the story of a mule shipped from the
United States to Greece, illustrated the Greek agricultural aid program for the American
public and thus helped to promote the Marshall Plan's achievements in Greece and other
European countries. US propaganda stressed the values of freedom and democracy and
promised a higher standard of living, but it also worked to restore the conservative Greek
monarchy. See the website of the Marshall Plan Filmography (www.marshallfilms.org/mpf.
asp) and also De Grazia (2005: 345–50).

13. Parry-Giles (2000: 106–8).

14. Parry-Giles (2002: vii; italics his).

15. Botsiou (2007: 223, 228–29); Lialiouti (2016b: 111–12); and Stefanidis (2007: 181–84).

16. Howard (1950: 9n64, 10, 23). Wittner illustrates the meek to complacent American
   position on the subject of the Greek mass executions of communists of the late 1940s

contested the Greek national election of 5 March 1950. General Plastiras, a Venizelist (supporter of Eleftherios Venizelos, the antiroyalist statesman from Crete), had served a short term as prime minister in early 1945, in the aftermath of the Dekemvriana, the communist insurgency of December 1944. He emerged from the 1950 election as the leader of the National Progressive Center Union (ΕΡΕΚ, Εθνική Προοδευτική Ένωση Κέντρου). Plastiras was not a left-winger, but he advocated for political liberalization and reconciliation between the Left and the Right at a time when the first post–Civil War governments (typically of short duration) were still deeply divided about how much leniency to extend to the (communist) rank-and-file members of the vanquished Democratic Army. The election of 9 September 1951 was again heavily contested but eventually placed Plastiras in an (unstable) premiership for the one year marked by the government of "reconciliation and national-mindedness." Plastiras's administration was being undermined by the Greek royal house, however, and he himself was gradually sidelined. The royalist Sofoklis Venizelos gained the upper hand and influenced the most important political decisions made from late October 1951 through 11 October 1952. This means that Sofoklis Venizelos and the monarchy prevailed during the most critical months for the communists arrested and put on trial. The execution of the four on 30 March 1952 was ironically followed, two days later, by governmental "pacification measures" (Law 2058), which transformed nearly all death sentences into sentences to life in prison.[17]

A new Greek constitution had gone into effect in January 1952, but this charter's supposedly liberal scope was promptly compromised by a "parallel" or "paraconstitution" that extended the validity of the "emergency measures" against communism issued in June 1946 and December 1947.[18] Nikos Alivizatos has incisively analyzed the "paraconstitutional" nature of this "emergency regime" created and maintained by the Greek right-wing state: it gave its executive powers the "right" to continue to suppress the Left, based on measures that contravened the guarantees of civil liberties of the January 1952 constitution. Also, military tribunals could penalize the leftist defendants' intentions as much as their actions.[19] To justify this exten-

---

(1982: 144–48). Sakkas documents the bolder British stance of public criticism (2013: 122–25).

17. Nikolakopoulos (2001: 154, 155, 157). Lilian Kalamaro, the widow of the executed Dimitris Batsis, describes the devastating effect of this historical irony in her personal memoir entitled *The Heaviest Possible Price* (original Greek title: *Βαρύτατο τίμημα 1941–1952*) (1981: 177).

18. Alivizatos (1981: 223, 228; 2011: 366–67, 373–75).

19. Alivizatos (1981; 1995: 463–65, 525–600, especially 528, 535–36, 583–87). See also Kazamias (unpublished ms.: 32).

sion of the "emergency regime," the Greek state resorted to the "theory of permanent civil war," which made the "rebellion" last until 1962.[20] Alivizatos affirms that, while Western European countries were building their domestic models of the "welfare state," the Greek Right and Left lived in what were essentially two different states, in which the political apartheid inflicted by the former on the latter continued to disfigure democratic institutions:[21]

> The liberal—at least in principle—1952 constitution regulated the relations of the state with the "nationally thinking" citizens (the ἐθνικόφρονες), while the "emergency" measures comprised a second constitution (a "paraconstitution" . . .) that dealt with the nonnationally thinking.[22]

The full range of Greek constitutional freedoms could be exercised only by the so-called *ethnikofrones*, those who branded leftists and communists as "antinationals" while they themselves "safeguarded" *ethnikofrosyni*, the "high" ground of nationalist patriotism. *Ethnikofrosyni* may be defined as a self-righteous "national conviction" or "national-mindedness," in a vocal to militant blend of political, cultural, religious, and moral conservatism.[23] By way of comparison, Minas Samatas has resorted to the notions of "anticommunist 'apartheid'" and "'Greek McCarthyism.'"[24] Downplaying any ideological differences or frictions on the side of the Left, the Greek rightwing establishment lumped Argyriadis, his comrades, and also his family into the "evil" category. With verve, historian Alexander Kitroeff describes the Greek state of 1952 as follows:

> The 1952 constitution was . . . a fig leaf, unable to hide a formidable undemocratic monster composed of the excessive constitutional powers of the king, the US-supported conservative political wing, and the repressive shadowstate mechanism (*parakratos* [the "parastate," "deep state," or secretive "parallel state"]) run by the army. For many Greek citizens, the situation was just

---

20. Alivizatos (1981: 227–28).
21. Alivizatos (2011: 364). Greece is regrettably absent from Béla Tomka's social history of Europe, in which he discusses the beginnings and the expansion of the welfare states (2013: 154–71). Kliafa outlines the postwar circumstances that delayed the Greek state's design of its own welfare state (2016: 41–50, 70). See further Stathopoulos (2005) and the volume edited by Venieris and Papatheodorou (2003).
22. Alivizatos (1981: 227–28).
23. Papadimitriou (2006) has studied the nationalist-conservative standard of *ethnikofrosyni* in its historical development from 1922 through 1967. See also Kazamias (unpublished ms.: 31, 32, 38–39, 70–73), who reflects on the conceptual and analytical potential of the discourse of *ethnikofrosyni*, especially in its multilayered relations to Greek state policy and the monarchy.
24. Samatas (2014: 57 and 52, respectively).

as bad as it would have been under a Papagos dictatorship or, ironically, one run by the Stalinist communist leaders imprisoned or banished into exile by the post–Civil War regime.[25]

Because the September 1951 Greek election results had proven to be inconclusive and had generated yet another unstable coalition government, John Peurifoy, the American ambassador to Greece, favored a change of the Greek electoral system from a proportional to a majority system.[26] Once this change had been implemented, it delivered the (eventually American-backed) victory of the Greek Rally party (ES, Ελληνικός Συναγερμός) of General Alexandros Papagos, who had been military commander-in-chief with wide-ranging powers during the final months of the Civil War.[27] The hard-liner Papagos won the decisive November 1952 election and served as prime minister from 1952 until his death in October 1955. His rule showed hardly any signs of the terror against the Left easing. In the same election of November 1952, the more liberal-minded Plastiras was not reelected to the Greek Parliament, and he died shortly afterward. Thus, the March 1952 executions jettisoned the last hopes of a true postwar reconciliation, and disappointment with political leaders ran deep. This malaise engendered a saying common at the time: "Τι Πλαστήρας τι Παπάγος; Όλοι οι σκύλοι μια γενιά," "What with Plastiras? What with Papagos? All dogs are of the same stock."[28]

---

25. Kitroeff, 1 February 2002. Kazamias situates the charged notion of the "parastate" in its historical context of the 1950s through early 1960s (unpublished ms.: 31–32).

26. Wittner uses the characterization of a "winner-take-all system" (1982: 290). See further Botsiou (2007: 219–20); Hatzivassiliou (2014: 96–97); and Stefanidis (2007: 178). Iatrides (2016) details the American interest in the Greek electoral system, which had surfaced about one year prior to the September 1951 election but affected outcomes only by November of 1952.

27. Iatrides (2016) documents how US Ambassador Henry Grady, Peurifoy's predecessor, had long tried to stall even a less authoritarian version of the "Papagos solution," for which the Greek royal couple had been pushing (up through spring 1951, when the relationship between Papagos and the palace soured). Grady feared the backlash of resentment that American entanglement in Greek internal politics would inevitably cause, given that the Greek election results had been showing only modest support for the agenda of any nationalist or anticommunist strongman. Even the more intrusive Peurifoy initially aligned himself with Washington's view of Papagos as the "last card for use only in great emergency," whose election would stand in the way of Greece's path to political normalization (Iatrides 2018: 38, quoting Peurifoy's characterization of the reluctant stance of the US Department of State and the American Embassy in Athens). But Peurifoy reached a level of frustration with Greek political wrangling that led him to seek more forceful solutions by mid-March of 1952 (Iatrides 2018: 41–43).

28. Paschaloudi (2013: 215). Cf. Hatzivassiliou (Chatzivasileiou) (2001: 43, 316). I owe the facts of this brief synopsis to Alivizatos (1981, 1995, and 2011: 365–66); Clogg (2013: *passim*); Gallant (2016: 257–59); Hatzivassiliou (2014); Iatrides (2016, with the most detailed analysis

The 1952 executions took place after months of court hearings, media speculation, and international activism, especially on behalf of Beloyannis, who was given the opportunity to speak out.[29] But in the morning of 30 March, the Greeks woke up to the startling news that four fellow citizens had been shot on a Sunday, the one day on which even the Nazi Germans had refrained from killing their opponents. Beloyannis had arrived in Greece clandestinely on 7 June 1950. He was arrested only six months later, on 20 December 1950.[30] His capture led to more searches, numerous arrests, and heftier charges, and to the tragic end of the four men to whom the military tribunals did not give prison sentences but the death penalty. The first trial, held by the "emergency" tribunal that dealt with alleged violations of the anticommunist law 509/1947, lasted for several weeks, from 19 October through 16 November 1951.[31] The second trial built on the prior charges of communist subversion but moved the case to the Permanent Military Court of Athens. It commenced on 15 February 1952, involved a total of twenty-eight defendants, and reached a verdict on 1 March 1952. This verdict was front-page news in the Greek papers: the *Akropolis* of the following day stressed that Beloyannis and Argyriadis received the harshest

---

and documentation); Kazamias (unpublished ms.: 44–47, 68–70, 74–91, 98); Kostis (2018: 331–41); Miller (2009); Paschaloudi (2013); Petropoulos and Chatzidimitrakos (2015a); and Wittner (1982: 283–96). Lymberatos (2015: 20–33, 44–49) outlines the 1951 emergence of the more moderate party of the United Democratic Left (EDA, Ενιαία Δημοκρατική Αριστερά) amid a climate of political confusion and failed communist regrouping. Van Boeschoten (2015) makes Greece a case study for an incisive theoretical reflection on the challenges posed by the demands of top-down reconstruction and reconciliation.

29. The Western European outcry set off by the Beloyannis trial is the point of departure of a recent mystery novel written by Nikos Davvetas, *The Painter of Beloyannis* (2013; original Greek title: *Ο ζωγράφος του Μπελογιάννη*), referring to Picasso's portrait of "the man with the carnation." The novel contains an excellent historical epilogue contributed by Eleni Paschaloudi and entitled "The Events Prior to the Myth" (2013: 209–15). In his book *The Man with the Carnation* (1990; original French title: *L'homme à l'œillet*), André Kédros writes from the perspective of an indignant Greek expatriate in France closely following the events of 1949–1956.

30. Kousidou and Stavropoulos (ca. 1998: 321, 343) and Petropoulos and Chatzidimitrakos (2015a: 32–33).

31. The volume edited by Petropoulos and Chatzidimitrakos (2015b) examines the preliminary phases of the prolonged trial and the state's interpretation of alleged communist infiltration (based on the prehearing exposé of the Security Police). The editors have identified the later dictator Giorgos Papadopoulos as one of the judges serving on the military tribunal that oversaw the first trial (Petropoulos and Chatzidimitrakos 2015a: 35; 2015b: 413). Publications such as Sakellaropoulos and Sakellaropoulos (2016) attest to further renewed interest in the trials. In March 2017, the leftist Greek prime minister Alexis Tsipras inaugurated a permanent exhibition on Beloyannis in the latter's native home in Amaliada, in the western Peloponnese.

penalty: "twice to death" ("εἰς θάνατον δίς").[32] On 30 and 31 March 1952, the executions of the four condemned to death made the front page again: the *Akropolis* came out with a special Sunday 30 March edition; the *Athinaïki* newspaper of 31 March 1952 noted also the reactions abroad, and especially in London. The front page of the *Akropolis* of 1 April 1952 featured a chilling "photo reportage" of the prisoner transport and the site of Goudi, and also a reconstruction drawing of the execution.

Just a couple of days before the end of the first trial, the Greek authorities had broadcast the "spectacular" seizure of two wireless sets, with which, they alleged, the defendants had been transmitting critical data to the communist leadership in Bucharest. The prosecution then invoked this "new," contrived information to push for a second trial that would be driven by the aggravated charges of espionage and high treason, even though several wireless sets had been in use throughout the 1940s war years and the authorities had known about them for at least one year.[33] The search for these wireless stations had been intensified only by the first trial's closing date, when new and graver accusations were needed to steer the court case in the direction willed by the state, that is, toward an irrevocable verdict of the death penalty. This irrevocable penalty exceeded the worst penalty carried by law 509/1947 of a death penalty verdict that could still be converted into a life sentence, if clemency were granted by the Greek king and his councilors on the Board of Pardons. The captured men's use of up to four wireless sets provided the prosecution with legal grounds for charges that far outweighed the initial accusations of illicit communist activity. The state predictably invoked law 375/1936 "on espionage," which dated back to the anticommunist policies of pre–World War II dictator Ioannis Metaxas and provided "much-needed" safeguards against external security threats.[34] Thus the second trial led to the 1 March 1952 verdict of the death penalty, which, it was rumored, was also prompted by interference from the United States.[35] "Liberalism and, needless to say, the concept of a fair trial were

---

32. Anon., *Akropolis*, 2 March 1952.
33. Kousidou and Stavropoulos (ca. 1998: 393–94); Lymberatos (2015: 30, 64–65); Paraskevopoulos (1980: 79–82, 88, 99); Petropoulos and Chatzidimitrakos (2015a: 25, 36–39); and Vournas (1981: 35–38, 42–47). See Anon. (1989) on espionage charges laid against Greek left-wingers of the early 1960s.
34. Alivizatos (2008: 52, 53; 2011: 390–91).
35. Lymberatos (2015: 64–66); Paschaloudi (2013: 214); Petropoulos and Chatzidimitrakos (2015a: 41); and Stathakis (2004: 391). The persistent suspicions of American interference in the grim outcome, however, are not borne out by any of the currently available evidence. Iatrides refers to a telegram that Ambassador Peurifoy dispatched to the US Department of State some thirty-six hours before the executions: in this internal communication, Peurifoy reported from the viewpoint of an observer of the trial's verdict, who actually

swept away in the name of the anticommunist crusade. Beloyiannis would become one of the earliest victims of the defeat of the project of national reconciliation," Kitroeff concludes.[36]

The execution of Beloyannis became emblematic of the heightened antileftist climate of early 1950s Greece, but it also raised questions about affiliations and disaffiliations within the group of the condemned, within the Greek Communist Party Bureau, and within the broader communist movement. Were Elias Argyriadis, his wife, and his children targeted twice, for being, inadvertently, on the wrong side of the party line and on the wrong side of Cold War history? Relating to subsequent historical revisionism, Kitroeff adds, "Beloyiannis and his comrades have been neatly extracted from the Stalinist context."[37] It remains difficult, however, to reconstruct the ideological alignment of the three executed individuals who were left out of the spotlight of international sympathy. Chronologically, the four men still belonged to the era of Stalin's rule, which started to crumble after Stalin's death on 5 March 1953. The process of "destalinization" began in earnest, however, in February 1956, when the Soviet Communist Party officially condemned the realities of power struggle and exploitation that had defined Stalinism. The higher echelons of the Greek Communist Party Bureau still worked within a Stalinist straitjacket, which no longer befitted the post–Civil War era. "[S]avage internal purges" were part of the "ugly Stalinist baggage" that dragged down the Greek Communist Party, "which to this day it has not officially disowned or apologized for," in the words of David Close.[38] André Kédros reflects, with a sense of wistfulness, that

> Beloyannis and his men may well have escaped something much worse than death. Ever since the 20th Congress [of the Communist Party of the Soviet Union, held 14–25 February 1956], I see around me only militants in a state of shock. Zombies and enraged people. People who cannot be recuperated.[39]

---

expected new turns of events. He did not discount the possibility that a "new expedient or compromise may be devised" that would avert the killings (Iatrides, email communication of 30 and 31 March 2016). Peurifoy's tone was, nonetheless, disparaging: he opened with "Fate of convicted Commies . . . seems to hang in wildly swinging balance," and he distinguished between "small fry" and "big shots including Beloyannis." Peurifoy's telegram of 28 March 1952 (tel. 4281) is part of the Department of State Records 781.00/3–2852, held at the National Archives and Records Administration at College Park, Maryland.

36. Kitroeff, 1 April 2002.
37. Kitroeff, 1 April 2002.
38. Close (2004: 264).
39. Kédros (1990: 340): "Béloyannis et les siens ont peut-être échappé à quelque chose de pire que la mort. Depuis le XXe Congrès, je ne vois autour de moi que des militants en état de choc. Des zombis ou des enragés. Irrécupérables."

The Ripple Effect of a Family Tragedy

We Were Little and Did Not Know

> Το μόνο που ήθελα ήταν να δω τις κόρες μου πριν πεθάνω. Μου το 'χαν
> υποσχεθεί αλλά με γέλασαν.
> The one thing I wanted was to see my daughters before I die. They had
> promised that to me, but they cheated me out of it.
>
> —Elias Argyriadis, in response to a priest's question as to whether he
> had a last wish, moments before his execution on 30 March 1952[40]

Communication between the Greek undercover communists and their leaders abroad depended on the use of the infamous wireless stations. The private home called "Avra" ("Breeze") of Elias Argyriadis, on 43 Artemis Street
in the Athenian suburb of (Ano) Glyfada, housed one of the wireless sets in
a secret, cellar-like space that Elias himself had built.[41] To the outside world,
however, it looked like Elias was operating a chicken farm on the property.
On 14 November 1951, the Greek General Security Police (Γενική Ασφάλεια)
discovered its suspect in this crypt, arrested him, and confiscated the equipment and any documents it could find. Leftist historian Tasos Vournas has
claimed that this wireless had not been operational for a while, which led
him to conclude that it was found out only through a cowardly or treason-
ous act from within.[42] The shock of the arrest and the stigma of betrayal
were not the only aspersions cast onto the Argyriadis family. On 27 November 1951, the thirty-four-year-old Katerina Dalla, Argyriadis's second wife
and mother of the two youngest daughters, committed suicide. Dalla (born
near Larisa in 1917) had met Elias when they were both serving with the
Greek resistance in the mountains, he as a guerrilla fighter against the occu-
pying forces, she as a cook for his team.[43] Before taking her own life, Dalla
had been interrogated for about ten days at the Athens headquarters of
the Security Police. On her return home, she took an overdose of pills and,
when she started to lose control over her body, she fell out of a window.[44]

---

40. Based on the Greek film version of the Beloyannis affair, produced by Nikos Tzimas and
    entitled *The Man with the Carnation* (also on DVD, 2010). The movie's first release in
    November of 1980 generated renewed interest in the trial and execution of Beloyannis and
    his comrades, as seen in a sequence of articles and interviews published in the Greek news-
    paper *Eleftherotypia*, which began on 6 December 1980 (Oikonomeas et al., 6 December
    1980–16 January 1981).
41. Paraskevopoulos (1980: 23, 79, 86, 88–90).
42. Vournas (1981: 42–43).
43. Anon., *Neologos Patron*, 20 November 1951, 1, 4.
44. Thus state the contemporary newspapers, quoting the police report of the incident along-

The Greek Right conceived of communism as a "virus" that infected not only individuals but entire families or social groups.[45] Similar to the ways in which the mother of the two Argyriadis girls had become known to the broader Greek populace, the identities of the girls themselves were no longer those of private persons but became those of political beings. After 30 March 1952, Efterpi Argyriadi (born in 1938) was old enough to go and live with relatives. Her two younger half-siblings, however, Ioanna (born 1945) and Olympia (born 1949), were now orphans from the "tainted" Argyriadis family, whose members were deemed unworthy (if not too dangerous) to act as guardians or substitute parents.[46] The two girls were committed first to a foster home in the southern Athenian suburb of Dafni. Then they were dispatched to a residential care facility situated on the Penteli mountain slopes, northeast of Athens, where they were kept together until shortly before their adoption case was finalized on 12 April 1955. The siblings were given to the loving adoptive parents George and Betty Alevras, Greek Americans who were both in their early forties and childless. The Alevrases had met the two sisters, probably in January of 1955, and they knew their prior family history.[47]

---

side a chilling picture of Dalla in agony. See, for instance, Anon., *Akropolis*, 28 November 1951, 1; Chatzianastasiou, *Ethnikos Kiryx*, 28 November 1951, 1. There may, of course, have been more to Dalla's bruises on the head and feet. But worse, arguably, than the physical mistreatment that Dalla might have suffered during the days of her interrogation must have been the papers' portrayal of her as collaborating with the authorities. This depiction, if there was truth to it, would have discredited her with the Left.

45. Samatas comments on the "guilt by association" that extended to the family of any left-wing suspect (2014: 55). The Greek Wikipedia entry on Elias Argyriadis supplies the name of Elias's first wife, Triantafyllia Petridou, with whom he had fathered two older daughters, Efterpi and Evangelia, who does not figure in the adoption narrative of Elias's second family. At the time of Elias's arrest, suspicions fell on Triantafyllia, her brother, and two cousins as well.

46. Born in late April 1945 in a village near Larisa (in Central Greece, where Elias spent time in detention), Ioanna's birth came at a time of renewed internal strife after the incidents of December 1944 (with only a temporary reprieve granted by the Varkiza Agreement), followed by the onslaught of violence called the "White Terror" (1945–1946), which again targeted leftists. Therefore, Ioanna is truly a child of white terror. Early childhood trauma is at the core of "*Where Is Your Mother, You?*" (1986; original Greek title: "Πού 'ναι η μάνα σου, μωρή;"), an autobiographical account written by survivor Dimitra Sotiri Petroula, whose (left-wing) family was killed by reactionary thugs when the Civil War was still raging. Gerolymatos (2004) situates the White Terror wave of violence in the context of Greece's role in the onset of the Cold War.

47. Oikonomeas and Oikonomidis quote extensively from the girls' adoption records and provide the final date in a lead article in *Eleftherotypia* of 16 December 1980, to which Efterpi Argyriadi contributed. The adoption papers stress that Ioanna and Olympia Argyriadi are not only orphans but also "illegitimate children" ("ἐξώγαμα τέκνα," literally: "children born out of wedlock"). To prove its case, the Greek court refers to the death certificate of

Interestingly, Efterpi vividly recalls the time that Ioanna and Olympia spent with their first foster mother in Dafni, who did what she could to block Efterpi's access to her half-sisters.[48] The Greek American adoptive mother recounts the story of visiting the girls' "really nice foster home in Sparta."[49] The Greek and the American versions of the years 1952–1955 are probably complementary, given the dearth of details on the year and a half prior to April 1955. Most decisively, however, the adoption records show that George and Betty Alevras petitioned the appropriate Greek court, that is, the Court of First Instance, to adopt Ioanna and Olympia Argyriadi on 31 March 1955. On 5 April, the adoptive parents and their Greek lawyer, G. Tsevas, were present at a scheduled court hearing in Athens. Exactly one week later, a court order sealed the case.[50] Based on this mandatory legal document, the

---

Katerina Dalla but also to the execution order against Elias Argyriadis. The use of these documents before the Greek court proves that the Alevrases were aware of who the girls' parents were and of the circumstances of their deaths. They were by no means unsuspecting or deluded would-be parents.

48. Once Efterpi had been granted visitation rights by the Greek police, she was able to see her siblings. Already on her first visit, however, she noticed that the foster mother did not take good care of the children and filed a formal complaint. A social worker from PIKPA looked into the matter and confirmed Efterpi's report.

There were no professional foster parents in Greece in the 1950s, nor were there sound legal provisions covering foster care. Foster families were offered allowances (of approximately 200 to 300 drachmas, or 7 to 10 USD, per child per month in the mid-1950s) to look after the children placed in their care based on a freelance type of arrangement. Wood-Ritsatakis comments on the poor to unsatisfactory living conditions provided by postwar Greek foster families, whose motives for taking in children were primarily economic (1970: 127). She nearly apologizes for Greece's social workers who, well aware of the problems, still "choose families in which they believe the children will not come to any physical, or mental harm, knowing that in many cases there is little chance of their receiving the emotional care and affection they need" (1970: 127). Theodoropoulou contextualizes the role of wet nurses and foster families in Greece of the mid-twentieth century (2006: 67–70). See further Anon., *Nieuwe Leidsche Courant*, 24 December 1956; Kliafa (2016: 92); Koussidou and Maganiotou (1991: 175); and Nanou (2011: 60), who stresses that formal foster care has remained rare for decades. With the issuance of Law 4538 of mid-May 2018, the Greek government only recently committed to supporting stronger domestic fosterage and adoption structures, but the law does not redress the institutional shortcomings of the past that disproportionally affected adoptees and birth mothers.

49. Betty Alevras is quoted by Whittemore, 1 February 2012. The correct location is not Sparta but Spata, to the east of Athens and close to the Penteli mountains and Agia Paraskevi, where the children stayed shortly before their departure for the States.

50. A two-step legal process was normal in those 1950s international adoption cases that began and ended in Greece: the preliminary court hearing established the consent of the child's natal family or guardian, whereas the decisive second hearing tended to grant the adoption based on the consent of the adoptive parents. If the prospective parents could not be present in a Greek court on a set date, the court could still proceed with the statement of consent, which they then had to file in advance at the Greek consulate closest to their home location. The suitability of the adoptive parents was, therefore, already estab-

girls were given a visa to enter the United States. They started the long journey by late April of 1955.

Ioanna and Olympia were far from silent subjects, however. Efterpi tells the moving story of how Ioanna had hidden a note in her pocket on a day in early April of 1955, when the siblings were to meet again with their would-be mother.[51] She paraphrases Ioanna's message (in Greek) as follows: "Effi, they're taking us to America. Little Olympia wants to go, but I don't want to. Come and get us!"[52] When the Greek intermediary, who was to hand over the children, found the note, she began to scold Ioanna. Olympia remembers how her new adoptive mother silenced the woman by insisting that her children should never be made to feel ashamed for loving their family. Efterpi stresses the negative role of this go-between, whose husband, with the last name of Zervoulakos (no first name given), was introduced to the children as an "uncle." In fact, both intermediaries were more distant relatives, who probably served as temporary caregivers. The children stayed with them in a house in Agia Paraskevi, northeast of Athens, during the two short weeks from the time their adoption was finalized until the day they departed for New York.[53]

Nothing indicates that adult relatives from the larger Argyriadis or Dallas families were able to adopt the orphaned children, even if only informally. Discussing similar cases of offspring of left-wing parents of Northern Greece, social anthropologist Aigli Brouskou cites counterexamples demonstrating that intervention by close relatives was possible, if they acted in a timely manner to retrieve their kin children before they entered the welfare system or adoption procedures began.[54] In most cases cited, however, those children were very young (up to five years old) and also from "less

---

lished in the preliminary hearing. I have yet to see a final act of adoption that revoked the preliminary decision in a 1950s adoption case of a US-bound Greek child. See also Athinogenis and Papathanasiou (1959: 30–31).

51. Efterpi Argyriadi, testimony of 13 July 2014, based on memories that Olympia has recounted to her.

52. Brouskou's work contextualizes the meaning of messages and objects associated with the very moment of children changing hands (2015: 203–7). Ioanna's message is an exception for being written by the child herself located at the very center of the transfer. However, her note shares the desire for ultimate reunification with the more conventional messages or tokens of "discovery" or "recognition" (the hoped-for *anagnorisis*) accompanying foundlings across time and space (2015: 206–7). One interviewee's illiterate mother asked a female friend to write the note, which she then pinned to the ten-day-old foundling: the note contained the baby's baptismal name and also a reassurance that the mother would later return to the orphanage to fetch her child (Maria, telephone communication of 1 February 2016).

53. Efterpi, testimony of 13 July 2014.

54. Brouskou (2015: 158–59).

political" families than the Argyriadis girls. Also, it was during the years 1947–1949 that the relatives who preempted further procedures managed to take action. The timing coincided with the worst upheaval of the Civil War and with the malleability of a child welfare system still in its infancy. When the articles concerning adoption of the 1946 Greek Civil Code were enforced, however, they stipulated that formal adoptive parents had to be childless and at least fifty years of age.[55] Moreover, the adoptive parents had to be politically conservative, Greek Orthodox Christians of some means.[56] These written and unwritten stipulations (under which also the Argyriadis and Dallas family members would have had to operate) unnecessarily complicated adoptions within Greece but remained in force for a quarter-century. New laws on adoptions, issued in 1966 and 1970, finally lifted some of the old restrictions, which Greek couples interested in adopting had long found hard to meet.[57] Through the 1950s and early 1960s, however, the old stipulations steered more Greek children than necessary toward the inter-country adoption system (where the minimum age requirement of fifty did not apply) and again toward established couples of Greek descent and of the Orthodox faith.[58]

The obstructive minimum age requirement of fifty traced its origins back to the "model" 1804 French Civil Code, itself informed by strictures

---

55. The Civil Code of Greece dated back to 23 February 1946, and it covered adoption in articles 1568 through 1588. The minimum age requirement of fifty could be waived, and it was lowered to thirty-five in 1966, as evidenced by the data collected by Maganiotou and Koussidou (1988: 387–88). See also Athinogenis and Papathanasiou (1959: 41); Kambylis (2008); Politakou (1958); Wood-Ritsatakis (1970: 127–28); and the Greek Legislative Decree 4532 of 17 August 1966, published in the *Government Gazette of the Kingdom of Greece*, the *Efimeris tis Kyverniseos tou Vasileiou tis Ellados*. In the case of Anthony (see below, p. 208), the Greek court was clearly willing to accept a little white lie about the age of his Greek-born but expatriate adoptive mother: Anthony's childless new mother was much younger than fifty when she declared in person that she was of the appropriate age, and the judge accepted her statement (Anthony, testimony of 4 February 2016). The volume edited by Venetia Kantsa (2013) traces developments in Greek notions of motherhood and also adoption. On adoption within Greece, see the chapter by Eirini Papadaki (2013), whose 2015 dissertation elaborates on the subject. Mastrogiannis (1962) and Kaloutsi-Tavlaridou (1970) reflect older Greek thinking about adoption practices. Handman (1993) offers a local case study with further historical references to traditional adoptions. Dedousi (2012) and Tatsopoulos (2006) present more recent and personal perspectives on domestic Greek adoptions. Carsten (2004: chs. 4 and 6) offers new theoretical perspectives on the study of kinship in anthropology through the lens of, among other foci, adoption and fostering.

56. Theodoropoulou (2006: 20).

57. Moschos (1981–1982: 385–89) and below, pp. 116–17.

58. Brouskou (2015: 159–60, 271, 274, 277–79). See also, prematurely: Anon., "Greece Is Revising Her Adoption Laws," *New York Times*, 12 July 1959.

stemming from ancient Roman law. Aiming to protect natural heirs, the requirement mainly served the succession system for which it was designed. It proved to be utterly impracticable for couples attempting to build or expand their young families. The succession-centered "old" adoption system did not gratify the wishes of hopeful would-be parents, and it did not provide care for children in need, either. Most of the child subjects of the old adoption system were young relatives of couples adopting within Greece. Their "simple" adoptions did not decrease, but rather extended family ties, rights, and duties, unlike the "full," "plenary," or "stranger" adoptions, which forever severed the child from the natal family.[59] The phenomenon of "full" adoptions, also called "new" or "Western-style" adoptions, was not widespread in Greece of the 1950s, but it became most common from 1970 on.[60] Importantly, adoption within Greece needed to be uncoupled from the stigma of illegitimacy and of birth mothers lacking judgment and strength.[61] E. Wayne Carp has noted the bias against the "feebleminded" unwed mother and her illegitimate child in American adoption history.[62] According to Michael Herzfeld, the Greeks' essentialist thinking about blood bonds and inheritance (of character as well as property) delayed the development of a domestic adoption movement of and by "strangers."[63] The developing inter-country adoption system involving Greek-born orphans preferred to place these children with Greek Americans, and it helped that Greek kinship relations proved to be elastic across oceans and continents as well. More than any other Americans, Greek American adoptive parents were thought to "guarantee" the children's continuity of language, culture, and especially religion. Even today, diaspora Greeks are still regarded as members of a kin group that weds familial to national identities and to claims of legacies: they are members of the ομογένεια, the "homogeny" or community that shares the marker of common ethnic Greek descent (broadly defined); that is, they belong to the extended family of Greeks abroad and their offspring.[64]

Based on her multiyear research at the Municipal Foundling Home of Thessaloniki named Saint Stylianos (Δημοτικό Βρεφοκομείο Θεσσαλονίκης "Άγιος Στυλιανός"), Brouskou lists the "criteria for exclusion" that have typ-

59. Handman (1993: 211); McKnight (2001: 312–13, 324–25, 328); Mignot (2019: 336); and Papa-
    daki (2015: 78–81).
60. Koussidou and Maganiotou (1991: 167–68, 169, 170, 175).
61. Kaloutsi-Tavlaridou (1970: 27, 103, *passim*).
62. Carp (2002: 9). Rossini discusses the long-standing bias against "fallen women" in Britain
    (2014: 28-38).
63. Herzfeld (1992: 138–39).
64. Leontis (1995) theorizes the Greek ties to the homeland across generations. I review these
    topics in part 2 of this book.

ically impaired available children's progress toward adoption.[65] The list of these factors impeding a "clean break" from the children's past leads me to conclude that the Greek American family that adopted the Argyriadis girls admirably showed the open-mindedness to discount all of them.[66] Brouskou defines these factors as "bolstering a child's identity as a member of a family": the existence of siblings, of known parents, and of name(s), and also the children's older age.[67] According to Brouskou, foundlings were the preferred category of children to be entered into the intercountry adoption network, precisely because they were entirely "ahistorical."[68] Even more than orphans, who had typically enjoyed close family ties in their early years, infant foundlings in particular lent themselves to adoptions characterized by irrevocability. This "guarantee" of finality, and thus of exclusive new kinship, was the kind of comforting result that most adopters hoped to secure via a cross-border placement. Irrevocability was, regrettably, a one-way street. It did not apply to those adoptive parents who, after a few days or even months, returned the adoptee, whether to an intermediary or to an institution.[69] The steady demand meant, too, that some authoritarian, government-funded Greek childcare institutions and organizations became so committed to sending adoptable children abroad that they started cooking the books: they designated more children as "foundlings" or "orphans," without the knowledge of some children's still-living biological parents, whose consent would otherwise have been legally required.[70] This method of sourcing adoptable children is known as "child laundering" or "making paper orphans."[71] Part 2 of this study revisits some of the above-mentioned issues.

---

65. Brouskou (2015: 281). The best English translation of *vrefokomeío* is, rather, "nursery," but common Greek parlance referred to this and similar institutions, which placed abandoned babies in the care of wet nurses, as "foundling homes" or as ορφανοτροφεία, "orphanages." Strictly speaking, however, Greek orphanages housed and educated older children, from approximately six years old through their midteens. American English usage refers to these postwar Greek institutions indiscriminately as "orphanages." Some English translations of Greek documents, however, refer to them as "children's asylums."

66. Admittedly, by the early 1950s, waiting periods for would-be adoptive parents who had been approved for domestic adoptions by US agencies had grown notoriously long. In 1953, waiting periods from one to more than four years were not exceptional. See Herman (2008: 143–44).

67. Brouskou (2015: 281).

68. Brouskou (2015: 65, 109, 280).

69. On such grievous cases, see below, p. 159 and p. 213.

70. Brouskou (2015: 109–10).

71. The latter expression is based on Oh (2015: 117–19, 208), reflecting on international adoption from Korea.

Little Did We Know

> An animal will not abandon its young, but I learned that some communist
> women would. One officer actually saw a woman throw her baby away. He
> picked the child up and handed it to us.
>
> —Queen Frederica, *A Measure of Understanding*, 1971: 138

This statement, taken from the autobiography of the Greek Queen Frederica, may provide further background to the story of the Argyriadis girls.
The girls' American adoption, which also cleared them for immigration
visas, was handled through a Greek state institution called PIKPA. PIKPA
was founded in 1914 as a women's philanthropic organization assisting poor
families, but by 1951, it had been consolidated under the purview of the
Greek Ministry of Social Welfare (itself founded in 1916), and it cared for
"unprotected" children as well. The agency's acronym stands for Πατριωτικό
Ίδρυμα Κοινωνικής Προνοίας και Αντίληψης, or Patriotic Institution for
Social Welfare and Awareness.[72] Under the auspices of Queen Frederica,
PIKPA intensified its efforts to provide support services for mothers and
children. Since 1933, the Adoptions Bureau of PIKPA had been involved in
domestic adoptions. By 1950, the Bureau was handling overseas adoptions as
well. Only from about 1955 on, however, did PIKPA start to add substantially
to the growing numbers of US-bound adoptions.[73] The trend's numbers rose
far more rapidly through the actions taken by the Ahepa, the International
Social Service (ISS), and by independent agents, who placed many more
Greek-born children in the States (see part 2 of this book). Assisted by the
first Greek social workers, PIKPA prioritized placing orphans with adoptive parents in the States, but it insisted that those parents belong to the
Greek Orthodox faith—that is, that the intercountry adoption still be an
intrareligious adoption. Many orphans spent a few months in Greek foster
homes, in the PIKPA residential care facility on the Penteli mountains, or
both before their overseas adoption process could be completed, as was the
case with the Argyriadis girls.

PIKPA had originated in crisis philanthropy, developed into a seminational agency that processed intercountry adoptions, and maintained ties

---

72. The name's various terms have been subject to change. Theodorou (2015) discusses the
    role of PIKPA's precursors through the 1930s. See further Kliafa (2016: 150–55); Theodoro-
    poulou (2006: 85, 96–98, *passim*); and Wood-Ritsatakis (1970: 124–25). English-language
    literature of the 1990s refers to the agency as the Public Institution of the Social Welfare
    Association, operating under the supervision of the Greek Ministry of Health and Social
    Welfare (Panera 1991: 145).
73. Athinogenis and Papathanasiou (1959: 13) and Tsitidis (1964: 13).

to the Greek queen. The same characteristics applied to three more of Queen Frederica's initiatives. The earliest ones were the *paidopoleis* (παιδοπόλεις) and the so-called Queen's Fund with roots in the Civil War. The latest one was the founding of the Babies' Center Metera, whose adoptions would fast become byproducts of social rather than political constraints. The *paidopoleis* or *paidoupoleis* were state-sponsored "child-towns" or children's homes founded by the queen. Frederica had stepped up to manage Greece's child welfare system through the Welfare Organization of the Northern Provinces, whose founding date of 1947 reveals its direct link to the Civil War. This organization was renamed the Royal Welfare Fund in 1955, but it was most commonly referred to as the Queen's Fund. It operated on the basis of a "combination of voluntary and imposed philanthropy."[74] Frederica honed the latter funding mechanism to turn Metera, her 1953 shelter for unwed and expecting mothers, into a showcase institution. PIKPA's Adoptions Bureau built on the *paidopoleis* and the Queen's Fund, and it intensified the push toward overseas placements that characterized Metera. Meanwhile, Frederica also strengthened her grasp on the emerging profession of Greek social work. Thus, the child-towns, the Royal Welfare Fund or the Queen's Fund, PIKPA and its social workers, and Metera established their combined network or genealogy of overseas adoptions, which originated in the competitive child-rescue campaigns of the Civil War but subsequently developed into an autocratic child welfare system. By the onset of the Cold War, international adoption no longer presented itself as a mere alternative; rather, it was a ready-made solution to the Greek state's weak planning for child welfare. This rapid development inevitably came at the expense of creating better family-support services and domestic fosterage and adoption structures. After I complete the story of the Argyriadis girls and their adoption through PIKPA, in the sections below I place all three platforms in their historical and political context.

From 1950 to 1956, when PIKPA operated under the auspices of the Greek queen, the right-wing Lina Tsaldari served as its president. In February 1956, the widow of the former prime minister Panagis Tsaldaris became the first female Greek minister, overseeing social welfare for the conservative government of Konstantinos Karamanlis.[75] Marriage ties linked Lina Tsaldari also to Konstantinos Tsaldaris, who on behalf of the Greek government had negotiated the issue of the endangered Greek children with Dwight P. Griswold, the chief of the American Mission for Aid to Greece

---

74. Vassiloudi and Theodorou (2012: 127).
75. Alivizatos (2011: 370–71).

(AMAG, 1947–1948). These discussions had raised the solution of the mass institutionalization of Greek children, but the search for in-country foster arrangements was also considered.[76] The latter alternative, of cultivating home-care models, was the route recommended by the Americans at this early stage. Reporting for AMAG on a 1948 study of the Greek Ministry of Social Welfare, Joseph LaRocca recommended deinstitutionalizing Greek childcare to the extent possible in favor of home-care models such as in-country adoptions and foster-home placements. Given these new priorities, he recommended that the ministry seek out and maintain connections with foreign organizations, to gain from their experience in providing noninstitutional, in-country childcare.[77]

Social standing, intense civic exposure, and the PIKPA presidency had prepared Lina Tsaldari for her even more influential post of minister of social welfare, and both positions let her shape an era. In mid-1957, Tsaldari proposed to create a centralized state service with an "ethnosocial" mandate to oversee all domestic and intercountry adoptions, limiting the latter to benefit only adoptive families of Greek descent and of the Orthodox faith.[78] Karamanlis himself had led the Ministry of Social Welfare in the formative months of November 1948 through early January 1950, during which he had capitalized on its power as gatekeeper in distributing US aid.[79] PIKPA president Tsaldari knew how to influence international public opinion. During the Civil War and after, she herself had acted as a spokesperson for the Greek royalist and nationalist position, denouncing communist "child abductions" at international venues such as the November 1948 United Nations General Assembly meeting and the May 1950 UN Commission on the Status of Women.[80] Social historian Tasoula Vervenioti adds that, between November 1948 and December 1950, the UN General Assembly unanimously approved three resolutions demanding the Greek children's repatriation from the Soviet Bloc countries to Greece.[81]

---

76. Vassiloudi and Theodorou (2012: 125).
77. LaRocca (1948: 1, 14–16).
78. Kliafa (2016: 92–93) discusses the nationalist underpinnings of Tsaldari's proposal, which did not come to fruition. See below, p. 120, n. 178.
79. Lazou (2012: 126, 135). In the subsequent Papagos administration (1952–1955), Karamanlis served in the critical role of minister of public works. Hatzivassiliou (Chatzivasileiou) (2001) describes Karamanlis's rise to power through the mid-1950s, focusing on October of 1955. Svolopoulos (2011) offers a longer historical perspective.
80. Tsaldari (1967: 1: 43).
81. Vervenioti (2002: 120). On the "child abductions," see below, p. 50. Vervenioti further discusses Tsaldari's contributions (2002: 115–16, 119–20, 122, 123, 124; 2009: 86–87, 98–99, 104–5). Nachmani (1990) details the United Nations' course of action in the Greek Civil War and the Balkans through 1952.

As early as November 1951, Tsaldari set out to shape domestic public opinion on the younger Argyriadis sisters. She pressed the question of what the Greek state should do to "save the Argyriadis children from communism," in the words of Efterpi Argyriadi, who was deeply perturbed by the PIKPA president's public declarations.[82] One of Tsaldari's statements was published on the front page of *Ta Nea* of 30 November 1951, a mere three days after Dalla's suicide, when the imprisoned Elias Argyriadis was still awaiting trial:

"THE CHILDREN OF DALA"

An Athenian lady belonging to the national-minded people [ἀνήκουσα εἰς τὸν ἐθνικόφρονα κόσμον]—and we emphasize that in order for the moral weight of her appeal to be appreciated—requests that we pose publicly the following question: "What will become of the children of Ekaterina Dala?" She herself has committed suicide. [Elias] Argyriadis, with whom she had the children, is being held at the Security headquarters, and of course rightly so. What will now become of those two small children, who are under age, as the newspapers write, and who now remain entirely unprotected? Will society let some suspect family round them up, so that they, too, will end up being poisoned? [Θὰ ἀφήσῃ ἡ κοινωνία νὰ τὰ περιμαζέψῃ καμμιὰ ὕποπτος οἰκογένεια, διὰ νὰ δηλητηριασθοῦν στὸ τέλος κι' ἐκεῖνα;] We cannot fathom the thought of that happening. At stake are Greek children: we want them to be given back to us [i.e., to Greece], regardless of whether they have lived in a communist climate; and it would, therefore, be inhumane if we were to leave those two unfortunate little children to their fate. These children are not at all to blame for being born out of an illegitimate relationship and in the crossfire of so many liabilities. [Τὰ ὁποῖα δὲν πταίουν σὲ τίποτα ἂν ἐγεννήθηκαν ἀπὸ μίαν παράνομον σχέσιν καὶ εἰς τὴν διασταύρωσιν τόσων εὐθυνῶν.] We pose and submit this question to the social organizations and to the women's organizations, in particular, being the proper authorities.

Tsaldari presented no evidence, only her authority. Her claims were profoundly political, even though the last sentence of her statement disingenuously redefines them as legitimate female concerns. Tsaldari's public call for action also declared that Elias Argyriadis and Dalla had been living together without being married. Back in the 1940s and 1950s, even an insinuation of this sort was enough to exacerbate the pariah status of "illegitimate" chil-

---

82. Efterpi Argyriadi, testimony of 13 July 2014.

dren, who were already regarded as the progeny of enemies and traitors to the nation. In the eyes of Greece's reactionaries, it further confirmed that communism was detrimental to traditional family life.[83]

The nefarious results of Tsaldari's statements followed swiftly. On 7 December 1951, a social worker from PIKPA, accompanied by the gendarmes of Glyfada, came to take the younger siblings away from Efterpi, who had been taking care of them at home.[84] For days, Efterpi's urgent requests for information about the whereabouts of her half-sisters went unanswered. The official explanation, stated in the paperwork that Efterpi discovered many years later, was that "the children were without protection and remained without the means necessary for their care."[85] Efterpi subsequently learned that her half-sisters had been placed in the foster home in Dafni and had thus been entered into PIKPA's welfare system. Efterpi could not reasonably have expected that the two younger children would be left in the care of a teenage stepsister, but there was no need for the agents' violent struggle, to which she attests.[86] Crucially, however, the children's removal was the direct result of political purges, whose results could never be undone.

From late March 1952 through late April 1955, Ioanna and Olympia Argyriadi were classified as the orphaned offspring of former (that is, deceased) communists. Orphanhood, institutionalized care, and adoption became plot drivers in the Argyriadis-Alevras family narrative. PIKPA and its social workers set the Argyriadis girls on an adoption track, which must be seen against the backdrop of an expansive, monarchist child welfare system that routinely diminished the roles and responsibilities of left-wing birth parents and their families. According to Brouskou, the first Greek employees in the new profession of social work became instruments of the state's authoritarian interference; the Greek legislation concerning adoptions, which dated back to 1946, allowed for official intervention in family

---

83. Mitsopoulou (2014: 222, *passim*). For an example of such anticommunist (and misogynist) rhetoric, see Thomopoulos, *Athinaïki*, 19 November 1951, 1, 5.

84. Ironically, common parlance of the interwar and postwar periods referred to social workers as "(ἐπισκέπτριες) ἀδελφές," "(visiting) sisters," and even as "περιστέρες τοῦ πολιτισμοῦ," "doves of civilization" (Theodorou 2015: 95–96, 98). In the presence of a teenage girl, official figures styled themselves as family relations and came with the authoritative appellation of "culture-bringers" or agents of modernization.

85. In her testimony of 13 July 2014, Efterpi cites the official Greek justification: "Ἔμειναν ἄνευ προστασίας καὶ χωρὶς τὰ ἀπαιτούμενα μέσα συντηρήσεως," as per the document issued by the director of the Glyfada gendarmerie, dated 8 December 1951 (part of the adoption dossier, a copy of which is currently in Efterpi's possession).

86. Efterpi Argyriadi, *To Vima*, 9 April 2017.

life.[87] The year 1946 also saw the founding of the first Greek school for social work, which was based on the physical premises of the private American College of Greece (Pierce).[88] Initially, the profession of social worker was open only to women, and attracted students from middle- and upper-class families of more conservative political leanings.[89] In another of her efforts to promote a "top-down alternative to the grassroots welfare that flourished during the resistance period,"[90] Queen Frederica made sure she could oversee the development of the profession and of the new field in general. Even though the first Greek social workers received an American-style education, their training and outlook were slow to professionalize in the sector of in-country social work.[91] The early development and the crude politicization (that is, the anticommunist prejudice) of the Greek social welfare system, a system that was generally feeble in the Civil War's hyperpoliticized climate, have remained somewhat understudied.[92]

---

87. Brouskou (2015: 110, 115).

88. Ioakimidis (2011: 3–4).

89. Ioakimidis (2011: 6–7).

90. Ioakimidis (2011: 4).

91. Brouskou (2015: 115–16); Kliafa (2016: 77–78n218); Papadaki (2015: 126–30); Theodoropoulou (2006: 60, 71); and Theodorou (2015: 98n59, 100). In his pioneering book *Family Matters*, E. Wayne Carp situates the casework methodology of Mary Richmond (1861–1928), the "founder of modern American social work," in the context of the postwar US adoption movement and its struggle to balance disclosure versus secrecy (1998: 111). Richmond applied a behaviorist-environmental model to social work's prior emphasis on individual psychology and personal emotional adjustment. See also Fehrenbach (2016: 213, 215, 219, 221) and Winslow (2015). As Fieldston observes, the perceived link between social work and democracy facilitated the export of the social work system in its early years (2015: 195). At times, however, the imposition of "modern" and interventionist (quasicolonialist) American methods deepened distinctions of class: the increased civic participation of middle- and upper-class women, through the venues of social work and "modern" childcare techniques, exacerbated the marginalization of poor and uneducated mothers (Fieldston 2015: 166, 172, 173).

92. Close (2002: 72–74). Ioakimidis (2011) has highlighted the Greek social welfare system's collaboration with or, rather, subservience to, oppressive right-wing governments and external hegemonic forces. He stresses the system's attempts to "establish its authority over the popular classes," while it preached the values of humanitarianism and (leftist) rehabilitation (2011: 2). A similar thematic thread runs through the second part of Theodoropoulou's book that presents short data on the range of Greek, mainly twentieth-century institutions involved in social welfare, maternity care, child protection, and adoption (2006: 30–123). Lazou (2012) offers an incisive treatment of the social welfare system of the late 1940s. This system was hampered by frequent changes of directors and other personnel, due to the turmoil caused by the Civil War, uneven foreign aid distribution, and short-lived and poorly coordinated governments. Stratakis's PhD dissertation (2003) studies the Crete-based records of the Ministry of Social Welfare, which do not, however, extend beyond the first months of 1949. Stratakis pays ample attention to the Royal Welfare Fund, the care of children and orphans through the 1940s, and the expanding role of

A Domestic Genealogy of Children's Institutionalized Care and Overseas Adoption

Technically, the PIKPA foster homes and the Penteli facility, where Ioanna and Olympia spent more than three years, were not incorporated into the better-known network of the *paidopoleis*, the child-towns sponsored by the Greek monarchy and the state. The PIKPA foster homes were nonetheless selected on the basis of similar, conservative principles and conditioned by some of the same disciplinary practices. From the summer of 1947 on, Queen Frederica had overseen the Welfare Organization of the Northern Provinces, known as the Queen's Fund in the postwar vernacular. Through the Civil War years, she had prioritized the founding of the *paidopoleis*, also called "children's villages" or "Queen's camps," to house and "protect" thousands of "endangered" or "abandoned" children evacuated from the war-torn regions of Northern Greece. Most children resided in these *paidopoleis* until the summer of 1950, when the authorities began to return hundreds of them to their home villages. While affecting thousands of young lives, the Greek nationalist and anticommunist establishment invoked the good of the children and, ultimately, the good of the nation. The so-called "Commissioned Ladies" (the Ἐντεταλμένες Κυρίες) helped the queen carry out this mission of the "παιδοσώσιμο" or "παιδοφύλαγμα," literally, the "child-saving" or "child-safeguarding." Lina Tsaldari figured prominently among this group of some seventy aristocratic women before she assumed the position of PIKPA president in 1950.

Frederica devoted three chapters of her autobiography to legitimizing the royal family's involvement in the Civil War and her own, semiofficial

---

seminational agencies such as PIKPA, as well as to the latter's anticommunist bias (2003: 9–10, 152–56, 169–81). A typical document issued by a regional PIKPA president in 1946 attests to the agency's intent to wage a propaganda (counter)war against the communists: the president requests vehicles to take Greek children out on excursions, "to provide an antidote against the communist subversion to which they have been exposed" (Stratakis 2003: 222, no. 21). This lack of a comprehensive understanding of the Greek social welfare system is not helped by the state of some of the postwar social welfare and public health archives, which reside at the General State Archives (GAK) in Athens and have not yet been opened to the academic community. They may, however, be consulted in their unclassified form. Amalia Pappa and Anna Koulikourdi, archivists at the GAK, Athens, email communications of 26 February 2015, 5 March 2015, and 29 May 2017. See also Theodorou (2015: 82). In 1964, N. Tsitidis, director of child welfare, approached the PIKPA president about the lack of any proper filing and storing of the adoption files that PIKPA's Adoptions Bureau had been accumulating since 1933 (1964: 13). Athinogenis and Papathanasiou reported that PIKPA, burdened by the many bureaucratic demands on its small staff, had not been keeping up its ledger of adoptees (1959: 15–16).

children's evacuation program.[93] The queen and her "Commissioned Ladies" consistently presented this royal "humanitarian" initiative as a "reaction" against the large-scale "abductions" or "kidnappings" of children (the "παιδομάζωμα," literally "child-gathering") carried out by the communist leadership. The Greek communists sent a host of youngsters across Greece's northern borders to countries of Central and Eastern Europe. Many of these children stayed there for decades or for the rest of their lives. However, a consensus has emerged claiming that it was not the communists, but the palace and the conservative government that took the first step in relocating large numbers of children.[94] At least 12,000 to 14,000 children were dispatched to the queen's *paidopoleis*.[95] Conservative estimates place the total number of "communist-abducted" children from Northern Greece at about 20,000; others cite a total of 28,000 children.[96] Several youngsters spent time in both types of internment.

In 1948, during the peak of the competing child evacuation programs, children were regarded as political and national capital.[97] The Greek Right of the first post–Civil War years symbolically linked the recovery of the "abducted" children to the recovery of its hegemony. It abandoned its efforts, however, when it deemed those children no longer capable of assimilating back into their home environment.[98] Also, the right-wing governments of the 1950s feared that the then-older children would return to Greece as trained communists. Had Lenin himself not stated, "Give us the child for eight years, and it will be a Bolshevist forever"?[99] Also, the Greek nationalists' demands for the return of the "kidnapped" children was inconsistent—they continued to facilitate mass placements of war orphans in the United States.

The realities of the two Civil War programs, both of which invoked humanitarian grounds and the parents' rights to make final decisions, are extremely complex—as is the ideologically charged rhetoric associated with both campaigns to this day. They have, however, received renewed scholarly attention in the work of Loring Danforth and Riki Van Boeschoten (2012),

---

93. Frederica, Queen of the Hellenes (1971: 95–139).
94. Voglis (2014: 323). See also Plakoudas (2017: 93) and Vassiloudi and Theodorou (2012: 124).
95. Damousi (2015: 146–47, 176); Danforth and Van Boeschoten (2012: 6, 45, 98); and Plakoudas (2017: 93–94).
96. Danforth and Van Boeschoten (2012: 4, 48) and Plakoudas (2017: 91–92).
97. Vassiloudi and Theodorou (2012: 141).
98. Anon., *New York Times*, 30 January 1952; Plakoudas (2017: 117).
99. Lenin, epigraph to an anonymous 15 March 1948 article in *Time Magazine* entitled "As the Twig Is Bent," which denounces the Greek communists' "indoctrination" of Greek children evacuated to Soviet Bloc countries.

who analyze the role of the children themselves as agents as well as victims in the war waged between the Right and the Left for the next generation. Fear of losing the younger generation to the other camp drove—and blinded—both sides of the Civil War conflict. Because Greek passions on the topics of "child protection/abduction" and "child education/indoctrination" run high even today, I refer the reader for further details to the nuanced work of these scholars and also of Loukianos Hassiotis.[100] I acknowledge their important work in restoring voice, agency, and subjectivity to the children of the deep Civil War.[101]

By the early 1950s, the network of *paidopoleis* had been reduced from fifty-three to nine in number.[102] The Queen's Fund and PIKPA entered many of the queen's remaining war orphans into the international adoption circuit, whereas host institutions in the Soviet Bloc countries did not pursue large-scale adoptions. Giannis Atzakas, the Greek writer of autobiographical novels, attests to a conversation on the subject of a US-bound adoption, which he, as a child who exerted some agency, refused to accept: "The head of the *paidopoli* . . . asked me if I wanted a kind and wealthy American family to take me. 'They'll treat you like a child of their own, and you'll have nice clothes and toys and anything else you might want,' she said."[103]

In most cases, however, childcare officials made top-down decisions about which children were to stay on in one of the few remaining *paidopoleis*, which would be dispatched to orphanages or foster facilities, and

---

100. Hassiotis [Chasiotis] (2011, 2013a, 2013b, 2014).
101. See further Baerentzen (1987) and Vervenioti (2009) for balanced introductions. A recent volume edited by Lagani and Bontila (2012) focuses on the children sent to Central and Eastern Europe. See also Kalyvas and Marantzidis (2015: 443–55, 459). Damousi (2012) has discussed the International Social Service's efforts to reunite Greek children taken to Soviet Bloc countries with their migrant parents in Australia. As Vasiloudi's article (2014) demonstrates, the printed magazines disseminated among the child residents of the communist and royalist homes or camps couched the propaganda war of the adult world in topics and images deemed more suitable for young readers. In the broader context of the Greek crown's extensive multiyear propaganda campaign, Hassiotis speaks of "anti-communism for kids" (2011: 278). His study of the children's magazine *Paidopolis* (1950–1951) further illustrates these tenets (2009). The autobiographical novel entitled *Muddy Bottom* (original Greek title: Θολός βυθός) of Giannis Atzakas describes scenes of *paidopoli* supervisors reading anticommunist stories to their young charges (2008: 151–55). The novel's title refers to the painful experience of recovering and processing childhood memories. *Muddy Bottom* is part of a richly nuanced trilogy that recounts the life of a village boy interned at various institutions and *paidopoleis*, where he gained an early education. The other two volumes are *Folded Wings* (2007; Διπλωμένα φτερά) and *Light of Fonia* (2013; Φως της Φονιάς). See further Hassiotis (2014) and Kaisidou (2019), both focusing on the interactions between literature and (the making of) public history.
102. Danforth and Van Boeschoten (2012: 97, 105) and Plakoudas (2017: 93).
103. Atzakas (2007: 116).

which of both groups were to be placed on the path to (preferably inter-country) adoption. These officials and their social workers acted under the supervision of Lina Tsaldari. But the buck stopped with the Greek queen. The domestic constituents of the long decade of the 1950s shaped a hege-monic and royalist system of institutionalized care that, driven by both pol-icy and biopolitical interests, built up the overseas adoption channel as an expedient and inexpensive solution.

The charged interior context of the early through mid-1950s caused the determining categories of "orphanhood" and "adoptability" to be politically defined long before they were tied to social or familial backgrounds. First, children did not have to be orphaned to be considered proper candidates for the Greek queen's evacuation program of the Civil War years. According to Danforth and Van Boeschoten, convincing evidence shows that the parents of many children who were evacuated to the *paidopoleis* had not died.[104] Rather, it sufficed for the children's parents to be left-wingers who were in prison or living in exile (in countries behind the Iron Curtain after mid-1949).[105] By the early 1950s, children whose parents had long been missing or had passed away (due to natural causes, deprivation, or violence) continued to linger in the few remaining *paidopoleis*, in PIKPA institutions, or in foster care. The Executive Committee of the Queen's Fund then stipulated that the Fund continue to "protect" the children of partisans to shield them from "anti-national" propaganda.[106] For all practical purposes, the Queen's Fund declared Greek communist parents "dead"; these deaths may have been real, but they were symbolic as well. Both in life and in death, Greek communists underwent a political as well as a social and familial death: thousands of communists lost their Greek citizenship in or after 1947.[107] Danforth and Van Boeschoten clarify: "By betraying the nation, they [partisan parents] had forfeited their rights as parents to care for their children. It became the responsibility of the Greek state, therefore, to intervene and take care of these 'orphan' children."[108]

Eftihia Voutira and Aigli Brouskou speak of the Greek queen's and the state's "interventionist child welfare policy that favoured the institutional-

---

104. Danforth and Van Boeschoten (2012: 98).
105. Danforth and Van Boeschoten (2012: 103, 105) and Vasiloudi (2014: 175).
106. Danforth and Van Boeschoten (2012: 103), with reference to Mela (n.d. 87).
107. The formal disenfranchisement, enacted by the Greek state on a massive scale, targeted especially the large numbers of Greek-born Slavomacedonians who had fled to countries belonging to the Soviet Bloc. See also Christopoulos (2012: 84–85, 86–87, 89, 90) and Balt-siotis, who explains, "It is not a matter of citizenship being taken away from Greeks but from 'EAM-Bulgarians,' 'Slav bandits,' and 'Slav communists'" (2004: 88).
108. Danforth and Van Boeschoten (2012: 103). See also Theodoropoulou (2006: 47, 48–49).

ization of children at all costs."[109] Inevitably, with institutionalization came bureaucratization and a fair degree of social, or rather, biopolitical, engineering (in the sense described by Foucault, referring to the state's managing its current and future citizen bodies). Hassiotis characterizes the persistent work of the Queen's Fund as a type of "militarized welfare," driven by a "monarchical paternalism" that tried to instill "patriotism, [and] loyalty to the monarchy and to the political and social system as a whole."[110] Shows of thankfulness to the institution, the royal house, the nation, and organized religion were expected from the interned youngsters through adulthood; gratitude, a well-rehearsed skill, was mandatory.

As Hassiotis avers, the queen's initiative did much to restore the image of the crown in postwar Greece—though not for long.[111] The strong-willed Queen Frederica, who used her patronizing social work, or reactionary charity, to contain or subvert the Left's sphere of influence, never won the battle for the hearts and minds of the Greek people. To this day, the Greeks like to remind students of their country's history and politics that a popular nickname for Frederica was "Friki" ("horror," "the horrible one"). Much of the popular resentment against the queen was subsequently transferred to her son, Crown Prince Constantine, who ascended to the throne on 6 March 1964. The Greek monarchy was abolished some ten years later by a (postdictatorship) plebiscite that registered an overwhelming vote against the kingship and in favor of a parliamentary republic. For years, though, the Greek royal house and the Right kept investing in the "nation-as-paternal metaphor," in the words of N. Potamitis, who has subjected the Right's postwar rhetoric to an in-depth discourse analysis.[112] He concludes that the conservatives were able to consolidate their power by denouncing communism not only as a political crime but also as a moral and/or religious sin and a betrayal of family, community, and society at large. This discursive framework allowed the queen with some effectiveness to present herself as the "mother" of all "abandoned" Greek children and "orphans." Thus the public invocation of essentially private family relations helped to disguise the autocratic imposition of reactionary political, social, and moral codes.

A 1957 report detailed the Queen's Fund's first ten years of operation and accompanied the 26 June opening of a special public exhibition held at the Zappeion, in central Athens.[113] The author(s) of the report invoked the "fam-

---

109. Voutira and Brouskou (2000: 105).
110. Hassiotis (2013b: 228 and 222, respectively).
111. Hassiotis (2011: 273, 284).
112. Potamitis (2008: 130).
113. Theodoropoulou (2006: 63).

ily atmosphere" of the *paidopoleis* and the "Greek blood that flowed in the children's veins," to guarantee that its alumni would become "model Greek children."[114] Were the Argyriadis girls thought to be beyond re-education, given their family legacy? Had they "imbibed communist teachings"?[115] Not necessarily, and there's no need to posit the question in such a biased way. Did ideological warfare play a role in the hastily conducted adoption process that placed a ten-year-old and a six-year-old in a North American home? Yes, most certainly. Was the adoption process illegal in the sense of being driven by greed? No, not by the legal standards and procedures of the mid-1950s. Paradoxically, the tragedy of the Argyriadis girls did not end with them being "repossessed" by the state and forced to adopt a new, more "desirable" way of thinking. It also entailed the queen and the conservative government debunking their effort to "convert" children to their own ideology as soon as US-bound adoptions could help unburden the state's strained resources. The American free-market culture would take care of the rest, as would the new family's relative wealth. Passing through the hands of the last few intermediaries, the two youngest daughters of the executed communist were whisked off to the States to become model Americans, breaking the last bonds to their roots. Ioanna and Olympia, now Gina and Helen Alevras, spent the next several years growing up together in a small town in Massachusetts. The overseas adoption and the ensuing "new life" depoliticized and dehistoricized the Argyriadis girls and many other Greek children whom PIKPA (and, indirectly, the Greek queen) set on a similar course to

---

114. Vasiliki Pronoia (1957a: 50), quoted by Danforth and Van Boeschoten (2012: 104). There are, in fact, two 1957 reports of the Royal Welfare Fund, but both are disappointing sources (1957a and 1957b): they provide hardly any real data and make their case for the Fund's success by presenting pretty pictures (especially 1957b). The same holds true of the 1963 report and of the thirty-year report (1977) by the National Welfare Organization (Εθνικός Οργανισμός Προνοίας, Ε.Ο.Π., the fund's name from 1972 on), even though the latter contains more text. According to the former report, the young inmates of the *paidopoleis* "relearned the meaning of laughter" (1963: caption accompanying a picture of a smiling child; no page number). In 1956, Panagis Zouvas published a "study" entitled *Queen Frederica in the Service of the Nation* (original Greek title: Ἡ Βασίλισσα Φρειδερίκη εἰς τὴν Ὑπηρεσίαν τοῦ Ἔθνους), amounting to 100 pages of eulogy for the queen's philanthropic initiatives and ongoing projects. Controversy surrounds the fate of the children housed in the Queen's homes. Two novels, one by Boutos (2000) and the other by Skroumbelos (2005), imply that rapes took place in the *paidopoleis*. The latter further ties the history of postwar adoptions from Greece to the thematic axis of the mythical Oedipus' quest for the truth about his identity. These novels have provoked angry reactions from alumni (Danforth and Van Boeschoten 2012: 220, 301–2). Theologis (2006) responds to a controversial television program featuring interviews with former residents of the *paidopoleis*. See also Kaisidou (2019).

115. The phrase cites the charged language of one official associated with the Queen's Fund, quoted by Hassiotis (2013b: 223).

America; they were severed from the political past of their birth parents and were "orphaned," too, of their natal cultures and ideas.

Some Like It Hot

Queen Frederica was well aware that her struggle for the next generation was an incendiary proposition, one that would benefit greatly from being validated by the West and the United States, Greece's superpower sponsor. She certainly knew how to relate to and manipulate American public opinion. First, a propagandistic holiday postcard of 29 December 1949, in English, has Frederica refer to the "little 'Lindberghs'" of Greece: she compares the communist "kidnapping" of Greek children to the criminal abduction case of the Lindbergh baby, the eldest son of the famous aviator Charles Lindbergh.[116] The case had shocked America in 1932, or rather, since 1932. This rhetorical positioning of a deeply wronged Greece, the victim of the communist baby-snatcher's criminal kidnapping, is no doubt an extreme case of "national self-definition through the bodies of children," as Karen Dubinsky has phrased it, using the shortcut of the "national baby" as well.[117] "Cold War children were a product of, and indeed advertising for, Cold War fault lines," Dubinsky notes, in terms that were not written about the contested Greek children but could hardly be more applicable.[118]

Second, *Muddy Bottom* (2008; Θολός βυθός), the autobiographical novel of Giannis Atzakas, features a copy of a brief Greek newspaper article announcing that Queen Frederica was given an award by the US-based organization called American Mothers. No date is attached to the article, and neither is the name of the newspaper. However, the (anonymous) reporter to the *Cincinnati Enquirer* of 8 May 1950 mentioned Greece as one of forty-two nations to nominate a woman for the "Mother of the Year" award, and the Greek delegation chose its queen. Frederica received a citation and a medal, but she did not win the grand prize for 1950.[119]

Third, the Greek royal couple, invited on a state visit, spent part of October through December 1953 in the United States. The queen strategically granted interviews to popular US magazines, which responded with full spreads on the visit. The 26 October 1953 issue of *Time* magazine placed

---

116. Holiday card reproduced in Hassiotis (2013a: fig. 9).
117. Dubinsky (2010: 6).
118. Dubinsky (2010: 12).
119. On 23 May 2015, I contacted the American Mothers organization in the hope that its librarian might be able to find documentary evidence of the 1950 ceremony. To date, however, my inquiry has not yielded any further results.

a flattering picture of Frederica on its front cover, sporting her motto, "My power is the love of the people." *Life* magazine of 16 November 1953 devoted a photo report to the monarchs' visit and also put the queen on its cover. However, the unnamed reporter for *Time* detected Frederica's unabashed blending of state affairs and formal appearances with Greece's campaign for more US aid, for the queen's charity projects, and for the crown. The reporter commented,

> This easy informality and Frederika's gift for bowling over generals, sergeants and congressmen alike has proved a major asset to a ruling house whose royal motto is: "My power is in the love of the people."

> Frederika organized and personally supervised every detail of The Queen's Fund, a vast charity whose original object was to find food and shelter for the thousands of homeless children wandering lost in her land. Her impassioned pleas for her pet causes seldom fell on deaf ears. "If you could have a vote taken at this minute," said Wisconsin's Senator [Alexander] Wiley after hearing Frederika talk at dinner one night, "you would get the American aid to Greece doubled."[120]

Also, Frederica took a keen interest in American cinema, and she realized its power. On her visit to the States, which included a stop in Hollywood, she even met with Marilyn Monroe. She was introduced to the queen of the silver screen by the Greek-born Spyros P. Skouras, Monroe's "godfather" in the movie business and long-time president of Twentieth Century Fox (1942–1962). Skouras and his wife were unwavering supporters of the Greek crown who organized (glamorous) fund-raising campaigns across the States for the "Queen's Fund for Greek Orphans, Inc."[121] May we suppose that Frederica was inspired, too, by the 1938 influential film *Boys Town*? The movie is largely fictional, but it is based on a historical founder, the Catholic priest Edward J. Flanagan, and a real community near Omaha, Nebraska. The term *paidopolis*, "child-town," and the official rhetoric promoting this type of institution certainly suggest that the queen may have embraced yet another American media and movie icon. Also, the shared emphasis on older children's "elective" institutionalization and on their education in moral values as well as practical skills resonates through Frederica's auto-

---

120. Anon., *Time Magazine*, 26 October 1953, 35, 39.
121. See Skouras (2013: *passim*) and also the miscellaneous correspondence held in the folders entitled "Donations," folder 65, and "Chief Court Mistress [Mary C. Carolou]," folder 1104, Archive of the Former Royal Palace (1861–1971), GAK, Athens.

biography.[122] The film's popularity certainly helped the queen present her own welfare work more effectively to a Western public.

The "Happy Orphans" of Queen Frederica

Frederica's Western outlook showed in one more important venture, which cared for the very young children of unmarried mothers whose families did not know of or did not support their single motherhood: the founding in 1953 of the Greek children's home Metera (conventionally spelled "Metera" but occasionally "Mitera"). Technically, the Babies' Center "The Mother" (Κέντρο Βρεφών "Η Μητέρα") became operational only in September of 1955, and it established branches in Irakleio, Crete, and also on the island of Corfu (Kerkyra).[123] Most mothers who were sheltered at Metera in Athens delivered their babies at the Alexandra maternity clinic, or else babies delivered and relinquished at the clinic were transferred to Metera, without their mothers ever staying in the Mothers' Home there. Other babies were brought over from the Greek countryside through the mediation of regional centers for social welfare, which fell under the purview of PIKPA and the Ministry of Social Welfare. From about 1962 onward, Metera and PIKPA tightened their collaboration with the *vrefokomeio* of the southern city of Kalamata, which became the Papadopouleio Babies' Center of Kalamata (Παπαδοπούλειο Κέντρο Βρεφών Καλαμάτας).[124]

The Metera network was funded partially by the Greek state and the Queen's Fund and partially by donations from abroad. Sponsored and favored by the queen, this institution soon took the lead in childcare and development, while simultaneously functioning as a training school for nursery and pediatric nurses and social workers. From Metera's early years, Spyros Doxiadis, professor of pediatrics, and Litsa (Charikleia) Alexandraki, a highly educated lawyer, social scientist, and social worker, put in practice there the ideal of infants' early bonding to a single mother figure that British child development expert John Bowlby had been promulgating and that became known as the "attachment theory."[125] Building on this theory, each "unprotected" child was to be provided with a family as soon as possi-

---

122. Frederica (1971: *passim*).
123. Agapitou (1958); Kliafa (2016: 163–65); and Theodoropoulou (2006: 119, 120–21).
124. This local and regional institution represented the legacy of the Papadopoulos merchant family, but its foundation in 1901 was facilitated also by other donations, including a large German gift. See also Theodoropoulou (2006: 118).
125. Koussidou and Maganiotou (1991: 171). On Doxiadis, see also Lapatsanis, Nakou, Pantelakis, and Valaes (1994) and Theodorou (2015: 96). Amera (2012) leaves a historical portrait of Alexandraki.

ble, even if the first "family" was the institutional "cottage family," in order to avoid "maternal deprivation."[126] Thus, the goal of adoption according to "modern" casework methods loomed large at Metera, but it often contravened the wishes of the young mothers.[127]

By 1960, the Mothers' Home at Metera accommodated approximately 100 birth mothers annually for stays lasting on average about two weeks. Hosting a mother at Metera cost about 51 drachmas daily (or less than $1.50 at the 1960 exchange rates, which is less than $10 today, for basic room and board). Newborns remained in the institution for an average of approximately 150 days. A child's daily maintenance cost the institution about 82.5 drachmas (some $2.50 then or $16 today). By comparison, a child's upkeep at one of the (underfunded) municipal orphanages cost about 20 drachmas per day, or one-fourth of the amount set by the "posh" institution.[128] All institutions, however, faced the higher cost of constructing, maintaining, and staffing their facilities, which required around-the-clock personnel. The large majority of Metera's infants were adopted out before their first birthday, whether to Greek parents or to foreign parents who traveled to Athens to "select" a child and acquaint themselves with it, or to parents who, unable to travel from overseas, had to submit home studies along with their application for a child. Unaccompanied by a child, most Metera mothers were able to restore relationships with their home environments and could eventually go back where they came from. Only about 10 percent of all babies returned to their birth mother or family.[129]

---

126. Carp (1998: 111) and Lapatsanis, Nakou, Pantelakis, and Valaes (1994: 1). Fieldston briefly discusses the "modern" orphanage laid out on the "cottage plan," which helped to create the children's first substitute or fictive families (2015: 156, 186). Nancy Newton Verrier has long described the range of emotions experienced by the adoptee and the other members of the "adoption triad." Her oft-reprinted book *The Primal Wound* (first published 1993) focuses on the effects on relinquished children of separation from the birth mother. See especially Verrier (2012: 20–21, 177–79).

127. Papadaki also credits Doxiadis with Metera's more advanced theories and practices in the realm of adoption and its follow-up (2015: 132–36). However, the need for proper casework in adoptions was first championed in Greece by the International Social Service (see below, p. 109). I thank Ohio-based pediatric psychologist Georgette M. Constantinou for sharing her experiences of a three-week internship period she spent at Metera in 1968, under the tutelage of leading child development specialists from Vassar College (among them L. Joseph Stone and Henrietta T. Smith, a pioneer African American psychologist who studied nurse-infant interactions at Metera). The young Constantinou was struck by the stark contrast between the Greek nurses' genuine care for the newborns and infants and their utter disdain for the unwed and therefore "fallen" birth mothers (email and telephone communications of August 2015). These impressions have been confirmed by Maria Selekou (testimony of 18 June 2016).

128. Athinogenis and Papathanasiou (1959: 40).

129. Papa-oikonomou (ca. 1962: 1–5).

The conditions that prevailed at Metera were said to be "optimal" for the babies and to limit the effects of institutionalization. They were certainly also advertised as such to the West (see figure 1). Metera was aggressively promoted as the prime Greek and even global institution whose state-of-the-art "home" model of childcare could guarantee to Western adopters that their chosen baby had received the best possible nurturing before being handed over to them.[130]

In a speech given on 26 June 1957, Queen Frederica herself boasted that "her" institution's adoption rate was 70 percent for infants less than six months old.[131] In those years, a white, healthy, and available newborn was considered to be a "blue-ribbon" baby, that is, the undeniable preference of hopeful adoptive parents. A. Athinogenis and F. Papathanasiou of the Greek Ministry of Social Welfare repeatedly praised American prospective parents for accepting children with physical "shortcomings," whereas most other adopters wanted to find a "little 'angel' with beautiful little eyes and rosy cheeks."[132] This coarse but not unsubstantiated generalization occurs in the section of their 1959 report describing Metera's adoption procedures and recent institutional history. Letitia DiVirgilio, a caseworker active in the Boston area, shrugged at the "perennial requests for the blonde blue-eyed child," but she also noticed the first positive changes in racial attitudes. She cited a typical reaction from applicant parents when they were told that a Northern European or German child would not be available for adoption but that Greek children were: "Aren't Greek children dark?" "Aren't they different?"[133]

---

130. In his article "The Happy Orphans of Metera," Milton Silverman did not fail to remark on the young, unmarried, and "highly attractive" nurses (*Saturday Evening Post*, 19 March 1960, 101)! Metera supported and even cosponsored a 1984 world conference, entitled "Infancy as Prevention," and also the subsequent production of two collective volumes on child development and adoption, both edited by Euthymia Hibbs (as per the acknowledgments, 1988: xvii, and 1991: xiii). The 1984 conference was hosted by the Greek Ministries of Culture and Science and of Health and Social Welfare in collaboration with Metera. The first volume (Hibbs 1988) contains a section on adoption comprised of three chapters, two of which deliver unabashed praise of Metera's adoption protocols articulated by close associates of the institution. Panos Palmos, president of Metera's administrative board, advertises his institution's reputation for being "the most demanding adoption agency in Greece [i.e., in selecting adoptive parents]" (1988: 383). Maganiotou and Koussidou (1988) offer an overall positive assessment of Greek adoptive parents' experience of taking in babies from Metera. In the second volume (Hibbs 1991), see the chapters by Koussidou and Maganiotou (1991) and Panera (1991). At the time of the 1991 publication, Koussidou held the position of Metera's Supervisor of the Adoption and Counseling Sections, while Maganiotou served as Metera's Head of Social Services (1991: ix–x). Their coauthored chapters thematize confidential or "full" domestic adoptions.
131. Theodoropoulou (2006: 63–64).
132. Athinogenis and Papathanasiou (1959: 35).
133. DiVirgilio (1956: 17).

Fig 1: "Playtime: Nurses sunning their charges in front of one of Metera's pavilions. The home now [in 1960] has accommodations for 110 infants." Credit: Eugene Kammerman (photograph) and Milton Silverman (text), "The Happy Orphans of Metera," *Saturday Evening Post*, 19 March 1960, 27.

From 1956 through 1970, a total number of 1,820 children were adopted from Metera. Only about one-third were adopted within Greece; 420 of them were adopted in the Attica region alone.[134] Almost 64 percent of the total number of 1,820 children (some 1,157 children) were adopted out internationally, mostly to the United States, the Netherlands, and Sweden.[135] Nearly 13 percent of the subtotal of 1,157 children adopted out overseas (approximately 150 in number) were taken in by families of Greek origin living abroad, typically in the States.[136] The Netherlands, a country with a comparatively small population, is a somewhat surprising destination, particularly since it had suffered severe deprivation during World War II and disastrous flood damage in 1953. The number of Greek-born children adopted out by Metera and its branches to the Netherlands between 1956 and 1970 is estimated to stand at approximately 480.[137] A catalyst in this process was the fall 1956 passage of the long-awaited Dutch "full" adoption legislation, which made intercountry as well as domestic adoptions legally possible and protected them by abolishing all judicial ties to the birth families.[138]

---

134. Maganiotou and Koussidou (1988: 386–87).
135. Koussidou and Maganiotou (1991: 175). See also Storsbergen, Juffer, van Son, 't Hart (2010: 192), based on personal communications with Metera's head of social services of 1994.
136. Koussidou and Maganiotou (1991: 175).
137. According to René Hoksbergen, 478 Greek-born children were adopted out to the Netherlands from 1957 through 1970. This influx, however, tapered off and then nearly stopped after 1975. The years of 1971 through 1980 saw only 113 Greek-to-Dutch adoption placements. The numbers still amount to a combined total of 591 Greek-born children adopted out to the Netherlands from 1957 through 1980, or over the course of two-and-a-half decades (Hoksbergen 2002: 7, 9, 10, 15; 2011: 65, 126, 143–44). Until 1968, the Dutch courts required a probation period of three years before any adoption process could be completed. Along with the professional agencies, they also preserve the most reliable sources (Hoksbergen 2002: 7, 9, 15). Metera and its branches delivered the vast majority of all Greek-born babies placed in the Netherlands. Significantly, Metera's supply approximated half of the total of 1,010 international adoptions that the Dutch courts saw through in the fifteen-year time span prior to 1970 (Hoksbergen 2011: 65). Bonds of friendship tied the Greek royal house to that of the Netherlands. Interviewees speak informally about a "bilateral understanding" among the royals and the organizations or mediators involved. The ISS Netherlands (founded in 1955) and also the Dutch Association for Foster Families (NVP, Nederlandse Vereniging voor Pleeggezinnen, founded in 1950) served as agencies in most of the Dutch cross-border cases, and they provided better-quality oversight than their (earlier) US counterparts (the weak spot remained the sourcing of the adoptable children). Some Dutch adopters, however, acted on their own initiative and responded to announcements published in the print media or to promotional materials issued by Metera (Antoinette De Boer, email communication of 15 April 2016). See also various pictures and postings on Ta Pedia, the Facebook site of the close-knit group of Greek-to-Dutch adoptees, https://www.facebook.com/ta.pedia.7. As per Metera's preferred way of operating in the 1960s, many Dutch couples traveled to Greece and stayed there long enough to acquaint themselves with the children and to see their adoptions through.
138. By 1989, however, further Dutch legislation had to institute much-needed protections pertaining to the international placements.

Couples adopting from Metera were asked to give money to the queen's showcase institution.[139] Metera received large donations also from a Dutch aid commission assisting Greek children (translated as "the Committee of Assistance of Greek Children in Holland"), from the Swedish Save the Children (Rädda Barnen), and from the Swedish Red Cross, among others.[140] When foreign states or some of their organizations donated substantial amounts of money to Metera, they could name one of its children's cottages or pavilions: the "Pavilion of Holland" and the "Pavilion of Sweden" attest to the kind of monetary gifts that greased long-lasting and officially sanctioned relations of give-and-take.[141] Holland donated laundry and kitchen equipment to Metera as well. Gifts from the oil-rich military dictatorship of Venezuela, through the mediation of Colonel Marcos Pérez Jiménez, inaugurated the "Pavilion of Venezuela."[142] To this day, Metera's big marble plaque listing all major benefactors acknowledges the "Republic of Venezuela," along with the anonymous donor who gave "in memory of his daughter Eleni." "American Citizens" were among the first to give money for building and equipping a children's pavilion. A Greek American organization called the "Order of the Three Hundred Knights of Thermopylae" also made generous donations to the Queen's Fund to benefit the "orphans of the modern heroes of Greece [i.e., of the National Army troops who had defeated the communists]."[143] If the "civilized" West owed a debt of gratitude to Greece, then the Greek monarchy and its Greek American supporters did not have a hard time "justifying," either, why they now called on the West to show its philanthropic side and to sponsor or adopt "orphans" from Greece.[144] In 1958, however, the "American Pavilion" had yet to be built. Even though US donations kept coming in, a pavilion naming the States never materialized, probably because, by the end of 1958, US-bound adoptions were rapidly gaining notoriety and American patronage in general was becoming increasingly suspect.[145]

---

139. Theodoropoulou (2006: 64, 120).

140. Agapitou (1958: 298) and the English-language brochures disseminated by Metera.

141. See Endt (1963: 137, 138, 139), whose words and images depict Greece as one of the most backward and unstable countries of an orientalized South and East.

142. Anon., *Nieuwe Leidsche Courant*, 24 December 1956. See also the related correspondence held in the folder entitled "Donations," folder 65, Archive of the Former Royal Palace (1861–1971), GAK, Athens.

143. Knights of Thermopylae Committee, *The Ahepan*, Oct.—Dec. 1952. See also Nikoloutsos (2013: 269–70 and n23).

144. Classical Greece was probably foremost on Westerners' minds. See Yalouri (2001: 82, 103–5). But the Greek acts of resistance and sacrifice on behalf of the Allies in World War II had left a deep impression on Great Britain and the United States as well.

145. Athinogenis and Papathanasiou (1959). See also Fieldston (2015: 169–70, 187) and part 2 of

The archival evidence attests to sizeable donations from the Niarchos family as well.[146] These gifts were lauded in contemporary newspapers, as in the following report of the Greek queen's formal speech delivered in Boston, where she christened the supertanker SS *Princess Sophie*, a 1958 addition to the Niarchos oil shipping fleet. The report also bespeaks the queen's fragile "popularity" among the Greek people:

> Queen Frederika . . . told how during troubled wartime, her chauffeur had accidentally knocked down a small child. She was alone in the back seat, threatening crowds were closing in when a band of young Greek naval officers pushed through and dispersed them. Their leader, she learned, was Stavros Niarchos. Her Majesty added that this former naval officer had just given her around $30,000 [approximately $200,000 today] to build a home for Greek orphans.[147]

Notably, the invocations of "Greek orphans," as of the child victims of recent earthquakes, continued to deliver monetary results for the Greek queen, who pushed hard to secure the full operation and expansion of Metera. But by 1958, Metera served not "orphans," but unwed mothers and their "illegitimate" offspring, and, inevitably, the lucrative intercountry adoption circuit.[148] The following 1957 news report, too, artificially perpetuated the "orphan" label and failed to note that the money benefited one pet institution that was *not* facing high operating expenses:

> The world première on April 10 . . . of the Twentieth Century-Fox film "Boy on a Dolphin" [produced by Spyros Skouras] will benefit Queen Frederika's Fund for Greek Orphans. . . . The Queen's Fund is dedicated to the care and rehabilitation of Greek orphans.[149]

---

this book. The year 1958 saw the publication of a runaway bestseller that exposed US arrogance in Southeast Asia: *The Ugly American*, by William J. Lederer and Eugene Burdick (1958).

146. Miscellaneous correspondence in the folder entitled "Donations," folder 65, Archive of the Former Royal Palace (1861–1971), GAK, Athens.

147. Mary V. R. Thayer, "Queen Frederika Bests Helen of Troy," *Washington Post and Times Herald*, 17 November 1958, B5.

148. E. J. Graff has unmasked the recurring fiction of "orphan" crises, which have primed the pump of the international adoption industry. Her anchor article, "The Lie We Love," focuses on more recent decades but contains valuable observations about the Cold War adoptions as well.

149. Anon., "Film Premiere to Aid Greece," *New York Times*, 31 March 1957.

The more formal foreign donations and agreements among partnering institutions, agencies, and states offered incentives for Metera to continue to give out children for adoption abroad, to the global West and North (if the Netherlands and Sweden may stand as token countries for the stable and prosperous North).[150] Unlike many of the US-bound placements, nearly all of the Greek-to-Dutch and Greek-to-Swedish adoptions were stranger or nonrelative placements with families that were not Greek Orthodox, but rather Catholic or Protestant. Pages 136–39 below revisit the Greek government's official position and the Greek Orthodox Church's stated preference for "culture-keeping" and coreligious placements, a contentious issue in the Greek-to-American adoptions of the 1950s through early 1960s. Regrettably, Metera rejected the Barrer family's petition of 1960 to bring a Greek child to the States because they were "Israelites."[151]

Greece of the 1950s was still a country of the starkest contrasts, and not just between rich and poor, ancient and modern, freedom and dependency. While Frederica and Metera basked in the international spotlight, other sectors of Greek social welfare and childcare remained desperately underfunded. Also, the country still allocated one-third of its financial resources to defense spending, as part of its obligations to the NATO alliance.[152] In 1955, Greece signed on to president Dwight Eisenhower's "Atoms for Peace" program, which was, once again, championed by Queen Frederica. She thus

---

150. A research report issued by the Ministry of Social Welfare of Sweden confirms that Greek-to-Swedish adoptees come from Metera. It even prints, in an appendix, the "Agreement between the Swedish National Social Welfare Board and the Babies' Centre Metera in Athens, Greece" dated 1965 (1967: 33, 99–101). This agreement stipulates that the Swedish adoptive parents "must appear in person at Metera . . . to facilitate the matching" (1967: 100). According to Yngvesson, an (unspecified) portion of a total of 240 international adoptions that occurred in Sweden from 1950 through 1966 were placements of Greek-born children (2010: 44). Fortunately, the Swedish government research report from 1967 delivers more precise numbers: 40 children from Greece were adopted by Swedish couples in the postwar years through 1966, which placed Greece in the second position as a sending nation after Korea (Ministry of Social Welfare of Sweden 1967: 22–23).

151. Spyros Doxiadis to Mary Carolou, letter of 10 November 1960. Typescript, 1 page, held in "Chief Court Mistress," folder 1119, Archive of the Former Royal Palace (1861–1971), GAK, Athens. The desire to preclude Jews from adopting Greek children was voiced also by Athinogenis and Papathanasiou (1959: 45). The typed minutes of a closed meeting discussion of a contested child placement with "Israelites" reveal that, in early 1966, the issue was still not resolved in favor of extrareligious and Jewish adoptions. See the "Minutes of the 43rd Meeting of the [Greek National] Council for Child Protection," held on 25 January 1966. This five-page document is held in the Archive of the National Council for Child Protection, "Minutes of the Years 1960–1968," box 299, folder D2, unclassified Archive of the Ministry of Health (and Social Welfare), GAK, Athens.

152. Lymberatos (2015: 191–97) and Richter (2013: 166, 167, 175).

earned the *Time* magazine's title of the "Atomic Queen."[153] The stakes for the Greek royal dynasty were very high: an (odd and contradictory) mix of advancing science and "peace," abetting US propaganda and geostrategic interests, building international alliances, and thus securing the unstable Greek throne.[154]

The years 1955–1956 saw a shift from politically driven adoptions, which advanced the all-consuming Cold War script and the "orphan" designation of older children, to economically and socially motivated adoptions of babies. The latter adoptions became characteristic of the new network of Metera and of the "second post–Civil War period" at large. The term has been coined by Hatzivassiliou, who ties the country's lived realities from 1955 on to the steady advance of Karamanlis.[155] Each of the intercountry adoption trends, however, was in its own right an "index of vulnerability" (to use Briggs's phrase).[156] Over several years, if not decades, the culture and praxis of Metera increased the use of the far more neutral term "infants" ("βρέφη") to proclaim the "available" babies' very young age. Age and confidentiality became prized assets in the cross-border movement of Greek adoptions, which by the mid-1950s, had moved beyond its origins in war, destruction, and anticommunism. Accordingly, the language of our analysis shifts from the political terms that characterized early postwar adoptions to concepts from social and sociological studies and even to metaphors of economic supply and demand. Many young women from the Greek lower classes, which suffered from the uneven American aid distribution, continued to struggle for subsistence in harsh new urban environments and under treacherous economic and social conditions.[157] Single women who had

---

153. Anon., 3 November 1958, 23.

154. Kourkouvelas (2011) and Rentezi (2009).

155. Hatzivassiliou (Chatzivasileiou) (2001: 284–88). For recent perspectives on the political and global meanings of the year 1956, see the special section in *ArcheioTaxio* 18 (November 2016).

156. Briggs (2012: 282).

157. Several older anthropological and historical studies reflect on Greek women's status in village environments and on their complex relations to family, power, and property, such as Cowan (1990), du Boulay (1974), Gallant (1991), Handman (1983), and the volumes edited by Dubisch (1986), Hirschon (1984), and by Loizos and Papataxiarchis (1991). See also McNeill (1957: 83–84, *passim*). Chantzaroula (2012) covers female domestic workers of the first half of the twentieth century. She analyzes the Greek institution of the "adopted daughters" or "foster daughters" (ψυχοκόρες), who were not legally adopted but were kept in often-exploitative live-in working relationships by well-to-do urban families (2012: 335–67, or her ch. 11, and 502–3). See also Bada and Hantzaroula (2017: 26). Greek employers expected their female domestic servants to be single and childless. Doxiadis's 2011 book traces these gender and socioeconomic interactions back to the transition from the Ottoman Empire to the Greek nation-state. Sant Cassia (1992) paints a comprehensive picture

unplanned pregnancies were routinely fired from their jobs, and children born out of wedlock were often abandoned. Shame, therefore, confounded the crisis of sheer financial survival. Institutional barriers, too, stood in the way of poorer women's access to social services and even to basic information about reproductive choices. Whenever orphanage administrators knew the mother of a child in their care, they made her sign a document in which she relinquished her child to the institution if she could not keep paying for its living expenses (τροφεία).[158] Brouskou notes the significant point that some birth mothers did not receive a straightforward answer regarding how much the upkeep of their child would cost: "it depends," was the director's typical response.[159] This uncertainty, along with seemingly insurmountable social and practical impediments, led more mothers to relinquish their children and may well be seen as an institutional strategy.[160] Occasionally, orphanage directors, delivery doctors, local mayors, and lawyers designated the offspring of a poor and socially disadvantaged mother as a "foundling" or as an "illegitimate" child, with or without the mother's consent and depending on the specific circumstances. Sometimes, a struggling unmarried mother could—conveniently—not be found when she was supposed to deny or consent to an adoption in court, in which case the adoption went through.[161]

The Greek state has long sanctioned the moral regulation of its families. The social taboos and the statutory disadvantages that Greek "illegitimate" children continued to endure were extremely hard to eradicate in a nation that disavowed maternity outside of the (idealized) normative family. The new Family Law of 18 February 1983 (Law 1329) finally abolished the terrible discrimination against "illegitimate" children and their mothers, which encouraged more mothers to keep their babies and raise them themselves.[162]

---

of marriage and family life in Greece through the nineteenth century. His chapter 5 (1992: 145–63), on adoption, fosterage, and spiritual kinship, is particularly relevant.

158. Daravinga (1963: 5) remarks on this practice at the Saint Stylianos Foundling Home in Thessaloniki.

159. Brouskou, email communication of 7 August 2016.

160. For an incisive, comparative analysis on the topic of child abandonment, see Tilly, Fuchs, Kertzer, and Ransel (1992).

161. Papadaki (2015: 116).

162. See Halkias (2004: 41); Papadaki (2015: 21, 49, 76–77, 80, 90–91, 107); and Van Steen (2003: 261–63, with extensive bibliography on feminism in twentieth-century Greece). According to Wood-Ritsatakis, Greece counted 15.1 illegitimate babies per 1,000 live-births in 1957; ten years later and with steady improvement in Greek living conditions, this figure had dropped to 10.0, also because many more women turned to abortion, which was illegal and unsafe yet within reach (1970: 125). In 1960, extramarital births accounted for only 1.2 percent of all births (Maratou-Alipranti 2004: 121). Papadaki presents similar statistics (2015: 107), but she rightly refers to two other postwar Greek phenomena: infanticide of illegitimate newborns and the failure to officially declare ille-

This law also prepared for the legalization of abortion, which was finalized in 1986. However, an estimated 300,000 illegal abortions had been taking place in Greece annually up through the mid-1980s. This estimate must be set against the then relatively stable number of Greek births per year: approximately 150,000.[163] The 1983 and 1986 legislation was key in stemming Greece's practice of adopting out overseas, by indirectly making far fewer children available for adoption. Efi Avdela, Aigli Brouskou, and Eirini Papadaki note the absence of in-depth discussions about "illegitimate" children in the decades-long tradition of anthropological and ethnographical literature written on modern Greece, which has perhaps overemphasized the interpretive axes of "honor" and "shame," of male versus female roles, and of rural versus urban life.[164] Avdela (2002) details the social and gender predicament of postwar Greece using honor killings as her reference point. The punitive conditions of the 1950s through 1960s drove many indigent and unwed mothers to institutions like Metera, where they found care, anonymity, and the prospect of cross-border adoptions that perpetuated this anonymity and also "legalized" children without proper status in their home society.[165]

gitimate births (2015: 97, 98, 100–101, 104–8, 111–12). On infanticide, see also Brouskou (2015: 85, *passim*). The ongoing research of social historian Violetta Hionidou, on the topics of abortion and birth control until the 1960s, will allow us to update the numbers given.

163. Maratou-Alipranti (2004: 120, 125). The anthropological studies by Halkias (2004, stressing Greece's high abortion rate), Georges (2008), and Paxson (2004) offer ample background material but touch on adoption only briefly (Paxson 2004: 61, 148, 192, 221–22, 233, 289n6).

164. Brouskou (2015: 81–85) and Papadaki (2015: 95–101). Contextualizing the notion of "undoing kinship" or "de-kinning," Papadaki (2018: 184–85, 194) invokes the terse mention of the illegitimate child by Campbell (1964: 187). Avdela (2002: 212–34) reviews the older literature of "Mediterranean anthropology" that, with its emphasis on men versus women, has never devoted much attention to children, let alone to offspring born out of wedlock. The threat of an illegitimate pregnancy or, rather, of "behavior conducive to it," has overshadowed the realities of actual illegitimate births and of the hardships suffered by surviving illegitimate children. Campbell (1964) and Friedl (1962) are among the "classic," English-language anthropological studies of postwar Greece, in addition to the ones listed in n. 157 above. John Peristiany codified the honor-versus-shame binary in the title of his collective volume, *Honour and Shame: The Values of Mediterranean Society* (1966). Herzfeld refuted this generalizing interpretive framework and also qualified the norms of chastity against which rural Greek women appeared to be measured (1980 and 1983, respectively). The latter article was part of the first issue of the *Journal of Modern Greek Studies*, a special issue entitled "Women and Men in Greece: A Society in Transition," which both reiterated and questioned some of the topics outlined above.

165. Premarital relations that lead to unwanted pregnancies (but rarely to adoptions) are common motifs in Greek film comedies of the 1950s through early 1960s. Delveroudi notes that, unlike in postwar reality, the movie couple ends up uniting in marriage, elusive fathers

American Adoption as Child Rescue or Child Abduction?

The dichotomy of "humanitarian rescue" versus "imperialist kidnap" or "colonialist exploitation," of "deliverance" and "reintegration" versus "rupture," is a recurring theme in the discourse on postwar intercountry adoptions.[166] The frequently invoked justification of children's "best interests" is notoriously ambiguous and reductive as well, and the Greek case is no exception. The student of any adoption policies and practices inevitably runs into the difficult conundrum of what constitutes children's "adoptability" and who has the right to define it. How did the climate of the 1950s influence those definitions? Can "adoptability" be conditioned by the free-market principles of supply and demand, or even by the well-intentioned question of what would happen to children who continued to live in grinding poverty?[167] This issue is far from settled, and it applies *a priori* to potential adoptees from underdeveloped countries and those on the brink of war or economic crisis. Moreover, the issue returns in full force after every major natural or man-made disaster. For Greece, the mid-1950s marked a turning point, but real-life exigencies kept overshadowing the country's transition from reconstruction to a phase of rapid development, in political and institutional as well as economic terms.

By the mid-1950s, the older competition of the royalist versus the communist child-evacuation campaigns was recast as a contest between US-bound adoptions versus domestic placements in rehabilitated and supported family networks. A protected in-country placement, however, was impossible for the Argyriadis relatives and many other left-wing families, which were often decimated and dispersed. The Greek Left regarded the process of "adopting out" to the United States as tantamount to placing chil-

---

assume their responsibilities, and punishing parents reconcile with the pair, who live happily ever after (2004: 226–31, 548). Visits to Greek orphanages and foundling homes, in particular, "enhanced" the plots of several Greek films, such as *Νταντά με το ζόρι* (1959; the title may translate as *Forced to Be a Nanny*) and *Δύο μάννες στο σταυρό του πόνου* (1962; *Two Mothers on the Cross of Pain*). The latter offers a detailed look inside of such an institution, which, for the purposes of the movie and of the viewers' conscience, is presented as well-staffed, well-equipped, and immaculate. In the 1968 comedy *Η Οικογένεια Χωραφά*, the international adoption of one of the newborn triplets of the Chorafa family is thwarted by the baby's many siblings. A wealthy Greek American couple enters negotiations with the birth parents through a private lawyer. The prospective parents had placed an ad in local papers looking for a child to adopt, but they fail to earn the Chorafa children's and the viewers' respect.

166. Dubinsky (2010: 3, 19–21); Marshall (2013: 481–84, 486); and Winslow (2015: 337, 342–43, 345).

167. Lovelock (2000: 941).

dren on the road to perdition. Throughout the Cold War era, they associated the States with wealth but also with "inequality, moral decline, [and] cultural inferiority," with the cruel or inhumane "alienation of individuals," and with unscrupulous or even violent threats to traditional values.[168] By sending its children to the States, Greece was seen as "selling out" to American money and power in the worst possible way. No such stigma was attached to the Greek children's export to the Netherlands, given this small country's non-hegemonic and nonthreatening position in the global balance of powers.

The Cold War was a clash of antithetical worldviews before the eyes of an international audience.[169] Placing Greek children with American parents was, therefore, an act of committing to one worldview over the other: it was about entrusting dependent children to the capitalist but democratic camp, rather than the leftist or communist camp. This ultimate leap of trust had to help legitimize the act of a very divisive choice—ironically, not of freedom, but of dependency, in either case. Greek children became part of the exchange of goods and services that the Marshall Plan had initiated and that spurred the Greek royal house and successive right-wing governments to unabashedly court the States for prolonged support and backing. William Hitchcock explains that the early foundations of the foreign aid program "represented the first stage in the construction of that community of ideas, economic links, and security ties between Europe and the United States we know simply as 'the West.'"[170] But the Greek establishment's calculated alignment with the States as the leader of the West did not come without domestic resentment about the growing American foothold. Zinovia Lialiouti has proposed a periodization of anti-Americanism in Greece: she posits a transition in the year 1954 from the "genetic phase," which started with the 1947 proclamation of the world-ordering Truman Doctrine and was grounded in the Civil War, to the decade of full development (1954–1965).[171] One of Lialiouti's prior studies of the phenomenon

168. Lialiouti (2010: 119). See further Lialiouti (2015: 45–46, 49) and Papadimitriou (2006: 179, 184).

169. Engerman (2010: 41).

170. Hitchcock (2010: 154).

171. Lialiouti (2015). See also Botsiou and Sakkas (2015) and Lialiouti (2016a, 2016b). Botsiou further contextualizes Greek anti-Americanism and the politics of aid, which helped shape an "endemic ideological cross-party current for nearly six decades" with "wide local recognition as a sound and legitimate 'narrative'" of twentieth-century Greek history (2007: 233–34). Stefanidis assesses the Greek political culture of the postwar period, focusing on the Cyprus question: the lack of US support for the Greek demand for the island's unification with Greece further fueled anti-American sentiment (2007: 27–54, or his ch. 1). The contested position of Cyprus marked the years 1955–1956 as a particularly low point in Greece's international relations (Hatzivassiliou 2006: 50–53; 2014: 93). See further

of Greek anti-Americanism clarifies this perspective: "It would be fair to say that the Left in the post-war period orchestrated a campaign against the myth of the American dream. Let's not forget that the Cold War was a cultural war, and a war of propaganda as well."[172]

Anti-American prejudice was cultivated by popular Greek authors, journalists, and filmmakers, who reinforced caricatures also of Greek Americans.[173] But these stereotypes reveal some of the dire domestic realities of postwar Greece as well. The example of one particular media representation strikes home how Greeks of the mid-1950s perceived an established and affluent American family and deemed its concerns to be trivial, if not arrogant, amid the deprivation that still plagued many Greek children. A front-page article in *Ta Nea* of 28 December 1956 has Dimitris Psathas, the well-known satirical journalist and playwright, railing against the insensitivity of the then-US Ambassador, George V. Allen, who had relocated his family to Athens.[174] Allen had been looking for the lost family dog. He had publicly complained that the "drama" of this loss had left his young son very distressed, around Christmas time, no less. Speaking for the "average Greek," Psathas lashes out at Allen's use of the word "drama" in these circumstances, which he contrasts with the "real drama" of the plight of the poverty-stricken children of Greece:

> There are much greater dramas in this country: here, the life of thousands of children is such that they truly envy the blessed conditions in which not the son of Mr Ambassador lives, but even . . . his dog.[175]

While Psathas spoke out caustically in 1956, many Greeks were reminded of their earlier, even harsher predicament with a sense of shame. At the time of the American debates on the Truman Doctrine and the Marshall Plan in 1947–1948, the designation of "Orphan Greece," of an entire country lacking food, clothing, and shelter, had been deployed to render Greece's dire needs intelligible to the US public. Rachel Winslow refers to an anonymous article, "Orphan Greece: Shall Uncle Sam Adopt This Problem Child?," published in the March 1947 issue of the *Senior Scholastic*, a widely disseminated maga-

---

Chourchoulis (2015: 111–19); Kazamias (unpublished ms.: chs. 4–6); and Kofas (1989).

172. Lialiouti (2010: 119).

173. Lialiouti (2010: 121–23).

174. Stefanidis offers more examples of the skeptical, anti-American voice of columnist Psathas (1907–1979) and his fictitious spokesperson, "Mr Naïve" (2007: 106, 116, 152–53, 182–83, 193, 195, 202–5, 227–28, 232, 233, 244, 245–46).

175. Psathas, *Ta Nea*, 28 December 1956 (in Greek).

zine geared toward seniors in American high schools.[176] Teachers could use this article to introduce their impressionable pupils to the Truman Doctrine and the Marshall Plan and their direct, near-parental—others might say "infantilizing"—relationship to a Greece ravaged by World War II and the Civil War. Greece is presented as the indigent and potentially problematic adoptee of the United States, itself the generous, more responsible, and more patient adoptive parent in a family of nations.[177] In the language of contemporary debates on US immigration policy, Greece posed the risk of becoming a "public charge" or burden on the hard-working American taxpayers.

The label and stigma of "orphan Greece" placed the United States in the parental power role and called out the new American claim to global leadership. Regrettably, this patronizing rhetoric permeated official communications through the 1950s, as in the following exchanges from 1951 through 1958. "[W]e are still as much loved as any Sugar Daddy ever is," claimed Charles Yost, acting chief of mission at the US Embassy in Athens, characterizing the relationship between the Americans and the Greek people on 11 June 1951.[178] "We [the United States] should and presumably will be able to continue to exercise guidance and leadership . . . but it should tend to become increasingly fraternal rather than paternal," averred John Peurifoy, US ambassador to Greece, in a dispatch to the US Department of State on 25 September 1952.[179] On 22 September 1958, the US Embassy in Athens still used similar language in its exchanges with the US Department of State: "It is probable that most thinking Greeks regard their country as the orphan of NATO, with all the repressed emotional reaction that that connotes."[180]

What's "Left"?

Ioanna and Olympia Argyriadi were "stolen" by the capitalist West and the prosperous "American way of life," at least according to their half-sister Eft-

---

176. Winslow (2012a: 102–3; 2017: 51).

177. Christina Klein illustrates how the States resorted to similar rhetorical tropes to legitimate its unequal power relations with Asian countries and with China and Vietnam, especially (2003: 175–78, 188–90).

178. *Foreign Relations of the United States, 1951, The Near East and Africa*, Vol. V, 483 n2, footnote to document (telegram) 4396, 611.81/6–1151 (V, 481–83): "The Ambassador in Greece (Peurifoy) to the Department of State, Athens, June 11, 1951." Available online at http://images.library.wisc.edu/FRUS/EFacs2/1951v05/reference/frus.frus1951v05.i0010.pdf.

179. *Foreign Relations of the United States 1952–1954, Vol. VIII, Eastern Europe; Soviet Union; Eastern Mediterranean*, document 434, 611.81/9–2552: "The Ambassador in Greece (Peurifoy) to the Department of State, Athens, September 25, 1952." Available online at https://history.state.gov/historicaldocuments/frus1952–54v08/d434.

180. Quoted by Botsiou (2007: 227).

erpi, who stayed behind with relatives in Athens, where she settled down and had a family of her own. The Greek state had dealt with Ioanna and Olympia as "endangered children," but it treated Efterpi as a "dangerous" young adult. Efterpi was forced to grow up quickly and to cut short her own teenage years. She never gave up hope, however, of reconnecting with her younger half-siblings, whose caregiver and protector she had become from the day of their mother's suicide. Efterpi displayed an extraordinary degree of perseverance in the search for Ioanna and Olympia: from 7 December 1951 on, when her half-sisters were violently taken away from her, she had been determined to extract them from PIKPA's web. She endured many painful encounters with the oppressive hierarchies of Cold War Greece. Through the mid-1970s, her resilience was seen as a challenge to the heavy-handed authoritarianism of the Greek establishment. In her difficult quest, Efterpi received hardly any help from Greek institutions or officials, who tried to silence her very legitimate questions or chased her away under a barrage of threats. It took until 1980 for her to finally receive news about her half-siblings. Efterpi infers that she was victimized by institutions and services that, being tainted themselves, further stigmatized the offspring of "criminal" communist parents.[181] Her more recent statements have been inspired by a desire to settle scores with the past. They have expressed, not strictly her personal ideological stance, but also that of other informant-representatives of the so-called Old Left, which was directly linked to the Occupation and the Civil War. Her story further illustrates the gendered experience of the political discrimination of the Cold War era, when brutal politics affected the societal standing of all leftists, but especially of women.

The communist's daughter, left-leaning Efterpi herself, was a "stigmatized supplicant whose opportunities were always conditional, rather than guaranteed" (in the wording of Cathy Frierson).[182] The antileftist bias of the Greek authorities intensified the typical degree of bureaucratic obstructionism and even spurred outright hostility. David Close has called the "standard" police repression of left-wingers "not merely irksome but intimidating."[183] In the case of the Argyriadis siblings, antileftist prejudice was exacerbated by the establishment's structural need to cover up the hasty or questionable adoption practices that marred maternity clinics and childcare institutions in several Greek cities.[184] As mentioned above, in its scheme to

---

181. Efterpi, testimony of 13 July 2014.
182. Frierson (2015: 17).
183. Close (2004: 263).
184. Brouskou (2015: 167). See also part 2 of this book.

free up more children for adoption, the Greek state profited from declaring biological parents or close relatives incapable of parenting, dangerous, or even "dead." Politically motivated adoptions must therefore be added to the long list of harmful Cold War practices through which the Greek right-wing establishment suppressed citizens whom it judged to be extraneous to the national body politic.

Other, psychological factors were at play in the Greek establishment's repeated refusal to respond to Efterpi's quest: the nation's sense of culpability was rooted also in feelings of shame. The Greek national body is seen as feminine, in persistent allegorical depictions as well as in rhetorical tropes. The name of Greece, too, is grammatically feminine: ή Ἑλλάς or η Ελλάδα. The Greek nation is often regarded as the motherland. Therefore, a nation giving up its children is perceived to be a suffering mother at best, but a shamed, "unnatural," or even "evil" mother at worst. The steady supply of adoptees of the 1950s and 1960s constituted proof of Greece's status as a "relinquishing" state, a status associated with underdeveloped countries that the establishment, therefore, preferred to push into oblivion.[185] Many Greeks recalled the dire postwar predicament of the "client state," "orphan Greece," with a sense of inadequacy or shame. Efterpi's pesky requests for information and assistance were a discomfiting reminder also of the Greek Right's own defiant and overused rhetoric of the nation-as-family. In practice, this rhetorical trope signified the nation as a traditional, self-righteous, and even punitive family, in which the positions staked out by its right-wing members were taken for granted. In contrast, the Greek family's "deviant" leftist members, like "fallen daughters," had seen their places erased, or they needed to earn them back the hard way.[186] Efterpi's gritty resolve strikes home just how powerfully the origins of adoption and the realms of relinquishing children are feminized and maternalized. Her tenacity clashed with the Greek sense of belonging and (re)acceptance into a family, which was often a paternal, even a patriarchal, decision in response to an all-too-feminine plea. Efterpi's questions stirred up memories of actions and psychological conditions that Greek leftists as well as right-wingers were in the end eager to forget. The Greek Left's public memory from the time of the Civil War was silenced or grew distorted. The Right imposed its own thirty-year silence on left-wing personal as well as public memory. Tellingly, Greek reactionaries continued

---

185. Hübinette has proposed a similar argument centered on Korea as the shamed motherland, with its women being the reproducers and bearers of a colonized and therefore feminized nation (2006: 105–28, or his ch. 4).

186. Van Steen (2011: 123, *passim*).

to refer to the internecine struggle as the "bandit war"; the war was only officially recognized as a civil war in 1989.[187]

Efterpi's experience of repeatedly—and violently—being denied information is, *mutatis mutandis*, akin to the enforced secrecy about the clandestine taking of children from political radicals in Latin American nations.[188] From the 1960s through the mid-1980s, many South and Central American countries witnessed dictatorships and state terrorism (among them Argentina, Bolivia, Brazil, Chile, Honduras, Panama, Peru, and Uruguay). Their military regimes, which were commonly known as juntas, were largely products of the Cold War. Many of their left-wing opponents shared principles of a Marxist ideology, despite the vast domestic and regional diversity that characterized the dissident movements. The babies and very young children of these left-wingers became prized commodities in the renegade (internal and international) adoption circuit, which was premised on a furtive abetting that disguised itself as the "greater good" of confidentiality. Well-known are the many cases of adopted offspring of leftist victims (alive, dead, or killed) of Argentina's "Dirty War," the country's military dictatorship of 1976–1983: many parents were "disappeared" (with the verb "to disappear" expressly used as a transitive verb), only to have their infants reappear as "ahistorical" children available for adoption. Adding insult to (fatal) injury, some of these children were taken in by parents who were either perpetrators or were in the know as "appropriators" (to invoke the term that describes many Latin American cases).[189] Briggs and Marre caution that many "well-meaning" transnational adopters inadvertently contributed to the "disappearances" of children in countries that for political reasons had violently cut off ties to the adoptees' birth parents and families.[190] Closer to Greece's paroxysm in space and time perhaps, present-day Spain has been shaken by revelations that hundreds of children with "red genes" were stolen during the nearly four-decade-long rule of General Franco.[191] The oppressive Greek state of

---

187. Close (2004: 271) and Voglis (2014: 383–84). The term "civil war" recognizes insurgents as part of an equal, opposing party, and it ends their stigmatization as outlawed rebels. See also Armitage (2017), who discusses civil war in ancient Greece but not in modern Greece.

188. Briggs and Marre (2009: 11) introduce this incendiary topic, which has generated a vast amount of recent literature, offering further references to the sources most relevant to the phenomenon of international adoption.

189. Briggs and Marre (2009: 21n12).

190. Briggs and Marre (2009: 11).

191. The Spanish revelations continue to generate a lot of media attention. Prominent and well-informed has been the work of Ricard Vinyes, which has validated personal testimonies and has inspired the 2005 documentary *The Lost Children of Francoism*. The attention given to the Irish state-sanctioned "adoption well" of illegitimate babies, which was "pumped" by punitive Catholic Church institutions, shows promising signs of leading

the late 1940s through the early 1960s and also Greece's own junta (1967–1974) did not engage in the extreme crime of multigenerational disappearances, but like the juntas of Latin America and Spain, it did practice terror tactics against left-wing parents and family members and made every effort to forcibly control or "disappear" information.

to sustained public investigations. See the 2013 movie *Philomena*, directed by Stephen Frears, and recent books by authors such as O'Reilly (2018), Redmond (2018), and Smith (2007).

PART 2

NATION OF ORPHANS, ORPHANED NATION

Where Have All the Children Gone? Greek Adoptees by the Numbers, Relatively Speaking

The exact number of intercountry adoptions from Greece is known only approximately, but the relative numbers are an eye-opener. Greece started to compile data more systematically only after 1967, which is when the number of Greek adoptees sent to the United States had steeply declined.[1] The data provided by the receiving agencies in the United States are more precise, but adoptees from Greece were sent to multiple international destinations in addition to the States. Howard Altstein and Rita Simon claim that between 1948 and 1962, a total of 3,116 Greek-born children were adopted by US parents.[2] The number of 3,200 Greek-to-American adoptees, therefore, is a safe grand total: it is derived from the baseline count of 3,116 US visas issued, and it adds several Greek cases granted through the US private law system. The chronological breakdown of the total of 3,200 US-bound adoptions of 1948–1962 runs as follows: 1,246 Greek children arrived in 1951 through mid-1952; another 506 to 510 joined that number by the end of 1956, and another 1,360 children had arrived by late 1962. The approximate grand total number of 3,200 Greek-to-American adoptions is a much-needed objective measure, since it takes into account US immigration figures, visa applications, and other governmental and administrative data.[3] Any num-

---

1. Brouskou (2015: 162) and Altstein and Simon (1991: 14).
2. Altstein and Simon (1991: 14).
3. See Altstein and Simon (1991: 17nn6, 7) and also Matthews (1987: 10, 40, his tables 5 and 6), but secondary sources lead back to Weil (1984: 280, his table 1). See, however, below pp. 103–4 n. 109, on the necessary addition to Weil's total of some 54 Greek cases. Weil alerts the reader to the relatively small numbers of intercountry adoption cases granted via the US system of private laws (pieces of legislation) that add to the baseline totals for any given country of origin (1984: 279). Karen Balcom estimates that the additional number of Greek-born adoptees, whose postwar migration was granted not via public laws but via such special, individualized legislation, amounts to about 30 to 40 cases, bringing the

ber, therefore, that exceeds by many hundreds or thousands this total of 3,200 Greek-born children adopted out to the United States from 1948 to 1962 shows the signs of exaggeration—and inflated figures do serve particular agendas, which I will revisit below.

When entered into a ranking based on absolute numbers, the bare total of 3,116 adoptees places Greece in second position as a country of origin, after (South) Korea.[4] Greece delivered circa 16 percent of the total number of 19,230 foreign-born children adopted by US parents between 1948 and 1962. Greece and Korea combined, however, offered up more than one-third during that same time period.[5] The Greek numbers remained strong through the early 1960s, but the absolute numbers have Korea in the lead almost consistently from 1948 through 1987.[6] The raw numbers confirm the common perception that the nascent intercountry adoption movement of the Cold War era was primarily a Korean adoption movement (which is also the trend that has been studied most extensively), but that popular perception certainly lacks nuance. Greece is the outlier whose relative figures must, belatedly, add a necessary corrective.[7]

Greek total to about 3,200 cases (email communication of 4 April 2017). Weil's numbers do not reflect, either, the occasional adoption that fell through after all the steps for the child's travel to the States had been taken. Therefore, the total sum of the 3,200 Greek adoptions of 1948–1962 remains an adequate ballpark figure to work and think with.

The private law system resolved many US adoption, immigration, and naturalization issues caused by unusual hardship or extraordinary circumstances, often on behalf of foreign-born children sponsored by American families (or single persons), their lawyers, and state representatives. When US legislation beginning in 1953 offered (nonquota) provisions for younger but not older Greek-born orphans entering the States, many Greek American families turned to the private law system in the hope of extending a tradition of kin migration (and family expansion rather than separation) with which they had long been familiar. They brought private bills before the US Congress "for the relief of" younger relatives, many of whom were not orphans or were beyond the age limitations. Not every proposed private bill passed; many failed when more comprehensive legislation that would resolve the special cases was expected to pass in the near future. The postwar US private law system is the subject of an ongoing research project by Balcom, who has kindly shared her preliminary conclusions and estimates with me (email communication of 4 April 2017). See also below, pp. 204–7 (Adamantia's case). Maguire (1997) discusses the history of private laws, their prevalence, and the rules and procedures by which they have been enacted (on adoption cases, see 1997: 87–88, 92, 96–97, 102–3, 108–9, 114, 118, 121, 123, 124–25, 126–27, 128, 518n48, *passim*).

4.   Altstein and Simon (1991: 14).
5.   Altstein and Simon (1991: 14).
6.   The figures provided by Altstein and Simon cut off in 1987 (1991: 14–16).
7.   Wide-ranging scholarly articles, such as those collected and edited by Diana Marre and Laura Briggs (2009), provide further details and make occasional attempts to establish absolute numbers. Arissa Oh has placed the subject of the Korean adoptions back in the spotlight with her recent book with the telling title *To Save the Children of Korea: The Cold*

The far left column at the top of table 1 below lists the five countries of origin that ranked highest numerically in the intercountry adoption movement of the first 15 years of the Cold War period. From 1948 through 1962, the countries that sent the most adoptees to the United States were, in descending order, Korea, Greece, Japan, (West) Germany, and Austria, followed by "other countries."[8] The total and annual figures of these adoptions are in columns 2 and 3, respectively. The United States regarded all these named countries as crisis countries where the need for postwar humanitarian assistance through adoption was felt to be most urgent. Greece was home to the "neediest group of orphaned European children."[9] Thousands of Greek children had lost their parents in the war decade of the 1940s, and their acute predicament constituted a forceful push factor. Also, for many years, Greece offered a steady supply of adoptable minors of a younger age, whose placement into American families could occur in a relatively "invisible" manner, that is, without stirring serious racial, ethnic, or religious objections.[10] Americans wanted to adopt Greek infants in large numbers "because of the growing cultural acceptance that Greeks were 'white,'" Rachel Winslow claims.[11] Until the 1940s, the dominant white population in America had been racializing the Greeks as an ethnic minority, swarthy in skin color. These charged statements are best explained in the context of US racial history and immigration politics and hierarchies (as, for instance, in the insightful 2009 study by Yiorgos Anagnostou). Greek-to-white-American placements did not cross any stubborn racial lines, although many of my interviewees reported feeling "somewhat different" or "not quite the same" when growing up.[12] US immigration policies realized

---

War Origins of International Adoption (2015). See also Kim (2010), Lee (2016), McKee (2019), Park Nelson (2016), and Pate (2014), who fuses military history with the adoption history of South Korea. Tobias Hübinette has studied postwar Korean adoption from the perspective of the land of origin and its popular culture (2006).

8.   Altstein and Simon (1991: 14).

9.   Altstein and Simon (1991: 3).

10. Peña (2014) has collected the most important bibliographical references on the subject of interracial adoptions that are also cross-border adoptions. See further Brian (2012); Briggs (2012); Gailey (2010); Herman (2008: 229–52); McKee (2019: 61–65, 69–76, *passim*); Melosh (2002: 158–200, or her ch. 4); Park Nelson (2016); Simon and Altstein (2000); and Yngvesson (2010).

11. Winslow (2012a: 104; 2017: 52).

12. By comparison, more Greek-to-Dutch adoptees characterized themselves as "the odd man out," *"een vreemde eend in de bijt,"* as per Marten van Haren (2006: 247) and Marina van Dongen (2013b: 11). My very general observations here are not based on scientific studies of my own or on any other measures of racial or broadly cultural assimilation (but see below for a few references). My observations are, rather, empirically informed by oral testimonies, but I do acknowledge the adult adoptees' objections against "specialists" articulating how they, the transplanted children themselves, "turned out."

American notions of national identity while furthering foreign policy goals. They even actualized long-cherished notions of American exceptionalism. Also, many Greek-born adoptees who were sent out, especially in the early 1950s, had Greek American relatives who had been seeking to adopt them and to whom they were known by first and last names.[13] These were typically referred to as "named" cases or as "known" children, who faced fewer bureaucratic obstacles, and their adoptions could be completed in the States (given the urgent conditions back home). However, the rankings, the absolute numbers, and even the various motivations or trends mentioned earlier do not tell the whole story, and each factor described above requires further elaboration. Important considerations shed new light on Greece's ranking in the second place—and must, regrettably, move Greece to first place in the list of crisis countries.

First, these bare lists of nations and numbers of adoptees must be weighed against the critical factor of the population size of the country in question. Column 4 shows population figures based on the record of 1960 for the named "sending," "relinquishing," or "supplying countries," as they

---

The psychological adjustment of Greek-born adoptees has only recently become the subject of systematic research, even though comprehensive models of so-called "outcome studies" started to appear decades ago. Herman defines this number-driven trend as the second of three modes of quantification in the "adoption research industry" (2009: 124, 125–30). Hester Storsbergen and her collaborators have studied more than fifty Greek-born adults who as infants from Metera were adopted by Dutch parents. Storsbergen's interviewees responded to questions related to mental health, well-being, and self-esteem. The outcomes showed a direct correlation between the adults' appraisal of their adoption (negative versus neutral or positive) and the levels of psychological adjustment they had attained (Storsbergen, Juffer, van Son, and 't Hart 2010). The published results of 2010 build on Storsbergen's doctoral research and fieldwork conducted in the mid- to late 1990s (2004) and also on her contributions to Hoksbergen, Storsbergen, and Brouwer-van Dalen (1995). Conversing with the Dutch teams, Panayiota Vorria has made further contributions to the longitudinal outcome studies pertaining to infants from Metera who had been raised in residential group care and were subsequently adopted (domestically). See, most recently, Vorria et al. (2015), who follow up on the "Greek Metera Study" with their quantitative assessment of their subjects' "attachment security." Interviewee Marten van Haren, who was born in 1970 on the island of Corfu and adopted out when he was four months old, recounts his overall positive experience in a volume of adoption stories collected by Hoksbergen (2006). See further the collective volumes of De Pauw, Hoksbergen, and Van Aelst (1998) and of Hoksbergen and Walenkamp (2000).

13. Winslow (2012a: 101, 111, 112, 114; 2017: 50, 55, 56, 57). The early and long-considered-authoritative history of Greek America by Saloutos does not touch on this postwar adoption phenomenon when mentioning the Greek Americans' lobbying to increase the number of compatriots allowed into the United States, whether in the refugee or the "relative preference group" (1964: 379). Laliotou offers a more comprehensive critique of Saloutos's erasure of gender, racial, and other culturally sensitive or family-specific topics (2004: 191–95). See also Korma (2017: 56–57).

Table 1. Total and annual adoptions and per capita ratio of foreign-born children adopted by US parents, 1948–1962.

	Adoptions (1948-1962)			
	Total	Annual	Population (in millions)	Annual adoptions per million people
Korea	4,162	277.5	25.012	11.1
Greece	**3,116**	**207.7**	8.332	24.9
Japan	2,987	199.1	92.501	2.2
Germany	1,845	123.0	72.815	1.7
Austria	744	49.6	7.048	7.0
Other	6,376			
Total	**19,230**			
	Annual adoptions per million people			
Greece	**24.9**			
Korea	11.1			
Austria	7.0			
Japan	2.2			
Germany	1.7			

were called.[14] After adjusting for population size, the number of annual adoptions per million people places Greece at the top: Greece has, unequivocally, the highest annual per capita adoption ratio from 1948 through 1962 (columns 5 and 6). Moreover, Greece's number of 24.9 is more than twice as high as the figure of 11.1 for Korea, whose postwar population was three times as large as Greece's. The Greek number of 24.9 is also more than 3.5 times higher than the number 7 of Austria, a country with a postwar population size only slightly smaller than Greece's.

It is precisely this huge proportional discrepancy that makes Greece a true outlier in the early Cold War period. From the late 1940s through the early 1960s, Greece was a sad exception for other reasons as well. In the early years, Japan, Germany, and Austria were probably not sending many children to other destinations. Greece, on the other hand, was still dispatch-

---

14. The figures in column 4 of table 1 are drawn from the World Bank Databank with total population numbers for all countries for the year 1960 (the earliest year listed). This databank is accessible online at http://databank.worldbank.org/data/views/reports/tableview.aspx?isshared=true. The demographic yearbooks issued by the United Nations are accessible online as well at http://unstats.un.org/unsd/demographic/products/dyb/dyb2.htm. The UN yearbooks typically show lower numbers (but also many estimates) from the late 1940s through the 1950s.

ing many adoptees to the Netherlands. Solid data from before 1967 are not available, other than the count of 478 Greek-born adoptees sent to the Netherlands from 1957 through 1970.[15] Sweden's take of Greek children (40 adoptees through 1966) was far smaller than that of the Netherlands, but it was not negligible. Contrary to common perception, Australia took only a "very small" number of Greek adoptees.[16] Moreover, Northern Greece had recently lost some 20,000 children (a conservative estimate) to the countries behind the Iron Curtain, where they had been taken by the communist forces during the Civil War. Only very few of these children were ever returned.[17] These facts are not obvious from the absolute numbers, and are simply overshadowed by the statistics of subsequent years.

Another important differential is not readily apparent from a reading of the absolute counts some six decades after the fact: Korea, Japan, (West) Germany, and Austria hosted scores of servicemen, relief workers, and other personnel of US government agencies and services. United Nations troops and staff, too, established a tangible presence in some of these countries— but not in Greece. The US soldiers and the other foreign men fathered many children, who were and are often indiscriminately referred to as the "G.I. babies" or "war babies." Many of these children, however, were marginalized in their home country for being of "mixed race" (according to the commonly used terminology of the 1950s). This was especially true in countries with strong patrilineal family structures, such as Korea and Japan, but a social stigma was attached to war children in Germany and Austria as well. Postwar US adoption policies, therefore, through a combination of official quotas and private laws, considered "orphans" from Korea, Japan, Germany, and Austria to be among the first candidates for intercountry adoption. This move toward cross-border adoption translated into temporary or special US legislation—in other words, into an American emergency response. The result was a more formal but still far from permanent process of immigration and refugee policymaking, but it did not constitute a direct path to citizenship.[18] Sue-Je Lee Gage explains how some governments used international adoption agencies for a political purpose, letting them deal with population groups that were marginalized within their countries.[19] She adds, "The pull factors were obligations felt by Americans in efforts to wipe the slate clean

---

15. See above, p. 61 n. 137.
16. Quartly, Swain, and Cuthbert (2013: 105).
17. Danforth and Van Boeschoten (2012: 4, 48) and Plakoudas (2017: 91–92).
18. Gage (2007: 94, 96, 97, 99) and Oh (2015: 147).
19. Gage (2007: 90).

for their own nation: that is, 'cleaning up' their boys' messes."[20] Richard Weil phrases the issue of expiating guilt and taking (paternal[istic]) responsibility more delicately: "significant numbers of children from one European country, West Germany, are still migrating to the U.S. as adoptees. It is possible that the large U.S. military presence there may be a factor. . . . this military presence was important in the 1940s and 1950s."[21]

On 25 June 1948, the United States issued the Displaced Persons Act (DPA or Public Law 774). This landmark act endeavoured to speed Europe's postwar reconstruction and admitted a general total of about 400,000 refugees over the course of four years.[22] The Displaced Persons Act helped to bring over the children of American fathers born in Germany and Austria.[23] Its dispensations actually contravened the rhetoric of US government spokespersons and the State Department, which resisted taking responsibility for the overseas partners as well as the children of American servicemen.[24] In general, however, Greek orphans did not qualify for special dispensations until 1950, when the DPA was extended and amended: Public Law 555 of 16 June 1950 accelerated the relief of war orphans from additional countries. Special US legislation was extended to benefit the "mixed-race" children of Korea and Japan only from 1953 onward.[25] This shift resulted from the changing global theaters of war and relief work as well as from timidly transforming race relations. Thus, the United States made special dispensations for children of American fathers born in four of the five sending countries that scored highest in adoptee counts. Greece, however, is the clear exception to the rule, because it never housed large numbers of American armed forces. The fact that Greece's orphans were not a target group for the initial

---

20. Gage (2007: 90). See also Oh (2015: 87–88).
21. Weil (1984: 285).
22. Bon Tempo (2008: 7–8, 12, 22–26) and Cohen (2012).
23. Weil (1984: 280, his table 1).
24. Gage (2007) devotes ample attention to the discriminations resulting from discrepancies between US government rhetoric and action, which treated various groups of "Amerasian" children differently over the many postwar years. The US military command on site helped prevent marriages that "crossed the color line."
25. Weil (1984: 281, his table 1 continued). These postwar laws began to erode the US national origins quota system, the linchpin of the Immigration Act of 1924 (the Johnson-Reed Act), which favored immigrants of certain ethnonational backgrounds and prohibited, for one, most Asian immigration (the long-lasting "Asian exclusion," on which see Park Nelson 2016: 52–53). The 1924 Act remained under attack throughout the 1950s and was finally abolished in 1965 (by the Immigration and Nationality Act of 1965, the Hart-Cellar Act). Here, Bon Tempo's (2008) introduction and chapters 1–2 prove helpful, even though they contain scant information on Greek immigrants and refugees. See also Oh (2015: 146–47, 148) and Winslow (2012b: 319–26, 340). The evolving US policies pertaining to unaccompanied refugee children have been outlined by Forbes and Fagen (1984: 9–11).

US legislation of 1948 again strengthens Greece's ranking among the other four countries.

The above conclusions about the absolute and relative Greek numbers must take an important mitigating factor into account. Greece's ranking in first place, relatively speaking, would probably not be changed much if we deducted the many Greek orphans who went to Greek American family members, since that scenario played out for orphans from other Western European countries as well. Such a hard-to-quantify subtraction would bring the Greek relative numbers at least closer to the Korean ratio, but Greece's adjusted ratio of 16 or higher still stays well above Korea's figure of 11.1.

The circumstances behind this mitigating factor must be traced back to the early 1950s and to the provisions made through the Displaced Persons Act. No fewer than *one-third* of the total number of 3,116 Greek-born children (of nominally 1948–1962) entered the United States under the non-quota DPA provisions between the summer of 1950 and the summer of 1952 (that is, under the DPA as amended). The sheer volume of this earliest phase of the Greek-to-American adoption movement, which might be better described as another Greek migration flow, brings the remaining two-thirds down far enough to begin to narrow the gap between Greece and the other sending countries from 1953 on (through 1962). The vast majority of the 1950–1952 arrivals of Greek minors were not small children, but youngsters with an average age of 16. The boys outnumbered the girls by two to one, and many of the girls traveled in sibling groups with their brothers. Some sibling groups were comprised of up to four children from the same natal family.[26] These Greek-born teenagers were typically sponsored by family members or more distant benefactors, among them many members of Greek American organizations. Even though these youngsters traveled from Greece to the States under the designation of "orphans" or "for adoption," large numbers of them received a less formal guardianship, and many eventually pursued naturalization and US citizenship on their own.[27] Only the youngest of these Greek-born children who arrived between 1950 and 1952 were formally adopted by their Greek American families or acquaintances. Therefore, this

---

26. I draw these numerical conclusions from an extensive study of the relevant New York Passenger Lists on Ancestry.com, in association with the National Archives at New York City, New York Arrival Records, 1820–1957.

27. Until the Child Citizenship Act of 2000 was issued, foreign adoptees were not automatically granted US citizenship. The American adoptive parents or the adoptees themselves had to formally apply for it. If they failed to do so, adoptees aged eighteen or older in 2000 were left without US citizen status, and many have since found themselves in immigration limbo.

mitigating first trend of the typically "named" or "known" children is one of conscious migration rather than of adoption or "orphan" care: extended and truly transnational Greek families saw in the DPA legislation an opportunity to implement (male) kin migration, allowing poorer Greek relatives to share in the "superior" living and working conditions of Greek immigrant families who had already settled in the States (typically in Chicago and New York). Thus, too, this earliest phase of the Greek "orphan" adoption movement built on prewar, well-established (and well-studied) patterns of migration from Greece to America.[28]

The common discourse about facilitating and accelerating the adoptions of "eligible orphans" from all supplying countries again indicates that the definition of "orphan" was meant to include "illegitimate," "fatherless," and abandoned children, and children relinquished by one or both parents. Many minors were not technically orphans but were only labeled as such because governments bilaterally were willing to use a very expansive and self-serving definition of the term "orphan."[29] The even more capacious notion of "war-handicapped children" also began to be used internationally in the aftermath of World War II.[30] This term was extended to incorporate those foreign-born children who benefited from the various relief acts, and also the young wards of the Greek foster homes, orphanages, and *paidopoleis* of the 1950s, victims of the lost decade of the 1940s. The conservative Greek government's favorite term was not (the Greek equivalent of) "war-handicapped" or "war-stricken children," but "rebel-stricken" or "bandit-stricken children," "ανταρτόπληκτα" or "συμμοριόπληκτα παιδιά," in further slurs against the opposing left-wing and communist camp.[31]

In sum, the number of adoptees that Greece sent to the United States in the postwar era differs from the popular perception, and they have yet to be studied more systematically. Before taking the relative figures into account, the reader might not have expected Greece to be listed with Korea, Japan,

---

28. For more recent, edited volumes devoted to the broader topics of the Greek diaspora and migration, see Clogg (1999) and Tziovas (2009). See also Laliotou (2004). Despite the prominence of intercountry adoption from Greece in migration management, the topic has remained virtually absent from Venturas (2015). I have benefited greatly from discussing the subject of kin migration with Karen Balcom (on 24 March 2017).

29. Winslow (2012a: 35–36; 2017: 13–14). Kim Park Nelson elaborates on the "clinical" use of the full sequence of "eligible alien orphan," in which the latter term connotes an "object of pity, and a subject for charity and salvation" (2016: 56–57). Rickie Solinger has drawn attention to those children rendered adoptable by way of legal or procedural definitions, policy decisions, economic constraints, social pressures, and other factors, which are often far removed from strict orphanhood (2001: 20–32).

30. Hassiotis (2011: 272).

31. Vassiloudi and Theodorou (2012: 123) and above, p. 52 n. 107.

and Germany as providers of children for international adoption—let alone for Greece to outrank those other countries of origin in the first fifteen years of the intercountry adoption movement. Granted that Greece sent scores of adoptees to Greek American family members (broadly defined), its numbers and rankings should be noticed by the "emerging community of historians" working on the history of adoption in the United States, Canada, and other parts of the world (in the words of Karen Balcom).[32] In their otherwise important introduction to the intercountry adoption movement's history, Laura Briggs and Diana Marre deal with the case of Greece as a relinquishing country in less than three lines: they invoke the Greek Civil War but fail to quote figures, let alone further bibliographical leads.[33] Greece is altogether absent from Ellen Herman's *Kinship by Design* (2008).[34] In her recent book, Arissa Oh reiterates the popular perception: she claims that "Korean children received the largest share of visas issued under subsequent [post-1953] temporary orphan laws [up through 1961]."[35] The total count of Korean-born adoptees dispatched to the United States was indeed the highest, but Korea's relative number still drops below even half of the per capita ratio of adoptions of Greek-born children. Lastly, the cautionary statement of Altstein and Simon merits repeating: even though the figures are based on the "best available primary (governmental) and secondary sources," gaps inevitably

---

32. Balcom (2011: x).
33. Briggs and Marre (2009: 5).
34. Greek children are absent, too, from Betty Jean Lifton's succinct pages on international adoption (2009: 276–77) and from Kirsten Lovelock's comparative analysis of intercountry adoption and immigration policy in three Western receiving nations (the United States, Canada, and New Zealand) (2000). Cf. Brian (2012) and Park Nelson (2016: 53), with a recent but less-than-accurate reference to the Greek adoption movement. Welcome exceptions are Catherine Ceniza Choy's *Global Families: A History of Asian International Adoption in America*, which summarily acknowledges the Greek adoptions (2013: 17, 30, 83, 103, 182), and also Fehrenbach's chapter (2016: 218, 220). Karen Balcom studies the nature and scope of the numerous 1950s efforts to resolve immigration issues for adopted or to-be-adopted foreign-born children by way of the US private law system, and also discusses the personal experiences behind them. Private bills also resolved many adoption and immigration issues for Greek children and their (typically) Greek American adoptive parents and relatives. Thus Balcom extends the Greek scope well beyond her previous book, *The Traffic in Babies*, which devoted a chapter to "criminal law and baby black markets" of the critical years 1954–1964 (2011: 166–94). Older sources that reflected thinking "on the ground," such as the written versions of mid-1950s conference presentations, delivered accurate data, but it failed to percolate into subsequent studies. Letitia DiVirgilio, a caseworker with the Boston-based Children's Aid Association, presented a paper at a May 1956 conference on social work in which she described the "initial adjustments" of twenty-four foreign-born children in their new homes in eastern Massachusetts. Half of these children came from Greece, only seven came from Korea. DiVirgilio's qualitative analysis of the Greek cases is also more detailed than that of the Korean cases.
35. Oh (2015: 148).

still exist "due to incomplete and fragmentary reporting, particularly in the early years of data collection."[36] It is to be hoped that, long after the faceless statistics have lost their meaning, the real lives of the actual adoptees will take the reader's grasp of US immigration policy and its impact on the Cold War history of Greece in a new, critical direction.

The Political Is Personal: Adoption and/as Anticommunism

> Little Violetta [reportedly abandoned by a communist mother] grew into a beautiful girl who was adopted by an American couple and taken to the States. Here she had a home, a radio, a car and all the clothes she wanted . . .
>
> —Queen Frederica, *A Measure of Understanding*, 1971: 138

At the onset of the Cold War, the US government came to understand the political, anticommunist power of international adoption from Greece and—later and more visibly—from Korea and Vietnam. At first, Washington was reluctant to jump on Greece's anticommunist bandwagon as long as it was driven by the issue of the "child abductions," mainly because many parents from Greece's rural North had "voluntarily" given up their children for evacuation to Soviet Bloc countries.[37] American reactions and solutions grew bolder, however, through the 1950s, when it became apparent that Greece was still divided ideologically and thus remained critical to the US containment strategy (and to its counterpart, the global expansion of American influence). A movement of adoption activism started to develop that was church-based or grounded in broader religious communities or ethnic interest groups. American evangelical Christians, for instance, spearheaded the drive to resettle war orphans from Korea. The mass adoptions of Korean orphans by Harry and Bertha Holt, a conservative evangelical pair from rural Oregon, spoke to the imagination of patriotic and faith communities across the States and shone perhaps too bright a light on independent or proxy initiatives in placing children.[38] The Holt couple even benefited from a special act passed by Congress that circumvented the regulatory protocols by stipulating that six of the interracial adoptees "be held and considered to be the natural-born alien children of Harry and Bertha Holt."[39]

---

36. Altstein and Simon (1991: 17n6).
37. Damousi (2017: 119–22, 128–34); Hassiotis (2011: 280–82); and Jones (1985).
38. Brian (2012: 10–13); Fehrenbach (2016: 227–29); Oh (2015: 89–104); Winslow (2012b: 326–41); and Woo (2015: 40–41).
39. *United States Statutes at Large* 69 (1955), Private Law 475 of 11 August 1955: "An Act for the Relief of Certain Korean War Orphans." Holt (1956: 83–84) and Winslow (2012b: 331–32).

Briggs and Marre explain that, during the 1950s, evangelical Protestant-ism was seeing a revival as a "key ally of a political anticommunism" (that is, the struggle against "godless communism" preached and promulgated by the leading evangelist Billy Graham, who rose to celebrity status in the late 1940s): "evangelical anticommunism became powerfully wed to con-servative international politics—and both became intimately entwined with transnational adoption."[40] American fundamentalist and missionary zeal met anticommunist foreign policy and security concerns in intercountry adoption, "while . . . giving ordinary Americans a sense of personal par-ticipation in the Cold War as family ties became a political obligation" (in the words of Hübinette).[41] Arissa Oh stresses how the US media pre-sented the Korean War as the struggle for survival of Christian South Korea against communist North Korea; therefore "the adoption of Christian South Korean babies was a deliberately anticommunist act."[42] Dubinsky cites the Cold War slogan of "fighting communism one child at a time," which urged Americans to make their own Cold War sacrifices by generously donating money to charities working for children living under communist regimes or by rescuing those children through international adoption.[43] Sporting the motto that parental love conquers all, America was staving off the commu-nists, who would otherwise find easy prey (and an inexhaustible flow of new recruits) in the world's poorest youth. Adopted children would grow up in a democratic and peaceful new country that prized traditional family life. Parental love, but certainly also prosperity, would exorcise any harm that communists had done to these children in their early years.

International adoption became the family-size metaphor of the expan-sive US democracy. Adoptive families "saved" and raised foreign children as prosperous America came to the rescue of foreign nations threatened by communism. An anonymous but typical article in the *Chicago Daily Tribune* of 13 November 1954, entitled "Shy Greek Girl Finds Loving Par-ents Here," drove home the point by erasing many of the domestic details: "The child whose natural father was murdered by communist gangs during the Greek civil war, was adopted by . . . . Her [birth] mother . . . has eight other children." When details were transmitted, they were often impossi-ble for well-meaning American parents to verify. A 1952 article in the *New York Times* set the newly arriving orphaned child up as a would-be warrior against communism:

---

40. Briggs and Marre (2009: 6).
41. Hübinette (2006: 44).
42. Oh (2015: 84 [quotation], 110).
43. Dubinsky (2010: 17).

[The American adoptive father] had been told that the child [a six-year-old boy from the "Queen Frederica Orphanage"] had been tossed by his mother into a flower garden . . . moments before the family was slaughtered by the [communist] invaders.

When the youngster stepped from the plane he was wearing a Greek uniform of the "Evzones"—mountain troops of the Greek army.[44]

Given Cold War global affairs and American foreign policy considerations, mass refugee admissions to the States bolstered anticommunist sentiment: they "saved" people who were fleeing communism and could compare and relate their experiences.[45] But the allegiance of child refugees was more secure. The States crafted into a compelling argument the perceived need to especially rescue children from Soviet and generally communist brutality. Hardly anything is as persuasive (and as powerful a legitimation) as being able to show the child victims of a regime's failure. In addition to dissipating any public objections, the fate of young and innocent victims bonded restrictionists and liberalizers in US immigration and refugee policymaking, who found common ground in anticommunist "rescue operations" of infants, the perfect, apolitical immigrant refugees, eminently worthy of admission and capable of quickly becoming "American." Established US citizens deemed infants and toddlers to be "the best possible immigrants" (quoting the apt title of Winslow's 2017 book). They did not expect the thorny issue of newcomers needing to "excise completely their immigrant roots" to rear its ugly head again.[46] Policymakers gave American families important positions in the rhetorical as well as the ideological battle lines by letting them take in such innocent child victims.

Through their commitment to child-rearing, adoptive families were happy to strike their blows against totalitarian communism and to help define the new democratic nation, ready to assume its role of world leader. Elaine Tyler May was the first to study the ties between Cold War anticommunist containment and the ensuing American tendency to reinvest in a strong family life focused on raising children.[47] She has situated 1950s family (self-)containment against the backdrop of a revived domes-

---

44. Anon., "Adopted War Orphan Flies in from Greece," *New York Times*, 15 June 1952.
45. Bon Tempo (2008: 3–4).
46. Bon Tempo defines the issue in the context of the 1950s public debates about mass entry for Hungarian refugees (2008: 23 and his ch. 3).
47. May (2008; first published 1988).

tic ideology, that is, of "the nuclear family in the nuclear age."[48] E. Wayne Carp and Anna Leon-Guerrero speak of the "baby boom pronatalism that put a premium on family and home life."[49] Christina Klein shifts the focus back to the upswing in adoptions and calls transethnic adoptive families instrumental in assigning "re-domesticated women a role in the national [American] project of global expansion."[50] International adoption responded forcefully to the stated will of many childless American couples who felt marginalized in a "celebratory" pronatalist society on a mission.[51] "[C]hildless couples besieged adoption agencies pleading for a child to add to their household," Carp maintains, underscoring the cause-effect relationship between the American dream of "personal happiness" and an "ideology of domesticity."[52] The number of postwar adoptions in the States skyrocketed as white, middle-class, and childless couples (re)discovered adoption, intercountry and domestic alike, as the pathway to familial bliss.[53] American society became increasingly preoccupied with adoption as a right as well as a duty. In despair, given the short supply of Caucasian children available through state-licensed agencies, some couples turned to nonregulated adoptions. In the prospective parents' judgment, licensed agencies and their social workers threw up unnecessary hurdles.[54] "My parents were desperate for a child," claimed Greek-born adoptee R.D. He volunteered, "My Jewish mom, a concentration camp survivor, went so far as to search Germany for a child."[55] Push and pull factors started to work in unison, adding nuance to the complicated but contingent relationships between sending and receiving countries.

> Little Violetta . . . had . . . all the clothes she wanted but she was so homesick for Greece that we had to take her back and return her to the Children's Home in which she had grown up. . . . [56]

---

48. May (2008: 1). Konstantinos Nikoloutsos discusses the reflection of these domestic(ity) politics of containment in American cinema of the early 1960s and its connections to the reconstruction of Cold War Greece (2013: 263, 278–79).

49. Carp and Leon-Guerrero (2002: 210).

50. Klein (2003: 190).

51. Carp (1998: 29; 2002: 12–13). See also Brian (2012: 9).

52. Carp (1998: 28).

53. Carp (1998: 29).

54. Carp (1998: 29–31, 113).

55. R. D., testimony of 14 August 2016.

56. Frederica (1971: 138).

Striking Close to Home: The Ahepa, 1940s

The anticommunist intercountry adoption movement, spearheaded by various nonstate actors and interest groups, including evangelical Christians, concentrated on Asian-born children. It had a contemporary or even a predecessor, however, in the Greek American and Greek Orthodox advocacy for policies sponsoring the adoption and resettlement of Greek-born children in the States. Various Greek and Greek American agents and intermediaries matched the push factors of an exhausted and ideologically divided Greece to the pull factor of US families wanting to take in Greek orphans as "objects of political rescue" (as per Winslow).[57] The lion's share of midcentury US-based activism on behalf of Greek orphans was undertaken by the Order of AHEPA, the American Hellenic Educational Progressive Association (spelled and read as the acronym "Ahepa" in the bulk of the association's literature, referring to its members as "Ahepans"). Founded in 1922 in Atlanta, Georgia, the Order of Ahepa grew in the course of a few decades into the largest and most influential Greek American voluntary and fraternal association.[58] Notably, the association's focal point was not the Greek Orthodox Church but the Greek American community and its acculturation, even though the activities of many local and regional chapters show substantial overlap between the two. George Leber, long-time executive secretary, collected the Ahepa's records and authored its official history on the occasion of the order's fiftieth anniversary in 1972. The Ahepa archives, as digested (selectively) by Leber, reveal samples of outspoken views on the problem of the communist "child abductions" but also, unilaterally, on the need to save and adopt Greek children. *The Ahepan*, the order's official magazine, which appeared every few months, resonated with similar sentiments.

During the early 1940s, the Ahepa was preoccupied with sending war relief to the home country suffering under Nazi German, Italian, and Bulgarian occupation forces.[59] Spyros Skouras, president of the Twentieth Century Fox Film Corporation, took the lead role in the mobilizing and fundraising efforts of the Greek War Relief Association (GWRA, founded as early as November 1940), which set up its headquarters in New York City.

---

57. Winslow (2012a: 112).
58. Laliotou (2004: 82–83); Moskos and Moskos (2014: 52–55); and Zervakis (1997: 306–7, 314).
59. Leber (1972: 336–37); Odzak (2006: 106); and the volume edited by Clogg (2008). Over the course of a decade, Ahepa members also collected donations to help build the "Ahepa Wing" of the Athenian Evangelismos Hospital, which was inaugurated in early April of 1950.

Before Skouras went on to relentlessly support Queen Frederica's charities, the GWRA joined forces with the Ahepa and other organizations, setting aside their political differences under the exigencies of World War II.[60] By the late 1940s, however, the Ahepa's rhetoric had markedly changed: it spoke with greater animosity against the communist-led Greek resistance than against the former occupiers, and it blamed the resistance for engaging in a "minor civil war."[61] In 1947, the Ahepa started to scrutinize all applications for "members of any subversive group," and it sought assurances that applicants were "free of any and all Communist taint," while pledging full support to the Truman Doctrine.[62] An anticommunist litmus test for admission was a common occurrence, however, in light of the Red Scare purges of the late 1940s and early 1950s. These purges were fueled by the outspoken hatred of communism of US Senator Joseph McCarthy, and the paranoia he instigated has since been known as McCarthyism. The Ahepa leadership took great pride in its postwar connection to the Greek monarchs, and it advertised the official welcomes and tokens of appreciation received from King Paul and Queen Frederica on its regular visits to Greece (as manifested by numerous articles and photographs in *The Ahepan* from the fall of 1946 on). The Ahepa's "patriotic" anticommunism, its outspoken royalist stance, and its care for or sponsorship of Greek children soon converged into a movement that peaked in the numerous Ahepa-sponsored adoptions of 1956 through 1958.

Through the Civil War years, the Ahepa conceived of various plans to bring relief to Greek war orphans, but after 1948, US government policy started to reshape and streamline such initiatives. Ahepa chapters sponsored meetings across the States to raise awareness about the cause of some "28,000 Greek children who had been abducted . . . by communist guerrillas and taken to various Iron Curtain nations," thereby denouncing "one of the most unspeakable campaigns in all human history."[63] In 1947 alone, no fewer

---

60. Kyrou (2008: 60–62, 74) and Saloutos (1964: 382–83). Martin (2014: 60–71) discusses the relief aid and services provided by UNRRA (1943–1947) and continued by the International Refugee Organization (IRO, late 1940s through early 1950s), both concentrating on refugees, displaced persons, and concentration-camp survivors in Western Europe. See also Fehrenbach (2016) and Palmieri and Herrmann (2016), on the broader international framework of war relief and aid to child victims.

61. Leber (1972: 364). As Zervakis has disclosed (1997: 316–18, 321), the Ahepa and its postwar Justice for Greece Committee were initially reluctant to acknowledge the full scope of the Greek Civil War, while they were strenuously lobbying for US support for the homeland.

62. Leber (1972: 366). On this anticommunist exclusion, see also Anagnostou (2009: 209) and Zervakis (1997: 334).

63. Leber (1972: 374). See also Anon., *The Ahepan*, Jan.–March 1950.

than twenty-six domestic camps for Greek children began to operate, "under the auspices of the Greek government and the Greek War Relief Association" (GWRA).[64] In the summer of 1946, the GWRA had launched its Orphan Support Program, which was geared toward finding foster and permanent homes for orphaned children in Greece itself.[65] The GWRA was soon superseded by the Ahepa, which focused far less on domestic placements, choosing, rather, to institutionalize intercountry adoptions from Greece.

In 1948, the Ahepa Supreme Convention endorsed the work of the international Foster Parents' Plan for War Children, thus first paving the way for mass *symbolic* adoptions of Greek orphans by Greek American and American parents.[66] The GWRA, the Foster Parents' Plan, and also CARE indisputably established bases of "soft power" in Greece along with their humanitarian platforms, and the Ahepa's 1950s US-bound adoptions were able to successfully build on that model. The symbolic adoptions of the Foster Parents' Plan entailed financial sponsorship of a known war-stricken child: the foster parents or other adopters (such as church or student groups, teams of soldiers, and even of prison inmates) committed to regularly sending money and occasional relief packages to a needy child identified by the central organization. The Foster Parents' Plan was founded in 1937 to help alleviate the impact of the Spanish Civil War on children.[67] Its charitable work was encouraged and recognized by the Greek state.[68] Sara Fieldston's recent book (2015) provides further context to such schemes of long-distance child welfare on the American paradigm, part of the Cold War battle for the hearts and minds of future citizens and leaders. Many child sponsorship programs led to loyal and durable relationships of solidarity between American and Greek families and to some formal adoptions of known Greek children. The support that Plan International (as it has long been called) extended to

---

64. Leber (1972: 367).

65. Anon., *The Ahepan*, Sept.–Oct. 1946, 15–16, 17. See also Winslow (2012a: 107–8; 2017: 54).

66. Leber (1972: 372).

67. Baughan mentions World War I versions of the "financial adoption" programs (2018: 196–97). She devotes special attention to the child sponsorship campaigns of the Near East Relief (NER, founded in 1915) on behalf of Armenian children in the aftermath of the Armenian genocide and through the 1920s (2018: 187–89, 196, 209–10). By the mid-1920s, the NER had pulled out of Anatolia and moved its office from Istanbul to Athens. Then the NER's "diplomacy of relief and refuge" became more Greece-centered in nature and appearance: it focused on the NER orphanages established in Greece to house formerly Ottoman Greek and Armenian children and teenagers (e.g., in Athens, in Corinth, on Syros), and it appealed to the Western admiration of (and "debt" to) ancient Greece in its fund-raising rhetoric. Lapidot-Firilla (2009: 165, 167 [quotation]).

68. See the Greek Legislative Decree no. 1102 of 28 September 1949. See also Kliafa (2016: 73).

Greece ceased in 1975, by which time it had assisted more than 17,000 of the country's children in need.[69]

Anonymous reports of 23 February 1950 and 28 November 1951 in *The Hi-Po*, the student newspaper of High Point College (now University) in North Carolina, detail the Plan sponsorship of Vassiliki, a Greek orphan girl (with picture) that the Methodist Student Fellowship (and later many more members of the student body) decided to take on. Vassiliki was urged to write grateful letters in response (which the central office collected and translated): "I received the money you sent me as well as 1 piece cloth, 1 pillow case, 1 pound lard and 5 bars soap. . . . You can't imagine how happy your presents have made me."[70] The Foster Parents' Plan also arranged for medical assistance and even for overseas surgery for a few of its badly maimed adoptees. The American media drew plenty of attention to such cases.[71] Other children were invited on longer-term stays with US families. Again, the American press was quick to add its own, paternalistic readings of such "heart-warming" cross-border contacts:

> Hoboken, N. J., Jan. 7 [1956]—Three war orphans from Greece came ashore here today to begin a year's visit with an American family. . . . The visit is designed to show youngsters from war-torn homes the democratic way of life, so they can cope with the lure of communism when they return to their native land.[72]

The Greek government and the Ahepa further endorsed the work of CARE, the Cooperative for American Remittances to Europe, which was founded in 1945. By 1953, the organization was renamed the Cooperative for American Relief Everywhere, and it is currently known as CARE International. From June 1946 on, CARE started sending tools and equipment kits to the struggling inhabitants of Greek rural areas, in accordance with its self-help philosophy. CARE dispatched massive amounts of food as well,

69. See Dijsselbloem, Fugle, and Gneiting (2014: 122–23, 124); Foster Parents' Plan (1957: 10–11, 21, 23); and Molumphy (1984: 91–95, his brief chapter on the Plan in Greece; 334–35, appendix D, his tables of enrollment by program country, including Greece). See also Anon., *I Thessalia*, 11 January 1950. Fieldston claims that "Greek authorities [of the early 1970s, i.e., of the Greek military dictatorship] were so embarrassed by photographs of ill-clad Greek children depicted in American advertisements" that they asked Plan International to phase out its Greek program (2015: 194).

70. Quoted by Anon., *The Hi-Po*, 28 November 1951.

71. See, among many others, Rusk, *New York Times*, 11 June 1950; Anon., *New York Times*, 21 July 1950; and Kerr in the 10 May 1952 edition of the *Pacific Stars and Stripes*, the newspaper of and for the US armed forces and their families.

72. Anon., *New York Times*, 8 January 1956.

including staples sent to Greek orphanages. The organization's aid to Greece lasted through September of 1973, by which time Greece had grown tired of its "orphan image."[73]

From Aiding Displaced Persons to Placing Adoptable Orphans: The Ahepa, Early 1950s

In the aftermath of the signing of the 1948 Displaced Persons Act (DPA), the 1949 Ahepa convention asked its leadership to urgently request that the US Senate and House of Representatives act to allow "at least 50,000 Greek orphans, and other refugees," victims of the "Communist war," to enter the States in 1949 and 1950.[74] The convention delegates urged the Ahepa leaders to also lobby for easing the adoption process of Greek minors and thus for expanding the geographical scope and subject categories of the 1948 DPA. Greek refugees were not a group targeted by the 1948 US government act, which aided, rather, Western and Central European victims of Nazi German persecution. The repeated pleas for help for Greek refugees and orphans met with moderate success: 1,246 Greek children were sponsored for adoption by US parents under the extended provisions of the 1948 DPA (as amended on 16 June 1950 by way of Public Law 555), which accelerated the relief of "Greek orphans" and "war orphans" from Greece through June of 1952. "(Eligible displaced) Greek orphans" and "war orphans" from Greece constituted two different legal categories of eligibility, addressed by section 2(e) and section 2(f) of Public Law 555, respectively. The maximum age for the first category was sixteen years (on 25 June 1948), whereas the age limit for the second category was ten years. Greek American relatives stepped up and pledged that they would initially assume guardianship over these Greek minors, and their formal assurances sufficed in many of the DPA cases and in the cases of (male) teenagers, especially.[75] The guardianship of American relatives prepared the children for eventual adoption in the youngsters' new home state. When formal adoption did not follow, however, the case replicated the 1940s crisis model of a symbolic and financial adoption, this time in close geographical proximity to the US sponsors.

The total of 1,246 DPA-sponsored adoptions of Greek-born children was the highest number compared to other countries; it was more than twice the

---

73. Fieldston (2015: 56, 194); Reuter, *The Ahepan*, August–Sept. 1959; www.care-international. org; and the CARE Records, Manuscripts and Archives Division, New York Public Library.

74. Leber (1972: 372).

75. United States Displaced Persons Commission (1952: 206–7, 366 tables 2 and 3, 376 table 30).

number of Italian-born children, for instance.[76] Given the necessary processing time, the bulk of the Greek DPA-sponsored orphans arrived in the States from mid-1951 through September 1952. These starting dates position the first wave of the Greek adoption movement firmly in the 1950s, not in the late 1940s, as per the popular misperception. Anecdotal evidence explains how the numbers added up so quickly in a relatively short time. *The Ahepan*, for one, featured (but did not question) some of the most extraordinary mass arrival stories:

> At 54, Bro. John Liaskos, a bachelor . . . , decided it was about time to have a large family. The restaurateur is pictured in front of his Hammond, Ind., home with 12 of the 25 orphans he has brought over from Greece and which will reside with him. The others have found homes in the Chicago area.[77]

Thus the earliest nonquota provisions for the adoption of Greek orphans, as for adoptees from other countries, stemmed from the dispensations made for refugees. These provisions defined the first wave of adoptions from Greece as a kin migratory trend and also as the good cause of finding families for children instead of finding children for families.[78] It bears repeating that the founding moment of the Greek-to-American adoption movement was not the post–World War II era but the turn of the new decade: the years 1950–1952 saw the movement's rise in a context of post–Civil War political rhetoric, humanitarian justifications, both push and pull factors, and old extended families as well as new Cold War alliances of do-gooders. Precisely because it was so new and partisan, the movement was marked not only by diverging standards and inconsistent methods, but by ethical dilemmas and moral transgressions. In 1953, C. G. Paris reported on the recent placements for adoption on behalf of the Ahepa Displaced Persons Committee:

> Orphans: As the original sponsors were not pleased with the behavior of a boy (Case # . . .), we effected his replacement to another home where the child is much happier. . . . [W]e placed at the Denver Jewish Hospital, a . . . girl who contracted tuberculosis. The girl was sponsored by someone who refused responsibility, as did two others for whom she worked as a domestic.[79]

---

76. Weil (1984: 280, his table 1) and also Krichefsky (1958: 19, 28, table; 1961: 43, and her table 1).
77. Anon. (picture caption), *The Ahepan*, April–June 1953.
78. I borrow the terms from Lovelock, who describes a transition that occurred later in time and in three different geographical contexts (2000: 908, 911–12, 942–43).
79. Paris (1953: 6).

The sequence of events that led to the Ahepa's role as a private "adoption agency" was complex: the 1948 DPA had delegated certain duties and screening procedures to the United States Committee for the Care of European Children (USCOM), a private nonprofit organization that had been commissioned by the State Department in July of 1940. As an umbrella agency, USCOM oversaw temporary and permanent orphan migration programs and adoptive placements through 1953, but it left most of the particulars (such as the identification and processing of foreign-born orphans for adoption) to private agencies or organizations, which, as per State Department rules, were not allowed to charge fees. In late spring of 1951, USCOM officially approved the Ahepa as a voluntary agency and granted its Displaced Persons Committee a license to place Greek orphans for adoption in American homes through the DPA as amended.[80] This formal acceptance paralleled the mid-November 1950 certification granted to the Ahepa by the State Department's Advisory Committee on Voluntary Foreign Aid, which concerned itself with displaced persons of all ages. Under the 1948 DPA, American individual sponsors had to furnish proof of shelter and employment for incoming adult refugees, and to offer assurances of adoption in the case of unaccompanied children. Members of neither category were to become public charges at the expense of the US taxpayer. Thus these assurances became the magic ticket for immigration to the States.

George A. Polos, chairman of the Ahepa Displaced Persons Committee, called the processing of orphans from Greece a "much more complicated matter" than the processing of displaced adults.[81] Apparently, however, the challenge of the "tremendous red tape involved in the processing of the orphans" could still be met in just two weeks to one month.[82] Polos also gave away what "orphan" meant in the early 1950s when he declared, "Many orphans were brought to Athens by either one of the parents."[83] In cases in which the parents were absent or dead, relatives, too, could and did deliver adoptable orphans to an institution in Athens that housed and cared for the minors for the duration of the processing period. The Ahepa had been assisting adult Greek immigrants for years, but it had not gained any experience in child welfare work, and its committee soon ran into problems.[84] Polos alluded to these problems but defined them as organizational and logistical challenges, such as the large numbers of applicants and personnel

80. Polos (1952: 75).
81. Polos, *The Ahepan*, Jan.–March 1952, 10.
82. Polos, *The Ahepan*, Jan.–March 1952, 11.
83. Polos, *The Ahepan*, Jan.–March 1952, 10.
84. Winslow (2012a: 79, 92–93, 111–12; 2017: 46, 55–56).

changes and shortages.[85] According to Winslow, the odd USCOM-Ahepa partnership "signaled the influence of [private] voluntarism on the structure of international adoption," which did not come into existence without some mishaps.[86]

To describe the problems resulting from the Ahepa's lead role in the 1950–1952 adoptions of Greek minors, I turn to the words of Winslow, who has carried out meticulous research in the relevant US archives:[87] "a country [Greece] with deplorable conditions and few resources" ("insufficient transportation, no local authority with extant records, overwhelmed staff, and inexperienced volunteers"); "inattention to proper casework"; "[Greek] children were routinely sent to the States without completed social histories"; "hundreds of [Greek] orphans arrived in the U.S. without being screened"; "other difficulties came from AHEPA's direct management of cases"; "the operations in Greece reeked of slipshod volunteerism, similar to commercial adoption practices in the United States"; and the "AHEPA's inflated fees and unprofessional services."[88] Not surprisingly, "[o]fficials [of USCOM] worked diligently to remove the fraternal order from the program so that the highest standards could be maintained."[89]

The opening paragraph of a "Memorandum of Conversation" initiated by the US Department of State, dated 4 October 1951, implies recalcitrance on both sides: on the one hand, the Ahepa Displaced Persons Committee was unwilling to admit its failure to follow up with adoptees who had trouble adjusting or whose sponsorship arrangements had fallen through. USCOM, on the other hand, could not comprehend the objections that various Greek institutions had raised against placing children with adoptive parents who were neither Greek nor Greek American:

> U.S. Committee has not been able to convince Ahepa of the fact that named children going to relatives or friends sometimes need special care when their placements were unsuccessful. . . . U.S. Committee hopes that the Greek Government and Church will allow unnamed Greek children to be placed in non-Greek homes in this country.[90]

---

85. Polos, *The Ahepan*, Jan.–March 1952, 10–11.
86. Winslow (2017: 56).
87. Among these archives are the Records of the Displaced Persons Commission, 1948–1952, and the Records of US Foreign Assistance Agencies, 1942–1963, both held at the National Archives and Records Administration (NARA) at College Park, Maryland.
88. All of these quotations are drawn from Winslow (2012a: 113–14). See also Winslow (2017: 57).
89. Winslow (2012a: 114).
90. United States Department of State, "Memorandum of Conversation. Subject: Meeting

Polos placed a different spin on the deteriorating working relationship: because his Ahepa committee "could do the job just as efficiently and much more economically than the U. S. Committee [USCOM]," it "availed itself of the termination privilege included in the contract."[91] In late December of 1951 and with numerous cases pending, the Ahepa cut off its relation ship with USCOM. By 1 January 1952, USCOM, which still served as the Ahepa Displaced Persons Committee's direct link to the US State Department, saw no other solution than to withdraw its recognition and accreditation from the order's committee.[92] However, the Ahepa Displaced Persons Committee sought and received a two-year extension to its orphan program and thus continued to bring over Greek minors.[93] By the end of January 1952, the Ahepa Displaced Persons Committee had to start reporting back to the State Department's Advisory Committee on Voluntary Foreign Aid (ACVFA). As per the ACVFA's basic requirements, the Ahepa Displaced Persons Committee finally had to employ a professional social worker at its national headquarters in Washington, DC. The committee also had to arrange for newly arriving Greek children in need of care to be accommodated temporarily at a reception center with medical facilities.[94] The Ahepa's actions, however, do not appear to have extended far beyond making promises about complying: input from social workers continued to be lacking. After USCOM itself was disbanded in late spring of 1953, oversight weakened considerably. A couple of years later, complaints were surging about the Ahepa's failure to properly evaluate the suitability of applicant parents and adoptive homes and about its refusal to collaborate with trained child welfare workers in Greece as well as the States.[95]

A collaboration between the Ahepa Displaced Persons Committee and the Jewish Center in Hoboken, New Jersey, led to a better reception of the Greek minors on arrival. The Ahepa's working relationship with the Jewish Center on 830 Hudson Street in Hoboken and also with the nearby Mary Stevens Hammond Memorial Home (for children's medical emergencies) did

---

with Miss Olsen re U.S. Committee for Care of European Children and Ahepa DP Committee," 4 October 1951. Typescript, 1 page, held in the Records of US Foreign Assistance Agencies, 1942–1963, box 9, folder "Displaced Persons Committee (Orphans Program) Order of AHEPA: Correspondence," NARA.

91. Polos (1952: 76).

92. Winslow (2012a: 115; 2017: 58).

93. Polos, *The Ahepan*, Jan.–March 1952, 11.

94. Polos, *The Ahepan*, Jan.–March 1952, 11; and Polos (1952: 76).

95. See the many letters held in the archives of the ISS, American Branch Papers, box 10, folder 10: "Independent Adoption Schemes: AHEPA 1954–1959," Social Welfare History Archives (SWHA), University of Minnesota Libraries.

not outlast, however, the flow of 1952 DPA arrivals still overseen by Chairman Polos. Through the summer of 1952 (and before the Ahepa switched to air travel to New York), the vast majority of the Ahepa-sponsored newcomers, children and adults alike, arrived on ocean liners such as the *Nea Hellas* that docked at the piers in Hoboken, across the Hudson River from Manhattan. The Jewish Center was very close to the piers and offered large available spaces as well as trained staff. The Ahepa preferred to pay for the Center's (temporary) services rather than equip a facility of its own.[96]

To add to Winslow's findings, let me quote from a four-page letter written by two American child welfare officers stationed in Greece in August of 1951. Lena E. Cochran and Helen McKay jointly wrote the long letter of 24 August 1951 to their supervisor, Robert J. Corkery, the European Coordinator of the US Displaced Persons Commission. Cochran and McKay had been questioned as to why they were unable to complete the social histories of many Greek orphans prior to their departure for the United States. They explained that they had been working on a huge case load: in July of 1951, they had an overwhelming count of 1,074 cases, "of which 267 ha[d] D.P. Commission validation numbers and 86 ha[d] AHEPA-U.S. Committee numbers [i.e., numbers given out by the Ahepa Displaced Persons Committee, chaired by Polos]"; by 20 August 1951, they counted 203 orphans on the list of the latter committee.[97] The cases of more than 700 Greek orphans were pending at the time of their writing. Then Cochran and McKay stated,

> Many orphans do not want to work with AHEPA and question the whole procedure. We are placed in the position of defending the AHEPA-U.S. Committee plan when in fact we disagree in many cases. Many people here think of AHEPA more as a "racket" than as anything else and resent sponsors' paying money when no help is given here except for travel plans which they don't want. . . . In many people's minds we are identified more with AHEPA at this point than with the D.P. Commission. We question seriously whether this is a desirable position for a government agency to be placed in.[98]

---

96. This information is based on sporadic budget lines in Ahepa meeting minutes of 1951–1952, part of the Ahepa archives, Washington, DC. See also Paris (1953: 6). I thank Rabbi Robert Scheinberg for confirming that the Jewish Center building had offices, classrooms, and a basement gym, which was often converted to serve other purposes (email communication of 3 April 2017).

97. Cochran and McKay (1951: 2).

98. Cochran and McKay (1951: 3), part of their letter to "Mr. Robert J. Corkery, European Coordinator U.S. Displaced Persons Commission, Frankfurt A/M, Germany." Typescript, 4 pages, held in the Records of the Displaced Persons Commission, 1948–1952, box 58,

One year later, however, all efforts since mid-June 1950 combined although they were far from collaborative, delivered the total of 1,246 DPA-sponsored adoptions of Greek war orphans and refugee children. Again, this first wave of Greek children comprised mainly teenagers who went to live with their Greek American relatives. Many, mature beyond their age, looked after younger siblings who traveled with them, and they often had strong opinions about or took charge of their own circumstances. What did such DPA-sponsored adoptions look like in the lives of real Greek people? The transnational placement of the orphaned "T." siblings may offer a typical example. Two brothers, one born in 1932 and the other in 1935, and their younger sister traveled on DPA visas from Greece to Pennsylvania, to join the family of their paternal uncle and his wife, who co-owned a restaurant. The three siblings traveled together by boat and arrived in late June of 1951, after a trip in "tourist class" that lasted for more than two weeks. The migration of the older brothers was prompted by USCOM's desire to keep siblings together. Even though the boys were older teenagers, all three of the children received orphan visas and emigrated "for adoption." A newspaper article published shortly after the children's arrival in Pittsburgh informs us that the children's natural parents had died under the Nazi Occupation and that, until mid-1951, the children had been the wards of another uncle still living in Greece. The article ends: "And that's why life will begin for C. at 18; for A. at 16, and for S. at 12." The young girl died in 1953.[99]

By late August 1952, the Ahepa had gained increasing visibility and influence, and it proudly took credit for up to one-third of the total of 1,246 DPA-sponsored Greek adoptions.[100] Organizations with broader missions, too, joined the cause of the Greek war orphans. One such effective operation was the women-led Immigrants' Protective League of Chicago, which, through 1952, brought over from Greece an estimated total of 350 orphans and refugee children.[101] These numbers should not make us lose sight of

folder "Orphan Procedures—Public Law 555," NARA. In 1955, McKay took her expertise to South Korea, to work on intercountry adoptions there (Lee 2016: 128).

99. Source kept confidential.

100. Polos (1952: 76).

101. The Immigrants' Protective League (IPL) of Chicago, which offered practical assistance and public services to scores of immigrants of all nationalities, was founded in 1908 by female activists and social workers based at the Hull House Settlement, under the leadership of prominent women such as Jane Addams and Grace Abbott. See Leonard (1973); Nackenoff (2014); and, in relation to Greek immigrants, Theodoropoulou (2006: 71–73). See also Nicholas and Robert Askounes Ashford (2000), on the pioneering work of their mother, Venette Askounes Ashford, a distinguished teacher, social worker, and community leader active on behalf of the IPL. In mid-June of 1952, Venette Askounes accompanied more than thirty orphans and some adult refugees on their long trip from Greece to

the fact that, before 1952, Greek minors, including some orphans, had been entering the States under the actual quota system and also under the private law system. Most, however, were again "named" children who went to known Greek American families of either extended kin or acquaintances of their parents. Nonetheless, in the course of the DPA orphan program's final year (summer 1951–summer 1952), hundreds of Greek minors were hastily processed for migration and adoption, with all parties negotiating their cases by the statutory deadlines. The process was further accelerated by the fact that 1951 was officially proclaimed "Greek Homecoming Year," which was aggressively promoted by the Homecoming Year Service, the Greek National Tourist Organization, the Greek monarchy, US administrators in Greece, and Greek American organizations such as the Ahepa. This initiative sent hundreds of Greek American families traveling back to their homeland, reacquainting them with their local cultures and relatives, and spending thousands of sought-after tourist dollars. Amid the 1951 euphoria of the new expatriate tourism and "diaspora politics," the Greek state, again in collaboration with the most influential diaspora organizations, attempted to reinvigorate the emigration of its "surplus" populations.[102] Orphaned children with prospects of being adopted by Greek American relatives naturally fell into that category. This rush meant that documentation of DPA cases today is minimal, obviating answers to many questions of Greek adoptees who came over typically in 1951 through mid-1952. It is hard to appreciate the "open records" of this first postwar wave of kin migration and adoption when there are barely any records. But, as Kathryn Close somewhat naively generalized, "[n]early all . . . were children requested by relatives or other Greek persons in the United States whom the [poor and widowed] mother knew or knew about, a factor which in many instances seemed to ease the pain of separation."[103] If the Greek parents were still alive, they were motivated by the better economic and educational opportunities that awaited their children in the States. Often guardians of Greek orphans made similar strategic decisions that privileged blood ties. The practice resembled shared fosterage more than *de facto* adoption, even though, for visa issuance purposes, the Greek American sponsors still had to formally declare that the child would be emigrating "for adoption."

Chicago (2000: 93, 102). Details on the IPL's engagement with newcomers from Greece can further be gleaned from the displaced persons arrival lists of 1946 through 1953, held in box 3, folder 27 of the Immigrants' Protective League Records, Special Collections and University Archives, University of Illinois at Chicago.

102. Vogli (2011: 25–26, 28).
103. Close (1953: 47).

From Placing to Gathering Eligible Alien Orphans: The Ahepa, Mid-1950s

Meanwhile, Greek American lobbying for special US legislation to facilitate the overseas adoptions of more Greek children had grown louder, despite complications and setbacks that originated in Cold War internal politics (such as the passage of the restrictionist 27 June 1952 Immigration and Nationality Act, or the McCarran-Walter Act).[104] On 27 June 1953, five leading members of the Woodlawn Chapter of the Ahepa in Chicago approached their Illinois senator to urge him to endorse Senate bill 1917, which the US Congress was then discussing and which included special provisions for Greek refugees and orphans.[105] This bill, sponsored by Republican Senator Arthur Watkins of Utah, was also recommended for approval by other Ahepa chapters and by many more US-based ethnic organizations. The desired result followed within a few weeks. On 29 July, the Senate passed the Refugee Relief Act (RRA) of 1953, which President Eisenhower signed into law on 7 August 1953 (Public Law 203, section 5. (a)).[106] This landmark act offered a crucial opening to European refugees who were victims and opponents of communism.[107] The high number of these beyond-quota immigrants and the numerous unfulfilled applications and aspirations discredited communist regimes, even though most of them were prompted by economic hardship at home. The 1953 RRA enabled a total of 17,000 Greeks to enter the United States. In practice, only a small segment of them turned out to be children migrating for adoption, a pattern that held true for other sending countries as well.[108] Significantly, by distinguishing adoptable children from other refugees, the 1953 RRA changed the landscape of intercountry adoption. It also marked the growing trend to redefine intercountry adoption as nonrelative and confidential adoption (with sealed records).

Specifically, the watershed RRA of 1953 allowed 4,000 special nonquota immigrant visas to be given out to eligible orphans under ten years of age who had been adopted abroad or who were to be adopted in the United States by US citizens and their spouses (with a two-petition limitation on the number of adoptable children per applicant couple).[109] This "Orphan

---

104. Bon Tempo discusses the McCarran-Walter Act and its effects at length (2008: 26–33, 41).
105. *Congressional Record*, Senate, 29 July 1953, p. 10,244.
106. 83rd Congress, S. 1917 and H.R. 6481. *Congressional Record*, Senate, 29 July 1953, p. 10,250.
107. Bon Tempo (2008: 38, 44).
108. Papadopoulos and Kourachanis (2015: 176–78) and Tourgeli and Venturas (2015: 224–25).
109. Leber (1972: 390, 392) and Winslow (2012a: 118–19; 2012b: 324–25; 2017: 60). Public Law 162 of the 83rd Congress, also approved on 29 July 1953, provided for (nonquota) admission for permanent residence of 500 eligible orphans adopted by US citizens serving abroad

Program," as it came to be known, covered German, Austrian, Italian, Japanese, Korean, and other orphans in addition to Greek children. It was set to expire on 31 December 1956, which explains why the Ahepa ramped up its search for Greek American foster parents and adoptive homes, complete with advertisements in the Greek American press. By late January 1954, the US State Department renewed the Ahepa's accreditation, but as a voluntary *refugee* service agency, the Ahepa Refugee Relief Committee (ARRC).[110] Winslow invokes the Ahepa's "political connections" and the extraordinarily heavy Greek caseload to explain this second unexpected renewal of the order's "mandate."[111] By the mid-1950s, however, the Ahepa had gained at least some rudimentary experience in adoptive placements, though not necessarily in the professional screening (let alone in the follow-up) of relinquishing Greek birth mothers, of local childcare institutions, or of American prospective adopters of Greek children.[112]

"Ahepans! Have You Joined the 'Crusade for Sponsors'?" reads one of the full-page calls in the fall 1954 issue of *The Ahepan*, undersigned by Leo J. Lamberson, chairman, Stephen S. Scopas, supreme president, and "Honorary Chairman His Eminence, Archbishop Michael of the Greek Archdiocese of North and South America."[113] The choice of the word "crusade," with its connotations of a prolonged religious and then anticommunist struggle, was not coincidental (even if the historical irony of its usage was lost on the committee's secular spokespersons and their supporters from the highest echelons of the Orthodox Church hierarchy). Lamberson also stated, in a propagandistic expression of entitlement that would now be deemed objectionable but that was accepted for publication within the culture of the Cold War:

---

in the armed forces or employed abroad by the federal government. Only 54 Greek cases availed themselves of the opportunities offered by Public Law 162, as opposed to 287 cases in Japan, where the American presence was much more prominent. See Weil (1984: 280–81, his table 1). For most sending countries, Weil included the cases stemming from Public Law 162 into the totals of US visas granted to foreign-born adoptees or adoptees-to-be. For Greece, he did not, and he gave no reasons why. I have included the 54 Greek cases of Public Law 162 by raising the working total for Greece from 3,116 to 3,200 US-bound adoptions of 1948–1962 (above, p. 77 n. 3). Some sources confuse Public Law 162 with the much broader "Orphan Program" of the RRA of 1953. On the intricacies of the 1950s through early 1960s legislation governing migration, see Anon., "The Immigration and Nationality Act of 1952 as Amended through 1961" (spring 1964).

110. Anon., *The Ahepan*, Jan.–March 1954; and Winslow (2012a: 118–19; 2017: 59–60).
111. Winslow (2012a: 118; 2017: 59).
112. Winslow (2012a: 120; 2017: 60–61).
113. Ahepa Refugee Relief Committee, *The Ahepan*, Oct.–Dec. 1954.

Hellenes have done their part through educational programs, contacts, and other means in accordance with the program of the United States Information Agency, to indoctrinate friends and relatives in Greece and Europe on "the menace of Communism and the fruits of the American way of life."[114]

The reader should remember the names and early interventions of Lamberson, Scopas, and Michael Tsaparis, because this and subsequent sections outline a reinvigorated adoption movement that turned from generous to greedy. In the spring of 1955, Lamberson proudly reported that the newly launched Orphans Program of the Ahepa Refugee Relief Committee had already received "scores of applications" from US citizens (among them many Greek Americans) eager to adopt Greek orphans. He boasted that his committee "guarantee[d] each orphan to be free from any infirmity or disease, and in perfect health." With the committee, its directors, and the order's headquarters supplying the necessary forms, applying was easy. Moreover, because the ARRC had been accredited by the State Department, the requirements to submit certain "documentary certifications," which applicants normally needed to fulfill, were being waived.[115] In June of 1955, Scopas was trying hard to convince policymakers in Washington to cut even more of the red tape and to confirm the order's authority to give out agency or "blanket assurances" on behalf of its refugee sponsors and prospective adopters.[116] Assurances of sponsorship or adoption continued to be required unless a voluntary agency, such as the Ahepa, could vouch for the newcomers.

Some 506 to 510 Greek "war-handicapped" children were admitted to the United States by the time the 1953 RRA expired and before its extension, and then the 11 September 1957 successor act went into effect.[117] Ioanna and

---

114. Lamberson, quoted by Anon., *The Ahepan*, Oct.–Dec. 1954.
115. Lamberson (March–April 1955).
116. Scopas (1955: 143, 145–46) argued his case before the Subcommittee of the Committee on the Judiciary of the US Senate, which in June 1955 discussed proposed amendments to the Refugee Relief Act of 1953. Scopas further advocated for increasing the Greek refugee and immigrant quotas, extending the Orphan Program, and augmenting the numbers of Greek orphans eligible for admission (by raising the age limit, for one) (1955: 141–42, 144). In May of 1956 (and with the Ahepa-sponsored Greek-to-American adoptions now underway), both Scopas and Lamberson made presentations before the same subcommittee, restating their case for increasing the number of eligible Greek orphans (Scopas 1956: 94). Lamberson followed up on Scopas's lobbying: in addition to the recommended increase, he asked for an allocation of 500 orphan visas "specifically for Greece" (Lamberson 1956b: 95). See Anon., *The Ahepan*, July–August 1955, 5–6. The age limit was raised in 1957, but Greece did not receive a special, additional allocation of US orphan visas.
117. Weil (1984: 280, his table 1) and Winslow (2012b: 337–38).

Olympia Argyriadi were just 2 of the more than 500 minors to arrive in the States under the RRA provisions. The vast majority of the cases representing the Greek adoption movement's second wave, however, consolidated the phenomenon of "stranger" or nonrelative adoptions, which followed the paradigm of "full" adoptions with closed records of (preferably "ahistorical") children selected by the applicant parents.

In a third wave, the now-unlimited nonquota provisions for eligible orphans of the Act of 1957 (Public Law 85–316, the Refugee-Escapee Act, section 4) allowed another 1,360 Greek-born children to come over, adding to a total count of 3,116 Greek children adopted by US parents from 1948 through 1962.[118] Also, the 1957 Act upped the age limit for eligible orphans from ten to fourteen years old. Very few "stranger" adoptions involved Greek children between the ages of ten and fourteen, unless they were the older ones in sibling groups that the new parents agreed to keep together. The increased age limit of the year 1957, rather, brought back a few of the traits previously associated with the first wave of Greek family or kin migration. A mere five to seven years earlier, this wave had characterized the Greek and Greek American recourse to the Displaced Persons Act as amended. But by the late 1950s, all intermediaries or agencies worked with sealed records, even on cases that were intended to be and to remain open, "nonstranger" placements. The disconnect between fluid Greek expectations and firm American practices resulted in cultural misunderstandings, and even in some human tragedies.[119] The 1957 Act was set to expire on 30 June 1959, but it was extended through the period ending 30 June 1961. After the latter date, the Act was permanently amended to grant nonquota status to eligible orphans. Thus the Ahepa's advocacy on behalf of Greek orphans did much to transform provisional or extraordinary legislation into permanent statutes. The association helped to transform Greek adoptions from an exceptional into an accepted phenomenon. Trial and much error, however, arose when the Ahepa began to seek out a supply of Greek children, whom it would place through the procedure of adoption by proxy:

> Yesterday, Mr Miltiadis Petsas arrived in our city [Patras]. Representing Mr Michael Tsaparis, the general director of the Ahepa office in Athens, Mr Petsas will, within the next few days, proceed with the selection of 126 children, ages two to seven, from the Municipal Orphanage of Patras. These children will be adopted by Americans of Greek descent residing in the United

---

118. Weil (1984: 280, his table 1).
119. See below, pp. 218–20 and 222–24.

States. Today, Mr Petsas is meeting with Mr P[anagiotis] Lontos, director of the Patras Orphanage. . . . [120]

Adoption by Proxy: The Ahepa versus the International Social Service

> [W]e turned our attention back to the small, black-and-white photo stapled to [the dossier]. The photo showed a sour-faced little girl with dark eyes and uncombed hair. . . . She looked sad, angry, and scared, probably all three. I don't know what I had expected, but I found the photo a bit unsettling. Adopting a child we had not met was scary. You never really knew what you were getting into, and I worried about taking a child with severe health or psychological issues. I shared my fears with Richard and suggested we might want to consider another child. He barked, "She's a doll. We're not going to ask for another dossier. We are going to get *her!*"
>
> —American mother of Greek adoptee Maria. Heckinger 2019:46

By today's standards, the number of Greek adoptions rose dramatically in a very short period in the mid-1950s. Key to this "success" was the formula of adoption by proxy or third-party adoption, which the Ahepa and also other independent or voluntary organizations practiced. It was Lamberson, a lawyer by profession, who designed the ARRC's Orphans Program and based it on proxy adoptions through the courts in Greece.[121] Until then, most adoptions of Greek children had been finalized in the United States, which had granted travel visas on assurances of subsequent adoption. Technically a lawful provision of the 1953 RRA, as the Ahepa leadership knew well, the proxy adoption system allowed US citizens to adopt in foreign courts *in absentia*, but it also let peddling agents enrich themselves in reckless and unethical ways. The system has been "credited" with placing intercountry adoptions on the fast track through the mid- to late 1950s, but it effectively bypassed the authority and expertise of social welfare agencies.[122] Social agencies could only help secure more careful placements if American couples chose to complete the foreign-born child's adoption within the States. The US Act of September 1959, which amended the 1957 Act, acknowledged the valid criticism that the administration of the prior federal laws had left a policy vacuum by failing to restrict or ban the controversial system of adoption by proxy. It took another two years, however, for the US Congress to

---

120. Anon., "Greek Americans Will Adopt 126 Children from the Orphanage," newspaper *Neologos Patron*, 13 May 1955 (in Greek); quoted by Theodoropoulou (2006: 110).
121. Lamberson (1955: 48).
122. Winslow (2012b: 324, 330–31, 334–41, 345n54).

close the loophole of proxy adoptions and to make permanent provisions for the immigration of foreign-born children for adoption, through the Immigration and Nationality Act of 1961.[123] The 1961 Act illustrates how the practice of international adoption far outpaced US law, and how perceived loopholes challenged the States to keep revising its adoption and immigration policies. The years 1961–1962, therefore, represent the first phase of procedural tightening, and this shift set the Greek-to-American adoptions on the path of declining numbers. Conversely, the numbers of the Greek-to-Dutch adoptions rose, based on the rapprochement between the Netherlands and the Babies' Center Metera, which remained the Greek queen's showcase institution and boasted better placements via more professional protocols.

Discussions before Congress in July and August of 1959 expressed both the senators' and the representatives' concerns about alleged abuses of the relief acts, or the "reprehensible practices which, unfortunately, have marred the program."[124] Without mentioning the names of any of the accused, the *Congressional Record* repeatedly called for an agency or other control mechanism to examine the suitability of the prospective adoptive parents and, more urgently, to investigate the abuses stemming from adoption by proxy (here formally defined as adoption through the mediation of an agent who matches would-be parents with foreign-born orphans, sight unseen, often "for the financial profit of the proxy").[125] In mid-July 1959, Senator Thomas Hennings denounced the "black marketeers' ill-gotten gains" with direct references to the Greek orphan victims, and on 27 August 1959, Senator Kenneth Keating from New York spoke openly about "international baby racketeers."[126] The mid-July Senate record also noted instances in which the termination of the rights of the biological parent(s) had been secured in dubious ways by "international baby dealers."[127] In the April 1960 issue of the *I and N Reporter*, the newsletter of the Immigration and Naturalization Service, Supervisory Immigrant Inspector John M. McWhorter referred

---

123. Public Law 87–301 of 26 September 1961. See Herman (2008: 218); Lovelock (2000: 917); Oh (2015: 106, 178–79, and her ch. 5); and Winslow (2012a: 191–93, 431; 2012b: 339–40; 2017: 7, 228).

124. *Congressional Record*, House, 16 July 1959, p. 13,593.

125. *Congressional Record*, Senate, 22 July 1959, p. 13,968. One year prior, Laurin and Virginia Hyde, experts in the fields of social services and family casework, clarified in plain terms that "proxy adoptions look back to an earlier time, when children could be deeded by one person to another, like parcels of real estate" (1958: 20). They stressed that adoptions are not merely individual affairs but also communal, social, and legal matters (1958: 2).

126. *Congressional Record*, Senate, 15 July 1959, pp. 13,450–13,451, and 27 August 1959, p. 17,143, respectively.

127. *Congressional Record*, Senate, 15 July 1959, p. 13,451.

to "allegations to Congress that children were being exploited for personal gain . . . , that tragedy had resulted from certain proxy adoptions . . . , and that the termination of the parental rights had been obtained in highly questionable ways."[128]

The proxy adoption system underpinned the so-called stranger or nonrelative adoptions, and it routinely sidestepped the legitimate work of recognized adoption agencies, which sounded the alarm. Among the more vocal agencies was the American Branch of the International Social Service (ISS), a nongovernmental and nonsectarian refugee and family organization founded by female social workers in 1924. This organization extended humanitarian aid and legal advice and had grown to become the "main representative of the social work establishment."[129] By the mid-1950s, the focus of the ISS had shifted from reuniting families across borders to creating new families through cross-border adoptions. The organization's humanitarian commitment to child welfare had taken on global dimensions and continued to address the needs of children affected by war, "illegitimacy," and "fatherlessness."[130] In the early Cold War years of intercountry adoption, the ISS advocated for interdependent legal and social safeguards to secure the "best interest" of the foreign-born child.[131] It also pursued an assimilationist ideal for the child, who was to be adopted typically by a white, middle-class, heteronormative American family. SooJin Pate has spoken of "normalizing the adopted child," which entailed overwriting of the child's complex international and often interracial identities.[132] The comparison that Susan T. Pettiss, associate director of the ISS-USA, drew between Greek and Chinese children is, tellingly, still couched in early 1960s assimilationist and also racialized language:

> An infant from Greece will have little feeling of change in culture and may visually fit into an American family of non-Greek ethnic origin, whereas a Chinese infant would have the same ease in shifting cultures but would

---

128. McWhorter (1960: 47).
129. Oh (2015: 107). A comprehensive and up-to-date history of the International Social Service has not yet been written. Fehrenbach's chapter (2016: 211–22), however, starts to fill this lacuna. Surprisingly, hardly any of the contemporary sources or subsequent studies on the abuses of the proxy system have placed their concerns and proposed solutions in the context of the United Nations' adoption of the Declaration of the Rights of the Child (20 November 1959, and long in preparation). See further Marshall (2013: 483) and Winslow (2017: 219).
130. Fehrenbach (2016: 220).
131. Hochfield (1963: 3–5).
132. Pate (2014: 101).

be visually different from his adoptive family unless they were of Oriental ethnic background.[133]

The ISS-USA collaborated with the ISS Hellenic Branch, which was set up in Athens to alleviate the 1920s Asia Minor Greek refugee crisis but was suspended from late 1940 through early 1953.[134] When the Athens office of the ISS reopened, it promptly inherited more than 200 Greek adoption cases from USCOM, which this agency formerly in charge had preferred not to transfer to the Ahepa Displaced Persons Committee.[135] Through the end of 1956, the ISS Hellenic Branch operated area offices in Thessaloniki and Ioannina as well. The ISS-USA and the ISS Hellenic Branch tried to match applications coming from either end, either from prospective American parents through the ISS-USA, or from Greek institutions, organizations, or birth families that contacted the Greek offices of the ISS when they sought to place adoptable children in the States. The ISS Greece never kept the children in question in its care for extended periods of time. Rather, all ISS-sponsored adoptees remained in their respective institutions until their adoptive families had been screened and cleared by the child welfare agencies of their home counties and states. The applicant family filled out and signed an assurance form that had to be endorsed by a local and licensed American social services agency. This three-page DSR-5 form, "Assurance of Adoption and Proper Care for Orphan," committed the prospective parents to financially sponsoring an orphan known to them. Form DSR-6 was required for a child that the ISS (or another designated agency) would match with the adoptive parents.[136] From 1963 on, form I-600, a "Petition to Classify Alien as an Eligible Orphan," served similar purposes, filing the

---

133. Pettiss (1962: 22). Pettiss had gained valuable experience working with refugees and orphaned or displaced children as a UNRRA welfare worker in Germany in the immediate aftermath of World War II. Her memoirs offer keen insight into what that kind of relief work entailed, and how much basic organizing needed to be done. See Pettiss and Taylor (2004). In an older letter cowritten by ISS-USA general director William T. Kirk and Pettiss on the subject of "'matching' eligible orphans," the issue of a Greek girl's "race" had emerged: "We were particularly interested in the family for this child because the [prospective] mother is Syrian and has similar dark eyes, hair and skin" (1955: 2; letter from the personal archive of Mitsos, dated 30 June 1955). Park Nelson discusses the problematic nature of the intercountry adoption movement's ideal of "assimilative salvation" (2016: 61 [quotation], 75–76, 79–83). As Carp (2002: 10) has pointed out, the long-lasting policy of "matching" resulted in the equally long-lasting exclusion of disabled children from adoption.

134. Larned (1956: 31–37, 95, 96).

135. Winslow (2012a: 118; 2017: 59–60).

136. See United States Committee on the Judiciary (1958: 118, 119); also Lee (2016: 185–88, or her appendix 8, which reproduces both the pages and the instructions of the DSR-5 form).

assurances of professional social workers on behalf of an adoptee specified by name, to clear this child's entrance into the States and its subsequent path to citizenship. The waiting American parents also paid a bond of $1,000 to cover any additional expenses in case the adoption plan did not work out and the ISS incurred the cost of accommodating and rehoming the foreign child in the States. The ISS returned this bond money to the new parents when the adoption process was legally completed in the child's new home state.[137] Over the course of typically two to three years, the legal guardianship of foundlings or of children otherwise available for adoption was transferred from the president of the Greek orphanage's board of directors, who consented to the children's emigration, to the ISS, and then to the American parents, following the formal adoption procedure.[138]

As Theodoropoulou clarifies, the ISS Hellenic Branch first notified Greek institutions about the active role it wanted to play in their intercountry adoptions.[139] The Branch invested much time and energy to educate Greek institutions about its preferred protocols.[140] The ISS found a belated champion in the well-known journalist and author Freddy Germanos, who published a three-part series on the swirling allegations of a Greek baby trade in the Greek paper *Eleftheria* (18, 20, and 21 January 1959). Germanos explained the risks associated with adoptions by proxy and consistently set the ISS apart for its more professional practices. Most Greek orphanages, however, ignored the ISS's invitation to collaborate: they preferred to handle the US-bound adoptions of their young wards themselves, with the help of lawyers of their own choosing and with less or no interference from social workers, who were the ISS's very visible public face.

As early as 1955, Pettiss, then assistant director of the ISS-USA, explicitly warned that "proxy adoption" meant "finalizing a legal parent-child relationship sight-unseen."[141] Even though Korea drew most of the attention in the dispute over proxy adoptions, Pettiss singled out the Ahepa, which had no child welfare staff, for arranging "unprotected placements" of Greek children "through distribution of pictures to eager adoptive families."[142] The earliest postwar proxy adoptions, however, involved not Korean but Greek children, as a result of the Ahepa's near-monopoly on Greek-to-American

---

137. See the papers related to a bond issued in the summer of 1955, from the personal archive of Mitsos.
138. Papers related to the legal guardianship of the foundling, from the personal archive of Mitsos.
139. Theodoropoulou (2006: 82–83).
140. Theodoropoulou (2006: 78–79).
141. Pettiss (1955: 20).
142. Pettiss (1955: 20).

placements since 1950.[143] But from the fall of 1955 on, or *prior* to the Ahepa's second wave of mass placements of 1956–1959, the ISS Hellenic Branch began to regularly send over small groups of Greek children for adoption in the States. The earliest Greek adoptions sponsored by the ISS took place in mid-September 1955, and they peaked by the end of the decade.[144]

For all its criticism of independent adoption schemes such as the Ahepa's, however, the ISS-USA itself was not averse to collaborating and especially fund-raising with Jane Russell, a contemporary Hollywood icon and one of the first "celebrity adopters." As the founder of the World Adoption International Fund (for lack of a more felicitous acronym called WAIF, founded in 1955), the actress sought to place needy foreign children, mainly those from Greece, Germany, and Korea, in American homes.[145] The early history of these two organizations' work in the field of intercountry adoption is intertwined, even though they eventually parted ways to concentrate on their respective remits.[146] "WAIF-ISS" defined itself as the "inter-country adoption division of International Social Service," and it kept headquarters in Hollywood.[147] The mid-1950s through early 1960s collaboration of WAIF-ISS, however, led to some odd encounters. The picture below (figure 2) features Russell, Princess Sophia of Greece, and ISS employees welcoming a group of eight Greek orphans to New York (and to media fanfare) on 29 October 1958.[148]

---

143. See also Winslow (2012a: 120; 2017: 60–61).
144. The Greek adoption movement marked a first, too, when measured against the timeline of the (lesser-known) ISS-sponsored adoptions of children from families who had fled to Hong Kong to escape the Chinese communist revolution. The ISS alone was instrumental in the immigration for adoption of more than 500 Chinese refugee and orphaned children from 1958 through 1962 (Pettiss 1962: 22–23).
145. Le Varn, *The Victoria Advocate*, 7 October 1957.
146. Larned (1960: 30) and Russell (1985: 141–43, 171–73, 322).
147. *ISS World News*, November 1957, 4.
148. In other news: on 27 November 1957, the Armstrong Circle Theatre (1950–1963) devoted one of its popular CBS-TV episodes to the WAIF-ISS intercountry adoption story. In search of three "typical" cases, writer Vance Bourjaily and director William Corrigan featured a Greek, an Italian, and a Korean-American child, whose US adoptions were eagerly anticipated, in the episode "*Have Jacket Will Travel.*" The producer was Robert Costello. See Anon., *ISS World News*, February 1958, 2; and Choy (2013: 30–35).

On 11 May 1962, a brief and anonymous blurb in the *New York Times* featured the 10,000[th] child to arrive in the States under the WAIF-ISS program. The baby happened to be Greek, and its new Greek American parents were welcomed in a ceremony at the White House, hosted by Jacqueline Kennedy. This report has led some Greek commentators to posit that 10,000 Greek adoptees were sent to America. But the WAIF-ISS program covered many countries and nationalities, of which Greek children constituted merely a part. An anonymous article in the *Pacific Stars and Stripes* (12 May 1962) with the telling title "Greek Orphan Arrives as Mother's Day Gift," comments on the same landmark adoption through WAIF-ISS.

Fig 2: Jane Russell, Princess Sophia of Greece, and ISS employees welcome a group of eight Greek orphans to New York on 29 October 1958. Credit: personal archive of Greek adoptee Ellen.

Theodoropoulou notes Russell's 1959 visit to Metera, the baby center favored by the Greek queen that was also the stage of Princess Sophia's professional training in childcare (during the academic years of 1956–1958, followed by several months of practical training).[149] In the presence of Queen Frederica, Russell gave a lecture in which she unabashedly pointed to the ways in which Greece could further benefit financially from adopting out to the States. Along with Russell, many of her compatriots had no qualms in justifying the Greek-to-American adoption movement (even of the late 1950s) as a veiled way to channel economic assistance to the children's insolvent home country. Through the early 1960s, Metera kept responding to the many inquiries from hopeful American parents by urging them to arrange for home studies through the ISS American Branch.[150]

---

149. Theodoropoulou (2006: 84–85).

150. Metera also accepted the basic home studies submitted by the Greek Orthodox Archdio-

It took the ISS full five years to gain clarity on the labyrinthine legal procedures that ruled adoptions from Greece. The fat folder (box 31, folder 13) of correspondence, reports, memoranda, questions, and clarifications held in the American Branch Papers attests to the agency's arduous efforts to acquire knowledge, even while its Greek adoption cases were well underway. Notably, by 1959, the Branch's thick folder informally changed labels from "legal procedures" to "legal problems." At stake was the issue of whether the ISS-sponsored adoptions of Greek children, which the ISS preferred to finalize in the States after a minimum probationary period of six to twelve months (in most states), would be considered legal by the Greek jurisdiction, which insisted on handling any adoptions of its subjects itself. Crucially, too, the ISS understood any adoption to be confidential and final, abolishing all ties to the natal parents or families. In contrast, the 1946 Greek Civil Code (articles 1581 and 1583) did not divest the birth parents of their basic rights when the Greek court granted a "simple" act of adoption pertaining to their child. The Greek "simple" adoptions, as opposed to the "full" or "new" adoptions on the ISS model, augmented and strengthened rather than restricted family affiliations: they brought the adopters into the original family circle if they were not already members of the extended family, as when the open family symbolically added the children's godparents or the relatives of the grown children's spouses.[151]

Contrary to the "simple" adoptions, which often involved children who were relatives, the "full" and largely "stranger" adoptions carried out by the ISS upheld the principle of keeping adoption records closed. Indirectly, these "American-style" adoptions rested also on the geographical distance and cultural difference resulting from the migratory dispensations of the

cese of North and South America (New York). See the miscellaneous correspondence held in the folders entitled "The Babies' Center Metera" and "Chief Court Mistress," folder 1104, Archive of the Former Royal Palace (1861–1971), GAK, Athens.

151. The debate about the misalignment of the American and the Greek legislation preoccupied the high-ranking participants in August 1957 committee meetings summoned by Lina Tsaldari, then the Greek minister of social welfare serving in the Karamanlis administration. But this ad hoc committee did not devise any satisfactory or timely solution. The ISS continued to treat any US-bound adoption as confidential and final for the sake of the child's "smooth development" (letter written by Aristotelis Koutsoumaris, president of the executive board of the ISS Hellenic Branch, 31 August 1957, 2). Various other written exchanges reflecting the debate may be found in the Lina Tsaldari Archive, folder 8, subfolder 4, especially items 2, 9, and 12–15: "Adoptions 1957–1958," held at the Konstantinos G. Karamanlis Foundation, Athens. See also Rousopoulou (February 1957). The dispute lasted through the spring of 1959. In April 1959, Athinogenis and Papathanasiou reported that the ISS was still hoping to see legal changes made to article 1583 of the Greek Civil Code (1959: 8, 18, 22).

1953 RRA and its successors. The RRA rapidly consolidated the "Western" model of nonrelative adoptions, which was still new to Greece and therefore prone to being misunderstood. Moreover, up through the summer of 1952, the migration provisions of the DPA as amended had done much to reinforce the older Greek model, that of the "simple" or "old-style" adoptions of relative or named orphans. The transition from an open and intrafamilial paradigm to the closed system of mainly "stranger" adoptions was brisk and had unexpected and nefarious consequences. It also generated animosity toward the ISS, which some Greeks accused of imposing an American imperialist model.[152] However, the sealed-records system of the "full" and final adoptions quickly caught on with the Ahepa presidents, private lawyers, and other go-betweens, who pushed this system even a step further: they eliminated, by way of proxy adoptions, the need for the prospective parents to ever make contact with the child's native country, let alone with its birth family.

The ISS carried the brunt of the mid-1950s Greek resistance to changing adoption terms, all still within the purview of Greek and US legislation. Also, for criticizing the proxy adoptions especially of the Ahepa, the ISS had placed itself in a position of isolation in Greece. By April 1959, a total of 344 Greek children had taken the ISS route abroad, though not all of them went to the United States. The number is given, not without marked resentment, in the official report compiled by Athinogenis and Papathanasiou of the Greek Ministry of Social Welfare.[153] In a letter of 11 February 1959 addressed to the Athens office, Pettiss disclosed that the ISS-USA had been trying to effect reform by going straight to the top: ISS officials had approached Queen Frederica when she and her daughter Sophia were visiting America in the fall of 1958. They "talked frankly" with the queen about "some of the problems" that the ISS had been facing when attempting to give "maximum protection" to the Greek-born children whom the agency aimed to move "expeditiously . . . into better living circumstances" and eventually overseas adoptions.[154]

Herman reiterates the risk and potential for abuse that ensued from the proxy adoption system: by the time the adopted children entered the United States, they were legally already the children of the adopting parents,

---

152. See, for instance, Athinogenis and Papathanasiou (1959: 20–23, 26, 28, 30–31, 34, 53, *passim*).

153. Athinogenis and Papathanasiou (1959: 27).

154. Susan T. Pettiss to ISS Greece—Mrs. King, letter of 11 February 1959. The letter is held in the archives of the ISS, American Branch Papers, box 31, folder 13: "Greece: Legal Procedures 1957–1962," SWHA, University of Minnesota Libraries.

who had yet to meet them in person. She concludes, "proxies circumvented investigatory and supervisory regulations and flouted the notion that child welfare was the dominant factor in adoption."[155] Herman further posits that proxy adoptions were no longer permitted after 1961, a position restated and further explored by other adoption scholars.[156] However, the Greek cases of Maria Kelmis and her sister, which were finalized in March of 1962, indicate otherwise. Perhaps Herman has overstated the power of Public Law 87–301 of 26 September 1961: the new stipulations that the would-be adoptive parents "personally see and observe the [foreign-born] child prior to or during the adoption proceedings" and "comply with the preadoption requirements, if any, of the State of such child's proposed residence" may have done much to weaken but may not have altogether abolished the proxy adoption system. According to Winslow, even the new legislation, which implicitly outlawed proxy adoptions, still allowed exceptions: couples from US states that permitted re-adoption could still adopt foreign-born children sight unseen— and all but four states allowed re-adoption![157] California, Minnesota, Ohio, and Michigan were the four states to ban re-adoption. Maria Kelmis and her sister were adopted in the state of New York, but, as a content adoptee and adult author, Kelmis does not reflect further on the added step to the process, of which she may not have been made aware.

In 1966, Greece started to legally require that prospective parents petitioning from abroad use authorized international adoption agencies. Article 14 of Legislative Decree 4532 of 17 August 1966 instructed that international adoptions be carried out by certified agencies and organizations, but without naming them. Along with other historical factors, the 1966 law caused the number of Greek-born adoptees bound for the States to plummet. But even after 1966, the Greek statutes did not insist on the need for a probationary or trial period, allowing would-be parents and children to adjust to each other before their adoptions were legally sanctioned.[158] Greek Royal Decree 795 of 1970 finally specified those authorized agencies, organizations, and institutions through which any future international adoptions of Greek children would have to take place, thus further curtailing the numbers.[159] Among those agencies and institutions were the ISS, PIKPA, the Babies'

---

155. Herman (2008: 218).
156. Herman (2008: 218). See, for instance, Oh (2015: 99, 106) and Winslow (2012a: 166, 190, 373; 2012b: 331, 340, 341).
157. Winslow (2012a: 190).
158. Maganiotou and Koussidou (1988: 386).
159. The decree was published in the 11 December 1970 issue of the *Government Gazette of the Kingdom of Greece* (signed by Regent Georgios Zoïtakis, under the Greek military dictatorship).

Center Metera, and the Municipal Orphanages of Athens, Patras, and Thessaloniki—but not the Ahepa. Once Greece had put these new laws in place and had also relaxed the minimum age requirement for Greek adoptive parents (from fifty to thirty-five years of age, in 1966), the number of cross-border adoptions steeply declined while the number of domestic adoptions steadily increased.[160] Desiderata and actual requirements for adopting, such as home studies, background checks and references, and social-worker visits and follow-up checks throughout a probationary period, became decisive factors in the Greek overseas adoption process from the 1970s on, while the profession of social worker gained greater recognition as well. It took many more years, however, before the United States and a host of other countries endorsed the *1993 Hague Convention on Protection of Children and Co-operation in Respect of Intercountry Adoption*, which stated a preference for in-country adoption over out-of-country adoption. In the latter case, the Convention put safeguards in place to protect children's fundamental rights (albeit still not enough).[161]

The Gray Market: The First External Investigations into the Ahepa's Practices of the Mid-1950s

> An important component of AHEPA's mission is to create an awareness of the principles of Hellenism to society. These principles include a commitment to humanity, freedom, and democracy. The preservation and promotion of these ideals is where AHEPA has, and always will be, deeply committed.
>
> (Part of the Ahepa's mission statement, www.ahepa.org)

The first wave of adoptions of Greek-born orphans (1950–1952) had emerged out of the postwar phenomenon of refugee migration and had sought to find families for children. After the passage of the 1953 Refugee Relief Act (RRA), or "Orphan Program," this wave transformed into an Ahepa-driven movement to find Greek children for (childless) families.[162] The RRA, in tandem with push factors such as conditions in Greece itself, marked an important new trend in intercountry adoption, which changed the face (literally and metaphorically) of the growing American adoptive family and rapidly

---

160. See also Brouskou (2015: 165) and Koussidou and Maganiotou (1991: 167–68, 169, 170, 175).
161. The US laws that implemented the mandates of the 1993 Hague Convention went into effect only in 2008. Fehrenbach (2016: 207–8); Fong, McRoy, and McGinnis (2016: 26–34); Lovelock (2000: 937–42); and Winslow (2017: 219).
162. Lovelock's terms apply very well to the Greek case (2000: 913). See also Lovelock (2000: 927, 929, 943).

consolidated cross-border adoption networks. With this second wave of the mid-1950s came the kind of abuses that mar adoption practices when pull factors start to prevail, or when demand outstrips supply. By 1955, the pull factor of the adoptive families, and also of relatives, friends, and local communities endorsing the upswing in Greek American adoption activism, had interlocked with the push factor of the efforts made by the Greek monarchy, the right-wing establishment, PIKPA and other (strained) child welfare services, all of which were eager to adopt out the minors who had been left languishing in the Greek system. This situation explains why the slightly older Greek orphans, the children who were not "ahistorical," were among the first to leave the Greek institutions or the foster homes in which they had lived until then. Add to that handsome sums of money in miscellaneous fees for middlemen to seal the deal.

Greece at the epicenter of corrupt adoption practices?! How come? Was it only a matter of lax standards on proxy and other adoptions? And where did the new awareness of a Greek baby bonanza originate? My research in specialized American archives may deliver further answers and insights. Among the most compelling items held in the files on Greece by the International Social Service American Branch in Minneapolis is the anonymous "Survey of Greek-U.S. Proxy Adoptions."[163] Received on 1 May 1959, this fifteen-page survey was based on a study conducted by the New York State Joint Legislative Committee on Matrimonial and Family Laws and prepared by Ernest A. Mitler, who served as a special consultant to the committee. Since the early 1950s, New York County assistant district attorney Mitler had moved to the forefront of the discussion about the lack of explicit federal statutes and state laws designed to criminalize baby sales. He had honed his expertise as a "master investigator" in dealing with dodgy cases of infants born in Canada but adopted by US parents.[164] The February 1954 discovery of a baby-selling ring that moved newborns from Montreal to the greater New York City area had sensitized Americans to the problem of cross-border trafficking.[165] Mitler's article in *Look* mag-

---

163. The typescript survey is held in the archives of the ISS, American Branch Papers, box 31, folder 2: "Greece: ISS Greek Branch Adoptions, 1959–1964," SWHA, University of Minnesota Libraries. See under "Anonymous [based on Ernest A. Mitler]" in this book's References.

164. Balcom (2011: 181). See further Balcom (2011: 167, 169, 181, 184–87, 193, 216); Herman (2008: 225); and Winslow (2012a: 72, 121–22; 2017: 34, 61–62, 68). Mitler also joined forces with Democratic Senator Estes Kefauver of Tennessee, who had built a reputation for battling organized crime. Zelizer (1985: ch. 6) has contextualized the twentieth-century phenomena of baby farms and black-market babies.

165. Balcom (2011: 166).

azine (coauthored with Bill Slocum) had drawn attention far and wide with its uncompromising title and content: "Babies: Our One Remaining Black Market" (28 December 1954). In 1959, Mitler was still lobbying to bolster federal adoption legislation that would curtail future infractions regarding the transfer of babies across national and interstate borders for profit.[166] A more formal but equally bold version of Mitler's survey of the adoptions of Greek-born children was published in the English-language Sunday edition of the Greek American newspaper *Atlantis* in six installments, from 1 November through 6 December 1959.[167] The more definitive imprint of Mitler's research is reflected in the 1962 published Report of the Committee on Matrimonial and Family Laws.[168] This report confirms that "commercialized traffic in children was taking place, particularly between Greece and the United States."[169] The committee had brought the evidence before the New York County District Attorney's Office and a Grand Jury investigation followed.[170]

Notably, the first page of Mitler's preliminary survey marked the year 1955 as a turning point: "An unprecedented, wholesale intercountry proxy adoption traffic has become firmly established between Greece and the United States since 1955." Before the Subcommittee on Immigration and Naturalization hearing held in Washington on 23 June 1959, Mitler declared that, in the case of Greece, "the baby selling racketeers . . . have secured practically a monopoly."[171] This small group of unprincipled individuals "took over our inter-country adoption program from Greece. They literally moved the recognized social agencies almost out of the picture."[172] Among the recognized agencies to which Mitler referred were the United States Children's Bureau (founded in 1912) and the International Social Service (1924): both agencies had established professional practices for intercountry adoptions, but they stood no chance of toppling the Ahepa's near-monopoly, let alone of controlling the flow of babies from Greece.[173] In the 1950s and through the mid-1960s, the Greek courts merely asked to see reference letters from priests or

---

166. See Bigart's article in the *New York Times* of 6 January 1959. Carp (2014a) offers a recent bibliographical guide to the history of adoption law in the United States and to the laws of various states individually.

167. Moskos and Moskos (2014: 47, 48, 49) briefly introduce the influential Greek American paper *Atlantis*, which acquired some readership in Greece as well.

168. State of New York (1962: 319–20).

169. State of New York (1962: 319).

170. State of New York (1962: 320).

171. Mitler, *Atlantis*, 8 November 1959.

172. Mitler, *Atlantis*, 29 November 1959; also Mitler, *Atlantis*, 6 December 1959.

173. Winslow (2012a: 126; 2017: 64).

clergymen and employers of the foreign couple. Mitler commented, "a court five thousand miles away is completely unable to evaluate the suitability of the couple they have never seen by a few letters of reference that might be adequate for a part-time summer job."[174] In some cases, the letters submitted to the Greek courts were hastily concocted or even forged.[175] From 1962 on, the then-director of the Athens Orphanage at least referred prospective adoptive parents to the ISS when they sent inquiries from the United States, Canada, Australia, the United Kingdom, Sweden, Cyprus, or any other countries, unless the petitioners were of Greek descent.[176]

In an attempt to streamline adoption protocols, the Greek Ministry of Justice had issued a circular order dated 5 December 1957 urging the Courts of First Instance to solicit the input of professional social workers in any adoption cases, overseas and internal alike.[177] In practice and through the early 1960s, however, any reports composed by social workers were rarely consulted, let alone acted on in court, and the same held true of reference letters. A typical one-liner from the Greek adoption court files reads that the prospective parents are "good and honorable people" ("καλοί και τίμιοι άνθρωποι"), who attend church and have adequate financial resources. Minister Papakonstantinou's circular order was the meager end result of an ambitious plan initiated by Lina Tsaldari, Karamanlis's minister of social welfare. In mid-1957, Tsaldari was trying to centralize Greek adoption protocols and practices by calling for a new state institution with an outspoken "ethnosocial" mandate: this new state organ would oversee all Greek adoption cases and would collect the proper amount of input from social workers. But Tsaldari's initiative never moved beyond the planning stages, and the ineffectual circular order was, by the end of 1957, all that remained.[178]

A subsequent short-lived attempt to centralize and professionalize Greek adoptions focused on PIKPA. In 1958, the Greek Ministry of Social Welfare issued a document (9.400/1958) that directed (through the Ministry of Internal Affairs) all municipal orphanages to handle their overseas

---

174. Mitler, *Atlantis*, 8 November 1959.

175. See below, p. 160.

176. See the miscellaneous correspondence held in the Archive of the Municipal Orphanage of Athens at the GAK, Athens.

177. Minister Konstantinos Papakonstantinou's "Circular Order 126899/84" of 5 December 1957 (two-page typescript) is held in the Lina Tsaldari Archive, folder 8, subfolder 4, item 17: "Adoptions 1957–1958," Konstantinos G. Karamanlis Foundation, Athens.

178. The relevant archival documentation may be found in the Lina Tsaldari Archive, folder 8, subfolder 4: "Adoptions 1957–1958," Konstantinos G. Karamanlis Foundation. See also Athinogenis and Papathanasiou (1959: 10–11) and Kliafa (2016: 92–93).

adoptions through PIKPA.[179] PIKPA's "special adoption service" promised to pursue Greek Orthodox placements, which would in turn secure a "happier future" for the child.[180] Given the bureaucratic hurdles associated with PIKPA adoptions, however, this measure, too, failed to produce the desired unified system and adequate oversight by social workers. Several municipal orphanages simply continued to handle US-bound placements the old way: they kept collaborating with preferred agents on adoptions by proxy and thereby thwarted the interference of state and social services; also, they thus avoided delays in sending the adoptees on their way.[181] The repeated calls for a viable form of centralization on the Greek end went unheeded through the early 1960s.[182] This structural vacuum left more room for the Greek American agents to fashion the overseas adoption movement.

The survey representing Mitler's research laid the responsibility for implementing the Ahepa's role under the 1953 RRA squarely with Leo Lamberson, the order's supreme president of 1953–1954. Lamberson had become the (second) chair of the Ahepa Refugee Relief Committee, which was formally recognized by the State Department on 27 January 1954.[183] In April of the same year, Lamberson traveled to Greece to open offices in Athens and Thessaloniki and to appoint local staff, to ensure that as many adult Greek refugees as possible be given a visa to emigrate to the States.[184] By the fall of 1954, however, he was issuing full-page calls in *The Ahepan* for Greek American foster parents and adoptive homes for orphans from Greece.[185] By late 1955, Lamberson was calling himself the chair not only of the Ahepa Refugee Relief Committee but also of the Greek Orphans Program, as in a blurb that he himself probably submitted to *The Ahepan* of November–December 1955 (p. 15). He personally honed the crucial trend of distinguishing children and orphans from other Ahepa-sponsored refugees. It was the late spring of 1956, however, before the Ahepa Refugee Relief Committee was ready to actually put adoptees on planes for New York.[186] This is an important tem-

---

179. Athinogenis and Papathanasiou (1959: 39).
180. Document 9.400/1958, quoted by Athinogenis and Papathanasiou (1959: 39).
181. Athinogenis and Papathanasiou (1959: 40).
182. Mastrogiannis (1962: 51, 54).
183. Anon., *The Ahepan*, Jan.–March 1954.
184. Anon. [Mitler], survey pp. 3–4. See also Mitler, *Atlantis*, 15 November 1959; and Leber (1972: 392, 393, 394).
185. Ahepa Refugee Relief Committee, *The Ahepan*, Oct.–Dec. 1954. See above, p. 104.
186. This conclusion is based on my compilation of data from adoptees' testimonies and personal archives. This extensive database, cross-checked against the New York Passenger Lists on Ancestry.com, allows me to draw a number of other chronological conclusions as well. I am much indebted to Merrill Jenkins for his generous assistance with this part of my research.

poral fact that does not stand out among the details of Mitler's exposé. Also, this chronology contradicts generalizations and outright misinformation about the Ahepa's Greek Orphans Program, whose starting date and scale some sources overstate (pushing the program back to an earlier date and exaggerating the numbers of adoptees).[187]

The logistical delay until the spring of 1956 was inevitable, but it was not for lack of trying on the part of Lamberson and also of Michael Tsaparis, the Greek attorney who oversaw the newly established Ahepa office in Athens (on 2 Fidiou Street and subsequently on 9 Dimokritou Street). A sequence of visits and letters attests to Lamberson's push for an Ahepa monopoly in US-bound orphan placements and to his pursuit of the Greek government's formal endorsement, to help secure the cooperation of child welfare institutions and organizations across Greece. On 10 May 1954, Lamberson wrote a letter to Ioannis Nikolitsas, minister of internal affairs under the Papagos administration, in which he referred to a prior personal visit during which he had outlined the Ahepa adoption program. In the letter, Lamberson affirmed that his organization would cosign and vouch for the applications submitted by American adoptive parents, who would be Greeks living in the United States or Greek Americans of the Orthodox faith. These couples would "raise the orphan in a Greek and Orthodox Christian environment, where the child will also be taught the Greek language, customs, and traditions."[188] Lamberson further asked the ministry to approve an "exceptional interpretation or even an adjustment of the Law on Orphans."[189] He hinted at the Greek government's facilitation of adoptions by proxy, but his letter does not enter into details. Rather, Lamberson goes on to request that the Ahepa's adoption program be granted a preferred or priority status over and above "any other organization or group." He closes by referring any further questions to Tsaparis.

Once Minister Nikolitsas had responded in the affirmative three months later, on 13 August 1954, Tsaparis promptly followed up with a request, dated 21 August 1954, to the Ministry of Social Welfare, to which he attached a

187. See, for instance, Bogiopoulos, *Rizospastis*, 21 April 1996.
188. Lamberson, letter to the Greek Minister of Internal Affairs, 10 May 1954, following up on a visit of 30 April 1954. A copy of this letter, translated from the original English into Greek, is attached to the correspondence discussed below, which is held in the Archive of the Child's Asylum of Volos, folder 2125, "Documents of the Ministry of Social Welfare and Other Ministries, 1954–1956," Archives of the Prefecture of Magnesia, GAK, Volos. Pages 136–39 below revisit the expectations of the Greek state and church that Greek children be placed with coreligious adoptive families. See also Mastrogiannis (1962: 51–54).
189. Lamberson, letter to the Greek Minister of Internal Affairs, 10 May 1954: "μίαν ἐξαιρετικήν ἑρμηνείαν ἤ καί τροποποίησιν τοῦ Νόμου περί Ὀρφανῶν."

copy of the formal endorsement letter. Tsaparis's two-page letter uses the bold subject line: "Adoptions of Greek orphans with the guarantee of the Ahepa."[190] The intrepid lawyer projected a target number of some 250–300 orphans, whose medical exam prior to their adoption and visa issuance would be carried out by "our doctor." The Ministry of Social Welfare may want to facilitate the US-bound adoptions of these children, Tsaparis asserted, by formally requesting the collaboration of all Greek orphanages and "the other philanthropic organizations." More specifically, Tsaparis suggested, the ministry may want to issue a circular letter "with the appropriate guidelines and introductions" and send it to all these institutions on the Ahepa's behalf. And could the ministry please forward a copy of this circular to the Ahepa's Athens office, "accompanied by the list of those institutions' names and exact addresses"? "As soon as your circular has been issued," Tsaparis promised, "we plan to visit" all institutions, including those in the provinces. The latter, he continues, could speed up the process "by sending us lists of how many boys and how many girls between the ages of one and seven they would be able to make available" ("ἠδύναντο νά διαθέσουν").[191] Christos Solomonidis, the Greek minister of social welfare, followed up with his verdict of approval. He addressed his circular letter of 27 September 1954 to all private as well as state institutions dedicated to child welfare, and he urged them to assist the Ahepa in its selection of some 250–300 orphans for adoption overseas.[192] Solomonidis also duly asked the institutions to lend "every possible assistance" to Tsaparis and to forward to him directly, as per his request, the lists of children ages one through seven, "sorted by sex."

Over the course of 1954 through mid-August 1956, Lamberson managed to shift his committee's role from serving refugees to bringing over Greek children adopted by proxy; that is, he exploited the loopholes opened up by legal provisions that did not require would-be parents to make personal

---

190. Tsaparis, letter to the Greek Ministry of Social Welfare, 21 August 1954, 1. A copy of this letter is held in the Archive of the Child's Asylum of Volos, folder 2125, "Documents of the Ministry of Social Welfare and Other Ministries, 1954–1956," Archives of the Prefecture of Magnesia, GAK, Volos. The quotations immediately following are taken and translated from the same letter.

191. In all likelihood, the Ahepa and Tsaparis themselves posited the children's upper age limit at seven years old, even though the 1953 RRA placed it at ten years old, because they were expecting further delays. They did not want to disappoint the American adoptive parents whose assigned children would, with the passage of time, have exceeded the age limit of ten.

192. Solomonidis, circular letter of 27 September 1954. A copy of this letter is held in the Archive of the Child's Asylum of Volos, folder 2125, "Documents of the Ministry of Social Welfare and Other Ministries, 1954–1956," Archives of the Prefecture of Magnesia, GAK, Volos. The quotations immediately following are taken and translated from the same letter.

appearances before Greek institutions or courts, but that let them relegate such duties to (paid) intermediaries.[193] While Lamberson was still operating in the "gray market,"[194] he did not hesitate to seek the national spotlight for his "airlifts" of Greek orphans. On 12 July 1956, he went to meet the reporters as well as the Swissair plane that had arrived at Idlewild Airport (later renamed JFK Airport) with twelve Greek orphans on board. There, he publicly vowed that he and the Ahepa would bring over another seventy Greek children in the following few months. The anonymous *New York Times* article of 13 July 1956 that documents the event is accompanied by a picture of twelve slightly bewildered children, ages three to eight, looking toward the camera (see figure 5).

The Black Market: Lamberson, August 1956–1959

> "It seems to me that a charity project turned into a money making scheme."
> —Complaint voiced by an Ahepa member from Charleston, SC

In mid-August of 1956, the Ahepa's New York convention terminated Lamberson's work on the Ahepa Refugee Relief Committee in response to a flood of external as well as internal complaints, which led its delegates to believe that Lamberson had been distorting the order's mission.[195] Under Lamberson, the program's component of orphan placements had started to degrade into a lucrative baby bazaar.[196] But Lamberson's practice grew into a full-blown black market for babies when he ignored the Ahepa's veto and carried on with his abuses through 1958. Moreover, a couple of Ahepa leaders kept in the know took over part of the "business."

Lamberson kept exploiting his former high office and the confidence that the Ahepa name inspired in Greece as well as in the States.[197] Among the misled Greek institutions was the Municipal Orphanage of Patras (Δημοτικό Βρεφοκομείο Πατρών, founded in 1873).[198] The directors of the Patras Orphanage, however, were no strangers to deceit themselves.[199] From 1955 until the late 1950s, these directors offered up an unusually large

---

193. Anon. [Mitler], survey pp. 3–4; Mitler, *Atlantis*, 1 November 1959.

194. Winslow (2012a: 123; 2017: 62).

195. Some complaints, such as the one of the epigraph, are quoted by Critzas (1957: 103).

196. Anon. [Mitler], survey p. 4.

197. Anon. [Mitler], survey p. 4.

198. Anon. [Mitler], survey p. 5.

199. Anon. [Mitler], survey pp. 10–11. See also Theodoropoulou (2006: 110).

number of "abandoned" infants to Lamberson and his accomplices. Mitler astutely observed, "it seems improbable that all of the unmarried mothers left almost an identical note attached to their children's clothing in Patras and that they almost never could be located for the purpose of getting their consents."[200]

Mitler rightly focused on the Ahepa's collusion with the Patras Orphanage, but a few additional words disclose the Greek side (and scale) of the deal and introduce the reader to the world of Greek orphanages. Greek orphanages and similar institutions were complex sites of power relations, but also of social and economic relations with their surrounding communities. The cast of male characters associated with the Patras Orphanage, in particular, illuminates the high level of interaction between municipal and state governments and between domestic courts and transnational organizations. On 26 February 1953, Vasileios [Basil] Thanos Roufos, mayor of Patras and president of the Patras Orphanage's board of directors, or "Brotherhood" (Αδελφάτο), reported that his institution was taking care of a total of 431 children, which made for crowded conditions, a powerful push factor. The Patras Orphanage, however, was the first to also identify the pull factor of the American demand for available white children. Roufos prided himself on modeling the rules and practices of the Patras Orphanage on those of the Municipal Orphanage of Athens (Δημοτικό Βρεφοκομείο Αθηνών, founded in 1859, hereafter "Athens Orphanage").[201] One of the standard rules charged

---

200. Anon. [Mitler], survey p. 11. The Patras Orphanage was located at 6 Sotiriadou Street, on a natural elevation named Sakketos. The orphanage shared a block with the church in which some foundlings were baptized, and it remained easily accessible from the nearby municipal hospital where numerous women gave birth. In 1972, the old and damaged orphanage building was replaced with a new one that today functions as a daycare center but that, through 2016, kept up a small "memorial room" to preserve and display token items from its former history. By the summer of 2017, the institution had dismantled this "memorial room" and merely left a few pieces of furniture sitting in the corridors. The obliteration of the institution's older history, which had been gaining new and unwanted public attention, was fast progressing.

    During its nearly century-long operation, the Patras Orphanage entered the names and data of some 11,000 children in its ledger books. See Theodoropoulou (2006: 107–10, 115–17). For images of the Patras Orphanage, see figures 13–14. The Patras Orphanage is not to be confused with the National Orphanage for Girls of Patras (Εθνικό Ορφανοτροφείο Θηλέων Πατρών, founded in 1925) or with the National Skagiopouleio Agricultural Orphanage for Boys of Patras (Εθνικό Σκαγιοπούλειο Αγροτικό Ορφανοτροφείο Αρρένων Πατρών, founded in 1926). The Skagiopouleio Orphanage (for short) functioned as a training school in agricultural methods and in discipline, and it housed male children through their teenage years.

201. Korasidou (1995: 111–12). For decades, the Municipal Orphanage of Athens was located at 51 Peiraios Street, that is, right on Eleftheria Square, aka Plateia Koumoundourou, near Omonoia Square. The institution stopped functioning as an orphanage in 1982, and its

the board of directors with facilitating adoptions, which is why Mayor Roufos could pursue more foreign adoptions than one would normally expect.[202]
Besides, a relinquished child's dependency on public support proffered suf-
ficient legal ground for the orphanage to make that child available for adoption. Through the 1940s, mortality rates among institutionalized infants had
been very high.[203] By the early 1950s, however, the ready availability of vaccinations, antibiotics, and artificial infant formula had let many more babies
survive.[204]

Overcrowded orphanages across Greece, eager to "reduce congestion,"[205]
found a ready solution in Greek-to-(Greek-)American adoptions. What did
"congestion" in a Greek orphanage look like? From 1950 through the end
of the decade, the Patras Orphanage entered, on average, one new child in
its ledgers every three to four days. The situation was worse at the Athens Orphanage, which saw averages of one child entering every two days in
some of the postwar years. The Saint Stylianos Foundling Home in Thessaloniki took in more than 120 children every single year through the 1950s.[206]

---

large neoclassical building was subsequently converted into a gallery space, colloquially
known as the "Old Municipal Art Gallery" (Παλιά Δημοτική Πινακοθήκη or, more formally, Πινακοθήκη Δήμου Αθηναίων, as per the engraving on the still-standing building).
Today, the name of Δημοτικό Βρεφοκομείο Αθηνών remains associated with a network of
daycare centers with headquarters in the Sepolia district of Athens.

By the late 1950s, the Athens Orphanage accommodated some 150 children in-house,
and it maintained external wet-nursing and foster family arrangements for another 180
children (Athinogenis and Papathanasiou 1959: 39; Skiadas 1999: 173). Theodoropoulou
covers the orphanage's history in great detail (2006: 35–42, 44, 56–57, 64–67, 70, 75–81,
121–23). Korasidou foregrounds the institution's role and struggle through the second half
of the nineteenth century (1995: 110–30). See also Kliafa (2016: 114–15); Marketou (1999);
the photobook by Papaioannou (ca. 1999); and Skiadas (1999). For an image of the Athens
Orphanage, see figure 15.

Kardamitsi Adami (1993) discusses the revolutionary history of the short-lived
orphanage for boys (1829–1834) on the island of Aegina, which, for a few years, housed the
first National Archaeological Museum. By 1880, the same building had been turned into a
prison. See further Kalliga (1990).

202. Theodoropoulou (2006: 150).
203. Infant mortality rates spiked up to 50 percent (and on occasion even 80 percent) during
the worst of the war years. Brouskou (2015: 254–57, *passim*) and Theodoropoulou (2006:
44, 55, 56, *passim*). Extreme rates of infant mortality reached the Greek news media and
triggered legal scrutiny. See, for instance, a 1950 investigation into the staggeringly high
90 percent mortality rate of the Baby Shelter of Piraeus (Βρεφική Στέγη Πειραιώς) of the
previous year, as reported by Anon., "The 'Baby Shelter (of Piraeus)' Has Been a Transit
Station to Death," *Tachydromos* (Volos), 21 January 1950 (in Greek). The Baby Shelter regularly transferred children to the Athens Orphanage. See Theodoropoulou (2006: 99–101).
204. Brouskou, testimony of 14 June 2016.
205. Petritsi (1952: 4), quoting Director Georgios Voutsis, who oversaw Greece's orphanages
and childcare centers on behalf of the Ministry of Social Welfare.
206. The sequential ledger numbers and corresponding entry dates allow us to calculate these

During the twelve decades of its operations, the Athens Orphanage entered some 47,000 children into its ledgers, or more than four times the number of names in the Patras Orphanage or the Saint Stylianos Foundling Home.[207] These numbers are a stark reminder that orphanages across Greece faced the challenge of keeping their charges alive before trying to meet their other, less basic needs.[208]

Not all of the children who entered Greek orphanages remained in these institutions or even survived, but the lack of space and money became a chronic problem that gnawed at any city's budget (and at its honor). All orphanages accepted (or even solicited) donations made in gratitude by couples who had received a child, which made Greek-to-American adoptions look more attractive than in-country adoptions.[209] Moreover, both types of adoption cost the Greek home institutions only a fraction of the costs of continuing to support dependent children beyond their board, in facilities that required staff throughout the day and night. To cultivate contacts, raise funds, and decrease expenses, Mayor Roufos of Patras sought out Greek American organizations such as the Ahepa with an eye to adopting out overseas.[210] In 1954 through 1955, Roufos was still willing to help facilitate US-bound adoptions via private lawyers and through the ISS Hellenic Branch. In 1956, he switched his allegiance to the Ahepa and subsequently to independent and disreputable agents. Again according to the Patras Orphanage rules, the institution had to keep records of all acts of adoption.[211] However, the current state of the archives of both the Patras and the Athens Orphanages (and of those of several other institutions) reveals that this rule was among the first to be broken.[212]

---

averages, but they do not tell the full story. Some mothers went to retrieve their children a few days or weeks after abandoning them, in which case the children's entries were merely updated, not deleted. Brouskou details the procedures of maintaining the ledgers of the Saint Stylianos Foundling Home (2015: 169–77, *passim*).

207. The latter with some 10,000 entries in its ledgers covered more than eight decades of operations since 1912. Brouskou, testimony of 14 June 2016.

208. Also, the figures play into the debate on whether access to orphanages (or similar institutions) and the availability of anonymous relinquishment do not, in fact, cause the total counts of abandoned children to rise. Tilly et al. further discuss such unintended consequences (1992: 6, 15, 17, 21). They have observed parents' increased use of institutional childcare (through child abandonment, temporary or not) as a substitute welfare system. See also Fieldston (2015: 186).

209. Zelizer (1985: 204–5) remarks on the long-standing efforts to define the exchange of money as a symbolic and elective gift rather than as a fee or price for obtaining a child.

210. Theodoropoulou (2006: 110, 112, 113–14).

211. Theodoropoulou (2006: 150).

212. Theodoropoulou pays ample attention to the history of the archives of the most important Greek institutions involved in childcare and maternity services. See Theodoropoulou

Buoyed by its success with the Patras Orphanage, the Ahepa Refugee Relief Committee under Lamberson approached the Athens Orphanage by mail, in the hope of establishing a similar productive collaboration. The ARRC's letter of 7 June 1956, written in Greek by Lamberson's right-hand man Tsaparis, was the subject of a meeting of the Athens Orphanage's board of directors about one week later. The minutes of this meeting, dated 15 June 1956, cite Tsaparis's letter in its entirety and also convey the board members' reactions.[213] The Ahepans ask for "25–30 orphans, ages 2–5" from the Athens Orphanage, for adoption by "American citizens, most of them members of the Ahepa." They boasted that the new Ahepa program, which had been fully operative for only about a year, had already achieved the legal adoptions of some 100 children from the Patras Orphanage, whose departures were underway. They took special pride in the fact that these had been proxy or predeparture adoptions "for the sake of complying with the pertinent Greek laws." Also, the Ahepa's in-country adoptions of children destined for the States "economically strengthen Greece": "this way, the country receives a considerable amount of foreign currency through payments to lawyers, the purchases of stamps for the lawcourts and for various other services, etc." This clumsy call for Greek economic solvency aside, Tsaparis's letter ends with the compelling promise that a normal US-bound Ahepa adoption case can be completed within three months.[214]

The Ahepa's mid-1956 proposal to the Athens Orphanage met with the stern reservations of only one board member, Georgios Garoufalias. He rightly questioned the orphanage's lack of oversight over the approval process of the petitioning parents. He also described the summary legal practices that the Greek lawyers working for the Ahepa were already following. "Just the other day," Garoufalias claimed, "[Ahepa] lawyer [Christos] Tountas brought a *list* of overseas adoption cases from the Patras Orphanage to the Court [of First Instance] in Athens. Only *one* witness was present to testify on behalf of *all* the cases, working down the list he was holding!"[215] All the other board members, however, refuted their colleague's objections,

---

(2006: 117) on the archives from the Patras Orphanage and Theodoropoulou (2006: 122) on those from the Athens Orphanage, both in a deplorable and incomplete state. Parish churches that have preserved baptismal records are not necessarily well-staffed or helpful, either. The same holds true of police stations, which had to draw up reports about babies that had been found and brought in (Theodoropoulou 2006: 117).

213. This letter and the proceedings, otherwise unpublished, are quoted at length by Theodoro-poulou (2006: 75–77).

214. Letter quoted by Theodoropoulou (2006: 75–76).

215. Proceedings in Greek quoted by Theodoropoulou (2006: 76).

invoked the Ahepa's prestige, and pushed the ARRC's proposal through.[216] One and a half years later, at the meeting of 3 December 1957, the board of the Athens Orphanage reconsidered its earlier decision and placed all its international adoptions on hold for six months (including those through the Ahepa), except in cases in which a specific child had already been selected or when the prospective parents were of Greek extraction.[217]

Maria Svolou, herself a feminist activist, labor specialist, and member of parliament for the reform party of the United Democratic Left, publicly applauded the suspension of the Athens Orphanage's international adoptions. In a heated parliamentary discussion of 16 July 1958, she denounced the "export of Greek children," along with the mass emigration of Greek youth, as "unacceptable."[218] She was one of the first voices to go on record condemning the unchecked flow of Greek children to America. The United Democratic Left (EDA, Ενιαία Δημοκρατική Αριστερά) had emerged from the 11 May 1958 election as the leading opposition party to Karamanlis's autocratic government, and it was growing more vocal on matters of political change and social welfare. On 11 July 1958, or after a seven-month interval, the board of the Athens Orphanage had duly returned to the topic of the suspended overseas adoptions. The cautious Garoufalias proposed that a maximum of only five orphanage wards per month be made available for adoption abroad, and that these adoptions be restricted to foreign applicants of Greek descent. His proposal now won the majority vote.[219] In the early 1960s, however, the Athens Orphanage relaxed its rules somewhat, as a handwritten record from its files may show (figure 3), to then suspend overseas adoptions again from 1964 until 1967.[220]

Coinciding with the tightening of the "supply line" from the Athens Orphanage, Lamberson's fees for procuring Greek children went up from an initial, "modest" $643 per adoption case to $2,800, with no questions asked, in less than three years.[221] Lamberson routinely charged the higher fee of New York Jewish couples, which leads Winslow to conclude that he "maintained his 'gray-market' adoption practice for U.S.-Greek couples, only covering his costs or asking for donations, while simultaneously extorting

---

216. Proceedings quoted by Theodoropoulou (2006: 76).
217. Proceedings quoted by Theodoropoulou (2006: 78–79). See also Athinogenis and Papathanasiou (1959: 12, 37, 41).
218. Hellenic Parliament, Official Minutes of the Special Committee of the Parliament of Article 35 of the Constitution, Period 5, Session 1, Meeting 4, 16 July 1958, 27. See further Bada and Hantzaroula (2017: 29) and Kliafa (2016: 171–79).
219. Proceedings in Greek quoted by Theodoropoulou (2006: 79–80).
220. Skiadas (1999: 172).
221. Anon. [Mitler], survey pp. 4, 7; also Mitler, *Atlantis*, 1 and 15 November 1959.

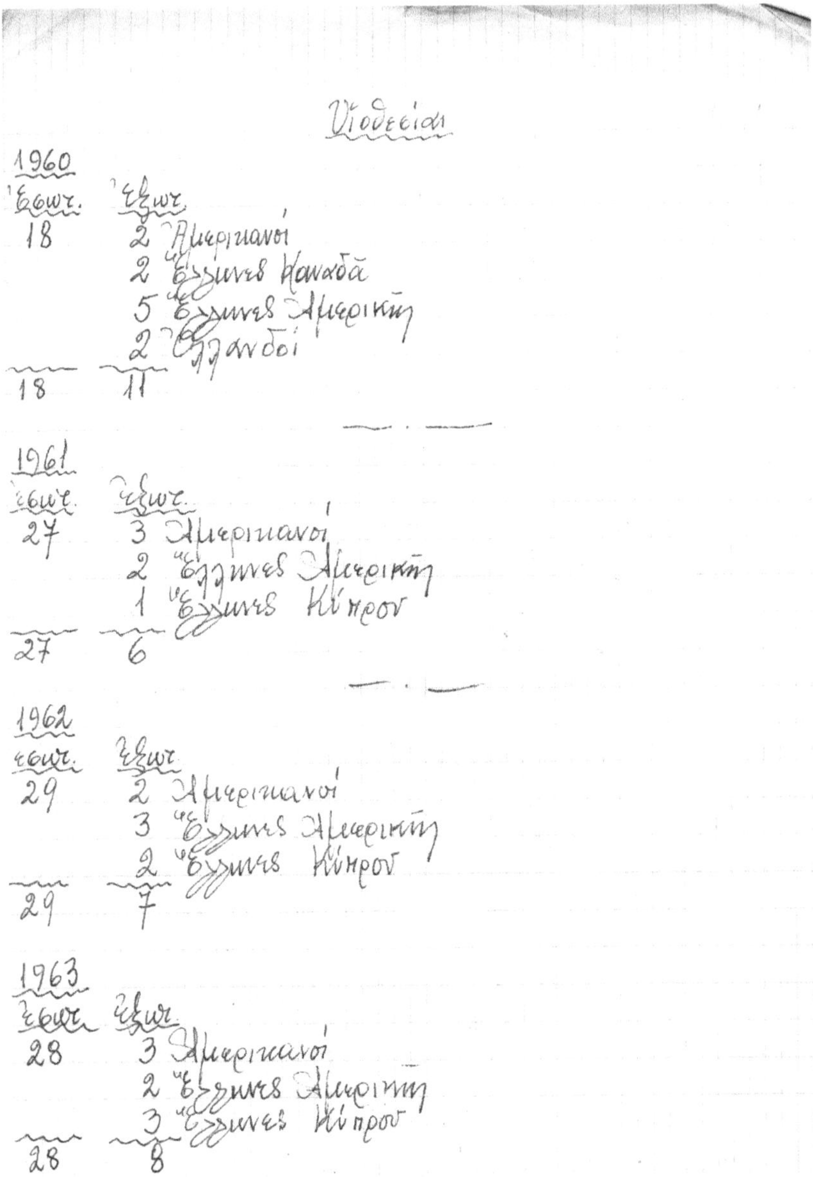

Υἱοθεσίαι

1960
Ἔσωτ.   Ἔξωτ.
18   2 Ἀμερικάνοι
        2 Ἕλληνες Καναδᾶ
        5 Ἕλληνες Ἀμερικῆ
        2 Ὀλλανδοί
——   ——
18   11

1961
Ἔσωτ.   Ἔξωτ.
27   3 Ἀμερικάνοι
        2 Ἕλληνες Ἀμερικῆ
        1 Ἕλληνες Κύπρου
——   ——
27   6

1962
Ἔσωτ.   Ἔξωτ.
29   2 Ἀμερικάνοι
        3 Ἕλληνες Ἀμερικῆ
        2 Ἕλληνες Κύπρου
——   ——
29   7

1963
Ἔσωτ.   Ἔξωτ.
28   3 Ἀμερικάνοι
        2 Ἕλληνες Ἀμερικῆ
        3 Ἕλληνες Κύπρου
——   ——
28   8

Fig 3: Record-keeping at the Municipal Orphanage of Athens: a handwritten page entitled "Adoptions" lists both the internal and the external adoptions that took place from 1960 through 1963, as well as the nationality of the adoptive parents ("Americans," "Greeks from Canada," "Greeks from America," "Dutch," etc.). Credit: Archive of the Municipal Orphanage of Athens, folder 94.6, General State Archives. Athens, Greece (with permission).

Jewish families. . . . [T]he well-documented desperation of childless Jewish couples proved too profitable for the Indiana lawyer to resist."[222] Lamberson himself explained: "It appears . . . that non-Hellenes are more interested in Greek orphans than Hellenes."[223] A US immigration official quoted by Balcom defined the middle income bracket in 1954 as "between $4000 and 7000 [annually]."[224] In the late 1950s, the sum of $2,800 generated some $2,000 in sheer profit for the perpetrators, given that the fees for securing a Greek child's adoption, board, medical clearance, passport and visa, and also the cost of airfare were low and sometimes even completely offset by charitable contributions (as per the calculations in Mitler's 1959 survey).[225] Moreover, when on 9 April 1953 the Papagos government devalued the Greek currency by 50 percent and introduced the "new" drachma (equal to 1,000 "old" drachmas), it also pegged the dollar to the rate of 30 drachmas, which was very beneficial for any American doing business with Greece.[226] The issue at stake, however, is not one of profit-making but of human rights: birth mothers and adoptive families were routinely deceived in this transnational scheme of baby brokering, which left children with little protection.

Scores of hopeful American parents fell into the trap of Lamberson's rogue operation, whose glossy newsletters helped to conceal a confidence game.[227] With demand rising, Lamberson tightened his collaboration with Tsaparis, who oversaw the ARRC's Athens office and kept building in-country connections. When called on, Tsaparis lent his services also to PIKPA, as when this organization, in 1958–1959, was seeking a Greek American family in which to place a baby born out of an incestuous relationship.[228] On a reg-

---

222. Winslow (2012a: 125); also Winslow (2017: 63–64).

223. Lamberson (1956a: 686).

224. Balcom (2011: 171). Carp and Leon-Guerrero clarify that these figures applied to white American families (2002: 203–4).

225. Anon. [Mitler], survey pp. 8–9. Children's airline tickets could be issued at half the price of adult passengers' tickets. From the late 1940s on, New York travel agencies advertised round-trips to Athens for approximately $900 (and "only" some twenty-six hours of travel time). One adoptee's single fare from Athens to New York in the early summer of 1956 cost $217.50. This precise amount is in a letter from the travel agency Acropole Express of N. J. Cassavetes, which, on behalf of the Ahepa, issued the children's visas and took care of the flight arrangements (letter dated 8 June 1956 and "Adoption Expenses—Maria," a list of expenses kept by Maria's adoptive mother, personal archive of Maria).

226. See Kazamias (unpublished ms.: 188–205, 208–14) and Volbert and Demopoulos (1989: 70–71, 77).

227. Mitler, *Atlantis*, 15 November 1959.

228. Athinogenis and Papathanasiou (1959: 17, 48). Athinogenis and Papathanasiou, who throughout their 1959 report stressed the importance of the coreligious adoptions to which PIKPA was committed, conveniently overlooked the fact that Tsaparis placed scores of children in non-Orthodox families. It sufficed that the young lawyer assisted with PIKPA's most sensitive cases.

ular basis, however, Tsaparis worked with the orphanages and through personal contacts to procure children for the Ahepa, and he also obtained the acts of adoption from the court in Athens.[229] On the American side, Lamberson soon co-opted Stephen S. Scopas, the Ahepa's supreme president of 1954–1956 and a prominent New York City magistrate, who covered the East Coast of the United States, while Lamberson retained his law practice in South Bend, Indiana, which he used as a base to cover the Midwest and the western states.[230] In 1956, Scopas had been honored with the Order of the Phoenix by King Paul, for service to his home country. After being named to the bench in April 1957, Scopas partnered with the Manhattan-based lawyer Jacob Cohen, as the "business" was clearly expanding in volume as well as territorial scope.[231] Among the ringleaders' areas of concentration were, in addition to New York State, California and especially the Los Angeles and San Diego regions, New Jersey, Massachusetts, Indiana, and Illinois.[232]

Racial thinking augmented the demand for white children, and Greek children fit the bill. Greek children ranked among the top of the racial hierarchies in adoption, after German children who scored highest on the preference scale of whiteness. Through the mid-1960s, US racial segregation and antimiscegenation laws were still on the books in many states, and they applied to ("mixed-race") Asian children as well, albeit not consistently.[233] Nobel Laureate Pearl S. Buck fought to improve the plight of "mixed-race" Asian children and, through her Welcome House foundation (1949) and her prolific writing, she became an early advocate also for transethnic and transracial adoption.[234] Through Buck's unrelenting work but also through cultural diplomacy initiatives such as Eisenhower's People-to-People Program and other soft-power practices,[235] Cold War national and racial boundaries were finally shaken and made way for greater internationalism and plu-

---

229. Lamberson (March–April 1955); Mitler, *Atlantis*, 1 and 8 November 1959; and Winslow (2012a: 119; 2017: 60). Tsaparis must have gathered lots of vital information on the Greek children made available for US-bound adoptions, but none of it has been preserved. A phone call of 2 June 2017 to his widow delivered the startling response that she had thrown out all of her husband's adoption-related paperwork some ten years after his premature death, because it was "no longer of any use." She also insisted that all of the adoptions enacted by her husband had "proven" to be "safe and successful."

230. Anon. [Mitler], survey p. 6; Mitler, *Atlantis*, 1 November 1959.

231. Anon. [Mitler], survey p. 8; Mitler, *Atlantis*, 1 November 1959. See also Mantzoros (1959: 2). Mantzoros was the vocal editor of the *Chicago Pnyx* semimonthly newspaper.

232. Mitler, *Atlantis*, 1 November 1959.

233. Gage (2007: 91) and Winslow (2012a: 28–30).

234. Klein (2003: 143–46, 174, 175, 178, 179) and also Conn (1996: 238, 312–14, 338, 346–47, 353–55, 364–65, 368, 374–75).

235. Klein (2003: 49–56, 59–60, 83–85, 187–88).

ralism. With some fanfare, the US president inaugurated his program in September of 1956: he aimed to enhance cross-border understanding and friendship through educational, social, and humanitarian activities among peoples from diverse cultures, thus engaging them in a "common effort to advance world peace."[236] Intercountry and interracial adoptions, however, were not immediately on Eisenhower's radar. The importance of the physical resemblance between parents and children continued to weigh heavily on "mixed-race" African American adoptees, whose placement became easier only by the end of the 1960s civil rights revolution (but again turned more complex in the 1970s).[237]

The demand for Greek children, invisible as adoptees, was high in Jewish circles of the upper East Coast. Jewish families who for whatever reason chose not to adopt Korean, Japanese, German, or Austrian children, were left with very few options. For them, adopting a Greek orphan was the logical default choice.[238] Like most prospective parents of the time, many Jewish adopters anticipated that this choice would obviate awkward comments or questions posed by strangers as to why their child did not "look like them."[239] Balcom further explains why Jewish couples figure so prominently in the stories about the adoptions of foreign-born children in the States. First, very few Jewish babies were available for adoption through agencies such as the Free Synagogue Child Adoption Committee in New York City at a time when many would-be Jewish adopters, impacted by the catastrophic Holocaust (which had especially targeted children), wanted to re-establish (coreligious) families.[240] The "law and practice of religious matching" meant that Jewish couples could locate very few children for adoption through "legitimate channels."[241] Therefore, Balcom concludes, "Jewish families desperate

---

236. Hagerty, "Immediate [Press] Release: The White House," 31 May 1956.
237. In 1972, the National Association of Black Social Workers (NABSW) publicly condemned interracial adoption, citing that African American adoptees risked developing a poor racial identity, given that they would grow up deprived of contact with role models of the same race and would fail to cultivate a sense of racial and cultural pride. The NABSW's strongly worded statement had a great impact. During the following years, the number of the placements of African American children in white homes plummeted. Carp (2002: 15–16) and Herman (2008: 248–52). Peña (2014) offers a guide to the most pertinent bibliography.
238. One retired US-based specialist in Greek roots searches claimed that, of all the requests for assistance that he had received over the course of some two decades, about 70 percent had come from Greek-born adoptees who had been placed with Jewish parents (telephone communication of 23 December 2015). I have, unfortunately, no good way to verify this high number.
239. Ellen, testimony of 4 February 2016.
240. Balcom (2011: 171); also Herman (2008: 127).
241. Balcom (2011: 171).

for children were turning, disproportionately, to domestic and transnational black markets."[242] Reflecting on the stream of babies taken from Catholic mothers in Quebec by callous baby traders and offered to Jewish couples, Balcom clarifies that, if Jewish parents wanted to "'legally' claim their children, they had to sever the religious tie between birth mother and child and re-create the Catholic waif as Jewish."[243] In practice, lawyers helped the Jewish couples find "rabbis who would register children presented to them as Jewish or even as 'born to' the adopting parents, thus obviating the need for an adoption and denying the very existence of the birthing mother."[244]

This practice of creating a different religious identity was extended to infants born to Greek Orthodox mothers. The case of Dionysios Dionou may illustrate this point. Dionou was raised Jewish but he reclaimed his Greek heritage as well as his Greek first name (or his actual baptismal name), and also a Greek-sounding last name of his own design. He was one of many Greek-born infants placed via proxy adoptions by Maurice A. Issachar and his sister, Rebecca Issachar. In 1957, the Issachars managed to stake out their own, independent share of the flourishing baby commerce.[245] They, too, cultivated institutional connections with the Patras Orphanage as well as personal contacts with maternity clinics and birth mothers. Maurice had worked as a legal advisor to the ISS,[246] and he had gained firsthand experience of the huge American and, in particular, New York Jewish demand for Greek babies. He handled the legal and administrative requirements for adoption from his home base in Athens. Rebecca, who was a secretary by profession and living in New York, occasionally traveled as a chaperone to the infants on their transatlantic flights.[247] The many Greek adoptions handled by the Issachars flouted even the minimum standards of social service work. In this and other respects, they resembled the Greek adoptions enacted by the Scopas-Cohen partnership, with which the Issachars competed for the eager clientele of the greater New York City area. This lack of due diligence and subsequent accountability was particularly nefarious given that 81 percent of the adoptions of Greek orphans that were processed after 9 September 1959 pertained to "half-orphans":[248] many of the "Issachar babies" had one remaining parent living whom they never got to know.

---

242. Balcom (2011: 171).
243. Balcom (2011: 171–72).
244. Balcom (2011: 172).
245. Anon. [Mitler], survey pp. 9–10; Mitler, *Atlantis*, 15 November 1959.
246. Athinogenis and Papathanasiou (1959: 47).
247. Theodoropoulou (2006: 69, 91, 114–15). See also below, pp. 155–60 ("Home Sweet Home").
248. The statistics are based on Krichefsky (1961: 45).

Mitler's May 1959 survey concludes by recommending, in the strongest possible terms, that the proxy adoption system, "which has led to the mail-order international baby-selling business," be abolished.[249] The survey further insists that certified social services and other qualified agencies must be given a more decisive role in the adoption process and especially in home studies and other procedures consistent with proper child welfare standards.[250] By August 1959, Lamberson had invoked the ire of nearly all prominent Ahepans, who suspected him of embezzlement in addition to baby trafficking. He had also been adding insult to injury: after the delegates of the Ahepa's New York convention had terminated the work of his ARRC in mid-August of 1956, Lamberson had gone on to present himself as the national chairman of a fake AHAPA (the acronym was occasionally spelled out as "American Hellenic Adoptive Parents Association"), thus exploiting the general trust placed in the only true association of the Ahepa.[251] Leber's official history of the Ahepa does not state the true reasons behind the order's decision to dissolve its ARRC in August of 1956, invoking instead the anticipated expiration date of the 1953 Refugee Relief Act in December of 1956.[252]

The Plot Thickens

> Χρόνια με χτυπάτε χρόνια στέκομαι
> Χρόνια με πουλάτε και τ' ανέχομαι
> Χρόνια ο σκοπός σας ν' αφανιστώ
> Έλληνας χαμένος πρόγραμμα βατό
> For years you beat me, for years I kept standing
> For years you sold me out, and I put up with it
> For years your goal was to make me disappear
> A lost Greek, a manageable plan
>
> —Singer Notis Sfakianakis, "Μα εγώ είμαι Έλληνας," "But I Am Greek," 2014; lyrics: Kostas Chorliafakis

Constantine P. Verinis, Ahepa supreme president of 1957–1959, followed the post-1956 developments closely but did little consulting with lower-ranking members. He reappointed Tsaparis, the insider lawyer and close collaborator of Lamberson, to the position of Athens-based director of the Ahepa Orphans Program as late as 17 October 1957. Shortly before, the 11 Sep-

---

249. Anon. [Mitler], survey p. 14; also Mitler, *Atlantis*, 1 November 1959.
250. Anon. [Mitler], survey pp. 14–15; also Mitler, *Atlantis*, 1, 22, and 29 November and 6 December 1959.
251. Mitler, *Atlantis*, 1 and 15 November 1959.
252. Leber (1972: 408–9).

tember 1957 successor Act to the 1953 RRA had made new orphan visas available, and the demand for Greek children kept growing steadily. Verinis refrained from referring to the post-1956 program as the Ahepa Refugee Relief Committee, but the September 1957 through spring 1959 version of the Orphans Program duplicated much of the old ARRC, without any level of transparency that the old program might still have maintained: Tsaparis took charge of finding adoptable children in Greece, and he cleared the administrative hurdles there. From his office in Indiana, Lamberson kept calling and even advertising for adoptive parents across the United States. He offered his private services as an attorney but also his Ahepa connections (signing off on documents as "P.S.P.," past supreme president of the Ahepa). Together Tsaparis and Lamberson secured power of attorney and adoption authorization and thus continued the system of proxy and predeparture adoptions. As a private lawyer representing American couples in such proxy cases, Lamberson could charge any legal and service fees he wanted; also, he could not be held accountable for these privately arranged fees by the Ahepa leadership.[253]

Supreme President Verinis duly signed the October 1957 reappointment letter addressed to Tsaparis and copied only to Lamberson. He starts by thanking them both for their assistance in the adoption of "little Peter," who has been a real source of "joy and happiness in our home for the past 15 months."[254] Verinis goes on to acknowledge the endorsement that "Archbishop Michael [of the Greek Orthodox Archdiocese of North and South America]" has lent to the Orphans Program.[255] The most startling part of the

---

253. Douris (1958: 2). Privately arranged adoptions are legal and very common in Greece to this day, despite the objections that social workers and certified adoption agencies have been raising. Prospective parents then do not avail themselves of social services, but they still hire a lawyer to steer their case through the court. Money cannot legally be part of such private arrangements, but in reality, it often is: monetary transactions appear under the guise of "gifts" given by the adopters to the birth mother (supposedly), and they raise legitimate concerns about baby trafficking. Nowadays, cases typically concern newborns. See Papadaki (2015: 192–204) and Papadopoulos, *Ta Nea*, 11 November 1984. Nanou (2011) concurs that risky and dishonest practices continue to affect domestic Greek adoptions.

254. As an adoptive father, Verinis had a personal stake in continuing the Ahepa's adoption program: in February 1959, he and his wife welcomed a second Greek adoptee, a five-year-old girl from the Patras Orphanage. The Ahepa president's adoptions were publicized, as by Anon., *The Ahepan*, March 1959, 10.

255. Several written statements attest to Archbishop Michael's formal endorsement of the Ahepa's immigrant sponsorship and adoption initiatives. See the encyclicals (formal letters to parishes) and documents compiled and edited by Constantelos (1976: 595–97, 599, 612–13, 616–18, 621–22). From January 1958 on, however, the newly created Welfare Department of the Greek Orthodox Archdiocese of North and South America (founded in 1921) started handling its own adoptions of Greek-born children in collaboration with PIKPA and occa-

appointment letter, however, is the penultimate paragraph, which contravenes the Ahepa convention's decision of mid-August 1956 to liquidate the ARRC: in no unclear terms, Verinis urges Tsaparis to go about gathering eligible orphans proactively, to meet the American demand for further adoptions, including "Proxy Adoptions" (capitalization as in the original letter):

> You are directed to contact various orphanages, Governmental Officials, and interested parties over there [in Greece], who have an available number of qualified orphans, (whether they be in Institutions or in private homes) who qualify under the Law, including medical, proper ages, etc.[256]

---

sionally with Metera. But its procedures were slow-moving and its placement numbers low. When Archbishop Iakovos took over in April 1959, the planning stages of the Church's adoption service were still under discussion (and they were further delayed by the May 1959 Scopas scandal, which spelled the beginning of the end of the Ahepa's adoption venture). On 17 April 1961, Archbishop Iakovos announced that the US government had granted the Archdiocese the formal status of adoption agency and counselor in the cases of Greek-born children, and also that the Church would continue to insist on coreligious placements. He further delegated the issuing of a "certificate of membership in the [Greek Orthodox] community" and of proof of a basic home study to an Adoption Committee comprised of select members of the philanthropic Greek Orthodox Ladies Philoptochos Society ("philoptochos" means "love for the poor"). The society was founded in 1902 but re-established in 1931 on a national basis with direct links to the Archdiocese. See further several encyclicals and documents edited by Constantelos (1976: 627–28, 633–34, 1018–19, 1024–26, 1030–31, 1037); Coumantaros (1984: 273); and Soumakis (2015: 46–47, 81–82, 123–24, 125). Until the time of this book's publication, I have been unable to consult the archives of the Greek Orthodox Archdiocese of North and South America, whose Department of Archives suffered water damage in 2016 (archivist Nikie Calles, telephone and email communications, January–March 2017).

The Archdiocese holds also the archives related to the founding (in 1944) and operation of the Saint Basil Academy (also: Saint Basil's Academy) in Garrison, New York, which was conceived as a home and elementary school for Greek Orthodox orphans and destitute children and also as a teacher-training school for Greek American women, to fulfill the needs of the Archdiocese's Greek language and broader educational and parish service programs (Soumakis 2015: 5–6, 18–19, 46–47, 57, 81–82, 122–58, 167–68, 178–79). The Ahepa engaged in aggressive fund-raising over many years on behalf of this philanthropic and educational institution, which it briefly considered as a possible reception center for needy adoptees (boys and girls) arriving from Greece. The Ahepa Hall for Boys was inaugurated at St. Basil's on 14 June 1959, a mere six weeks after the outbreak of the Scopas scandal. See Anon., *The Ahepan*, June–July 1959; various encyclicals and documents edited by Constantelos (1976: 623, 625–26, 637, 1020–21, 1022–23, 1024); and Prodromidis, who referred to the "Acropolis on the Hudson," in *The Ahepan*, January 1959.

256. Verinis, appointment letter to Tsaparis, 17 October 1957, referring to Public Law 85–316 of 11 September 1957. The original letter, written in English and typed on Ahepa letterhead, is held in the *Atlantis*, National Daily Greek Newspaper Records, MSS 43, box 31, folder 4, "Scopas #2," Historical Society of Pennsylvania (HSP), Philadelphia.

Lamberson did not lag behind in his own efforts to solicit children for adoption on the ground in Greece. In 1958, he visited the Municipal Orphanage of Irakleio, Crete, and he reportedly brought "attractive proposals" to the table in exchange for "all the babies available for adoption."[257] The orphanage board was duly impressed: it agreed to consider Lamberson's proposals and to follow up with Tsaparis. Tsaparis promptly forwarded the applications for ten children submitted by hopeful American parents. But the Metropolitan of Crete, who also served as president of the orphanage's board, raised objections because the prospective adopters were not Orthodox and not of Greek descent. Tsaparis then quickly proceeded with ten new applications, this time forwarded by Greek Americans and presumably Orthodox Christians. The ten adoptions were approved but had yet to pass through the local court. Then the "Scopas scandal" of May 1959 broke, which prevented them from happening.[258]

From mid-August 1956 through the spring of 1959, the Ahepa top leadership kept up a semiofficial form of the Orphans Program, by reappointing Tsaparis while simultaneously appointing committee after committee to investigate the abuses of the old program. A first internal investigating committee, appointed by the 1957 Ahepa convention and chaired by New York newsman George Douris, began its work in late August 1957. One year later, at the Ahepa's Boston convention of mid-August 1958, this committee publicly condemned Lamberson's shady practices. The committee members especially decried Lamberson's unabashed soliciting of further applications from hopeful American parents as the self-made chair of the bogus AHAPA, the American Hellenic Adoptive Parents Association.[259] Also, the investigating committee sharply criticized Lamberson's stubborn lack of cooperation and his unwillingness to hand over the records and accounting books from before and after August 1956.[260] Another bone of contention was Lamberson's indiscriminate placing of Greek Orthodox children with couples of a different faith. Douris alluded to Jewish recipients of Greek adoptees,

---

257. Anon., *To Vima*, 9 May 1959.

258. See below, pp. 140–42. Anon., "The Plan to Send 10 Babies for Adoption from the Municipal Orphanage of Irakleio, Crete, to the United States Has Been Canceled," *To Vima*, 9 May 1959 (in Greek).

259. Douris (1958: 2–3; 1959: 4, 6). See also Mitler, *Atlantis*, 1 and 15 November 1959. Douris's first report (five-page typescript) is held in the *Atlantis*, National Daily Greek Newspaper Records, MSS 43, box 31, folder 4, "Scopas #2," HSP, Philadelphia. Leber's summaries of the 1958 and 1959 convention proceedings fail to mention either the 1958 formal report or Douris's follow-up report of 1959 (Leber 1972: 414–21). The verbatim convention proceedings, however, which were not intended for wide circulation but were kept at the Ahepa headquarters, do reflect Douris's delivery of his reports of 1958 and 1959.

260. Douris (1958; 1959: 2–4, 6, 7, 8–9); also Critzas (1957: 101–4, 108, 112–13).

whom Lamberson had favored over desperate Greek American couples.[261] According to Douris, the Greek government did not sanction the repeated placements of Greek Orthodox children with families that were not coreligious; such placements had left Archbishop Michael "HORRIFIED."[262]

Even against the backdrop of the Ahepa's ideal of acculturation, the Greek and the Greek American condemnation of child placements that were not coreligious was as persistent as it was outspoken. A few chronologically organized examples from the 1950s through mid-1960s will illustrate my point. First, in a confidential letter of 16 November 1950 addressed to the Greek Ministry of Foreign Affairs, Ambassador Athanasios G. Politis noted the opportunities provided by the 1948 Displaced Persons Act (as amended) and also by the Ahepa's willingness to help clear the path of immigration for Greek refugees and orphans. Politis urged his colleagues to weigh principle against need in the case of orphans, but professed that

> Catholic organizations [here] in America have asked to act as mediators, to facilitate the immigration of orphaned Greek children and their settling in the United States. Of course, we cannot object on principle and decline such a service.

> However, we should take timely steps to demand a Greek authority's pre-approval in each case of "protecting" an orphan, so that we can quietly steer clear of the proselytism that the Catholics have been pursuing.[263]

Second, in May of 1959, the Holy Synod of the Greek Orthodox Church sternly warned against adopting out to non-Orthodox foreign families, and it appealed to its congregations to help turn the tide.[264] PIKPA took the same line but allowed for exceptions.[265] By 1965, however, *Ekklisia*, the official bulletin of the Greek Orthodox Church, concluded that "the infants sold were an irrevocable loss not only for Greece but also for Orthodoxy."[266]

---

261. Douris (1958: 4–5).

262. Douris (1958: 4; capitalization his).

263. Politis, letter of 16 November 1950, p. 3. Politis's three-page letter in Greek is held in the unclassified Archive of the Ministry of Health (and Social Welfare), box 5, GAK, Athens.

264. Anon., *Makedonia*, 10 May 1959.

265. Athinogenis and Papathanasiou (1959: 13, 15, 50, *passim*) and Tsitidis (1964: 11–12).

266. Anon., *Ekklisia*, 15 February 1965, 124: "Τὰ πωλούμενα βρέφη ἀπόλλυνται ἀνεπιστρεπτὶ τόσον διὰ τὴν Ἑλλάδα, ὅσον καὶ διὰ τὴν Ὀρθοδοξίαν." See Anon., *I Avgi*, 9 May 1959; Anon., *I Avgi*, 10 May 1959; Constantelos (1976: 1018–19, Archbishop Iakovos, 1 July 1959); and Politakou (1958: 315–16).

The damning internal report of Lamberson's abuses fell on deaf ears, even though Douris presented it before the hundreds of delegates of the Ahepa's 1958 Boston convention. Also, it reported problems dating back to 1955, that is, to the first months of Lamberson's involvement in the Ahepa's Orphans Program. Flouting the Ahepa's rules against profiting from the order's name, Lamberson retorted, "I don't know what's wrong with having an American Hellenic Adopted [*sic*] Parents Association."[267] An experienced lawyer, he pulled out all the rhetorical stops, referring to the "Ahepa Family," to his faith and model citizenship, and also to the first Greek orphan boys who were adopted by American Philhellenes during the Greek War of Independence (1820s) and who went on to distinguish themselves in their new homeland.[268] Lamberson further conjured up images of hungry and malnourished Greek children, who "have now come over to a paradise in America; they had nothing like it in Greece."[269] But, to clinch his appeal, he invoked his role of placeholder-father during the children's transfers from Greece: "we have changed their diapers, if necessary."[270]

Ironically, it was left to the *New York Times* to break the story and put the spotlight on Stephen Scopas, long-time collaborator of Lamberson, partner of Cohen, and rival of the Issachars. Jack Roth published his front-page article, "Scopas Arrested in Sale of Babies," in the *New York Times* of 5 May 1959, within days of the conclusion of the Grand Jury investigation into Scopas's practices. According to Roth, the New York State prosecutor charged that the Scopas ring had been offering Greek babies for sale on the "installment plan"—the ultimate act of commodifying children. The formal charges stated that Scopas had been placing Greek infants with New York couples for some two years, and that he had been receiving compensation for these allegedly unauthorized placements. The initial charges also noted "conspiracy" with Lamberson, Cohen, and Tsaparis, who were named as accomplices. The nationwide attention fell on Scopas, however, not because he was past supreme president of the Ahepa but because he was a prominent New York City judge. As an official magistrate, Scopas should have acted with integrity and should have discontinued his services as a private lawyer in Greek adoption cases. Scopas was soon released; his case did not go to trial. He petitioned for the charges to be dismissed one year later, by June 1960, upon which the New York State prosecutor took the case into appeal on principles of law. In March 1962, however, the Appeals Court upheld the earlier dismissal of the charges.

---

267. Lamberson (1958: 978).
268. Lamberson (1958: 982). See Soumakis (2015: 22).
269. Lamberson (1958: 984).
270. Lamberson (1958: 982).

Back in early May of 1959, a guilty verdict for Scopas looked imminent. Roth's *New York Times* article was the first to widely disseminate news about the scandal in the United States.[271] Within Ahepa circles, however, the abuses had been known—but not acted on—for at least a couple of years. Therefore, the "ahepagram" that "shocked" Supreme President Verinis sent out to the order's members precisely on 5 May 1959 did and does very little to alleviate the impression that the Ahepa leadership was more preoccupied with doing damage control than with eradicating the problem from within:

> I am shocked at the recent indictments in New York City stating that high legal fees were charged in connection with the adoption of Greek orphan children, and their being placed in non-Greek Orthodox homes.

> I am looking into the facts alleged by the Grand Jury as publicized in the press.[272]

At a five-hour-long emergency meeting of the Ahepa's Supreme Lodge, chaired by Verinis on 16 May 1959, the charges against Scopas were read out verbatim. They comprise alleged violations of the state laws of New York, where Scopas was based, but their ramifications crossed state lines:

> This was a crime of conspiracy, and the defendants were charged with receiving compensation in violation of Section 487A of the statutes of New York, and with the placement of children for adoption in violation of state

---

271. See also the anonymous article entitled "The Market in Orphans," in *Newsweek* of 25 May 1959, and, significantly, a preliminary, anonymous news report in the *New York Times* of 28 February 1959, entitled "Orphan Inquiry on: Magistrate [Scopas] May Face Queries on Greek War Children." Stories of "adoption tourism," however, such as "The Lad and I Came Through," by American adoptive father Philip Clarke (*Saturday Evening Post*, 3 May 1958), should have sent up red flags much sooner. With verve, Clarke recounts how his wife demanded that he not return from a two-week professional trip to Greece without bringing back a Greek baby (1958: 33, 72)! His (smartly illustrated) article advertises itself as follows (1958: 32):

> Here's a true story with everything: international "smuggling" of a beautiful baby, suspense, mother love and a fantastic battle with bureaucrats. No other husband ever had an adventure quite like this.

Clarke's adventure was reenacted by the Armstrong Circle Theatre for a television show called "And Bring Home a Baby!," which was widely advertised in newspapers of early January 1959.

272. Verinis, ahepagram of 5 May 1959. An "ahepagram" is a brief, telegram-style letter sent out by the Ahepa leadership to the officers of the order's many chapters, to be further distributed or otherwise disseminated among the chapters' regular members.

laws. This also included the charge that the defendants acted in adoption cases without being a recognized agency of the state of New York.[273]

The more than thirty participants in the lodge's emergency meeting then decided to issue a public statement declaring that the Order of Ahepa was "in NO way, directly or indirectly, involved in the recent unfortunate developments concerning certain of [its] members."[274] However, as Ahepan Victor Chebithes, a prominent attorney and past supreme president, admitted in the summer of 1959, a few months after the scandal of Scopas's baby business had been unleashed,

> [The Ahepa] is involved because the Ahepa used its influence to pave the way for these people [Scopas and Lamberson] to exploit the public. It was the Ahepa who acted [to facilitate proxy adoption in Greece and to lobby for more generous allotments of orphan visas on the US side] . . . to provide for their [the Greeks'] children to come here.[275]

News of the Scopas scandal traveled back to Greece and spread there like wildfire.[276] Critical Greek voices had been raised since 1955, but they had been ignored for being "journalistic" or anti-American, decrying the haphazard adoptions along with many other US "interferences."[277] A three-month-long investigation, conducted by inspectors Athinogenis and Papathanasiou of the Greek Ministry of Social Welfare, had generated the uneven, fifty-eight-page report of 10 April 1959, to which I have already referred at several points. Instead of examining the media reports about a Greek baby trade, however,

---

273. Doukas, Minutes, 16 May 1959, 2.

274. Doukas, Minutes, 16 May 1959, 4; capitalization his.

275. Chebithes (1959: 482).

276. The following list offers a mere sampling of related Greek newspaper articles, most of which, notably, made the front page: Anon., *To Vima*, 5 May 1959, 1; with follow-up, for instance, by Zotos, *To Vima*, 6 May 1959, 1; Anon., *I Kathimerini*, 5 May 1959, 1; Voultepsis, *I Avgi*, 6 May 1959, 1, 5; Anon., *I Avgi*, 7 May 1959, 1, 6; Anon., *I Avgi*, 8 May 1959, 5; Anon., *I Avgi*, 9 May 1959, 5; Anon., *I Avgi*, 10 May 1959, 1, 5; Nikolopoulos, *I Avgi*, 13 May 1959, 1, 5; Anon., *I Avgi*, 27 May 1959.

277. See Grigoris, *I Avgi*, 13 May 1955; Anon., *I Avgi*, 19 October 1955; and Anon., *I Avgi*, 23 and 24 June 1956. The well-known journalist and author Freddy Germanos published a three-part series on the alleged Greek baby trade in *Eleftheria* (18, 20, and 21 January 1959). His articles show the influence of Mitler's reporting but overstate the case. Mitler's research outcomes converged with the results of a survey conducted by Laurin and Virginia P. Hyde (for the Child Welfare League of America in collaboration with the ISS), which focused almost exclusively on Korean and Japanese adoptees (June 1958) (Choy 2013: 93–94). By the time their conclusions had trickled through in Germanos's reporting, however, the strict national distinctions had fallen by the wayside, to the detriment of a more accurate or balanced picture of the Greek-to-American adoptions.

the coauthors at every turn highlighted the advantages of PIKPA's (coreligious) placements, the shortcomings of the procedures enacted by the ISS, and the exaggerated numbers of exported Greek children that the press had recently been citing. The inspectors did denounce the "open-door policy" of the municipal orphanages that had been collaborating with "private intermediaries" and the "preferential treatment," especially, that they had bestowed on some of these agents.[278] The inspectors' scrutiny, however, did not reach far beyond greater Athens, and missed Thessaloniki and Patras altogether. They underestimated the size and reach of the adoption networks of the Ahepa and of the Issachars, but also the degree of autonomy of the boards of orphanages located in city centers in the provinces. Some four weeks after Athinogenis and Papathanasiou filed their report downplaying the numbers and the media's suspicions, the Scopas scandal erupted, which hurled the Ahepa and the Patras Orphanage back into the spotlight.

In May 1959, Andreas Stratos, the Greek minister of social welfare, called for a new investigation. By the end of May, Stratos announced that the outcomes of this investigation would not be made public, given its "confidential content," and besides "it was not of any interest to the public."[279] Stratos explained the motivation of his decision by again downplaying the number of overseas-bound adoptees until that date: "only some 400 to 500 children had become objects of trade, but even of those only a small percentage must have come out unlucky."[280] Most likely, the left-wing reporting on this issue was colored by its stance of opposition to the conservative Karamanlis administration, but it still fruitfully raised the all-too-common legitimation of calling adults' poor placements a matter of adoptees' bad luck. By the end of June 1959, Stratos's investigation revealed that "Greek laws on adoption ha[d] been observed faithfully"; it disclosed "no violation of existing legislation in Greece" and "no charges were made against anyone in connection with a similar investigation made in the United States," as per an article in the *Chicago Daily Tribune* of 1 July 1959.[281] A set of

---

278. Athinogenis and Papathanasiou (1959: 55).
279. "Δὲν ἐνδιαφέρει τὸ κοινόν!," at least as reported by Anon., *I Avgi*, 27 May 1959.
280. "Μικρὸ ποσοστὸ πρέπει νὰ ἀτύχησε," again as per Anon., *I Avgi*, 27 May 1959.
281. Anon., "Greeks Probe Procedures of Adoption: 'Hear Black Market Reports from U.S.,'" *Chicago Daily Tribune*, 1 July 1959, based on Reuters news reporting of 30 June 1959. See also Anon., *I Avgi*, 9 May 1959; Kairofylas (1993: 250); and Theodoropoulou (2006: 87). In December of 1962, Minister Stratos resigned in protest over the government's prolonged unwillingness to allocate adequate resources to matters of public health and social welfare (Sakkas 2010: 389–90). Lamberson promptly mailed a copy of the 1959 *Chicago Daily Tribune* article to Solon G. Vlasto(s), then the director of the Greek American paper *Atlantis*, which a few months later published Mitler's extensive report (in installments from 1 November through 6 December 1959; see above, p. 119). Aware of the fast unfolding revelations, the publishers of the *Atlantis* did not heed Lamberson's telling note of "cleared,"

dust-gathering Greek reports had now been added to the ineffectual Greek American reports.

On 2 June 1959, Supreme President Verinis suddenly charged another special committee with investigating the Ahepa's adoption history "independently" (from Douris's committee). The second Greek American investigative report was due by the time of the association's Hollywood convention of mid-August 1959.[282] Suspicions that some of the order's top leaders continued to profit from the adoptee placements were hard to quell. Resentment built up in the rank and file against Verinis and Lamberson in particular. After the Ahepa leadership had ignored (and even stymied) his first report of 1958, Douris presented his own second, now-caustic report to the Ahepa's 1959 convention. This eleven-page report speaks to infighting among the order's leadership as well as to the wrath of its members: many Ahepans are furious not only about Lamberson's abuses but about the cover-up, which by then appears to have lasted some three to four years.[283]

In June of 1959, with New York State criminal investigations underway, Lamberson didn't so much turn against his detractors from within the Ahepa circles, but he tried, rather, to divert attention to the ISS. He insinuated that the ISS was entangled in a sordid conspiracy that had penetrated and undermined the "Ahepa Family," and he alleged that the agency wanted to thwart Ahepa adoptions from Greece. In this vein, Lamberson prepared a defensive letter addressed to US congressmen: if he had previously tolerated the ISS as a slow competitor for "his" Orphans Program, he now declared outright war against the agency and accused it of having instigated a slander campaign against him:

> The I.S.S. et al. want a VIRTUAL MONOPOLY ON ALL ORPHANS OUT-SIDE U.S.A. Their propaganda is loaded with CONNIVERY, DECEIT, & UNMITIGATED FALSEHOODS ABOUT BLACK MARKET & MAIL ORDER ADOPTIONS, (guilt by Ass[ociatio]n.) PERPETRATED & DESIGNED TO KILL PROXY ADOPTIONS, under P[ublic] L[aw] 85–316.[284]

---

which he wrote in his characteristic handwriting underneath the article. The *Atlantis*, National Daily Greek Newspaper Records (MSS 43, box 31, folder 4, "Scopas #2"), held in the archives of the HSP, Philadelphia, contain an adequate number of notes in Lamberson's handwriting to allow me to conclude with certainty that the note proclaiming himself "cleared" is his.

282. Verinis, ahepagram of 2 June 1959.

283. This untitled report is held in the *Atlantis*, National Daily Greek Newspaper Records, MSS 43, box 31, folder 5, "Scopas #3," HSP, Philadelphia.

284. Lamberson, "My Dear Congressman: [blank]" (capitalization his). An original of Lamber-

By late 1959, Lamberson had become persona non grata in Ahepa circles, but he still saw through a few adoption cases on behalf of close relatives (through 1963). The Ahepa suspended his membership for five years. Already in August of 1961, however, the then Supreme Lodge reduced that suspension to just one year (and declared its term completed based on time elapsed).[285] Nonetheless, the scandal of alleged child trafficking shook the Ahepa to the core.[286] Accepting the truth was hard, even though the Ahepa could and can confidently claim that, once made aware of the problems and their cover-up, it finally took action to eradicate them. "Did I hear her accuse the Ahepa of baby trafficking?," asked a startled Ahepa member after I gave a first presentation on this topic at a mid-October 2016 conference in Tarpon Springs, Florida. "No," the Greek consul general in attendance replied, "You heard her talk about a few bad apples, and then you heard her emphasize that the association itself addressed the problems."

Immaculate Deception: Pretty Pictures and Orphan Planes

"Two Years in U.S., Greek Orphan Likes School, Crooners, Friends, Singing—and New Family."

—Headline from *ISS World News*, June 1958, p. 2

Leber's official history of the Ahepa kept the dirty laundry inside. He did reproduce, however, three "appealing" photographs of wide-eyed Greek orphans and beaming Ahepans, conjuring up the better days of the association's Orphans Program, which had lasted through mid-August of 1956.[287] Such photographs, numerous others like them, and endless "great-progress" stories have created the "happy end" illusion with which US-bound adoption has inscribed itself in America's collective memory. But happy ends to the long journey were no guarantee of happy "beginnings" to life in the States, especially in cases in which the adoptees' prior history was ignored.

Leber's first photograph (figure 4) is set against the backdrop of the Swissair plane on which five youngsters and two female caregivers are about to travel from Athens to New York. The editors of *The Ahepan*, who first printed this picture in mid-1956, identified the male character as Michael

---

son's letter to US congressmen is held in the *Atlantis*, National Daily Greek Newspaper Records, MSS 43, box 31, folder 4, "Scopas #2," HSP, Philadelphia.

285. Chirekos, Minutes, 16 August 1961.

286. See, for instance, Anon., *The Ahepan*, May–July 1957, VII, XIII–XIV, XXII–XXIII; and Manta, Feb.–April 1957, 9.

287. Leber (1972: 403).

Tsaparis, the Greek attorney managing the Athens office of the Ahepa Refugee Relief Committee. They also called this transport the first group of Greek orphans arriving under the Ahepa Refugee Relief Program.[288] Through mid-August of 1956, Lamberson, Tsaparis, Scopas, and also Verinis were basking in the nationwide attention that their "airlifts" were receiving, competing with those of Korean orphans arranged by the Holts. Allow me to call these transports the Ahepa's "orphan planes." With this coinage, I pun on "orphan trains," or the vehicles of the mass migration of urban poor children (not necessarily orphans) to rural areas of the American Midwest and West, which took place from the mid-nineteenth century through the 1920s.[289] The second photograph (figure 5) shows beaming Ahepans towering over eleven Greek orphans of the 12 July 1956 transatlantic arrival, which was met by Lamberson in person. They are the same children whose arrival was documented by the *New York Times* in an impressive photo op published on the following day.

But the pictures belie a deeper reality. The letter below, written by Susan Pettiss of the ISS-USA, expresses concern about a particular proxy and predeparture adoption. Accompanying the letter is a photograph of a Greek "bundle of joy" and its new mother (who left only a last name and an address), seated underneath a sign advertising TWA, Trans World Airlines:

On January 15, 1957, the last group of children processed by the International Social Service under the Refugee Relief Act [of 1953, which expired 31 December 1956] came to New York by plane from Greece. All the children on this flight were for approved families for whom we [the ISS] had suggested the child, except one. The one was a proxy adoption carried out by an adoptive mother from Texas. She was most demanding and irritated that our consultants were not giving her attention and special help. She insisted that she did not have to follow procedure (i.e., immigration) that the other parents did because she had already adopted her child! The consultants who talked with her said she appeared to be drunk, and she appeared to be over 50 years of age. She made the comment at one point that she must be rushed through because she had another baby at home. She also commented that she wished she had adopted all of the babies. Although we realize this child has already been legally adopted, we think that this child may be in need of

---

288. The Editors, *The Ahepan*, July–August 56, 5.

289. This supervised welfare program removed tens of thousands of children from crowded East Coast cities and thus laid the foundations of organized foster care in the United States. Carp (2014b) supplies a recent bibliographical guide to this movement and to the history of orphans and orphanages in the States.

1956—Greek orphans brought from Greece to the United States for adoption under the Ahepa Refugee Relief Program.

Fig 4: Five Greek orphans and their two female caregivers as they are about to start the journey by plane from Athens to New York. Credit: Leber (1972: 403).

Fig 5: Beaming Ahepans tower over eleven wide-eyed Greek adoptees. These children and one more orphan arrived on 12 July 1956 after a transatlantic plane trip. Credit: Leber (1972: 403).

protection. In fact, it was the feeling of the consultants that this woman was not the type to keep the baby herself and that she may have in mind to give it to someone else.[290]

290. Susan T. Pettiss to Rosalind Giles, letter of 8 February 1957. The letter is held in the archives of the ISS, American Branch Papers, box 10, folder 3: "Adoption 1955–1958," SWHA, University of Minnesota Libraries. Rosalind Giles served as director of the Child Welfare Divi-

Fig 6: A TWA flight attendant takes special care of a young Greek orphan girl. Another three Greek youngsters pose on their arrival in New York in June 1956. All children were adopted through the Ahepa Refugee Relief Committee. Credit: *Skyliner, Trans World Airlines Weekly Employee Publication*, 23 August 1956, 4.

TWA itself saw an opportunity to advertise its flights and services, as in the picture above of a doting air hostess (as a flight attendant was then called) and four Greek orphans (figure 6). The photograph is taken from the

---

sion of the state of Texas, and she followed up on this and other problematic placements for at least three and a half years. On 6 February 2017, I spoke to the very woman whose fate as a baby had been at stake. She confirmed that the clear-eyed assessment of Pettiss was "spot on," and that her adoptive mother spent a lifetime struggling with alcoholism, to the detriment of her two adopted children. The grown adoptee later volunteered:

> I have a memory of my mom and I walking through the supermarket and I was holding her up because she was drunk. I was embarrassed because people in the store were looking at us. I wonder now why no one called the police when they saw this. . . . I was about six years old
> (source kept confidential, testimony of 30 July 2017).

It brought great relief to my interviewee to learn that some people had noticed and cared. She understands that, in 1950s Texas, a very drastic intervention would have been required to remove a foreign adopted child, left without any other familiar environment, from a well-to-do couple of professionals. Also, the family strategically moved to get away from concerned social services and relatives.

Fig 7: TWA secretary Cleo Lefouses volunteered to bring over two Greek adoptees in either fall or winter of 1957–1958. Credit: *Skyliner, Trans World Airlines Weekly Employee Publication*, 3 April 1958, 5.

"TWA Photo Parade" in the airline's *Skyliner* magazine of 23 August 1956, and it documents a June 1956 transatlantic arrival via Paris, followed by a domestic connection, all organized by the Ahepa Refugee Relief Committee. As the *Skyliner* magazine was proud to announce, Cleo Lefouses, devoted TWA secretary (and member of the Ahepa-affiliated Daughters of Penelope), volunteered her time to fly from New York to Athens and back to fetch two little Greek orphans either in the fall or the winter of 1957–1958 (figure 7).

The ISS used charter flights with Flying Tiger Line (aka Flying Tigers) to transport people from Athens to New York (with layovers en route). Most planes landed at Idlewild Airport the day after leaving, but some flights took two days and three or four stops. Each flight held some seventy people, but only a handful of them were ISS-sponsored children for adoption. Among the documented arrivals are the larger ones of 5 October 1955 and of 22 April, 30 August, and 22 October 1956, each bringing over about ten to twelve children for adoption. Books devoted to the legendary Flying Tiger Line, which advertised flying "anything, anytime, anywhere," speak of the company outfitting cargo planes for chartered passenger transports to address the mid-1950s need for cheap charter flights. Regrettably, they fail to mention the ISS's orphan planes from Greece.[291]

---

291. See, for instance, Cameron (1964: 191, 251–52) and Chin (1993: 54, 267–68). See also Hudson, *New York Times*, 3 June 1956.

The pictures of "jet-setting" Greek orphans not only familiarized but also romanticized and glamorized Greek children in the eyes of the American public. Add to this the mid- to late-1950s images of Marlon Brando holding a Greek orphan up close, set against the backdrop of the Acropolis. Or Danny Kaye walking down from the Parthenon with eight Greek orphan girls in white aprons in tow, on a visit sponsored by the United Service Organizations (USO). The young descendants of an ancient culture that kept inspiring the West had a long and rich history, but like their aprons, they came supposedly untainted by recent events. The intense celebrity attention made the cause of "saving" quintessentially innocent Greek orphans widely known, and it also rendered its one-way direction acceptable, even admirable. Viviana Zelizer speaks of the "sentimentalization of adoption," which turned infant adoption into "the latest American fad."[292] The majority of American adoptive homes sought little girls for their "domestic sentimental value."[293]

So influential was the flood of media images of Greek children arriving, little boys being embraced, and little girls being kissed and handed dolls, that one well-meaning American mother kept referring to the time of her new daughter's arrival as her own "*Life* magazine moment."[294] Airlines and other companies saw opportunities for "product placement." Agents or politicians who had helped to facilitate the adoptions had their names acknowledged in the papers. But nothing was deemed as compelling as the studied combination of an orphan girl, a glamorous actress, and all-American comfort food (preferably ice cream):

"WAR ORPHAN FROM GREECE"

12-year-old [girl's name], whose foster parent is actress Tallulah Bankhead, flashes a made-in-America smile as she eats her favorite food in a NY Chinatown restaurant. She landed in the US 4 months ago from her native Greece, an almost blind and half-starved orphan.[295]

---

292. Zelizer (1985: 192).
293. Zelizer (1985: 193).
294. Heckinger (2019: 57).
295. *Baltimore Sun*, photo caption, no date (ca. 1950). In late 1948, this girl became the first Greek child to benefit from support extended through the Foster Parents' Plan for War Children (see above, pp. 93–94, and Molumphy 1984: 91). After about a dozen years of worthwhile international operations, the Plan had also honed its fund-raising formula of matching orphans, "disabled children and celebrity sponsors" (Dijsselbloem, Fugle, and Gneiting 2014: 123).

The media glare shone the limelight on the celebrity charity initiatives to benefit Greece. It easily picked up where the publicity surrounding the Truman Doctrine and the implementation of the Marshall Plan had left off. Greece continued to be in a most intense Cold War spotlight.[296] In fact, the Greek need for humanitarian and other aid had been broadcast widely even earlier, during the war years: Skouras had placed his vast business assets in the Hollywood motion picture industry and his many contacts with movie stars and entertainers in the service of fund-raising for his occupied and famine-stricken home country (and subsequently for the Queen's Fund).[297] Americans had—arguably—been gawking at needy Greek orphans since the early 1940s, and these children continued to be called "war orphans" for some ten years after the Civil War, too, had ended.[298] But if celebrities fostered and adopted Greek children, then ordinary Americans, too, would want to invite these children into their homes, even if only figuratively, by accessing the many popular news stories and media images that brought them up close and personal (but did not bring into focus the orphans' backgrounds, let alone recent and traumatic Greek history). Public fanfare animated the Greek orphan project with positive energy, which kicked in at the very moment of the planes' touchdown. The Greek orphan became the "must have" innocent, lovable, and worthy adoptee, who would thrive on the consumer comforts of the (domesticating) American way. The "easy-to-Americanize" Greek children affirmed average (white) fellow citizens in their visions of rescue and rehabilitation. The rights of the child had to yield to the right to the child on international adoption's one-way street.

"WANT TO ADOPT GREEK ORPHAN—STOP"

The desire among Americans to adopt Greek children kept growing steadily: the well-publicized 1956 arrivals by plane, cultivated by the Ahepa, made this adoption movement look successful and trendy—a win-win solution for both adoptees and adopters. A reliable Cold War ally to the United States, Greece delivered smiling, properly dressed youngsters, who stepped off airplanes and into a "fairy-tale" new life, under the approving eyes of queens, princesses, community leaders, flight attendants, and even movie stars. The

---

296. Jeffery (2000: 98, 125).
297. Kyrou (2008: 62) and above, pp. 56, 63.
298. Fehrenbach (2015: 167) has been studying the "'humanitarian eye,'" accounting for the prevalence of images of (unaccompanied) child victims in the official postwar publications of UNESCO and UNICEF and in the printed materials disseminated by NGOs for fundraising purposes. See also Fehrenbach (2016).

supply of Greek children for adoption could hardly keep up with the insatiable American demand:

> La Jolla, California
> *April 4, 1957*
> Honorable Bob Wilson
> House Office Building
> Washington, D.C.
>
> Dear Sir:
>
> It is very important to many of us adoptive parents that the additional Greek quota law allowing orphaned Greek children under ten years of age to be admitted into the United States be passed.
>
> People here, including ourselves, have homes waiting for these children—homes that will otherwise be forever barren of children.
>
> We beseech you to do everything in your power which will help pass this law. We are not Greek but have already adopted one Greek child, who is everything one could want in a child, and are desperately desirous of adopting another one.
>
> Thank you for your assistance.
>
> Sincerely yours,
>
> [signatures]
> Mr. and Mrs. [names][299]

In December 1956 and through the early months of 1957, the Ahepa did everything it could to ensure the passage of a new act that would let the immigration of Greek refugees and orphans resume (as indeed happened in September 1957). The association's efforts reached some of the farthest corners of the continental United States, among them San Diego, California, not known for its extensive Greek or Greek American presence. A good measure of the Ahepa's pervasive activism may be found in the papers of Congressman Robert (Bob) Carlton Wilson, held at San Diego State University. These papers, the source of the quotations above and below, contain

---

299. Quoted from a letter written by a San Diego couple to Congressman Bob Wilson, held in the Robert Carlton Wilson Papers, 1953–1980, box 38, folder 18: "Immigration and Naturalization: Adopted Alien Children, 1957–1958," Special Collections and University Archives, San Diego State University.

about twenty written appeals by local constituents urging their congressman to support 1957 emergency legislation adding another 7,500 Greek refugees to the quota. Most of these written requests were preprinted (mimeographed) cards lobbying for "Greek Veterans, Orphans and Relatives" (see
figure 8). Such postcards were widely disseminated by the Ahepa, and with
special zeal by Lamberson, even after the mid-August 1956 Ahepa convention had abolished his committee.[300] The postcards unmistakably link the
Ahepa campaign to Cold War anticommunism and to the future of adoptable orphans. They also still tie the association's sponsoring of adoptions
to the very person of Lamberson, especially in the perception of the many
trusting people who received their cards or stacks of cards from his private Indiana office, where they were printed.[301] Other residents of Wilson's
congressional district, who crafted letters of their own, directly connected
their appeal to their desire to adopt a Greek child. Not all of the authors
of these requests were Greek or Greek American. Some non-Greeks mentioned a "Mrs Poulos," a San Diego resident of Greek extraction who mediated between the Ahepa, the prospective parents, and Wilson.[302] Figure
8 offers an example of a non-Greek woman who used one of the Ahepa's
postal cards to support her own bid. She crossed out everything on the card
that she deemed non-applicable.

Some requests received at Bob Wilson's office were phrased more
curtly. One telegram of 17 January 1957 reads: "WANT TO ADOPT GREEK
ORPHAN" and "WANT LEGISLATION INCREASING IMIGRATION
[sic] QUOTA STRONG LOCAL INTEREST."[303] In the summer of 1959,
requests to adopt children from Greece were still coming in, and Congressman Wilson duly responded to all letters and cards. The Scopas scandal
had broken in May of 1959, but interest in adopting Greek children did not
diminish. Like the orphan planes, perhaps the scandal pointed to a supply
source that appeared flexible and inexhaustible. The Greek "baby scoop"
promised to fulfill even the kind of self-serving desires to adopt that would

---

300. Lamberson (1956a: 689; 1958: 981).
301. Lamberson (1958: 978–82, 983–84).
302. Maria, email communication of 15 February 2016. According to Lamberson, his committee
    asked American adoptive parents who were not Greek if they knew any Ahepans, who
    could endorse the couple's application sent to his office (1958: 983). Mrs. Poulos was such
    a local and informal sponsor.
303. Quoted from a Western Union telegram sent by a San Diego couple to Congressman Bob
    Wilson, held in the Robert Carlton Wilson Papers, 1953–1980, box 38, folder 18: "Immigra-
    tion and Naturalization: Adopted Alien Children, 1957–1958."

Dear Congressman: _Jan 17_, 1957
Our Hellenic community and Phil-Hellenes of this Area join
the Ahepa appeal, urging you to voice your approval and give
full support to 7,500 additional Greek Refugee quotas (to be
transferred from undersubscribed quotas) for ~~Greek Veterans~~,
Orphans and ~~Relatives~~. Since Greek quotas were exhausted
last summer, it is most urgent to give support to this (or
similar legislation) and to petition to get out of committee
for favorable vote by Congress as emergency legislation.
Such action will reaffirm to Heroic Greece, America's friendship and appreciation for the Hellenic stand in the cold war
against Communism. ~~The attention of Hellenism and the~~ eyes
~~of Eastern Orthodoxy are focused upon your action on this~~
~~important legis~~lation.   Sincerely yours,

SIGNED _Mrs. D. M. Hickethie (non Greek) Street_ /5735 Florida

Business _Housewife sent form_ City _San Diego_
                          1-24-57

Fig 8: A preprinted postal card, issued and distributed by the Ahepa (Lamberson). This
card was sent to Congressman Robert (Bob) Carlton Wilson by a woman who identified herself as a non-Greek housewife. Credit: Robert Carlton Wilson Papers, 1953–1980,
box 38, folder 18: "Immigration and Naturalization: Adopted Alien Children, 1957–1958,"
Special Collections and University Archives, San Diego State University.

alarm professional social workers today.[304] In a letter dated 26 July 1959, one
non-Greek San Diego woman and business owner wrote to Wilson,

> Please inform me as to the method to follow to get a little Greek girl into this
> country. Due to the recent death of my brother I am alone in the world and
> am most lonely. . . .

> At present I own the . . . Motel . . . I also recently bought nine apartments . . .
> where I plan to live as soon as I can sell the motel and secure a little girl to
> live there with me. Please add my plea for the admission of the Greek child
> to that of Mrs. Poulos.[305]

---

304. Without suggesting a close comparison with the troubling Greek case, I refer to the phrases
"Sixties Scoop" or "Canada Scoops" that have been used to denote the mass placements
of aboriginal children in institutional care and with white middle-class parents in Canada.
See Fournier and Crey (1997). Similar events occurred for many decades in Australia with
the "stolen generations" or "stolen children" (Read 2010). The term "baby scoop" has since
referred to the large number of postwar US babies stemming from premarital pregnancies
whose single (white) mothers faced all sorts of moral, socioeconomic, and family pressures
that coerced them to give up their babies for adoption. See Fessler (2006); Solinger (2000
and 2001); and also the website http://babyscoopera.com/.
305. Quoted from a letter written by a San Diego woman to Congressman Bob Wilson, held in

Fig 9: Congressman Bob Wilson (far left) and Leo Lamberson (middle) at a reunion of the adoptive parents of Greek-born adoptees and the children themselves (fall 1956, private home in San Diego, California). Credit: personal archive of Greek adoptee Maria.

In the fall of 1956, Wilson attended a West Coast reunion of the adoptive parents of Greek-born adoptees and the children themselves. Most of these youngsters had come over through the Ahepa Refugee Relief Committee under Lamberson, and some also had Wilson's assistance. As figure 9 shows, Lamberson, too, was a guest of honor at this reunion, which was hosted at a private home in San Diego.

Home Sweet Home: The Issachars in Action, 1957–1962

Χωρὶς περίσκεψιν, χωρὶς λύπην, χωρὶς αἰδῶ
Without consideration, pity, or shame
　　—Cavafy, "Walls"

By the late 1950s, Lamberson and other Ahepa leaders had been feeling the heat of ongoing investigations, and they curtailed their involvement in adoptions. At that point, the brother-and-sister team of Maurice and Rebecca Issachar, which had been active in the Greek adoption circuit since

the Robert Carlton Wilson Papers, 1953–1980, box 38, folder 19: "Immigration and Naturalization: Adopted Alien Children, 1959–1962."

1957 (independent of the Ahepa), stepped up the pace and filled the vacuum. Rebecca was known to make the rounds in New York Jewish circles with a picture book of little Greek children. Maurice's name came to stand out among the unethical lawyers who handled Greek adoption cases of the late 1950s through early 1960s. The Issachars developed a business model that could boast of the fast and efficient delivery of a highly sought-after "product." Lori was an "Issachar baby" from the Patras Orphanage, with which Maurice maintained close ties. Born in mid-April 1958, her adoption was approved in Greece three and a half months later, and Issachar delivered her to New York on 2 September 1958. Ellen was born in January 1958, was placed in the Patras Orphanage in March 1958, and was a New York resident by the end of May 1958. Ellen's adoptive parents told her that they paid the Issachars $2,500 to handle the adoption by proxy. The childless Jewish couple saw this as a reasonable fee, given that they did not qualify financially for a domestic coreligious adoption. But when the time came for Maurice to hand over the baby, he asked for more money, which Ellen's adoptive father refused to pay. Also, Ellen had a full biological sibling who was older, but they were not delivered to the orphanage at the same time. The Issachars could not have known about this sibling connection.[306]

Which adoptee cases, then, led to the 1959 scandal and to the subsequent US criminal investigations? This piece of the puzzle is hard to find: the proceedings of Grand Jury hearings on sensitive matters are kept confidential, and many legal records are not preserved beyond a fifty-year time period. But court action was first taken in the County of New York, responding to Mitler's report and to complaints filed by adoptive parents from New York City. One legal intervention then led to the investigation of several circuits, and the spotlight of scrutiny kept resting on the "bigger players," Scopas and the Issachars. Summaries of the Issachars' court case and of the prolonged one of Scopas, both heard in New York, are on file.[307] In both court cases, however, the prosecution had to concede a startling fact: because the adoptions, as predeparture adoptions, were finalized in Greece (by way of Greek court orders, which American courts recognized on the principle of international comity or reciprocity), US legislation had left a loophole open to people trafficking in babies that it had not yet been able to proscribe by appropriate language. Unsurprisingly, the case of the People v. Scopas became notorious,

---

306. Ellen, testimony of 4 February 2016.

307. See the People v. Issachar (12 May 1960), 24 Misc.2d 826, 203 N.Y.S.2d 667 (Ct. Gen. Sess., N.Y. Cnty. 1960), and the People v. Scopas (June 1959, June 1960, and March 1962, on appeal), People v. Scopas, 11 N.Y.2d 120, 181 N.E.2d 754 (1962). Online case briefs at www. leagle.com.

given that he had been charged with 30 counts of arranging illegal adoptions. The quotation below, taken from the 1978 court proceedings of a different case invoking legal precedent, explains how the decision not to prosecute Scopas was technically possible but far from compelling:

> In *Scopas*, the adoption took place in Greece and was then followed by the placement within this State [New York]. The majority concluded that since the adoption had been previously accomplished, the placement was with parents and not in violation of law. The minority wrote that this loophole should not be available and stated "a trade in human beings was not intended to be permitted, and cannot be condoned, regardless of by how circuitous a route the practice is conducted."[308]

In the 1960 case of Maurice Issachar and his sister Rebecca, the court proceedings state explicitly,

> I decry the methods used by these defendants to obtain the legal adoption of these children.

> It seems that the operation of some sort of "black market" prevailed in the placing in foster homes of unwanted infants and that the operation turned into a flourishing business—an evil, if presently existing, that calls for supplemental legislation of a more effective remedial nature. But, so far as I, as a Judge, am concerned, I, for my part, have no alternative other than to follow the law as it is now written.[309]

All adult parties involved realized that, for Greek adoptions to be accepted by the United States, they needed to be formalized or completed within Greece (as when the US, honoring the principle of reciprocity, recognizes the validity of foreign birth or marriage certificates). This drive toward finalization in Greece created new beginnings for the adoptee, for better or worse: the act of adoption came to signify not the end of a long or laborious process (which it seldom was), but the start of new and accelerated adult action in pursuit of the child's medical clearance, its visa, and its passage to a foreign destination. If these requirements could not be fulfilled quickly enough, American adopters tended to call on politicians to speed up the process. Also, this haste excluded child welfare officials from

---

308. Quoted from the court proceedings on the People v. Michelman, by Jonet (1990: 328).
309. Quoted from the court proceedings on the People v. Issachar.

becoming involved, sometimes with drawn-out procedures, as they were in US domestic adoptions and in intercountry placements through certified public agencies. The entire process did not leave room for a thorough investigation into the child's origins or status: Was the adoptee really a foundling or an orphan? Was the baby stolen? Were its papers real and consistent? Was the birth mother's consent to the adoption genuinely voluntary? Had she been truthfully informed about other options or about access to assistance, if any? The Greek courts did not go back to examine how the adoptees had been sourced—and herein lay the system's endemic weakness. But neither did the foreign adoptive parents, the Ahepa, the lawyers, or the ISS, for that matter.[310] The need for speed and confidentiality, which accelerated the process for the waiting new parents, was rebranded as most beneficial for the children themselves, who did not linger in their respective institutions any longer than necessary. The Greek way presented itself to hopeful couples as the less circuitous "fast track" to "guaranteed" adoptions, unlikely to be interrupted or revoked. Some Greek adoptions resulted from illicit agreements and transactions, but they were final and their records had been closed. Thus these Greek-to-American adoptions continued to escape US jurisdiction and the purview of the State Department, for which they became *de facto* cases of immigration policy and practice. In other words, these instances became cases, not of migration for adoption, but of adoption for migration, while the standards of children's "adoptability" were left to the country of origin to define. The State Department long treated cross-border adoptions as the internal or "private matters" of supplying countries, not as a public matter of the United States as the prime receiving nation. As Lovelock clarifies,

> The INS [US Immigration and Naturalization Service], in most instances, then deal[s] with a *fait accompli*. The reluctance to "interfere" with the process in another country is understandable. However, it creates a situation whereby the procurement of children by less than legitimate means can remain "private."[311]

For all their determination to obtain a quick and irrevocable Greek adoption, a few overwhelmed American parents returned their new child to the intermediaries who had procured it. The drive for "finality" may have

---

310. I thank Dr. Felicity Sackville Northcott, director of external partnerships and international services at the ISS-USA in Baltimore, for her most candid conversation on this topic (telephone communication of 27 April 2016).
311. Lovelock (2000: 928); also Carro (1994: 143).

sped along over legal ground back then, but it did not reckon with some adopters' recourse elsewhere and with their own lack of preparedness, especially when dealing with older adoptees who had suffered the stresses of war, institutionalization, or both. "And so, some couples took back the 'faulty product,'" in the self-deprecating words of one Greek adoptee abandoned in the States. Several such cases are known within the Ahepa and the Issachar circles, but charged as they are with disappointment, shame, and guilt, they are still too painful and too private to discuss. A Greek girl was returned to the Ahepa after her first few months in the States. Lamberson reassigned her, for a new steep fee, to a family located at the other end of the country. The girl's childhood was traumatic. Her second pair of adoptive parents later admitted that they had failed to secure a child through the regular channels of certified agencies and had turned to the Ahepa as a last resort.[312] This and a few other cases lay bare the blatant chasm of accountability that ensued when, as reputable agencies rightfully feared, proxy adoptions did not work out and "rehoming" children became necessary.[313]

The 2003 collective volume, *Welcome Home! An International and Nontraditional Adoption Reader*, edited by Lita Linzer Schwartz and Florence W. Kaslow, illustrates the trials and tribulations American parents have gone through to adopt foreign-born children. One published story details the many hoops a well-meaning US couple had to jump through to bring a Greek baby girl home to the East Coast, after they had been unable to adopt domestically because theirs was a mixed-faith marriage (Jewish and Christian). From the perspective of the adoptive parents, Naomi Moessinger describes a sequence of procedural steps that took place in Greece in the spring of 1962 and that amount to a baby-trade transaction.[314] This process was entirely driven by one lawyer's willingness to lie to and bribe Greek officials while charging a handsome sum of hard currency for his services. The story of the Greek-born Deborah Johnson's adoption by the Moessingers reveals that the couple was prepped to lie (even under oath) before the Greek authorities if necessary, and that lawyer "Maurice" repeatedly referred to monetary "gifts" as tools to grease the system. Naomi Moessinger declared herself ready to deny her Jewish faith, "as no court in Greece would allow

---

312. Source kept confidential, testimony of 4 August 2016.

313. See Winslow (2012a: 121; 2017: 61) on a different case, also kept confidential. For several more troublesome cases, see Aristotelis Koutsoumaris to William T. Kirk, letter of 13 June 1958. The letter is held in the archives of the ISS, American Branch Papers, box 10, folder 37: "Proxy Adoptions 1954–1956," SWHA, University of Minnesota Libraries. The current term is "rehoming." It is no longer "re-placement," or plain and problematic "replacement."

314. Moessinger (2003).

a Greek child to be adopted by a Jewish parent."[315] In a hearing before the newly appointed head of the Greek Passport Division, Naomi falsely promised to have her new baby baptized in the States.[316] Afterward, when "Maurice" realized that the new appointee might continue to stand in the way of his transactions, he shrugged that "it was going to be difficult to deal with him on matters of religion until some money changed hands."[317] As an adult, Deborah Johnson expressed her growing awareness of the shadowy route leading to her 1962 adoption, which, more than half a century later, may be summed up as a race to rubber-stamp Greek documents and to skirt intimidating but otherwise innocuous bureaucratic hurdles.[318] By spring 1962, the Issachars' case had already been brought before and dismissed by a New York court. Maurice Issachar continued to operate from his Greek home base and handled Johnson's adoption with the confidence of a seasoned pro.

In his tragicomic book of 2011, *Twentieth-Century Janissary: An Orphan's Search for Freedom, Family, and Heritage*, Dionysios Dionou describes with verve how he became a pawn in a dollar-fueled adoption scheme that, in its ruthlessness, constituted child trafficking. He speaks out about the shady entanglement of Maurice and Rebecca Issachar in his own 1959 adoption, and he provides copies of original and translated documents to make his case.[319] These records include a letter from a Presbyterian minister falsely attesting to the Christian faith of his Jewish parents.[320] The adoption story of Maria Kelmis, which she relates in *Golden Strangers: An Adoption Memoir* (2012), is far happier than that of Dionou. Maria and her adoptive sister Kathy left Athens together as infants in March of 1962.[321] Both Dionou and Kelmis noted the (casual) word-of-mouth advertising that promoted the business of adopting from Greece. Kelmis recounts, "when they [her adoptive parents] found out that a friend of theirs adopted a baby from Greece in a short amount of time, they changed their plans [to adopt within the US]. . . . They used the same lawyer in Greece as their friend and completed the entire process through the mail and over the phone."[322]

---

315. Moessinger (2003: 39).
316. Moessinger (2003: 43).
317. Moessinger (2003: 44).
318. Johnson (2003).
319. Dionou (2011: 63–64, 72–73, 75); the reproductions of the documents in the appendix start on p. 239.
320. Dionou (2011: 63, 72, and letter in appendix).
321. Kelmis (2012: 9).
322. Kelmis (2012: 6).

The Hand That Robbed the Cradle

> As you all well know, it is Greeks from the lower classes who, for the most
> part, seek to adopt children from the [Athens] Orphanage. That means,
> they themselves do not have enough to live on, and the children, therefore,
> are bound to become tramps [ἀλῆτες]. In contrast, our wards who are
> adopted by parents from foreign countries are headed for wealth.
>
> —Nina Tsimikali, speaking at a 11 July 1958 meeting of the board of
>   directors of the Athens Orphanage[323]

An anonymous cartoon published on the front page of the Greek newspaper
Makedonia of 8 May 1959, entitled "The Black Market in Babies [Sent] to
America" ("Ἡ μαύρη ἀγορὰ τῶν βρεφῶν εἰς τὴν Ἀμερικήν"), strikingly conveys the politics and economics of international adoption. It delivers a blis-
tering rebuke to the asymmetrical relationship between the United States
and Greece, suggesting that the latter has fallen to the nadir of submission.
By taking children in exchange for money or material goods, Stephen Scopas, the cartoon's stereotypical "ugly American," has engaged in a policy of
expropriation, which is nonetheless presented as a mutually agreed-upon
deal. Perfidious American entities have been conducting and concealing the
neocolonialist exploitation of their poorer partner; they have used humanitarian rhetoric as a smokescreen, which Greece's political elite has condoned. Scopas has found his match in soulless Greek officials, who have
accepted that economic aid and trade programs entail "return shipments" of
children, which are conducted with impunity (see figure 10).

In a move of cheap servility, the conservative Greek Prime Minister
Konstantinos Karamanlis (the larger figure in black with the characteristic
bushy eyebrows) presents a little boy to Scopas, here depicted as a cari-
cature of a Texas businessman. Before a mock tribunal of faceless Greek
"masterminds" ("ἐγκέφαλοι"), Karamanlis, who was at that time still loyal
to the monarchy, is preparing to ship another cargo of happy-looking babies
to New York. Ironically, those who admired Karamanlis's autocratic leadership style have called him "ethnarch" of the Greek people. All the brokers
of the child exports are men, reflecting the deep patriarchal structures that
underpinned the unlawful adoption traffic from Greece to the States. The
toddler in the foreground holds a sign that marks the scandalous transactions as necessary under "the five-year [economic program]" ("τὸ πενταετές

---

323. Proceedings in Greek quoted by Theodoropoulou (2006: 79). Similar prejudice against
    relinquished and institutionalized children was stated in official writing by Athinogenis
    and Papathanasiou (1959: 54).

Fig 10: An anonymous cartoon from the Greek newspaper *Makedonia* (*Macedonia*) of 8 May 1959, entitled "The Black Market in Babies [Sent] to America."

[πρόγραμμα]"), itself dependent on Greece's siding with the sinister forces of American imperialism. In late April of 1959, Karamanlis indeed announced his ambitious Preliminary Five-year Program for Economic Development (1960–1964), which aimed to increase Greece's agricultural and industrial production, promote tourism, and, with continued US aid and foreign capital, invest heavily in the country's infrastructure.[324] Greece's anticipated economic self-sufficiency is utterly deflated by new, insidious forms of dependency, and lasting transformation is nowhere in sight. In the words of Susie Woo (pertaining to Korea), wartime violence and postwar dominance are recast as "American altruism," premised on the superior partner's belief that the orphans of its weaker counterpart are better off under its own nurturing care.[325] This humanitarian or moral superiority is, however, a thinly veiled manifestation of economic and military supremacy. The cartoon's caption reads, with Karamanlis speaking:

Πάρ' τὸ κι' αὐτό, μίστερ Σκόπα. Ἀπὸ ἔκθετα . . . ἄλλο τίποτα; Οἱ κύριοι ἀπὸ δῶ μᾶς σκαρώνουν ὅσα θέλεις!

---

324. Botsiou (2010: 99, 103). Svolopoulos provides the full text of Karamanlis's announcements of 27 April 1959 (preliminary program) and of 9 April 1960 (final program) (1992–1997: 4:51–57, 275–82).
325. Woo (2015: 48).

Take this one, too, Mr Scopas. Any more foundlings [you might want]? The gentlemen over here can make up as many as you want!

How did Greek children figure in a Cold War economy of emigration and adoption, which was condoned by the Karamanlis administration? Was there a literal or formal agreement between Greece and the United States to trade children for aid? No, but one may argue that the Greek government stepped into the trap of expected compliance once it started to accept massive amounts of economic and other support from the States, while counting on receiving more aid in the future. When a country's national sovereignty suffers a protracted crisis, relief missions from abroad tend to grow into more intrusive and longer-lasting rehabilitation projects, in which the balance of decision-making power shifts. Greece of the late 1940s through 1950s was no exception. The rehabilitation of Greek child victims continued to use war terminology, however: rehabilitation was enacted through overseas adoption, itself a thinly disguised new form of evacuation, but one that conveniently responded to American parents' yearning for children to adopt. Successive infusions of US support and official agreements among the "partnering" states cemented reciprocities: they offered lasting incentives for Greek institutions to give out children for adoption to Americans, for local courts and administrations to facilitate the one-way flow, and for the Greek state to keep applying expansive definitions of "(war) orphans," "foundlings," and "adoptable children." Barbara Yngvesson has insightfully termed this phenomenon the state's "production of adoptability," and she has shown how it works to the advantage of everyone except perhaps the adoptee.[326] She explains that the adoptable child "is not sold, but is given to other states in exchange for a donation of money," through a transaction that reifies the hegemonic position in which the richer state stands to the poorer one.[327] Kristi Brian speaks of "kowtow[ing] to the dominance of capital and the enticement of meager charity."[328] Also, in the Cold War climate in which every adult party took for granted that this type of collaboration and exchange was wholly beneficial and that the child's best interest was "evidently" served, no party (except the ISS and some enlightened adoptive parents) saw the need to keep detailed records. After all, "real life" began in America.

---

326. Yngvesson (2002: 236).
327. Yngvesson (2002: 237).
328. Brian (2012: 179).

Of Scandal, Truth, and Consequences

> The trial of three people charged with involvement in a case of illegal adoption, dating back to 1968, opened at a Thessaloniki appeals court yesterday. Former clinic director Nikolaos Sourmelides, the child's adoptive mother Fotini Navrozidou, and the latter's sister allegedly adopted Isaac Navrozidis, now 33, through the city's Aghios Stylianos orphanage. The issue came to light after former appeals judge Daniil Daniil brought charges against the trio, supplying DNA test results proving he was the natural father. At the time, many parents were told by the home that their children had died, whereas the children had been given up for adoption.
>
> —Anon., "Adoption Trial," *I Kathimerini*, 17 January 2002

The December 1962 discovery of child trafficking at the Saint Stylianos Foundling Home in Thessaloniki remained somewhat contained, even though the trade had probably begun in the postwar era and probably lasted for fifteen years. The foundling's home director and eight employees appeared before a Thessaloniki court in mid-June of 1964, where they were charged with falsifying documents and profiteering from selling babies for adoption. Despite their confessions, they got off with light or no sentences.[329] But the scandal broke with a vengeance in May of 1995, more than three decades later.[330] On this occasion, and unlike the revelations of May 1959, the outcry started in Greece[331] and then reverberated back in the United States.[332] The new publicity and the wide availability of the internet led to self-organizing initiatives among Greek-born adoptees, both in Greece and in the States.[333]

---

329. Giannoulaki (2018) and Van Steen (2016). Giannoulaki describes how appeals procedures took the case well into the spring of 1965 (2018: 12–13, 75–76, 89–90).

330. Brouskou (2015: 25, 31–32, 159–68, 289).

331. See, for instance, Grapsas, *Eleftherotypia*, 16 April 1996; Sroiter, *Apogevmatini*, 16 April 1996; and Mathioudaki, *Eleftheros Typos*, 17 April 1996, with the misleading title of "List with 'Official' Illegal Adoptions" (in Greek). I am much obliged to Constantine Buhayer for sharing his research on the Greek reactions of 1995–1996, including his notes, contacts, and newspaper articles of the time.

332. See, for instance, Bonner, *New York Times*, 13 April 1996; Fields-Meyer, *People Magazine*, 28 October 1996; and Konstandaras, *Seattle Times*, 22 September 1996, and *Los Angeles Times*, 29 September 1996. These are the articles that routinely come up in interviews with Greek-born adoptees who have started to search for their roots later in life: the articles have been copied and disseminated widely, but they have also shaped adoptees' perceptions that all postwar Greek adoptions must have been irregular.

333. Greek-born but New York-based adoptee Maxine Deller (now deceased) led many of these efforts, which delivered knowledge, self-affirmation, and the occasional family reunification. Her name and those of her contacts and friends, along with the names of her two younger biological sisters, appear in many of the 1996 US media reports. Greek journal-

Frequently, newborns and very young children were (re)registered as foundlings, and parents were told that their baby had died but were not shown a body or a death certificate.[334] This abusive practice may at least partially account for the fact that, from the mid-1950s through the early 1960s, Greece's rate of infant deaths (that is, its declared rate, and therefore probably an incomplete count) was more than twice as high as the infant death rates of the United Kingdom and of the Scandinavian countries.[335] Also, numerous mothers of children born out of wedlock were being denied any meaningful consent in adoption proceedings. Many, too, realized how bleak the future was for young mothers at risk of losing their family and support network, because of the unforgiving taboos that still targeted single motherhood and "illegitimate" offspring. Young mothers' chances of making a living by themselves and of raising their children independently were very slim. Given also the dearth of appropriate and discreet social services, these women had no other choice than to give up their babies for adoption.[336] Occasionally, delivery doctors registered a newborn as the offspring

---

ist Fanis Papathanasiou was instrumental in establishing further contacts with the Greek media on the group's behalf. In the *Athens News* of 8 November 1996, reporter Nikos Konstandaras described how the initial media hype propelled the cause:

> Greece's combative private television channels seized the story and public interest, along with the successful reunions that were achieved, led authorities to lift much of the secrecy that hindered earlier efforts by adopted children to discover their blood relatives.

The first spotlight fell on adoptees from the Patras Orphanage, stolen and sold children, and on the nefarious roles of Scopas and the Issachars. Eleni Liarakou and other founding members of the Adoptee Search Association S.E.A.S.Y.P. (Σύλλογος Έρευνας κι Αποκάλυψης Στοιχείων Υιοθετημένων Παιδιών, Research Association for the Disclosure of Information on Adopted Children, founded in 1995) were able to provide assistance, cutting through some of the red tape in Greece. Adoptee Amalia Balch started publishing a newsletter that offered information and moral support and that also presented the cases of the first Greek-born adoptees publicly searching. The inaugural issue of *Greek Jubilee: The Newsletter of Adoptees in Motion* appeared in May 1997, but the newsletter was discontinued afterward (Balch, testimony of 27 April 2018). I am deeply grateful to Ellen, who granted me the best possible introduction to the history and memory of the first Greek adoptee support groups, covering the East Coast and also the West Coast of the States. In her testimony of 19 October 2016, Ellen professed:

> In the mid- to late 1990s, our story in magazines and TV programs was one of emotion and was about the need to find our roots. . . . But as the years passed, our story developed into a more coherent description of a time in history that others need to know about.

334. Brouskou (2015: 164, 167, 181, 257, 259–60, 290–92).
335. Wood-Ritsatakis (1970: 122–23, and her table 4.7). See the official Greek statistics on infant deaths since 1956: http://www.statistics.gr/el/statistics/-/publication/SPO09/.
336. Brouskou (2015: 196–97, 263–64).

of another couple: clinics and hospitals colluded in attributing a "natural birth" to a woman who wanted to have a baby but was not pregnant at the time, while, again, the biological mother (typically poor, young, and unmarried) was misled into believing that her child had died. This fraudulent practice has commonly been referred to as a "virtual delivery" or "virtual birth" ("εικονική γέννα") after a third party's faked pregnancy, premised on the need for a newborn (which had died a "virtual death" for its real mother).[337] Thus the innocent baby, passed off as the legitimate offspring of an unrelated woman, becomes a supposititious child, who is typically kept in the dark about his or her true origins. Time and again, Greek foundling homes, orphanages, midwives' practices, public maternity clinics, and even regular hospitals reappear in stories of exploitative adoption deals as places lacking in safety, professionalism, and integrity. Such unregistered adoptions have always fallen outside the purview of the state, the court, and the social welfare system. They have also forever associated large segments of the domestic Greek adoption movement with trafficking. According to Brouskou, abuses have been alleged or documented in all of Greece's largest cities (Thessaloniki, Athens, Patras, and Irakleio).[338]

Brouskou observes that Greek adoptions have typically been clouded by reticence, if not secrecy. The various levels of impervious confidentiality were supposed to ensure that bonds between adoptive parents and their new children would be forged in the most "natural" way possible.[339] Of course, the quest for "spontaneity," "authenticity," or exclusivity in family relations often comes at a time when the institution of the family itself, adoptive or otherwise, is in transition. The Western family, and the Greek family, saw plenty of changes throughout the second half of the twentieth century, and forms of open and variant kinship have become acceptable in most democratic societies. The scandal of May 1995 was addressed (partly and belatedly) by changes in the Greek adoption legislation that were promulgated in December of 1996. The much-anticipated open-records law, however, did not completely undo the *mystikotita* (confidentiality but inevitably mystification) in which Greek adoptions have long been held, and that used to disproportionally impede the adoptee.[340] Article 1559 of Decree no.

---

337. Theodoropoulou (2006: 30, 88, 89). Note also the numerous alleged cases of virtual births and illegal domestic adoptions related on Greek Facebook sites, where self-help groups have, for years now, been discussing individual instances from (typically) the 1970s and onward. Some of these Facebook groups are listed below on pp. 275–76, but their configurations and dynamics change rapidly.

338. Brouskou (2015: 167).

339. Brouskou (2015: 286).

340. Brouskou (2015: 27–28, 30, 31, 111–13, 217, 236–37, 276, 290–92, 293, 295).

2447, published in the 30 December 1996 issue of the *Government Gazette of the Greek Republic*, only briefly addresses the charged notion of *mystikotita*, which has affected adoptees, birth parents, and adoptive parents in varying (declining) degrees.[341] Under this article of the new law, adopted children can request full information from their adoptive parents and from the proper authorities, but only after they have come of age at eighteen years old. This does not mean that Greek authorities always collaborate: adoptees looking for their roots had better brace themselves for what experienced searchers have called the bureaucracy of social repression, silence, or indifference.[342] Also, the legal clause presumes that children would know about being adopted in the first place, which is itself often the missing piece of information and the ultimate stalling factor:

Μυστικότητα της υιοθεσίας. Η υιοθεσία ανηλίκων τηρείται μυστική. . . .

Το θετό τέκνο έχει, μετά την ενηλικίωσή του, το δικαίωμα να πληροφορείται πλήρως από τους θετούς γονείς και από κάθε αρμόδια αρχή τα στοιχεία των φυσικών γονέων του.

Confidentiality of the adoption. The adoption of non-adults is kept secret. . . .

Upon coming of age, the child given out for adoption has the right to be fully informed by its adoptive parents and by every appropriate authority of the data on its biological parents.

Since the mid-1990s, agencies and self-help groups as well as television programs and websites have assisted Greek adoptees in tracing their roots.[343] Under the pressure of time running out, stories kept private or untold have been surfacing, and some tellers have agreed to place them in the (often sensationalized) public domain. The typical Greek TV show, however, drops the curtain immediately after the birth-family reunion has taken place. Amid the euphoria that romanticizes kinship via bloodlines and

---

341. *Efimeris tis Kyverniseos tis Ellinikis Dimokratias* N/2447/96. Fountedaki (2010) covers Greek adoptions from a legislative viewpoint in light of Law 2447/96. See also the volume edited by Kousidou (2000) and sponsored by Metera.

342. Herzfeld (1992: 40–44, 134–49) offers an older but eloquent discussion of the power of Greek bureaucracy. Greek-born adoptees who grew up abroad and return to Greece on root searches tell horror stories of bureaucratic obstructionism. But for every damaging incident, there is a counterexample of a helpful or otherwise positive intervention, of the spontaneous kindness of Greek and other strangers.

343. Brouskou (2015: 166–67, 289–304). See below, pp. 275–76. The phenomenon of reality TV shows attempting to reunite separated families is well known in South Korea and in other countries.

that spawns social fantasies of unbreakable bonds among members of the would-be nuclear and forever-happy family, blind spots having to do with falsehood and broken trust reveal themselves. New facts may easily nullify official accounts of events, but so might facile emotional versions. Many birth parents have endeavored to mediate the past through redemptive narration; many adoptive parents have kept information concealed from their children for far too long. The deferred narratives have not only recounted the past, they have added layered meanings to the aftereffects of duress and trauma. Also, for some searching adults, the notoriety surrounding the unlawful Greek adoptions has become an all-absorbing interpretive framework that must explain their own lives' trajectories. If the adoptee has a psychological need for it, the actions of biological parents may be whitewashed. But the documented occurrence of past illegalities does not necessarily presuppose a criminal scenario in every hastily conducted adoption case or every instance of a "stillborn" or missing baby. Brouskou concludes with a word of caution to all those who may have invested too much in the tales of stolen children and deceived birth parents and siblings:

> All those people who are searching for "the truth" expect to find it within an idealized construction of kinship, culturally construed in such a way as to prevent them in the end from speaking out about what really happened. They remain once more invisible, voiceless, and exposed.[344]

Illegal Greek Adoptions by the Numbers: Of Checks and Balances

The total number of the illegal Greek adoptions will forever remain hard to establish. Litsa Kyrellis, a Miami-based consultant turned roots search expert, has claimed that estimates of the number of stolen Greek children begin at 3,500, but that the true figures are unknown and may well be higher. "[R]ecords have often been switched or altered," she continues, "making it impossible to trace birth families."[345] On the other hand, the figures proposed by the early activist Ifigeneia Kalfopoulou, which speak to 8,000 to 10,000 babies stolen from Greece, must be huge exaggerations.[346] Similarly, Kalfopoulou takes credit for reuniting some 1,000 adoptees with their Greek birth families in the two decades since 1995.[347] Equally over-

---

344. Brouskou (2015: 302–3). The closing term, έκθετοι, is a play on exposed or abandoned children or foundlings.
345. Kyrellis is quoted by Laura Aymond (2000).
346. Kalfopoulou is quoted by DeLand, *St. Cloud Times*, 13 and 14 September 2015.
347. DeLand, *St. Cloud Times*, 13 and 14 September 2015.

stated are the numbers cited by Greek left-wing newspapers in the frenzy of the mid-1990s outcry: 15,000 adoptees sent to the United States alone in the 1950s, "at $4,000 a head," not by plane but via the regular voyages of ocean liners such as the SS *Queen Frederica*, as stated by journalist Nikos Bogiopoulos (Nick Boyopoulos) in the *Rizospastis* of 21 April 1996 (without references to credible sources). Bogiopoulos sported the charged term of "παιδομάζωμα," or "child-gathering," which the Greek establishment used to denounce the child evacuation campaigns organized by the communists of the Civil War. He turns this slur against the very establishment that overused it, to characterize a collusion of Queen Frederica with the Ahepa, an operation of an unprecedented scale—but also an unsubstantiated one.[348]

The number of US visas issued to Greek-born adoptees apply a reality check on the claims of Kalfopoulou and the leftist papers. That number is known: a total of 3,116 Greek-born adoptees entered the United States between 1948 and 1962. The number of US-bound adoptions from Greece dropped sharply after the early 1960s, by which time adoptions by Greeks themselves had grown more common. A large portion of that total of 3,116 US adoptions of Greek children must have been entirely legal, as when birth parents gave full and informed consent, and when Greek American families adopted orphans or child refugees who were related to them (that is, in

---

348. Journalist N. Garantzioti launched similar exaggerated numbers, with an article in the Greek newspaper *Ethnos* of 17 April 1996 provocatively entitled "Child-Gathering ("Παιδομάζωμα") with the Itineraries of the [SS *Queen*] *Frederica*." The personal details divulged in this article appear to have inspired the plotlines of the 2005 novel *The Lost Gene* by Vaxevanis (see above, p. 20). The extravagant numbers far exceed the total number of orphan visas granted, with which this part 2 opened. A few purely factual objections further undermine the hyperbolic claims, which Bogiopoulos repeated in a near-identical online newspaper article of 9 September 2016 (in the online Greek paper *Imerodromos* at http://www.imerodromos.gr/paidomazwma-freiderikh-douleborio-ethnikofrosynhs/): the SS *Queen Frederica* began its voyages from Piraeus to New York only as early as January 1955. By that time, the Ahepa Refugee Relief Committee was still handling the paperwork on refugees and adoptees; it was not yet fully operative when it came to making travel arrangements (and recruiting female chaperones) for the children, which included babies. Once the ARRC was ready to send over adoptees, by the late spring of 1956, it preferred flights to sea voyages. It even nudged the adoptive parents toward paying for airfare, which would secure a faster delivery of the much-desired child (personal archive of Efthalia; Adamantia, testimony of 28 December 2015). One informant did report that his adoptive parents took a cruise on the TSS *Olympia* Greek Line from New York to Piraeus, but they then flew back with their new baby. The year was 1964, and the adoption was finalized in Greece (A.K., testimony on Facebook site, 2014–2015). I have thus far discovered only a handful of Greek-born adoptees who made the three-week-long voyage from Piraeus to New York on the *Queen Frederica*, and they did so after January 1955 when all the others were arriving by plane.

the "named" cases). The latter scenario was most common in the cases of the 1,246 Greek orphans and refugee children to whom the United States granted visas from June 1950 through June of 1952.[349] This first flow of Greek-born adoptees was, in essence, still part of the postwar refugee placement campaigns. Also, to accelerate the process for minors at risk, such campaigns preferred to legally settle their adoptions in the States rather than in the countries of origin. Deducting the first wave, then, brings the total down to 1,870 children for the remaining decade of 1953–1962 (again confirmed by US immigration data). During the eight active years of this decade, the Ahepa-affiliated attorneys and also lawyers operating independently or through PIKPA finalized a combined average of approximately 150 Greek-to-American adoptions per year, with the Ahepa taking the lion's share of some two-thirds. Another circa 80 orphan visas per year were given out to ISS-sponsored adoptees.

The average total of about 230 US-bound adoptions of Greek-born children per (active) year correlates with the number of the 506 to 510 Greek orphans who arrived in the States under the 1953 Refugee Relief Act (and its *de facto* window of opportunity of less than two and a half years). This average correlates also with the figure quoted by Lamberson in mid-August of 1956, namely that 348 Greek orphan cases had been processed since the Refugee Relief Act was issued three summers earlier (taking into account several months for preparing those cases).[350] Of this count of 348 cases, Lamberson credited about 100 cases to the work of his own committee and to its relations with the Patras Orphanage in particular. He further boasted that 60 of these Ahepa-sponsored adoptees had, by mid-August 1956, actually arrived in the States, and an equivalent number would travel within the following few months.[351] These figures align with the newspaper reports of the 1956 arrivals of Greek children, typically in groups of about 6 to 10 children. In June of 1959, however, Lamberson defiantly argued that, over the course of the five prior years, the Ahepa had placed some 390 Greek orphans as adoptees in American homes in two-thirds of the lower forty-eight states and also in Alaska. As proof of the success of "all Greek Proxy Adoptions," he invoked "SCORES OF UNSOLICITED TESTIMONIALS" and "scores of appealing photos."[352] By mid-1959, however, Lamberson was facing the

---

349. See above, p. 95, for the provisions of the 1948 DPA as amended in June 1950, in the context of the first migratory wave of Greek youngsters to the States.

350. Lamberson (1956a: 685–86).

351. Lamberson (1956a: 685–86); also Critzas (1957: 108).

352. Lamberson, "My Dear Congressman: [blank]"; capitalization his. An original of Lamberson's letter to US congressmen is held in the *Atlantis*, National Daily Greek Newspaper

threat of permanent expulsion from the Ahepa. He had been feeling the heat of the external as well as the various internal investigations. Therefore, he had everything to gain from shining a more positive (hyperbolic) light on the numbers and on his role in the Ahepa's recent history of placing Greek adoptees. Numerical discrepancies plague the record of the Ahepa Refugee Relief Committee, chaired by Lamberson. When it suited him, he added to the ARRC's annual figure of approximately 100 adoptions the number of those adoptions that he arranged as a private lawyer while still availing himself of the Ahepa name and of the assistance of Tsaparis. The May 1959 depositions of Tsaparis, which he delivered to Greek investigators and journalists in the aftermath of the Scopas scandal, confirm this picture.[353] Working with the yearly average of 230 US adoptions of Greek-born children, however, may not be the best approach, given that certain years saw spikes in adoption placements: 1956 and 1958–1959.[354]

Again, plenty of these adoptions would have been above-board. Additionally, the demand from Greek American parents and relatives hardly decreased. Admittedly, some Greek children were still sent to the United States after 1962, and some were taken in by parents from other countries altogether (such as the nearly 600 Greek children who grew up with Dutch adoptive parents). Therefore, the US visa issuance requirement provides only a limited means of checking on the figures of Greek adoptees leaving their home country. Two Athens-based clinics became notorious for selling newborns to Greek women who pretended to be pregnant: one in the Plaka district and the other, the "clinic" of midwife Thekla, in Ambelokipoi. The extent of their fraudulent practices, which locals called a "public secret," may never be estimated correctly, given that these clinics' records are not preserved, if they ever existed.[355] It is highly unlikely, however, that such clinics would have catered to many women from overseas. Perhaps the more effective checking mechanism on unlawful transnational adoptions was the apprehension of the adoptive parents themselves: worse than the agony of remaining childless would have been the fear of losing an adopted child once it had become a member of the family, if it were discovered that this child had been procured clandestinely.[356] Thus, the administrative checks in

---

Records, MSS 43, box 31, folder 4, "Scopas #2," HSP, Philadelphia.

353. Anon., *I Avgi*, 8 May 1959.

354. I posit these peak years based on my compilation of data from adoptees' testimonies and personal archives. Also, according to Athinogenis and Papathanasiou, the year 1958 saw a total of forty-nine US-bound adoptions from the Athens Orphanage alone (1959: 42). That number dropped to a mere seven in 1960 (see figure 3).

355. Athinogenis and Papathanasiou (1959: 48–49) and Theodoropoulou (2006: 88–89).

356. Upon the explicit request of a Greek lawyer who was feeling the heat of the 1959 investi-

tandem with the psychological and ethical inhibitions lead us to conclude that illegal adoption from Greece was *not* the more common scenario. We will never know the absolute numbers of children stolen from Greece and sent abroad. Nonetheless, the total count for cross-border adoptions based on fraudulent sourcing and placement can hardly have been higher than several hundred—but that does not diminish the gravity of the matter.[357]

Mary Theodoropoulou, cofounder of the reunification site and NGO Roots Research Center (founded in 1999), attests to the frequent occurrence of illicit placement schemes from 1949 through 1962.[358] After about a dozen years of activity since the 1996 legislation was issued and allowed adult adoptees to search for their Greek birth families, Theodoropoulou estimated that the Roots Research Center had received approximately 600 requests from people looking for their biological parents, another 350 requests from parents claiming that their children were taken from them in maternity hospitals, and another 200 requests from various other relatives seeking adopted children (mostly siblings).[359] Theodoropoulou was also quick to warn that the success rate of such searches is only about 15 percent, depending heavily on the availability and the quality of the documentation: "For most, the truth is never revealed."[360] Today, Theodoropoulou might add, "unless DNA results let adoptees make a critical breakthrough, if they find not only close

gations, one Texas couple wrote a letter testifying to the legality of the adoption by proxy of their Greek baby girl. The same attorney's unlawful practices, which entailed reporting the fake news of the Greek mother's death in childbirth, came to light nearly six decades later, when the adoptee found her birth mother, aunts, uncles, and cousins in the tiny Greek mountain village where she was born (even though her "official" documents, again, reported her being from Athens). The baby girl of 1958 was never available for adoption. The American parents had no way of knowing what exactly transpired on the Greek end of 1950s arrangements, which were kept at arm's length by the competitive proxy system. Uneasy about the follow-up, however, they moved home and cut ties with the contact persons in Texas who had helped to facilitate the placement. Based on Eftychia, telephone and email communications and joint search efforts, March–June 2017; also papers from her personal archive.

357. I remain most willing to revisit these preliminary conclusions as new evidence becomes available, especially of the (far fewer) Greek-to-American adoptions of the late 1960s through early 1970s, which await further scrutiny.

358. Theodoropoulou (2006: 81–82, 86, 87–89, 90–93). See the volumes issued by the Roots Research Center for more comprehensive data and early assessments (2002a and 2002b).

359. Theodoropoulou is quoted by Onisenko, 12 March 2008. Brouskou notes that older siblings of Greek adoptees have often displayed great determination to reunite family members. This holds true of older sisters, especially, as in the case of the Argyriadis family. For Brouskou, this phenomenon attests to the strength of the sibling relationship in the making of children's identity and personal history—a topic that merits further study (2015: 288, 295–96). See also Athanasiou, *Ta Nea*, 11 January 2003, and Kalmoukos, *Ethnikos Kiryx*, 25–26 September 1993.

360. Theodoropoulou is quoted by Onisenko, 12 March 2008.

genetic matches but also close relatives willing to respond to questions probing into an intimate past."[361] Recently, too, Theodoropoulou has posited that the total number of US-bound adoptees from the Patras Orphanage alone amounts to approximately 350 to 370, a number that represents a combination of legal, questionable, and simply illegal adoptions, most of them handled by the Ahepa, Lamberson, Scopas, and the Issachars.[362] These figures must be weighed against the total number of 431 orphanage wards, as reported on 26 February 1953 by Basil Roufos, mayor of Patras, president of the institution's board of directors, and active collaborator with the Ahepa and with Maurice Issachar.[363] Two years later, the total count stood at only 470 Patras orphans, despite the fact that, every three to four days, one new child was entered into the institution. The total figure did not increase much precisely because the years 1954–1955 saw a considerable number of adoptees leaving (or preparing to leave) the Patras Orphanage.[364]

The ISS Hellenic Branch, which was held (but did not always live up) to international professional standards, collaborated closely first with the Patras Orphanage, then with Thessaloniki's Saint Stylianos Foundling Home, and through subsequent years, with Queen Frederica's Metera center. According to Brouskou, the ISS handled about one-fifth of the 84 case files of adoptees sent out by the Saint Stylianos Foundling Home during the time span of 1956 through 1977; of those eighty-four cases, however, fifty-nine adoptions were concluded in the first eight years, from 1956 through 1963.[365] Again, the large majority of the ISS-sponsored children were formally released for migration and were issued travel visas on assurances of subsequent adoption; their adoptions were postdeparture adoptions, expected to take place in their country of destination. The ISS-USA scaled down its involvement with international adoption through the 1970s and beyond, and that trend was felt in Greece as well. Of the ISS's fourteen (prospective) adoption cases from the Saint Stylianos Foundling Home in 1956, the first beneficiary was a seven-year-old boy, who had already spent three years living at the institution. Most of the adoptees, however, were about two to three years old. The boy and the other thirteen adoptees of 1956 were handed over to a "representative of the ISS."[366] Interestingly, too, eight of the fourteen ISS-

---

361. Theodoropoulou, testimony on Facebook of 3 September 2018.
362. Theodoropoulou, email communication of 11 August 2015.
363. Theodoropoulou (2006: 109, 110).
364. Theodoropoulou (2006: 116).
365. This paragraph owes much to Brouskou, who has generously shared her deep knowledge of the foundling home's ledgers (email communications of 19 and 21–22 December 2015, and 31 July 2016).
366. Once the 1959 Scopas scandal had been unleashed, however, the board of the Saint Stylia-

sponsored adoptees of 1956 were children who had been relocated from the Municipal Orphanage of Volos (Δημοτικό Βρεφοκομείο Βόλου), which had suffered severe damage in a series of earthquakes (30 April 1954, 21 February 1955, and 19 and 21 April 1955) and floods (mid-October 1955). Local officials and social services acted on the urgency of their situation.[367]

The ISS and any other organizations were unable to control what happened at the very source. The sad record of postwar irregularities associated especially with the Saint Stylianos Foundling Home suggests that not even reputable organizations could fully investigate how children were designated as "up for adoption," or how babies came to be foundlings and were therefore easier to adopt. At least the ISS devoted far more time and resources to the handling of its adoption cases compared to the Ahepa ring or the Issachar duo. The best numbers on the ISS-sponsored adoptions from Greece may well be those given by Aristotelis Koutsoumaris, president of the executive board of the ISS Hellenic Branch, in a letter dated 31 August 1957 and addressed to the Greek Ministry of Social Welfare. In the course of the three years prior to his writing, he claimed, the ISS placed a total of 292 Greek-born children, of whom 287 went to the United States, 2 to the Netherlands, 2 to Canada, and 1 to Switzerland.[368] By April 1959, a total of

---

nos Foundling Home prided itself on having thwarted the adoption agreements with the ISS pertaining to fifteen children and probably dating back to 1956. Anon., *I Avgi*, 20 May 1959. But Brouskou raises legitimate doubts about the veracity of these claims.

367. Theodoropoulou (2006: 101–2). Barboudaki (2015) insightfully assesses the impact of the sequence of natural disasters that afflicted the Volos region in the mid-1950s. Several records from among the numerous itemized decisions of the Municipal Councils of the City of Volos attest to the reimbursements issued to Volos Orphanage employees or contacts who, in the immediate aftermath of the April 1955 earthquakes and through 1956, transferred the institution's displaced children to the Athens Orphanage and to the Saint Stylianos Foundling Home in Thessaloniki. Both institutions, already crowded themselves, appear to have given the Volos children up for adoption faster than some of their own wards. As repairs on its badly damaged building kept being delayed through 1956, the Volos Orphanage continued to send recent foundlings and new "illegitimate" children to Saint Stylianos. It dispatched them typically one by one, as these very young babies kept coming in. The records are held in the Archive of the Municipality of Volos, at the Municipal Center for Historical Research and Documentation of Volos: see, for instance, acts of 24 June, 19 September, 31 October, and 8 December 1955, and of 27 February, 6 April, and 16 May 1956. The number of young wards kept at the Volos Orphanage in the mid-1950s and before the disastrous earthquakes was about thirty-seven to forty (see, for instance, acts of 4 September 1953, 2 June 1954, and 4 June 1955, all pertaining to finances and budgetary approvals). Until the worst quakes, there were thirty-nine children at the Volos Orphanage (act of 15 June 1955), and all or nearly all of them were transferred to Athens or Thessaloniki (act of 19 July 1955). After the first mass transfer, the orphanage developed a closer working relationship with Thessaloniki.

368. Koutsoumaris, letter of 31 August 1957, p. 1. Koutsoumaris's typescript letter (four pages) is held in the Lina Tsaldari Archive, folder 8, subfolder 4, item 14: "Adoptions 1957–1958,"

344 Greek children had taken the ISS route abroad, and another 30 cases were pending.[369] During these first few peak years, nearly 30 percent of the ISS placements in the States were still with families of Greek descent.[370] The database of Greek case records maintained by the ISS today shows 128 cases in 1955 but only 46 cases in 1956, of which the large majority were adoption cases.[371] The year 1955, which counted 128 Greek cases, is an exception, but it can easily be explained. By 1955, and again in 1958, the numbers of ISS-sponsored adoptions climbed in response to the US provisions made for the immigration of foreign orphans, each time after a spell of "pent-up demand." The US laws responsible for these boosts were passed in 1953 and 1957, respectively, but ISS placements required many months of preparation.

As long as demand outstripped supply, the sourcing of Greek children remained the Achilles heel of all operations. Here, too, Brouskou's numbers are striking: from 1957 through November 1962, numerous babies were "found in the front garden" of the Saint Stylianos Foundling Home, according to its ledgers, and a total of twenty-eight of these babies were prepared for adoption to the United States.[372] The overuse of the designation of "foundling from the front garden" masked the criminal transactions of the institution's upper administration, which probably robbed many of these children of their earliest history to speed up their adoption process. In at least four cases dating back to 1960–1961 alone, Director Dimitrios Papadopoulos entered a child of known parentage into the ledgers as a "foundling from the front garden" ("ἔκθετον προαυλίου"), thus paving the way for more fast-track adoptions. The document of the trial's verdict on appeal refers to the cases of these paper foundlings, but it fails to reach back in time to

---

Konstantinos G. Karamanlis Foundation, Athens. Documents found in the ISS Netherlands Branch Papers (held in the Nationaal Archief, The Hague) allow us to further break down the total of 287 Greek children dispatched to the United States for adoption: 94 children came from the Patras Orphanage; 55 from the Babies' Center Metera, 26 from Thessaloniki's Saint Stylianos Foundling Home; 10 from PIKPA; and a final 102 children came to the ISS Hellenic Branch through a combination of individual referrals, referrals by Greek welfare centers, and a few also through the Athens Orphanage, with which the collaboration revealed "difficulties." See Maria King-Tsileni's typescript report (two pages) of 11 May 1957, which is held in the ISS Netherlands Branch Papers, folder 8: "ISS—Afdelingen 1956–1957 (en correspondenten), l. Griekenland," Nationaal Archief, The Hague.

369. Athinogenis and Papathanasiou (1959: 27).
370. Koutsoumaris, letter of 31 August 1957, p. 2.
371. Archivist Linnea Anderson has graciously provided the counts of (registered or archived) ISS case files on Greek subjects for the crucial years of 1954 through 1962, for a total of 332 case files listed (email communication of 11 March 2016).
372. Here and below, see Brouskou, email communications of 22 December 2015 and 31 July 2016.

the months and years prior to 1960.[373] The appeals judges stopped short of examining the adoption cases that the Thessaloniki court passed in April 1959, for instance, of which at least six pertained to young foundlings from Saint Stylianos. Tellingly, such fake and uninspired mentions of "foundlings from the front garden" do not reappear in the institution's ledgers after its scandal broke in December of 1962.[374]

The year 1957 saw no intercountry adoptions from the Saint Stylianos Foundling Home, which stemmed from the uncertainty and delay with which the United States made new orphan visas available. From 1958 on, the number of overseas adoptions from the foundling home picks up again, but the ISS is no longer explicitly mentioned; the ledgers do not mention the Ahepa, or any other agency. Since May of 1959, the Ahepa leaders' entanglement in Greek adoptions had drawn much legal and negative attention. Therefore, the foundling home would probably not have initiated or strengthened any collaboration with the Ahepa. However, the institution still concluded many post-1957 adoptions as proxy adoptions through the court of Thessaloniki, before dispatching the children abroad. It terminated this system of proxy adoptions by late 1961, which coincided with the enforcement of US Public Law 87–301 of 26 September 1961, requiring that would-be adoptive parents "personally see and observe the [foreign-born] child prior to or during the adoption proceedings." The model of proxy and predeparture adoptions carried out in the nearest Court of First Instance does not mesh with the ISS's protocols. Rather, it leads us to uncover one more important go-between.

One more independent agent of the mid-1950s sourced his babies, including several "foundlings from the front garden," from the Saint Stylianos Foundling Home, and his numbers may affect the count otherwise credited by default to the ISS. Father Spyridon (Spyros) Diavatis served as the parish priest of the St. Sophia Greek Orthodox Church in San Antonio, Texas. His proxy adoptions of Greek-born children covered the geographical area of San Antonio, Austin, and Houston. Around 1955, a young non-Greek couple approached Father Diavatis, who, according to his son, ended up placing "maybe 30–40 or more" Greek adoptees in Southern Texas. Harry Diavatis adds: "My father, to the best of my knowledge, never turned down any couple, nor profited financially."[375] Father Diavatis himself

373. "Proceedings and Decision of the Thessaloniki Court of Appeals Judges," 6 February 1965, 56–57. This sixty-two-page typescript document in Greek is held in the Records of the Court Case of the Saint Stylianos Foundling Home (GRGSA-IAM JUS 008.02), Historical Archive of Macedonia, Thessaloniki.

374. Giannoulaki (2018) and Van Steen (2016).

375. H. Diavatis (2012: 2–3); also his testimony of 16 January 2016. Greek parish priests are not

did not travel to Greece to select the children but collaborated with Fotios Bouras, an Athens-based lawyer and close friend who, through the spring of 1959, helped to place the first adoptees from the Athens Orphanage. From 1958 on, a second Greek lawyer-proxy named Dimitrios Kazakis worked on Diavatis's behalf with the Saint Stylianos Foundling Home. Kazakis processed numerous orphans and "foundlings" through the Thessaloniki court in 1959 and 1960. The adoptive parents, who received their children between late 1956 and 1962, founded a regional association named Parents of Greek Orphans (POGO), which also covered a few placements in Kansas and Mississippi. One POGO adoptee homed with a family in Texas explains how "matching" worked for the two Greek lawyers who made the final "selection" on site:

> Mom said they were asked to decide if they wanted a girl or a boy—if a girl, send a picture of the [adoptive] mom, if a boy, send a picture of the dad. I thank God every day that when they held that picture of mom next to me [at 3–4 months of age], they decided we were a match.[376]

Bouras and Kazakis soon specialized in Greek-to-American adoptions by proxy. By late 1958, Bouras's tactics were known to the Greek Ministry of Social Welfare, whose inspectors, Athinogenis and Papathanasiou, described them in their report dated 10 April 1959: in addition to working with the Athens Orphanage, "Bouras . . . follows young unwed mothers to ensure that they hand over their newborn to him for an overseas adoption."[377] Also, Bouras took his wife along on frequent visits to an underage, unwed, and pregnant inmate at the Averof Prison, in the Gkyzi neighborhood of Athens. He followed up once the mother had delivered her baby at the nearby Alexandra clinic. There the young woman shared her reluctance to give up the baby with the institution's social worker. She finally did relinquish the child, but by then she preferred to work out a solution with the social worker. When the latter broke the news to Bouras, he felt cheated out of a deal and threatened that "he'd fix her good" (literally: θά τήν "κανονίσῃ").[378]

In the winter of 1958–1959, Bouras and Kazakis came under Greek scrutiny, which stemmed from the revelations made by Mitler in New York. They turned to W.S., the then-president of POGO, for help in soliciting affi-

---

held to a vow of celibacy. Most of them marry and have children. The ominous name of Diavatis is not a pseudonym.

376. Eftychia, email communication of 28 March 2017.

377. Athinogenis and Papathanasiou (1959: 46).

378. Athinogenis and Papathanasiou (1959: 46).

davits from the American adoptive parents whom they had been serving for more than two years. Also, several Texas couples were now in the process of adopting a second child from either Athens or Thessaloniki with these lawyers' assistance. The POGO president uncritically championed the Greek lawyers' cause, and he ordered the organization's members to help out "as [they] were helped." Given the "very undesirable situation," the president urged the adoptive parents to state "in [their] own words" that "Rev. Spyros Diavatis of the Greek Orthodox Church . . . charged nothing for his services. Expenses were Legal Fees for the adoption, Board of the Child, and Transportation Fees from Greece to the United States."[379] The parents' missives had to be unequivocal in their uniform defense of Father Diavatis and of the two attorneys who had been handling the predeparture adoptions. Also, the president himself wished to receive all the letters at the POGO office in San Antonio, and he would forward them to the Greek lawyers. Nonetheless, the parents' letters needed to be addressed to "The Greek Courts." The adopters had to also dwell on their "feelings regarding [their] child" and had to include the child's picture, using only its Greek first name. "Do not put your return address on [the] letter or picture," the president warned. "Do not address the letter To Whom it May Concern or to the former parent."[380]

No (centralized) case files on "Diavatis babies" have been preserved apart from those that are in the adoptees' personal possession. However, a report produced by Valdemar Gonzales, a child welfare worker for the ISS, contains details that differ from the testimony of Harry Diavatis cited above. This ISS record indicates that Father Diavatis and POGO arranged for sixty-seven adoptions of Greek children by Texas residents (by 27 July 1960, the report's date, after which the total count kept climbing for at least one and a half more years to approximately ninety adoptions). Lawyer "Kayakis" (a misspelling of "Kazakis") received a flat fee of $425 per adoption.[381] Also, POGO lacked "social service concepts and techniques" to secure the best possible placements for its adoptees.[382] It let the petitioners' financial credentials outweigh their moral credentials. Reportedly, the "good Chris-

---

379. Letter from the personal archive of Pam, dated 27 January 1959; capitalization as in the original.

380. Letters from the personal archive of Pam, dated 15 and 27 January 1959 and undated.

381. Airfare and the cost of the child's board (from the formal adoption date until the child departed for the States) would have raised the total amount per adoption to approximately $750–$800. This total is also the amount stated by Father Diavatis in a San Antonio newspaper article of 1958 (?; unidentified newspaper clipping from the personal archive of Robyn). This total cost, however, does not add up to what some Texas adoptees have been told by their adoptive parents, who cited much higher amounts.

382. Gonzales (1960: 1, 2, 6 [quotation]).

tians" of POGO did insist that each adoptable Greek child be seen by four Greek and one American doctor and that "[t]he child must be free of Negro blood."[383]

"Mail-Order Children," Delicate Cargo

> And now the transition is complete, and J.H. no longer exists. The boy's name is being changed legally to . . .
>
> —Anon., *The Troy Record*, Troy, New York, 4 May 1954, 14

Our preliminary conclusions about the questionable legality of many Greek adoptions, their perpetrators, numbers, and time frames, require further explanation. The best clarifications, however, may well stem from the case studies themselves, which are presented in part 3 of this book. These case studies also show what it means to resignify fragile children or to conceal their origins. The sections above have tried to situate specific records, allegations, and actions and reactions in the context of the late 1940s through early 1960s. They have found multiple gravity points: Greece and the United States, history and biopolitics, the adoption and immigration nexus, the political as well as the socioeconomic rationales underlying relinquishment, separation, adoption, and thus social engineering. Part 2 pivots on less tangible axes of analysis as well: generosity and greed, ideology and jurisprudence, heartfelt testimony versus officialdom's impenetrable language, first-generation lived relationships and second-generation inherited experiences. Most central to part 2, however, have been the intercountry adoptions of two organizations, the Ahepa and the ISS. While both have by now revealed their strengths and their weaknesses, the Ahepa deserved further scrutiny for promoting for decades a brand of transnationalism that its own adoption praxis came to jeopardize. Striving to satisfy its Greek American and American adoptive public through the finite exports of children, the Ahepa of the 1950s lost track of the political, economic, and social vulnerabilities of the homeland; it could have helped pursue alternative, in-country childcare solutions. Also, the Ahepa never accepted the need for proper adoption casework, let alone for follow-up on its placements.

---

383. Gonzales (1960: 2). A copy of Gonzales's typescript report (six pages) is held in the archives of the ISS, American Branch Papers, box 10, folder 18: "Independent Adoption Schemes: Diavitis [*sic*], Reverend Spyrus 1960," SWHA, University of Minnesota Libraries. See Van Steen (2016). I have thus far discovered only one postwar case of a Greek-born biracial child of African descent, who was given up for adoption through the Volos Orphanage (Barboudaki, testimony of 4 December 2016).

To its credit, the association did let the very vocal critics make their case. It engaged in a multiyear phase of self-examination, which was, however, superseded by external investigation procedures. Lastly, the Ahepa poorly documented its life-changing adoptions, seeing adoption as a one-time-only and one-directional "transaction," with no further questions asked. For many "orphans," however, the "clean break" was not what the adult parties promised and expected it to be, and the memories and postmemories of the scars of early years live on:

> New York: Greek orphan M., 10, of Serres, Greece, gets welcoming kisses on arrival here 12/30[/57] via TWA from her new foster mother . . . and her foster brother, Nicholas, Jr., 12. Young Nicholas, also a Greek orphan, arrived in this country in 1954. Mrs. . . . said that the girl's name would be changed to Diane, because Nicholas wanted a sister named Diane.[384]

Suspicions about illegal Greek adoptions of the postwar decades have been raised in reports in newspapers and popular magazines, in television blurbs, on blog sites, in social media, and in chat rooms through recent years. However, this discussion of a crime of long duration has rarely taken place in any scholarly venue or forum. Here, I can only scratch the surface of what remains an immensely complex history of underhanded postwar Greek adoptions, given the many constraints of confidentiality regarding the adoption files of informants who are still living. Add to that some bureaucratic red tape and the corrosive effect of the current economic crisis on the workings of Greece's libraries and archives. To this day, many topics may be avoided for personal or psychological reasons, and it remains important to protect the privacy of interviewees. Much more remains to be done and can be done, however, with the memoirs written and published by the adoptive children or parents affected, including the personal records that they or their own descendants have wanted to share with readers across the globe. This kind of material is analytically significant if we want to add further nuance to the experiences from memory and postmemory. It prompts us to reconsider the value of testimonies generated on the American side of the Atlantic and to reckon with the impressions and reactions of the post-adoptees (if we may so characterize the deferred experience of adoption by those of the second generation). The desired level of minute detail, however, may only be uncovered later, when more classified files and life stories are accessible.

---

384. UP Telephoto caption, 30 December 1957.

Winslow has analyzed the postwar and Cold War Greek adoptions from a US history and policy perspective.[385] She has called out the Ahepa's incompetence and lack of professionalism in its handling of the Greek cases, but she still defines Lamberson's brokering as merely a "gray market" operation and does not cover subsequent agents.[386] The 2006 book by Mary Theodoropoulou of the NGO Roots Research Center provides a wealth of personal testimonies (including her own, hence the book's title, *Maria 43668*) and data related to Greek institutions involved in social welfare, childcare, and adoption. This Greek-language study adumbrates the scope of the black market in babies from Greece, but the author did not have access to US-based sources and policy records. Thus, the book's presentation of the Ahepa's involvement is confined to a mere three pages.[387] However, the English-language and revised version of Theodoropoulou's book is forthcoming. Brouskou is, therefore, the first author to combine historical documentation with critical analysis of our delicate subject, which she integrated into the broader discussion of her multiyear doctoral research at Thessaloniki's Saint Stylianos Foundling Home.[388] Brouskou rightly sees the many US-bound adoptions from Greece of the Cold War era as the first harbingers of the intercountry adoption movement, and she incisively critiques the general conditions that facilitated this "philanthropic" but hegemonic praxis.[389] "Transnational adoption emerged out of war," Briggs and Marre concur,[390] and Greece of the 1940s saw not one but two devastating wars.

The fate of the Greek adoptees of the Cold War, if discussed at all, has for far too long been treated as ancillary to the kind of grand political questions that historians have been investigating. In these children's fate, journalists and political commentators on the deep Civil War may be looking more for ammunition for anti-Right or Cold War rhetoric than for signs of the complicity or guilt of specific individuals or groups or of the trauma inflicted on the next generation(s). The narratives centered on infants and youngsters adopted out to the West have, nonetheless, remained largely absent also from the victim-focused historiography and commentary of the Greek Left. The phenomenon of twentieth-century Greek history-writing severing itself from the lived realities and memories of Greek children sent abroad,

---

385. Winslow (2012a and 2017).
386. Winslow (2012a: 123; 2017: 62).
387. Theodoropoulou (2006: 89–92).
388. Brouskou (2015, in Greek).
389. Brouskou (2015: 109, 162) and email communication of 6 January 2015. See Altstein and Simon (1991: 3); Herman (2008: 216–18); Howell (2006: 17); Lovelock (2000: 907–8, 911, 912); Oh (2015: 4–5); and Zahra (2011: 169–71, 237–39).
390. Briggs and Marre (2009: 1).

not to communist countries but to capitalist ones, is inevitably problematic. The adoptees' experiences and remembrances have not yet been integrated into any serious historical inquiry into the Civil War's aftermath through the early 1960s, let alone into the history of Greek America. Greek America especially may discover here new geographies of childhood and kinship that reach far beyond the migration-adoption nexus.[391] Undoubtedly, the private histories of Greek-born adoptees deserve to be assessed more positively and to be fully incorporated: they illuminate a variety of otherwise ignored issues and are reliable mediated memories. The variety of examples presented in part 3 may begin to draw a broader picture, which is overall a picture not of separation but of reintegration.

---

391. See the 2015 special issue of *Social & Cultural Geography*, edited by Jessaca Leinaweaver and Sonja van Wichelen, and the co-editors' contributions in particular. Catherine Nash has coined the term "geographies of relatedness" (2005), accounting for the dimensions of space, scale, direction, time, and context in the study of kinship.

PART 3

INSIGHTS FROM GREEK ADOPTION CASES

There Is Power in Knowing Your Story

> The children that you have chosen, and that we, too, have come to regard as yours, are truly special in every respect. We pray . . . that they may become worthy and honorable citizens. We want them to be true assets as much to their homeland, small but heroic Greece, as to our friend and ally America . . .
>
> > —Panagiotis Lontos, director of the Patras Orphanage, to the American adoptive parents of two of his young wards; letter from the personal archive of Pam, dated 23 July 1954
>
> I am number 43668—that's my name. The name Maria was added later.
>
> —Mary Theodoropoulou 2006: 7

Part 3 of this book features Greek adoption stories and personal testimonies that represent a sample of different experiences (see figure 11). It evokes the many ways in which adoption might be understood as a range of places, motions, emotions, realities, and reconfigurations. It was precisely the search for depth and diversity that helped me to decide which experiences to include here and which to deploy in the overall framing of my argument. My analysis of the stories and testimonies is based on extensive interviews and other communications from the summer of 2015 through September 2018. I have preserved the adoption terminology used by my interviewees, even when some usages may by now appear dated or controversial. One adoptee, Dionysios Dionou, preferred to speak for himself. His testimony opens this part of the book, which revisits and rewrites the public through the personal. It is the voices of the adoptees that interest me. Their stories or microhistories transcend time, space, and nation, and they power a sense of self perennially open to new information and therefore renewal. These stories do not press home political themes, but they do pose the question of how Greece is currently reacting to the persistent inquiries of its aging adoptees. They point up issues of shared agency, but therefore also of shared responsibility—which official Greek accounts have thus far failed to acknowledge. If there is an unofficial strategy of "ignore!" or "deny till they die," then may these stories at least help break the silence.

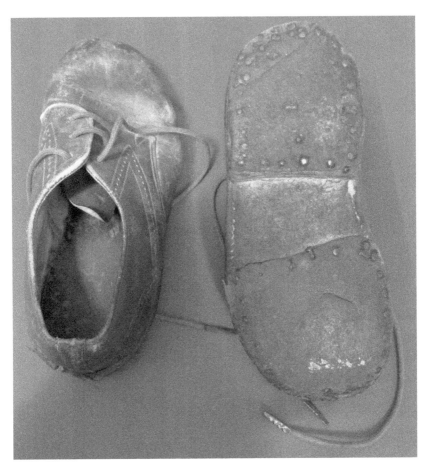

Fig 11: Pictures of the shoes in which Petros Koutoulas traveled from the Patras Orphanage to the state of Washington. Petros held on to these shoes because they symbolize a journey full of both potential and pain. Credit: personal archive of Greek adoptee Petros Koutoulas.

Part 3 also presents a gender balance between Greek-born male and female informants. This balance arose very naturally, given that, contrary to expectations, girls were *not* abandoned in higher numbers in postwar Greece. In fact, Brouskou has shown that Greek child relinquishment was not gender-driven but age-driven: newborns were more likely to be abandoned, indicating that the mother (or her family) had made the decision to give up her child well before its actual birth, as often happened with babies born out of wedlock.[1] Some of the details of the stories that follow may

---

1. Brouskou (2015: 208–10). Gallant adduces comparative data from other, nineteenth-

trigger discomfort. I have changed the names of my informants to protect their anonymity, if they so desired. As Winslow warns, "[t]he story of international adoption involves many characters, plot lines, climaxes, denouements, scene changes, and resolutions."[2] I add that these stories conjure up a lot of pain as well, and that my purpose has been to recognize but not exhibit this pain.

C. Dionysios Dionou: *Twentieth-Century Janissary*

> You find out you were out of the loop when the most crucial events in your life were set in motion.
>
> —Steve Jobs, as per screenwriter Aaron Sorkin,
>   in the 2015 eponymous film

I am a stolen child. The pain of this reality is imprinted upon my soul. Nothing, not even the passage of time, will ever lessen this pain, which I carry with me—always. I have never known my mother, father, siblings, or extended family. Within a fortnight of my birth I was abandoned. I do not know why. For a child to be abandoned is trauma more than enough, but in my case it was just the beginning. At the age of five months I was sold. Yes, you read the line correctly: *I was sold.* An infant sold in one of the many black markets that flourished in post–Civil War Greece. I was not alone or unique in this tragedy. Thousands of other Greek infants, boys and girls from all over the nation, were sold. Many children are abandoned or orphaned, and you might now be thinking, "If this infant was sold to a family, surely this must have alleviated the harsh reality of being abandoned." That may well hold for the lucky few. However, I write for nobody but myself. What I do know is that, for the many sold children to whom I have spoken and with whom I have corresponded, such was not the case. Rather, the exact opposite holds true for most of us, "the lost souls of Hellas." For many, this payment for a child marked only the beginning of a nightmarish childhood and also of teen years filled with abuse at the hands of our *purchasers.* I use the latter word for the maladjusted (at best) or too wretchedly evil (at worst)—these individuals can hardly be called "parents."

I personally spent the better part of my childhood and teen years suffering emotional and at times physical abuse. The two individuals who *purchased* me were neither loving, Greek, nor wise. They stripped me of any

---

century foundling homes in Europe and Russia (1991: 484–85, 487, 492, 493). See also Tilly et al. (1992: 8, 11).
2.   Winslow (2012b: 341).

and all traces of my birth culture and faith. They erased my name, my heritage, my birth religion, and they substituted all of that with a culture and a faith that never moved me. They did not really live; they existed, and I was expected to exist with them—keeping up appearances. I had to live a daily lie in order to appease them, so that their *purchase* of me could be deemed worth their while. I, as a thinking, feeling individual, meant absolutely nothing to them. This charade had a devastating effect on me as a child, teen, and adult human being. Once I learned by accident, however, of my true background, faith, and heritage, and once I began to see myself for who I truly was, then finally things changed for the better. But only after I took charge of my own life. The response from those two persons and, to a lesser extent, from members of their extended families, was a torrent of insults, mockeries, threats, and violent physical acts of the kind I had been enduring for years.

Obviously, I was able to find a way to survive, and, more importantly, to transcend this dismal period in my life. Today, I am a proud American of Greek ancestry, a practicing member of the Orthodox Church, and I have a wonderful family of my own. I found a wonderful woman, and I am a proud, loving, and sometimes strict father to my children. I try to be the father that I never knew or had. This triumph of my spirit, of my will, is bittersweet. The toll it took to survive was huge. I am covered with scars to this day: some are very visible, the ones that cannot be seen I feel deep inside me, and they are more painful than the physical scars ever were. After much reflection, I decided to write the story of my life, a memoir dedicated to "the lost souls of Hellas" and to all who have been uprooted, orphaned, or trafficked. *Twentieth-Century Janissary: An Orphan's Search for Freedom, Family, and Heritage* was published in 2011, and I am more than pleased with the reception that my memoir has received. It is through the publication of my memoir that I first had the pleasure of meeting the author of this book, a book that is long overdue.

For many decades, the subject of the Greek children sold on black markets has been a dirty secret in Greece and in the Greek diaspora alike. It has been an embarrassing stain on twentieth-century Greek history that many wished would quietly fade away. We, the children stolen from Greece, need to finally receive the recognition and the justice that we deserve. Today, Greece is in turmoil economically and politically. A nation that has given so much to the world is about to become undone. I do not believe that kind of calamity will happen. After all, the Greek people's strength runs strong and deep. The country's history is replete with great triumphs as well as profound tragedies. I do believe, however, that the current crisis affecting

Greece stands in direct correlation to the country's trade in orphans. Simply stated, any nation, people, or government that can willingly sell its children, like goats in a village market, can sell out the entire country to the highest bidder: its farms, hills, rivers, ports, antiquities, its entire economy. "Cash and carry," as we say in New York City slang. Therefore, the Greeks must come to terms with the reality of what was done to their brothers and sisters. And when "the lost souls of Hellas" return to their land of origin, to their homes and villages, they must be given unhindered access, so they can find their heritage and possibly their birth families. There are many monuments in Greece, and deservedly so. Now we need a monument to this postwar catastrophe. The Orthodox Church may want to declare a day of prayer to commemorate this tragic episode in our history. I ask our clergy to consider this initiative. The Greek state could open a museum to display our histories in an informative and sensitive manner, and it could grant us input in the making of such a museum. In sum, this dark chapter of Greece's past must not be forgotten.

George: The Fork in the Road at Distomo

In the summer of 1945, a Greek American husband and wife went on a visit to his brother's home in war-torn Distomo and met the newborn son of the family. The father of the growing family had escaped the massacre perpetrated by the Nazi Germans on 10 June 1944, but the village was still reeling from the shock of the many civilian losses; it would take decades to recover. The husband of the pair visiting was a successful restaurant-owner in Indiana, but he and his wife had remained childless. Over the next ten years, as baby George grew up in Distomo, the two brothers and their wives hatched a plan: George was to become his uncle's and aunt's adoptive son; he would benefit from an American-style upbringing and advanced education; and the childless couple would enjoy raising as their own a clever young boy from a known background. And so it happened that ten-year-old George was told that he would be moving to America rather than commute to the nearby city of Leivadia to attend high school.

Adopting George in Leivadia was easy and straightforward, but bringing him to the United States was a different matter, which took two additional years. The standard Greek quota for migration to the States were heavily oversubscribed. Also, George soon exceeded the age limit set by the non-quota orphan provisions of the 1953 US Refugee Relief Act, and he was not technically an orphan. With the help of an attorney and also of Congressman Charles A. Halleck of Indiana, the adoptive parents had a private bill introduced to the US House of Representatives in 1956. This bill, which the 85th US Congress eventually passed and which the president then signed into law, did not plead economic hardship (as most other private adoption bills did); it emphasized, rather, the mutual consent among all adult parties. Once the bill had become private law, George was issued a visa to travel to the States, and he arrived in November of 1957. Nobody in his close surroundings ever made his adoption a secret or a taboo topic, and George's family ties to Distomo remained strong. He traveled back for the first time five years after his arrival, and he has maintained close contacts since. George stresses that the adoption worked out well for all parties involved, and that the entire family's openness about it was very beneficial.

George became a science professor and, as fate would have it, he married another Greek-born adoptee whom he met in college. The two of them did not have any children, but they, in turn, (informally) adopted their Greek nephew and saw him through his studies at the university where George taught for many years. Both George and his wife enjoyed their role of substitute parents, and he, especially, took on additional duties as uncle-provider. George's wife did not pursue answers to the questions left pending about her earliest family history. Her own Greek American family had brought her to the States in 1958, after adopting her, at age four, from an orphanage in Athens. Reportedly, her indigent mother had left her there after she and the girl's biological father, a taxi driver, could no longer afford to raise her. George's wife, afraid of hurting the feelings of her loving adoptive parents, the only parents she had ever known, never delved deeper into the details of what was probably a privately arranged adoption through the mediation of a Greek professional contact, who became a friend of the family.

When I ask George about "the road not taken" at Distomo, he conjectures that he would probably have had a more "ambition-free" Greek village childhood (in both the positive and the negative sense, he stresses) and that he would have finished high school in Leivadia, as planned. Then, he would probably have gone to work in the bauxite mining industry in or around his hometown, where several of his close relatives found permanent employment, including his biological father and brother. George admits that he always grew up "between two families and between two different worlds," but he reiterates that, if anything, this twofold identity left him better equipped to deal with life's vicissitudes. He hastens to say, "I would not have been the person I am now without the adoption."[3]

---

3.   Based on George, telephone communication of 11 April 2017 and subsequent email communications.

Dean: The Deal of a Lifetime

"ο Θεός ορφανά κάνει, άμοιρα δεν κάνει"
"God makes orphans, but he does not leave them to their fate."

  —Giannis Atzakas, *Light of Fonia* [in Greek], 2013: 373, invoking a
  popular proverb

Dean was born in Greece on or around 1 October 1953, probably in or near Patras. Nothing is known about his natal family. He was relinquished to the Patras Orphanage and was entered into the registers there as a foundling. Dean was still a toddler when he, along with eleven other youngsters, was placed on one of the Ahepa's "orphan planes" and flown over to Idlewild Airport (JFK Airport), where he landed on 12 July 1956. By then, the Ahepa leadership had consolidated its cozy relationship with the Patras Orphanage and was regularly meeting flights carrying its charges (see figures 4–6). Dean's overjoyed Greek American adoptive parents greeted him in New York, and they promptly took him by car to Philadelphia, where they lived. Dean grew up as an only child but was surrounded by a large extended family and by a supportive Greek American community. As was common during the mid-1950s heyday of the proxy adoption system, Dean's would-be parents had been able to select a child based on pictures provided by the Ahepa Refugee Relief Committee, whose contact person was Leo Lamberson. The prospective parents could also state their preferences as to the child's sex, age, and other physical features.

Dean must have been about eight or nine years old when his parents told him that he was adopted from Greece. By then, he had no recollection of the Patras Orphanage, the long plane ride, or his arrival in New York. The match between Dean and his adoptive parents was a very successful one. For as long as his mother lived, she and Dean could joke that she got a "deal" for only $500 in adoption fees. According to Dean, his mother's cousin, who was an attorney on the rise in the nationwide Ahepa ranks, looked out for the family's best interests. Dean's adoptive father was an active Ahepan as well. These direct family connections to the Ahepa might explain why the sum of $500 was reasonable and probably just about covered the expenses for all the necessary arrangements. After the Ahepa Refugee Relief Committee had cashed the check and the bank had returned it to the family (as was customary in those days), Dean's mother carefully held on to the canceled check: for her, it symbolized the "transaction" that had brought her an abundance of happiness. Dean and his wife, who have long had their

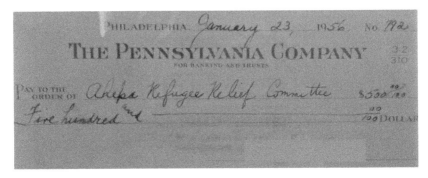

Fig 12: Payment of adoption fees to the Ahepa Refugee Relief Committee, issued by Dean's adoptive mother on 23 January 1956 (canceled check). Credit: personal archive of Greek adoptee Dean.

own children and now have a second grandchild, have framed the check and generously share the story behind it (figure 12).[4]

M./Mitsos: "When I Typed 'Patras Orphanage' into Google, Everything Changed"

> The [American adoptive] parents know little of the history of the child except that both of her parents are dead, believed to be victims of either an earthquake or some sporadic warfare. She was found abandoned on the steps of a police station in Patras and turned over to the orphanage. . . . [Her] past is something which is probably locked in the graves of her parents and [the girl] is here to begin a new life, as a member of an American family devoted to her, and in a country about which she is already showing amazement.
>
> —Ruth W. Ducker, "Little Greek Girl Becomes American," unidentified newspaper, 1958

A foundling who was reportedly abandoned in 1952 and today wishes to remain anonymous has been holding on to the above news clipping for what little it reveals. But the Ionian earthquake did not occur until August 1953. Also, major Civil War fighting ended in 1949. If this girl of a few days old was indeed a foundling (without any identifying markers or notes), there is no way of knowing what fate befell her parents. It was mere speculation to presume that her parents had died. Such self-serving presumptions, how-

---

4.   Based on Dean, telephone communication of 23 July 2015 and subsequent email communications; also testimony of 10 January 2016 and papers from his personal archive.

ever, eased the transatlantic adoption route originating in mid-1950s Patras. The girl came to the United States courtesy of Lamberson and the Ahepa. Several more Ahepa-sponsored adoptees arrived with her in January of 1958. Patras officials invoked the orphan-producing earthquake also in the case of Maria, who found her Greek mother decades later. Maria's illiterate mother had even gone to the Patras city hall to file (with a clerk's assistance) a document in which she recognized her child and explained her personal circumstances. She had left this document, which identified her by name and address, with her baby girl at the orphanage, with the stated intention to come back and fetch her. This act was highly unusual, but it was still ignored. When the Athens Court of First Instance was presented with Maria's 1956 adoption case, the Patras Orphanage and the Ahepa lawyer declared her to be of "unknown parents" (with the agent noun "parents" in the plural).[5]

Like Dean and these girls, Mitsos was probably born in Patras and was abandoned on the steps of a church near the orphanage there (see figures 13 and 14). It was late November 1954, and the foundling of approximately fifteen days old was discovered by the local police and then handed over to Andreas Frangoulias, the orphanage's janitor and gardener, whose name resurfaces in stories of other adoptees from Patras. In Mitsos's case and in many more instances, the record of Frangoulias's official declaration of having found or been given the child substituted for a birth certificate, and it thus served as a legal document during the foundling's adoption process.[6] As a healthy, white newborn "without a past," Mitsos was cleared quickly for an overseas adoption that was finalized in the States. Courtesy of Flying Tiger Line (aka Flying Tigers), he arrived at Idlewild Airport on 5 October 1955, not even one year old. The 4 October 1955 departure from Athens to New York was one of the first flights to bring over Greek adoptees sponsored by the International Social Service. It predated by some nine months the more visible orphan planes scheduled by the Ahepa. The ISS flights were paid for by the Intergovernmental Committee for European Migration (ICEM, founded in 1951), which helped resettle refugees and displaced per-

---

5. With the help of her adoptive mother, Maria has collected the full dossier on her case, including the signed statement that her birth mother filed at the Patras city hall. She will be publishing her own story (testimony of 1 February and 15 May 2016).

6. Theodoropoulou (2006: 33, 150). A contributor to a Facebook group of Greek-born adoptees (whose name and date of posting will be kept confidential), expresses her frustration about her inability to obtain a "real" birth certificate as opposed to a foundling registration:

   Who among you is unable to obtain a real birth certificate . . . ? I . . . cannot get one. Apparently, I sprouted up, but I was not born. . . . The issue is not where, after I die, my death will be recorded but, rather, what to do if I need that birth certificate while still alive.

sons in the aftermath of the war.[7] Mitsos's adoptive parents paid a nominal processing fee of only $115, as did many other American couples on behalf of their ISS-sponsored babies. Mitsos's new parents, Presbyterians of German descent living in the Midwest, had actually been looking to adopt a German child, but they quickly fell for the blond Greek boy with the curly hair, who was described to them as "happy," "good-natured," and "with a ready smile."[8]

Like more than 500 other Greek children, Mitsos entered the United States under the 1953 Refugee Relief Act. The ISS collected several reports on both Mitsos and his future parents as well as extensive correspondence from before, during, and after the child's placement. Also, the ISS needed Mayor Roufos of Patras to sign official forms consenting first to Mitsos's emigration and then, by relinquishing his own guardianship, to the boy's adoption within his American home state. Mitsos's adoption was finalized in January of 1957, or about 15.5 months after his arrival (even though only a 9-month waiting period was required). This baby's placement through the ISS, which released the bulky file on his case, is noteworthy: first, in its early days of adoption casework in Greece, the ISS collaborated with the Patras Orphanage. From May 1955 on, Patras switched its allegiance to the Ahepa. Meanwhile, the ISS started building closer contacts with the Babies' Center Metera in Athens and with the Saint Stylianos Foundling Home in Thessaloniki. Its office staff members were approached, too, by Greek mothers or families in distress who pursued US-bound adoptions for their children.

The ISS made a genuine effort to ease Mitsos's transition from an institution in Greece to a home in the American Midwest. Among the many papers in Mitsos's thick file is a four-page leaflet titled "Simple Phonetic Greek/English Vocabulary": it had to serve as a mini-phrasebook from English to Greek covering the basic lines of communication between the adoptive parents and the child. The ISS case consultant wished the new parents luck in "acquiring a fluency comparable to that of little Mitsos" (letter from the personal archive of Mitsos, dated 23 September 1955). The leaflet opens another window on adoptive parenting and on the contemporary (lack of) understanding of Greek and Greece, as the following quotations may show:

---

7.   Letter from the personal archive of Mitsos, dated 22 August 1955. ICEM (currently the International Organization for Migration, IOM) began its work in Athens in March 1952. By 31 January 1957, some 43,000 Greeks, adults and children alike, had left the country under ICEM, but not all of them migrated to the United States. Other destinations included Australia, Canada, Argentina, Brazil, and Venezuela. Intergovernmental Committee for European Migration (1957: 406) and Vogli (2011: 26).

8.   This emphasis on physical features, while unthinkable today, was common and accepted in the postwar adoption practice of "choosing" and "matching." See Papadaki (2015: 136–37).

Fig 13: The old building of the Municipal Orphanage of Patras; it was demolished in the early 1970s. Credit: exact date and source unknown (despite my best efforts, I have not found any attribution on the web page presenting this photograph).

FAMILY

Mother	Mitera OR Mamma
I am your mother.	Ego ime ee mamma sou.
Father	Patera OR Babba
He is your father.	Aftos ine o babba sou.

. . .

FOOD

. . .

Meat	Kreas

. . .

Cocoa	Kakao

NEEDS

. . .

Are you hungry?	Binas?

. . .

OTHER

I love you.	S'arapo
Do you love me?	M'arapas
. . .	
Sorry	Sekuris
Thanks	Efharisto
Please	Parakal

BODY

. . .	
Stomach	Stomaki OR keelia
My stomach hurts.	Panai i keelia mou.[9]

Mitsos had been found with some extra clothing and a note attached to it stating his first name: his birth mother herself may have penned the name she gave her newborn at the time of his baptism (which is when Greek name-giving traditionally occurs). Because the baby boy still needed a last name, the Patras Orphanage assigned him the name of Dimitriou, probably because his estimated date of birth (11 November 1954) followed closely upon the Orthodox feast day of Saint Dimitrios (October 26). "Mitsos" itself is a common nickname derived from Dimitrios or Dimitris. To prevent foundlings from being stigmatized, Greek law stipulated that orphanages had to give their wards a last name as well as a first name, if no name or names had been communicated to them via a message of any kind.[10]

Mitsos, now M., has long known that he was adopted, but he did not begin searching until March of 2011. Meanwhile, he has learned of a last name that may have been his birth mother's, if a link can be established

9.   ISS, "Simple Phonetic Greek/English Vocabulary" (ca. 1955: 2–4). I refrained from correcting the numerous errors. Given the faulty (and gender-biased) nature of the Greek here, the adoptive parents must barely have made themselves understood. Mitsos told me none of the Greek words "stuck."

10. Theodoropoulou (2006: 82, 99, 120, 150). Brouskou adds a most interesting section on mid-twentieth-century name-giving strategies, which offered up endless creative possibilities (2015: 227–31). The nurses and caregivers of the various institutions doled out nicknames to their charges as well. One little boy reared at the Saint Stylianos Foundling Home was nicknamed "Occupation" ("Κατοχή"), because the last two digits of his ledger number, the digits 41, reminded the nurses of the year in which Thessaloniki had first endured the World War II Occupation (Daravinga 1963: 7). Constantinou recalled that, in 1968, the nurses of Metera had named several children after members of the Kennedy family (telephone communication, 16 August 2015). These poor or ominous choices aside, name changes or discrepancies between official names and nicknames must have created confusion and might even have hampered the children's bonding process.

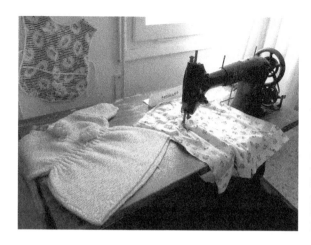

Fig 14: Until 2016, the Patras Municipal Daycare Center kept up a small room with mementoes from the former orphanage and its young wards. Credit: personal photograph collection of Greek adoptee Mitsos.

between him and a woman who was young and unmarried in 1954. In 2017, Mitsos attempted a DNA match with a family from northwestern Greece looking for a child who went missing around the time he was born. When the results came back negative, they left all parties disappointed but also enriched by a bond of solidarity. The word is still out on his case, but Mitsos remains hopeful. Assisted by Mary Theodoropoulou of the Roots Research Center, Mitsos went on a June 2016 search trip to Patras. Many other Greek-to-American adoptees vicariously traveled with him, as they closely followed his daily posts of pictures and comments on Facebook. However, no new information has thus far challenged Mitsos's status as a Patras foundling. Mitsos may not yet have found a birth family, or the truth for that matter, but he has newly discovered a native country and its millennia-long history and culture. Mitsos has sought and found multiple new answers to his questions about the Greek adoption phenomenon, and he has become the center of many rewarding exchanges among the ever-growing community of Greek adoptees finding each other. The members of this new, supportive community are perennially ready to remake themselves: unable to know their birth families for decades, they are now using every tool available to search for those families and for knowledge in general. Yet Mitsos's own case may serve as a reminder that, even for a very young adoptee who has never really known another life, adoption opens up an ongoing identity-seeking process. Mitsos's son is quick to add: "[My dad's] story is my story. Where he came from is where I came from. . . . I've got something on the line here, too."[11]

---

11. Based on Mitsos, extensive email communications, August—September 2015 and March—October 2017, and on papers and photographs from his personal archive. Mitsos's son, testimony of 14 May 2018.

Efthalia: Carrying (Foster) Sibling Affection to the Next Generation

> Maria had learned to eat soft foods on her own. . . . That's when I noticed
> a new troubling attitude. When she sat at the table, her head hovered just
> above her dish, and she wrapped her arms around her plate, guarding it
> like it might be pulled away at any moment. Was this what mealtime in
> Patras had been like for her? How awful for a three-year-old to have to
> fend for her food like that. I was not prepared to see this aggressive sign of
> self-preservation, and it left me very sad. Frankly, I was more than a little
> shaken when I realized such behavior might well have been necessary.
>
> —American mother of Greek adoptee Maria. Heckinger 2019: 66

Efthalia (born November 1951) was just over four and a half years of age
when, on 21 June of 1956, she was placed on a Swissair flight to America. She
recalls some of the emotions that shook her during the long plane ride and
the subsequent transfer by car to small-town Ohio. Like Dean's, Efthalia's
adoption from the Patras Orphanage was instigated by an Ahepan from
among her close family members (adoptive mother's father). It was again
both relational and transactional, and it was Lamberson himself who handled the correspondence with and the payments by the new parents and
also the transportation arrangements. The young parents, both in their late
twenties, who adopted Efthalia by proxy, had only ever seen a picture of
their toddler, before driving out to meet her and bring her home to Ohio.
Because Lamberson had kept the childless couple waiting much longer than
promised, they asked a local, high-placed politician to intervene on their
behalf. Subsequently, Efthalia's parents always credited this politician with
accelerating the adoption procedure. The entire process took about one full
year—a long time when measured against Lamberson's assurances of those
days. Notably, a letter of 7 May 1956 signed by Lamberson and mailed to
Efthalia's adoptive parents is a form letter on Ahepa letterhead (or typed
mimeographed "template" from the precomputer era) in which he or his
secretary could fill out the specifics of the receiving couple's last name, date,
and a few numbers identifying the promised child. As a general rule, one
only uses such a fill-out copy or template if one anticipates dealing with
many similar cases within a short period, to avoid having to retype the
entire letter. In the spring of 1956, Lamberson did indeed have many adoption cases going, and nearly all of them were predeparture adoptions by
proxy. In his boilerplate letter, too, Lamberson charged for the clothes in
which the orphans would be traveling.[12] This explains how and why pictures

---

12. Lamberson, letter of 7 May 1956, from the personal archive of Efthalia.

such as figure 6 show the Ahepa-sponsored orphans arriving in new shoes and white socks, and many of the shoes and socks look identical.

Efthalia's case is somewhat peculiar, however, and its peculiarities may well point to irregularities. First, Efthalia has the name and a few basic details of her birth mother and also the names of her Greek godmother and of the priest who baptized her. This means that she has more information than is customary for adoptees from the Patras Orphanage. These data are all listed on the Greek document that substitutes for Efthalia's birth certificate; dated 16 February 1952, it represents the declaration made by another janitor of the Patras Orphanage to the local Office of Vital Statistics. Therefore, it attests to the date on which the baby entered the institution's care, not to the baby's actual date of birth (which occurred three months earlier). This kind of formal declaration was common with foundlings, but not when the birth mother's name was known, as was the case in Efthalia's situation. Moreover, the document of February 1952 does not refer to an original birth certificate (which would have been issued in mid-November 1951); in fact, it ignores the existence of an original birth certificate altogether, even though the latter probably existed, given that the birth mother arranged or agreed to a proper baptism. Rather, the foundling record or substitute birth certificate cites a formal order issued by Mayor Roufos of Patras that the baby be entered into the institution he oversaw. This decision appears to be motivated by a (vague) reference to the birth mother's poor physical health, in addition to her unmarried status. Because Efthalia was an "illegitimate" child from a "stolen marriage" ("τέκνο ἐκ κλεψιγαμίας"), as the Greek says, the mayor probably considered her to be a child "at risk."[13] Local notables on the boards of orphanages could indeed steer certain "unprotected children" toward institutional care—and could abuse that power, too. Also, once children had entered the Patras Orphanage, they fell under the legal guardianship of the same mayor, who could act on behalf of the child's absent, incapacitated, or unknown biological parents.[14] Even if the mayor of

---

13. Theodoropoulou (2006: 36).
14. Evidence can be found in papers from the personal archive of Mitsos, dated 4 August 1955, and referring to the very same Roufos. As mayor of Patras, Roufos was also in charge of the city's Office of Vital Statistics, and he signed off on entry or foundling records substituting for birth certificates (entry record from the personal archive of Efthalia, dated 16 February 1952; foundling record from the personal archive of Pam, dated 26 August 1953; foundling record from the personal archive of Mitsos, dated 29 November 1954; foundling record from the personal archive of C.P., dated 3 August 1955; and foundling record from the personal archive of R.R., dated 6 November 1956). Also, Mayor Roufos was a descendant of Georgios Roufos, who himself served as mayor of Patras and presided over the orphanage's board when the institution was founded on 13 July 1873. One more mid-1950s professional relationship was too close for comfort: Giorgos Lontos, a public notary in the service of Mayor Roufos, was the brother of Panagiotis Lontos, the then-director of

Patras adopted out the baby for all the possible right reasons, Efthalia's birth mother would have had very little of a say in the matter. She may not have had her parents' support to fight the decision, either.

In March of 1956, the Athens Court of First Instance issued the act of adoption that assigned Efthalia to her new American parents. However, the court recorded a different date of birth (which is off by five days) and listed the child as "of unknown parents" ("parents" in the plural)—both signs of the kind of fabrication needed to make an illegal adoption possible. Michael Tsaparis, Lamberson's right-hand man in Athens, appeared before the court as attorney-in-fact and proxy holder for the parents-to-be. He saw the adoption through the court and arranged for the passport, the visa, the required medical examinations, the transfer from Patras to Athens, and the overseas airfare. Without the need for the birth mother's consent, Tsaparis was able to wrap up the process within three months. How did Tsaparis circumvent the stipulation that the known birth mother appear in person to give her explicit consent? Was she so "ill" as to be no longer legally competent? Was Efthalia at some point reregistered under a different date of birth and declared a foundling and orphan, so that Tsaparis and Lamberson could speed up the adoption process? The aim was, after all, to meet the deadline of the 31 December 1956 expiration date of the Refugee Relief Act. The allotment of available orphan visas was quickly running out. Seeking the birth mother's stated consent would only have delayed the process further. And what if she recanted or put up a legal fight? Did Tsaparis and Lamberson simply sideline Efthalia's birth mother to avoid one last hurdle, especially when trying to appease adoptive parents and a US politician who had expressed some impatience? Also, critical voices within the Ahepa were growing louder and, again, time was of the essence.

Efthalia's early history differs from that of many others in one more aspect: once she, at three months old, had been entered into the ledgers of the Patras Orphanage, its administrators placed her with a Greek foster family living in the vicinity. In early 1952, the orphanage suffered from overcrowding and "outsourced" the care of some children to nearby foster families. Efthalia spent about four years with her foster parents and their two boys before the orphanage's director abruptly retrieved her just prior to her journey from Athens to New York. Efthalia has been looking for her

---

the Patras Orphanage. The cast of these Patras characters, typically men in charge while women served as caregivers, illuminates the dense level of interactions between paperwork and power, between municipal and state governments, and between domestic courts and transnational organizations.

biological parents since 2001. She has, however, reunited with her loving foster family and has befriended even the foster parents' grandchildren.[15]

In several instances, foster mothers tried to maintain a connection with their foster children. They and other intermediaries sent along notes with the US-bound adoptees, tucked in the children's clothing or in a small, pouch-like amulet or charm (φυλαχτό). The typical note states the foster mother's name and address and conveys a message of affection, need, or both (by way of the Greek equivalent of "I seek your protection"). Foster mothers and families tended to be very poor, and some saw an opportunity to send along a request for financial support. Most American adoptive parents ignored or were advised to ignore such pleas.[16]

Myrto: "Processing the Information Is Nothing Compared to Processing the Lies"

> A few days later they [the people in charge at the Municipal Orphanage of Athens] told me not to come back [to nurse her newborn baby]: "Your baby is lost to you. You'll get your life back in order. You'll have more children."
> I never had more children. And I never got my life in order, either.
>
> —Birth mother Argyro describing how she was treated by the Athens Orphanage in the 1950s, quoted by Theodoropoulou 2006: 67

Greek-born adoptee Myrto entered the United States under the 1953 Refugee Relief Act: her passport shows her admitted on 12 October 1955. Myrto arrived in New York with a sign around her neck saying "Please deliver to [names of her adoptive parents]." Myrto's adoption process had been legally finalized in Athens about four months earlier. It was a privately arranged adoption by proxy: a Greek lawyer friend and the two brothers of Myrto's adoptive father acted on behalf of the latter. One of the brothers actually picked out the little girl: Myrto reached out to touch him when he and his wife were visiting the Athens Orphanage (figure 15), which made him decide that she was the child that the family wanted. The adoptive family followed up privately with Myrto's mother, who had, in the meantime, retrieved her baby from the orphanage (a not uncommon scenario). The other brother

---

15. Based on Efthalia, telephone communications of 27 December 2015 and 30 July 2017, and communications via email and regular mail (including papers from her personal archive), January 2016.

16. See the testimonies of Dean, Petros Koutoulas, and the one quoted by Theodoropoulou (2006: 69).

Fig 15: The old building of the Municipal Orphanage of Athens, located on 51 Peiraios Street, on Eleftheria Square (aka Plateia Koumoundourou), near Omonoia Square. In the 1980s, this neoclassical building was converted into a gallery space, colloquially known as the "Old Municipal Art Gallery." Credit: exact date and source unknown (despite my best efforts, I have not found any attribution on the web page presenting this photograph).

of Myrto's father-to-be was a priest who was rising in the ranks of the Greek Orthodox Church. He was on good terms with the orphanage director, which helped to speed matters along. Before Myrto's departure for the States, this uncle priest personally baptized her in a "real" church (not in the tiny orphanage church) in an elaborate ceremony attended by all the new relatives. Myrto's adoptive father had migrated from a Greek island to the States, and he had made his home in Ohio with his Greek American wife. The couple was childless and had been actively looking to adopt a Greek baby girl.

Myrto was sixteen when she learned, quite unexpectedly and shockingly, that she was adopted. The Greek relatives and the priest, in particular, had strongly advised her parents not to tell her. Myrto learned the news from someone outside of the family, who added the characteristic ". . . but everyone knows you're adopted." Since then, Myrto has worked hard to contravene the sense of being cut off from events of the past that have, nonetheless, anchored her present life. Since childhood, Myrto had been celebrating her birthday on 16 June 1954, the date she had been given by her Greek American parents. In September of 2015, however, and for the first time, she laid eyes on her actual Greek birth certificate, which showed the date of 19 June 1954 as the correct date of birth. The document states the name of her unwed mother, who even declared the names of her own parents, which was rather unusual. It does not mention the name of Myrto's biological father, which was common: unless a father recognized his offspring born out of wedlock (which rarely happened), a birth mother could not legally give the name of any father, and her child was forever "illegitimate." The law prevented natal mothers from "casting a slur" onto any male, who (in the era before paternity and DNA tests) could not easily defend himself against allegations.[17] Historically, all the blame and shame associated with a premarital pregnancy has rested on women alone, and Greece of the mid-twentieth century was no exception.[18] The typical Greek birth certificate listed the biological father who failed to recognize his child as "unknown," which heaped even more disgrace onto the unwed mother, as if she, as a less-than-reputable woman, had been engaged in promiscuous relationships.

Lack of information, deliberate avoidance, and old "white" lies have been part of Myrto's long quest to learn the truth from her (now-deceased) adoptive parents, Greek relatives, and officials in pertinent positions. The circumstances of her search have given new meaning to the notion of "identity politics" as family politics. Throughout her life, Myrto has heard all sorts of different and contradictory stories: that she was a foundling from "an Athens orphanage whose records room burned down"; that she was relinquished there some forty days after her birth; that her remorseful mother returned to the orphanage looking for her, only to be told that her little girl had already left for America; that her adoptive parents sent her mother a very handsome sum of money, to help her out because she was so destitute, and that they never heard back. Add to that that some family lore remains at odds with unmistakable pieces of recorded information, and the bigger picture does not become any clearer: a high-placed cleric and brother of the adoptive father used his connections strategically; the legal and final adoption papers state that Myrto's birth mother appeared in person before the court and that she alone formally consented to surrendering her child, given the impossibility of achieving the "unknown" father's consent.

At some point Myrto learned that she had been delivered to the Athens Orphanage via the infamous baby hatch (or baby box, βρεφοδόχος).[19] The Greek "wheels" or baby hatches, the boxes with revolving doors that facilitated anonymous child abandonment, spoke the language of shaming in no unclear terms: the baby hatches of both the Athens and the Patras orphanages were adorned with the Biblical quotation of "ὁ πατήρ μου καὶ ἡ μήτηρ μου ἐγκατέλιπόν με, ὁ δὲ Κύριος προσελάβετό με," "My father and

---

17. Brouskou (2015: 183) and Moschos (1981–1982: 368, 369, 376, 398).
18. Theodoropoulou (2006: 128–29).
19. Dos Guimarães locates some of the earliest "wheels" or "tours" in medieval Italy (1991: 542).

my mother have forsaken me, but the Lord took me in" (*Psalm* 27:10). The quotation in Biblical Greek would still have been readily understood by a native speaker of modern Greek of the mid-1950s.

By early 2016, however, and with the assistance of search expert Mary Theodoropoulou of the Roots Research Center, Myrto was finally able to close in on some of the facts. She discovered who her birth mother was, but also that this woman, mother of another two boys (half-brothers to Myrto), had died three years earlier, after a harsh life marked first by rejection and shame and, in her later years, by a debilitating disease. Unmarried and pregnant at a very young age, Myrto's mother had been abandoned by most of her family members and had, in desperation, even contemplated suicide. Unable to produce milk and to keep the baby while working at a hospital, she had consented to an independently arranged adoption among known families, which left her with basic information about the Greek American adoptive parents. Myrto's mother had gone on to marry a husband who knew and supported her; nonetheless, the pain of losing her first child and only daughter gnawed at her through her final days. She knew her daughter's new name, but she always felt that it was inappropriate to go and "disturb" her life faraway. She consoled herself by saying, "One day my girl will come looking for me."

After more than six decades, the pieces of the puzzle are finally falling into place. In the early summer of 2016, Myrto went on a "root trip," as it is called in adoption lingo, to meet some of the long-lost blood relatives. Myrto, who grew up as an only child, now thrives on the contact with her half-brothers, her stepfather, and the new extended Greek family. In the winter of 2017, Myrto's maternal aunt helped her to retrieve the name of her biological father, who had three more children. Because he, too, has passed away, Myrto is pondering whether to act on this new information or not. She may not contact those half-siblings, mainly out of circumspection for her father's widow, who is still living.[20]

Dena (Polites) Poulias: Gone (on) Missing

The adoption story of Dena Polites (born 1958), who grew up in Ohio, has the contours of a parable, and some details may have been burnished in the many acts of retelling. When Dena was about seven years old, her Greek American parents divulged that they had adopted her from Greece after

---

20. Based on Myrto, extensive email communications, August–September 2015, March–July 2016, and February 2017, and on papers from her personal archive.

her mother had died in childbirth. Decades later, Dena read about the shady adoption practices that had plagued placements from Greece, in the 28 October 1996 issue of *People* magazine (the article by Thomas Fields-Meyer, entitled "A Sense of Belonging"). However, Dena only started to question her own story and records when, after sorting through her deceased adoptive parents' papers and preparing for probate court, she noticed that the data did not add up: she had been informed that she was born in a small village near Sparta, and that she had been taken to an orphanage there. But there never was an orphanage in Sparta. Besides, some papers gave Athens as her place of birth. Family lore revealed that the Ahepa had been involved: members of the association probably arranged for Dena's travel to New York in July of 1959, when she was only fourteen months old. By the summer of 1959, the scandal of the Ahepa's entanglement had broken and prominent Ahepans were under investigation.

Dena's papers did reveal the maiden name of her biological mother, who was twenty-one and unwed when she gave birth to her first child. With the help of a Greek roots search specialist, Dena was able to locate her birth parents within two to three weeks: they had continued to live near Arta in northwestern Greece, which proved to be Dena's true birthplace.[21] Struggling with the lack of acceptance from older relatives, conservative fellow villagers, and especially from her boyfriend's parents, Dena's destitute mother had placed her baby girl in an orphanage or shelter temporarily, only to be told that she had fallen ill, had been transferred to Athens for treatment, and had probably succumbed. There the trail ended, and the news of another stolen baby and irregular adoption was kept from Dena's natal family for four decades. Nevertheless, her birth parents kept searching relentlessly. They had married and had been raising a boy and another girl, full siblings to Dena. When the reunion finally came about, Dena and her husband could introduce her birth parents to their first two grandchildren, who speak Greek, no less. Making up for lost time, the entire family is now in very frequent and loving contact with all of its members.[22]

---

21. The confusion between Arta and Sparta is understandable: Arta was the more sizeable provincial town but Sparta was the better-known place among those with only a cursory knowledge of modern Greece. Ironically, the name of Sparta even conjured up an ancient tradition of relinquishing and exposing infants (in a crevasse at the foot of Mount Taygetus). See Ogden (1996: 106–10, 231, 259) and also Plutarch, *Life of Lycurgus* 16.1. Standard works on childhood in Greek antiquity include Golden (2015) and Evans Grubbs and Parkin (2013): Evans Grubbs (2013) studies infant exposure and infanticide, while Huebner (2013) discusses adoption and fosterage in the ancient Mediterranean.

22. Based on Dena (Polites) Poulias, testimony of 5 December 2015; Hoover (2000); and Synadinos (November 2000, and email and telephone communications of 7 and 17 November 2015).

Adamantia: "My Dad Always Joked That I Cost Him a House"

Adamantia was born in August of 1956, but she has never seen her Greek birth certificate. Her Jewish adoptive father, a police officer in New York City, had met Stephen Scopas through work. Scopas promised the childless Jewish couple that he could arrange a proxy adoption of a Greek-born foundling in a short span of time. The couple kept every piece of paperwork related to the case, which Adamantia has generously shared with me. Her personal archive sheds light on unusual as well as regular procedures, scheduled payments and additional fees, and the parameters of US immigration policies and special dispensations.

On 20 December 1956, Scopas sent the committed couple a detailed letter stating the four installments for a payment amounting to a total of $1,750. This "contract letter" and the follow-up letters do not contain any mention of the (by then dissolved) Ahepa Refugee Relief Committee. In a letter of 2 January 1957, the US State Department let Scopas know that "the four thousand special nonquota immigrant visas, provided in the Refugee Relief Act of 1953, as amended, for alien orphan children, ha[d] been issued or allotted." The RRA had expired and the successor Act of 11 September 1957 was not yet in effect, leaving cases such as Adamantia's vulnerable to delays. The State Department's letter proposed a parole procedure, but the would-be parents could no longer meet its deadline, either. On the last day of January, Scopas informed the parents-in-limbo that he had communicated on their behalf with "a member of the United States Congress or Senate, and the White House" to "reserve a visa" before the adoption would be completed and given the anticipated extension of the Orphan Program. One month later, Scopas mailed the Greek preliminary act of adoption to the waiting parents, who then needed to appear in person at the nearest Greek consulate to declare their mutual consent to the adoption (letter of 25 February 1957). With these depositions on file, the Athens Court of First Instance finalized Adamantia's adoption on 20 March 1957, but it would still take nine months before she could be flown over to New York.

With the final act of adoption in hand, Scopas asked, on 1 April 1957, for more money than had initially been agreed to, to cover "additional expenses incurred or to be incurred in connection with the obtainment of a special bill or private law and parole visa." From late 1956 on and through the summer of 1957, adoptions in Greece naturally went ahead but visa numbers for US-bound orphans had been exhausted. Under these conditions but also previously, under other mitigating circumstances, American adoptive parents turned to politicians to seek waivers of the visa or quota restrictions on behalf of family members and "named orphans," especially. Thus, on 15 May 1957, the US House of Representatives was asked to consider "A Bill for the Relief of Certain Alien Children," introduced by "Mr. Walter (by request)" at the 1st Session of the 85th Congress (H.R. 7597). This special bill contains the names of twelve Greek orphans and their American adoptive parents, and Scopas handled nearly all of these cases. This bill, and the many others like it, states its purpose clearly:

> Be it enacted . . . [t]hat, [f]or the purposes of sections 101 (a) (27) (A) and 205 of the Immigration and Nationality Act, the minor child, [name], shall be held and considered to be the natural-born alien child of [names of the adoptive parents], citizens of the United States.

Given that the 1952 US Immigration and Nationality Act granted the child of a US citizen *nonquota* immigrant status, as per sections 101 (a) (27) (A), at a time when regular Greek immigrant quota were over-subscribed and orphan visas had run out, attorneys petitioned that the adopted child be "considered to be the natural-born alien child" of the American couple. Adoptive parents and their lawyers essentially tried a "backdoor" policy that redefined the origins of the (underage) Greek-born adoptee, and that often proved successful, unless pending legislation was expected to resolve the issue as a matter of policy and not of particulars.[23]

Many mid-1950s bills for the "relief of minor children" passed, but Adamantia's bill failed to become private law, because the Act of 11 September 1957, which made new orphan visas available, was already in the works.[24] The frequency with which petitioning parents and their congressmen or senators resorted to the solution of sponsoring private bills or private laws is astounding: it shows from the private laws section of any volume of the *United States Statutes at Large* of the mid- through late 1950s, and these private laws refer to both the adoptees and the adopters by name.[25] The

---

23. See Balcom (2012). Her past presentation entitled "The Back Door In" and ongoing research have done much to help clarify the issues, definitions, and procedures (section 205) at stake in the private immigration bills.

24. According to Doughty (1964: 50), 108 orphans from Greece were granted emergency parole to enter the United States between late October 1956 and the summer of 1957. Their status was subsequently regularized under provisions of the 11 September 1957 Act.

25. See also various written exchanges held in the Robert Carlton Wilson Papers, 1953–1980, box 38, folder 19: "Immigration and Naturalization: Adopted Alien Children, 1959–1962," Special Collections and University Archives, San Diego State University.

sharp increase in the use of special bills and private laws may have been spurred by the known success of the August 1955 bill issued on behalf of the Korean War orphans adopted by the Holt family (see above, p. 87). Also, members of Congress saw opportunities to engage in constituent service that reached well beyond adoption and immigration cases. Already in February of 1956, President Eisenhower complained to the US House Committee on the Judiciary that "undue and largely useless burdens [we]re placed upon the Congress and the President by the avalanche in recent years of private bills for the relief of aliens." To "eliminate the need for private legislative redress," Eisenhower recommended that the attorney general be invested with "limited discretionary powers to grant relief with respect to admission and deportation of aliens" and that a "ceiling" should further determine the number of cases in which such authority could be exercised.[26]

On 11 September 1957, the Orphan Program was formally extended. On the very next day, Scopas shared this good news with Adamantia's hopeful and still patient parents. He promptly asked for "the balance of fees, transportation, escort service, etc., in the sum of $1,150.00." How this sum meshes with the original "contract letter" of nine months earlier is unclear. But Scopas, by now a New York City judge, exuded confidence: "The sooner your check is received the sooner we will be able to make transportation arrangements." While serving on the bench, Scopas should technically have discontinued his services as a private attorney, thus avoiding any conflict of interest. He solved that problem by crossing out "Law offices of" on his firm's letterhead in all of his correspondence with the adoptive parents from May 1957 on. Scopas further invoked the cost of Adamantia's short stay in Athens "after being brought and cared for in Athens by *our people* from the Patras Orphanage."[27] For about one month, Adamantia's adoptive parents left the balance unpaid, given that they were presented with an unexpected new charge. But Scopas calculated correctly that they would not back

---

26. Eisenhower, 8 February 1956, 3–4. A copy of this official message is held in the Robert S. Kerr Collection, 1871–1970, series 3: Legislative, 1935–1962, box 11, folder 6: "Immigration, 1956–1959," Carl Albert Center Archives, University of Oklahoma. Eisenhower bolstered his case by citing the following numbers, which covered many adult aliens in addition to minors: in the first session of the 84th Congress (5 January–2 August 1955), 3,059 private immigration bills were introduced; the prior Congress saw 4,797 such bills introduced (3–4). The president pointedly added:

> The Nation's interest would surely be better served if the bulk of these private immigration claims were handled through suitable administrative machinery and if the Congress and the Executive could thus give their full attention to more urgent national problems.

(Eisenhower, 8 February 1956, 4)

27. Letter of 12 September 1957; italics mine.

out, now that they had come that far (and had already invested so much). Also, as far as the Greek jurisdiction was concerned, Adamantia was by now legally their child. Scopas had his secretary ask for the money again: "[M]ay we be favored with your remittance, by return mail, as per letter dated September 12, 1957, to you, in order that there may be no delay in paying final fees to Greece and making transportation arrangements, which must be paid in advance" (letter of 10 October 1957). By the end of October, Scopas informed the adoptive parents that the issuance of Adamantia's visa had been held up. To resolve this new delay, they needed to swiftly provide an affidavit of support that was current and also other updated documentation of their financial status. On receipt of the necessary documents, Scopas promised, he would duly forward them with the request that the "issuance of the visa be expedited" (letter of 30 October 1957). Finally, Adamantia's nonquota immigrant visa was granted one month later. The fifteen-month-old girl arrived in New York in early December of 1957, became a member of the Jewish faith shortly thereafter, and was naturalized as a US citizen in March of 1960.[28]

The case of Aristotelis runs parallel to that of Adamantia, except that his adoptive parents started receiving the same sequence of letters a few days later, by which time Scopas had raised his fees by 15 percent. Scopas handled this adoption case, too, while serving on the bench. Because Aristotelis's name had to be added to the same private bill, Scopas again asked for an ever-rising payment, which exceeded what he or the Ahepa leadership had been charging of Greek Americans. Once again, Scopas took advantage of the desperation of a childless Jewish couple, who did, however, not protest (or could not compare notes with other adopters). Aristotelis is another Patras foundling, whose documents reveal three different estimated dates of birth falling between March and September of 1956. At the time of his arrival in New York in November 1957, he was in very poor physical condition, which was remedied relatively quickly.[29]

Anthony: Four Adoptions and a Funeral

The story of Anthony (born February 1956) starts with the funeral of his biological parents, who both succumbed to tuberculosis when he was just under two years old and living on the island of Crete. A teenaged uncle took

---

28. Based on Adamantia, testimony of 28 December 2015, and on papers from her personal archive.
29. The couple that adopted Aristotelis also turned to influential politicians to help cut the red tape. Based on Aristotelis, testimony of 16 August 2016, and on papers from his personal archive.

care of him and his two older sisters, but given the family's dire financial situation, he eventually had to find different solutions for all three of the children. At age nine, the eldest girl was informally adopted into a Greek family, to serve as a helping hand. Thereafter, she was placed in a local monastery, where she received a good education and made connections that proved valuable in later life. Anthony's middle sister, aged seven, was adopted by childless Cretan parents, who shielded her from her early childhood history and never confirmed for her that she was not biologically theirs.

As a toddler who had just turned two, Anthony himself was left anonymously at the Geronymakeio Orphanage in Crete's capital city of Irakleio (Γερονυμάκειο Βρεφοκομείο Ηρακλείου Κρήτης).[30] The orphanage gave the foundling a new last name and declared him available for adoption. A feisty woman from Crete, who had already built a life with her husband in the States, made all the arrangements with a local lawyer to adopt Anthony through the Court of First Instance of Irakleio. She was able to legally conclude the adoption in June of 1959, and she herself traveled with her new son from Athens to Chicago, where they arrived on 10 July 1959. Anthony's adoptive mother did, however, have to tell the court that she was (at least) fifty years old, which she was not. The judges did not press her on the issue, or they let it slide knowing that this antiquated minimum age requirement did not apply in the United States.

Anthony grew up as an only child in a very loving household. His adoptive parents told him that he was adopted when, as a teenager, he needed a birth certificate, which, as he discovered at that time, he did not have. His parents also encouraged him to go looking for his natal family in Greece; they knew of one biological sister but were not aware of the birth parents' deaths. Anthony had no desire to start searching until, one day in 2005, he received a phone call from Petros Koutoulas. Petros asked Anthony's adoptive father if his son wanted to be located, on behalf of two biological sisters and an uncle who had been looking for him for years. Anthony's Greek family had received invaluable assistance from search specialist Mary Theodoropoulou, who had communicated the near-final results to Petros. Then Anthony eagerly said yes, and he has been building meaningful relations with his birth family ever since. He has also gone to see the humble house near Chania in which he was born: a three-room structure, consisting of a kitchen, a bedroom, and a stable. It has meant a lot for Anthony to learn more about the circumstances in which he was given to the orphanage,

---

30. The orphanage was founded in 1921 by benefactor Georgios Geronymakis. Theodoropoulou (2006: 118–19).

not by his biological parents but by a struggling teenage uncle who could not manage raising three children on his own. Anthony has been able to reassure this uncle, whose deed kept tormenting him, that everything has turned out well. Anthony visits Crete every few years, and he works hard on improving his Greek.[31]

It was not unusual for slightly older girls to be sent to and "adopted by" monasteries. Some Greek monasteries and nunneries oversaw small orphanages, from which they also recruited novices (and an unpaid labor force). One poignant case reveals the "logic" behind the scheme, in a collaboration between representatives of the Athens Orphanage and of the Monastery of Saint Nikolaos Galataki on the island of Evia. When in 1962 the US-bound adoption of Maria fell through, the administrators of the Athens Orphanage first moved heaven and earth to force the Greek American parents to continue to cover the boarding expenses for this child who was legally theirs but whom they had left to linger in the institution's care. They sent letters to the Greek Ministry of Foreign Affairs, to the Greek consul in New York, and through the latter to the social welfare office and the public prosecutor of the US state where the girl's adoptive parents were then living. When the nuns of the Monastery of Saint Nikolaos Galataki proposed to take in little Maria, the board members of the Athens Orphanage welcomed this solution wholeheartedly and rationalized their decision as follows:

> Because of her lively character, Maria has thus far been placed with an external foster mother.

> Maria's unruly character will . . . be tamed (θά δαμασθῆ) if we place her in the above-mentioned monastery from which we can always retrieve her whenever we want.[32]

Joseph: DNA Delivers

> Some of the travel bureaus are even advertising in newspapers that they have Greek children available for adoption.
> —Mitler, *Atlantis*, 1 November 1959

Joseph's story is one of much duress and little love and also of a frequently delayed search, precisely because the wounds have remained so raw. In the

---

31. Based on Anthony, testimony of 4 February 2016.
32. Source kept confidential.

summer of 1953, Joseph was abandoned in a residential neighborhood of Athens and taken to the local police station, which, on the next day, delivered him to the Athens Orphanage. There, he was promptly baptized in the little church affiliated with the institution. To this day, this church is dedicated to the "Anargyroi" Saints, that is, to Saints Cosmas and Damian, benefactor-physicians "who did not take silver (payment) (for their services)." Many others in Joseph's early life were less generous. The first inquiries that Joseph made in the mid-1980s did not lead to satisfactory results. Before the Greek legislative changes of December 1996 went into effect, the Greek authorities had no legal obligation to provide adopted children with the full information from their files, however thin those might have been, even on the adult adoptees' explicit requests. Joseph and his adoptive sister shared *one* Greek passport and visa for their travel from Athens to New York in February of 1958. Given that the children were not biologically related but were merely traveling to the same household, this oddity was another negation of their individuality. Prior to the children's departure for the States, however, the Athens Court of First Instance necessarily dealt with the petitions and the adoption dossiers that were brought in. Nonetheless, by mid-1957, this court, especially, should have been suspicious about the many foundlings who were presented without proper paperwork. But the court focused more on the applications submitted by the prospective parents than on the origins of the minors in question. Joseph's act of adoption emphasizes that his American parents have the financial resources to support two children, but it does not question those children's "unknown parentage" or the inadequate paper trail.

By late May of 1957, a Greek lawyer had shepherded the double proxy adoption of Joseph and his little orphanage sister through the Athens Court of First Instance. The children's travel, however, was delayed until early February of the next year, for the same reason as in the case of Adamantia: the shortage of orphan visas before the 11 September 1957 Act made new ones available. As in Adamantia's case, the waiting parents turned to a high-placed politician to intervene on their behalf. Newspaper articles issued on the children's arrival gave Representative Stuyvesant Wainwright of New York credit for helping to cut the red tape. Joseph and his sister were adopted by parents from Long Island, who made all the arrangements through a New York travel agency specializing in trips to Greece in collaboration with its branch office in downtown Athens. Chris Peters, the Greek American travel agent, was a prominent Ahepan with only a distant connection to Scopas (see figures 16a, b). By the spring of 1959, Peters was under investigation for

Phones: LOngacre 5-3236, 7, 8   CHRIS PETERS, Pres.

Loucas & Peters Travel Agency, Inc.
301 WEST 41st STREET, NEW YORK 36, N. Y.   № 6540

RECEIPT
Date _Aug. 17/56_

Received From

For: _service & fee for adoption of 3 children / from Greece_

Greek Lawer and court fee | 475 | 00
for the petition fee | 100 | 00
Service charges for Athens office / and NY office | 100 | 00

Balance to be paid when everything is ready.

By Clerk   Total | 675 | 00
                                            Amount Received | 525 | 00
                                            Balance Due | 150 | 00

Phone: CIRCLE 5-0550   № 1583

Crown Peters Travel Service, Inc.
711 EIGHTH AVENUE, NEW YORK 36, N. Y.

RECEIPT
Date _Jan-24/57_

Received From

For:
SERVICE FOR , 2 orphans

Also Greek attoreys fee and / other consular expenses for the orphans | 879 | 20

CROWN PETERS TRAVEL SERVICE, INC.   Total | 879 | 20
Per: Amount Received | 879 | 20
BALANCE DUE NOT LATER THAN   Balance Due

Fig 16a-b: Receipts issued by the same New York travel agent under two different company names. The receipts acknowledge payment for the agent's services in handling the adoptions of two or three Greek children in 1956 and 1957. The text of the first receipt, dated 17 August 1956, states: "Service & fee for addoption [*sic*] of 3 children / from Greece / Greek lawer [*sic*] and court fee / petition fee / Service charges for Athens office / and NY office / Balance to be paid when everything is ready." The second receipt, dated 24 January 1957, lists the cost of "SERVICE FOR 2 orphans / [names] / Also Greek attorey's [*sic*] fee and / other consular expenses for the orphans." Credit: personal archive of Greek adoptee Joseph.

his role in selling two children for $3,000; it was probably his preliminary case that led to the much-publicized arrest of Scopas in early May of 1959.[33]

Joseph's father had a child from his first marriage, and he and his new wife were also raising an older son. This family configuration made the couple a low priority on the long waiting lists of US-based agencies, and it would have given the Greek court grounds for exclusion if the couple had honestly disclosed all the family facts. This did not happen. "Adoption is too difficult in this country, so we turned to Greece," Joseph's adoptive father is quoted as stating in one of the many newspaper articles that he kept to document his "philanthropy." By early 1958, then, the travel agent booked the flights for both of the couple's newly adopted children to be transferred to New York. Joseph recalls his arrival at Idlewild Airport (after an exhausting Sabena flight), and he criticizes the publicity that surrounded it, which left him and his sister utterly startled:

> I remember sitting on the lap of a stranger who played the part of father speaking a strange tongue while big camera lenses shone in my face as they took pictures. I made the newspaper headlines the next day. I was on every major New York broadsheet. Bringing over a baby from Greece to America was big news; but bringing over two Greek orphans at our age was even bigger news. . . .
>
> At the age of 13, I was rudely thrust out of their home for good. There was no media attention, no photo shoots, no grabbing headlines. I was sent from institution to institution . . .

The popular media and the local press, especially, celebrated "heroic" adoptive parents in sentimental, feel-good language, but they seldom followed up on the supposedly "lucky" children.[34] The match between the two Greek children and the adoptive parents was not a good one. After four and a half years of growing up in a Greek institution, Joseph was no longer allowed to act on his Greek language and culture. His new parents had wanted infant children, and they let their disappointment show. They did enjoy, however, the media glare that came with being celebrity do-gooders.

---

33. See above, pp. 140–42. See Mantzoros (1959: 2); Roth, *New York Times*, 5 May 1959, 24; and Anon., *The Panama American*, 6 May 1959. The Greek version of Peters's last name turns out to be the same as that of the Greek contact who served as a proxy for Joseph's adoptive parents in the Athens Court of First Instance. The role of agent family networks in the Greek adoption circuit is not to be underestimated.

34. Park Nelson (2016: 5–6, 59).

Also, they did what abusive parents do so well: turn every day into a competition among the children for what little parental affection or affirmation might be available. They cultivated distinctions between the natural children, the adopted children, and the short-term foster children, or the residents from the Fresh Air Fund for urban youngsters, who came through the house as well. Joseph could never be sure what any given day would bring: some level of coexistence or another one of his father's irrational outbursts, complete with heavy-handed physical punishment.

The cruelty and unpredictability cast long shadows over the few better days, and Joseph began to lash out in frustration. Conditions at home soon became untenable. New York social workers looked into the situation of the two adopted children, but they did not take any decisive action. At age ten, Joseph asked his father if his adoption was the reason why he treated him differently from the "real" children. Startled that his major flaw had been called out by his child, the father resorted to further violence. The parents also boarded Joseph in various places for months on end. They formally rejected him at age thirteen. Faced with this second abandonment, the teenager was sent to foster homes and lived in institutional care again, this time in the States.

Once he became an adult, Joseph changed his name, location, religion, and adopted country. He only ever refers to his adoptive parents by their actual names, unable to grant them the title of "parents," let alone "father" and "mother." Joseph built his own happiness, but questions about his origins kept nagging at him. While many answers may still not be available to Joseph, he has gained a lot from learning that his story is part of a larger history. He admits:

> It is very maddening . . . that I've been denied a basic and given right of all born people. This then is my quest: not so much to see my biological mother, but to find out the truth and the reasons behind so many crazy discrepancies and lies that I have been told. It's confusing but I do not even know if I am looking at the real me. Even though I am 65, it's still very raw for me. I still feel I was wrenched away or torn apart; that is something I'll take to the grave . . .

June 2018 DNA test results finally delivered some answers to Joseph. At first, these answers were cast in the numerical language of the critical amount of centimorgans that identified a half-sister on his paternal side. Next, Joseph discovered a welcoming, close-knit family, an ancestral mountain village, an uncanny physical resemblance, and his real last name, in which he exults. He promptly announced on Facebook:

> I was an orphan for over six decades and searched for such a long time for my birth family, but not any longer! DNA results have come in and I have a sister . . . , a stepmother, aunts, uncles, nieces, nephews, second cousins, and on and on! . . . I have no words to express how I feel right now!

The questions of what and how remain open, however, as does the challenge of building new family relations across geographical, cultural, and language boundaries. But Joseph has been uplifted by the recent breakthrough, and he hopes it will lead to further clues about his birth mother.

When I asked this interviewee which pseudonym he preferred to use, he and his wife chose "Joseph," after Joseph from the *Book of Genesis*, whom they recognize as a guiding symbol. Faith has been an inspiring force in the lives of many Greek-to-American adoptees who consider their "uprooting" (their social and ideological displacement, in addition to their forced geographical relocation) to have been a damaging to traumatic experience. The Biblical Joseph, my informant explained, was sold by his own brothers to serve and suffer as a slave in a foreign land. In Egypt, Joseph lived the life of a man who was dead to his birth family, but his personal strength made him rise from slavery to a position of great influence with the then-pharaoh. When Joseph's brothers tried to escape the famine back home in Israel and went to ask Joseph for food, unaware that he was their sibling, Joseph responded with generosity and declared that what they had meant for evil, God had meant for good.[35]

Petros Koutoulas: "I Will Take the Bad and Turn It into Good"

> "The Seven-Year-Old in Patras Was Not Tortured"

> Yesterday's news reported that [name], the seven-year-old ward of the Municipal Orphanage of Patras, had been tortured by his foster mother. It has now been ascertained, however, that he was simply beaten (ἀπλῶς ἐδάρη) by her, because he was being unruly. The youngster himself has now acknowledged that as well.

> —Anon., *Eleftheria*, 15 September 1966

> We never forget where we come from.

> —Petros Koutoulas at age nine

---

35. Based on Joseph, email communications of April through July 2016 and of June through September 2018, on papers from his personal archive, and on some of his own writings (with permission).

Petros Koutoulas was six and a half years of age when he was adopted from the Patras Orphanage, where his unmarried birth mother had left him when he was only six days old (born March 1950). He was part of the Ahepa arrival in New York on 22 June 1956, and he then continued on to the West Coast. Petros remembers the cruelty and the deprivation he suffered as an older child in institutional care, and he has identified the signs of trauma in his own experience as well as that of fellow adoptees whose placement was not successful. Petros is also very open about what "medical clearance" from the Patras Orphanage entailed, and we have discussed the scant details of his form's mere ten lines of Greek text. The required "full" medical exam was supposedly comprised of various tests and vaccinations (e.g., against smallpox). It further checked for physical deformities, infectious diseases (such as trachoma), and signs of epilepsy, sleepwalking, bed-wetting, or syphilis (via the then-standard Wassermann test). However, Asimakis Stratopoulos, the pediatrician on staff at the Patras Orphanage, merely had to fill out the mimeographed form by adding the child's name and number and a few dates. This template form was the size of an insert in a regular international passport, and Petros's form was indeed stapled to the back of his Greek passport. The doctor's medical clearance was not verified independently.

The shoes featured at the opening of part 3 of this book belong to Petros (see figure 11): they are the shoes in which he traveled from Patras to the state of Washington, and they symbolize a journey of both potential and pain. Rather than dwelling on the negative baggage, however, Petros has made it his life's mission to help other Greek orphans and to assist in the search for their birth families. In 1983, he founded the Greek Orphans Birthright Center (GOBC), a roots search center and reunion assistance program that he personally funded. GOBC was active online from 2003 through mid-2012 from Petros's home office in Seattle, Washington. For several years, it collaborated with Theodoropoulou's Athens-based Roots Research Center (after its founding date of 1999). As director of the GOBC, Petros collected much material and fielded hundreds of questions from Greek-born adoptees worldwide, while also pursuing the intricacies of his own story. He further spearheaded a campaign for the rehabilitation of Greek birth mothers who relinquished children in the aftermath of the Civil War. He firmly believes that all parties to the Greek adoption history deserve the recognition of having their story told. Single-handedly, Petros has made important breakthroughs drawing the attention of the Ahepa and of the Greek Church in the United States to many of the unresolved issues concerning the postwar export of Greek adoptees to foreign countries.

Petros has supported my research project since our first exchange (in late December of 2015), and he has contributed much to its depth and scope

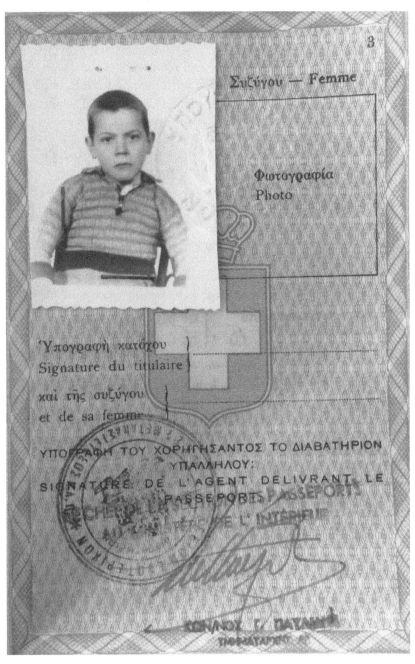

Fig 17: Passport picture of Petros Koutoulas at age six. Credit: personal archive of Greek adoptee Petros Koutoulas.

Fig 18: In a photo shoot with Constantine Verinis, supreme vice-president of the Ahepa, three Greek adoptees are sound asleep in a bed at the Hotel St. Moritz in New York City and two older children look into the camera. The date is 23 June 1956. All five adoptees are scheduled to continue their journey to the West Coast of the United States. Credit: personal archive of Greek adoptee Petros Koutoulas.

by raising thorny matters and by questioning some of my views. I found Petros because the Ahepa leadership used him as a "poster child" (literally and metaphorically), featuring him in several of its photographs of orphan arrivals. In the summer of 1956, the Ahepa regularly commissioned high-quality pictures from Olympic Press Photo, a Greek-owned photo studio in New York City. In some of these pictures, Petros gives the viewer a very generous, cheeky smile. But other, noncommercial pictures reveal Petros's true state: his passport picture, for instance, shows a feisty youngster with a scrutinizing look on his face, ready to challenge the world (figure 17).

According to Petros, Constantine Verinis, the Ahepa's supreme vice-president of 1956 who went on to become supreme president the following year, "hand-delivered" him to his childless, non-Greek adoptive parents, who then lived north of Seattle. Before starting the long plane ride across the States, Petros and four more adoptees were given a chance to rest in the classy (Greek-owned) Hotel St. Moritz near Central Park (figure 18).

From the day of his arrival, Petros's adoptive parents started to call him by a new first name. The desire among new parents to drop the Greek given name of their adopted child and to choose a name of their own (sometimes with the new father's name added as a middle name or initial) was common; it was, however, particularly unwelcome to adoptees who, like Petros, were old enough to feel strongly about their Greek name. Equally harsh was the adoptive parents' refusal to let Petros speak Greek, the only language he had ever known. The father was very disappointed that his new son did not know a word of English yet. The adoptive parents and also their local Ahepa contact (named G.R.) later admitted to Petros that his adoption was not entirely above-board, that he had, in fact, been used to meet the parents' wish for a speedy adoption (which they had been unable to achieve via regular domestic channels). Petros further reported that his adoptive parents needed to go and "check in" with this local but influential Ahepa sponsor about once a year.

Petros left home when he was sixteen. He took his Greek name back and avoided using his adopted first and last name whenever he could. Despite his critical stance toward certain high-placed representatives of the Greek Orthodox Church, Petros did rejoin the Orthodox faith, from which he had been severed since leaving Greece. Petros also put himself through school and went on to commit to a family, a career, and a mission: bringing knowledge and justice to the Greek orphans and their birth mothers who were unwillingly separated in the aftermath of the Greek Civil War. Petros did meet a Greek woman who claimed to be his birth mother. The details of her story, however, did not add up. Also, the mother and other relatives promptly made unreasonable demands from him, and they did not manage to establish a meaningful relationship.[36]

Linking Self, (A)kin, and Other

How are stories of troubling adoptions received? How does notoriety affect narration? These questions should leave the researcher constantly on the alert. Below is an example of a letter sent in late 1959 to the leading Greek American newspaper *Atlantis* by a distraught Greek parent in search of no less than three of his children. In the mid-1950s, the siblings, two boys and a girl, were sent to the United States for adoption after spending their first few years in a small village not too far from Thessaloniki. George Minouvides,

---

36. Based on Petros Koutoulas, extensive mail, email, and telephone communications, 19 December 2015 through July 2017, and on papers from his personal archive.

the father, wrote a first letter and, on the newspaper's request, followed up with additional information. Without much of an introduction, he pours his heart out in the opening letter, translated into English by the *Atlantis* office staff (here in its unedited form using pseudonyms):

Newspaper *Atlantis*
Greek Daily Newspaper
New York

I beg you to publish who is the American doctor who has taken under his protection, the on the reverse side mentioned my children because it is impossible for me to find out where they are and you will oblige me.
Respectfully

(signature)   George Minouvides
From Gian[n]itsa

9 years old Siderni [Sideris] Minouvides of George[37]
7 years old Athanasios Minouvides of George
3 years old Antonia Minouvides of George

They were taken in Salonica by the AHEPA in the year 1955 and I do not know their fate[.] I will be very much obliged if you will be able to find out for me where they are. I am a poor farmer and laborer.

My address is
George Minouvides
Giannitsa
Pellis [Pella], Thessaloniki, Greece

(The above is a direct translation).[38]

This wrenching case is also thoroughly problematic. In his follow-up letter of 8 January 1960, George Minouvides named the responsible party with great accuracy, leading the reader to conclude that he was only then consulting the formal papers he had received (and had probably signed, whether or not

37. The quotation's items in square brackets mark the slight differences between Minouvides's first and second letter.
38. Letter mailed from Greece on 4 November 1959 and received by the Greek American paper *Atlantis* on 10 December 1959.

he had grasped the full consequences of his action). Thus, when not merely (mis)remembering, Minouvides named the Διεθνής Κοινωνική Υπηρεσία, Τμήμα Ελλάδος–Έδρα Ελβετία–Βέρνη, in other words, the International Social Service Hellenic Branch, reporting to its main office in Bern, Switzerland. Minouvides may have been caught up in the outcry about the Ahepa leaders' entanglement in irregular adoptions, which might explain why the Ahepa readily came to mind in his initial letter. Given that the Ahepa and the ISS chose not to collaborate, because they represented very different philosophies about and practical approaches to intercountry adoptions, the ISS Hellenic Branch was the mediating party most likely to have been involved in this family's case.[39] Moreover, one of the gravity points of the activities of the ISS Hellenic Branch was indeed Thessaloniki (and its environs).

In all of my conversations with today's staff members of the ISS, both in Greece and in the United States, they have insisted that representatives of their organization never went out to actively seek or solicit children for adoption. But that principle may not have applied to provincial Greece of the mid-1950s. An anonymous article on the front page of the newspaper *I Thessalia* of 2 February 1956 stresses the dire need that has gripped the Volos region, especially after the devastating earthquakes, and it proposes US-bound adoption through the ISS as a viable solution. The relevant passage holds out the option of emigration, blends it with the topic of adoption overseas, and adds the names of the contact persons whom poor families might wish to seek out:

Ms [Ianthi] Meza has again arrived in our city. She is a representative of the International Social Service, and she is interested in [facilitating] the emigration and adoption of children to the United States. Accompanied by Mr Bornezis, this organization's lawyer with power of attorney here [in Volos], Ms Meza visited the Center for Social Welfare. . . . Ms Meza has already selected three little children who will be adopted by American families. Yesterday she left for Athens, taking with her one of the children, which was accompanied by its mother.

---

39. My conclusion is based on what philologists would argue is the *lectio difficilior* (Latin for the "more difficult reading"), which textual criticism traditionally credits with being the stronger ("*potior*") or more authoritative reading. I follow the rationale that, when Minouvides wrote his first letter and relied on informal memory, he blamed the Ahepa. But when the *Atlantis* staff pressed him for more specific details and he responded with a second, more carefully written letter, he probably did not haphazardly refer to the Hellenic Branch of the ISS, using its official and complete Greek name and all of its coordinates. The second reference is more unusual, more deliberate, or "more difficult," and therefore more credible.

Ms Meza will be coming back to Volos to take care of the adoption of other children as well. Interested families may apply to receive relevant guidelines and information at the Center for Social Welfare and from Mr Bornezis. Please note that the organization is interested in children of all kinds, up to age 10, whether they have parents or not.[40]

The suspicion that Greek families may have adopted out an older child (or children) to the United States to then use it as an "anchor child" (admittedly an anachronistic term), which would ease the chain migration of its parents and younger siblings, is prevalent but is seldom expressed in writing. The following (typical) affidavit given by a Greek birth mother and attached to a US private bill report of 1962 preempts the misgivings that many among the American decision-makers had been raising:

I hereby state . . . that I consent to the adoption and emigration of my said child, understanding that by my act of so releasing my child I shall never receive any right, privilege or status for entry into the United States of America.

The possible incentive of Greek chain migration, whether suppressed or openly addressed, reemerges in my conversations with parties who seek to augment the birth parents' agency and to diminish the role of willing mediators, be they the ISS or the Ahepa. In 1963, Eugenie Hochfield, supervisor at the ISS-USA, discussed a related case in which a Greek girl's temporary migration had been confused with her permanent adoption. The case points up a market psychology originating on the Greek side, whose dynamics complicate the blanket assumption that children move from sending to receiving countries in the one-way-only direction of American capitalist commodification:

In giving permission for the child to emigrate to the United States, he [the Greek biological father] had in mind a boarding home arrangement and really wanted the child to have better opportunities in the United States, hoping that some day his own immigration would become a reality.[41]

---

40. Anon., *I Thessalia*, 2 February 1956. I owe this reference to the generous assistance of Eleni Barboudaki, who guided me through the resources and holdings of the Municipal Center for Historical Research and Documentation of Volos. Notably, Ms Meza did not visit the Municipal Orphanage of Volos: by early February 1956, its earthquake-stricken building had still not been repaired. Of course, this situation only added to the desperation of some parents. We do not know what response Ms Meza's call received at this critical time for the city.

41. Hochfield (1963: 5).

Η αλήθεια στη χώρα των θαυμάτων, "Truth in Wonderland"

The only extensive personal memoirs written and published thus far are those of adoptees who were victims of the imprudent to illicit Greek adoption practices of the late 1950s through early 1960s.[42] Dionou's narrative in *Twentieth-Century Janissary* is particularly interesting for being the more complex one that not only cracks but actually breaks the formulaic mold in which adoption stories have typically been forged. Dionou reproduces a document showing that, as a newborn, he was found by Andreas Frangoulias—the same Frangoulias who delivered Mitsos to the Patras Orphanage. On 23 December 1958, Frangoulias discovered Dionou "at the doorstep of the Institution."[43] As in Mitsos's case, the record of Frangoulias's formal declaration of having found the child substituted for an official birth certificate. Dionou, too, came with a note attached, requesting that he be given the name Dionysios at the time of his baptism. Frangoulias then served as the godfather to the baby boy, who was indeed named Dionysios in a simple baptism ceremony performed at the orphanage.[44] It was common for a foundling home employee to accept to become a child's godparent, especially if he or she had already established some connection to the child. Also, this one-time commitment did not impose any future obligations on the casual godparent—unlike in the Orthodox communities and families beyond the institution.[45] Surely, Frangoulias, the janitor, gardener, and ad hoc godfather, wore many hats around the Patras Orphanage.

Joanna Giangardella wrote up her Greek adoption story in a book that is far more autobiographical than fictional: *The Girl from the Tower: A Journey of Lies* (2011) traces the cross-border trajectory and subsequent experience of nine-year-old Yiannoula (in 1957; born 1947). Yiannoula left from her northern Greek home village of Pergos (Pyrgos), which was later renamed Ouranoupoli. The older name referred to the formidable Byzantine stone watchtower, known as the Prosforion Tower, that sits on the shoreline of the easternmost Chalkidiki peninsula extending into Mount Athos. Yiannoula developed strong roots in her remote seashore village before being sent to a dysfunctional home in Los Angeles. There, her adoptive parents reacted with intolerance to her language, religion, and culture, and they unjustly favored her nonbiological but Greek-born brother, who had been adopted at an older age as well.

---

42. Dionou (2011), Giangardella (2011), and Kelmis (2012).
43. Dionou (2011: document "Deed of Birth" in appendix).
44. Dionou (2011: 63). The last name Dionou is the adult author's choice and plays on his first name.
45. Brouskou (2015: 231–38).

Yiannoula herself had asked to go to America, enticed by images of speaking dolls and abundant chocolate. An (unnamed) official and ISS social workers persuaded her widowed mother to let her go, arguing that superior living conditions awaited the adoptee in a new home in the States and that regular contact between mother and daughter would continue. With some bitterness, Joanna surmises that her mother, who herself stemmed from a family of Greek refugees displaced from Asia Minor, was probably deluded by a well-regarded foreign contact residing in her village into giving up her daughter for adoption.[46] Her mother was also unaware—or did not believe—that such a drastic decision would cut off all communication. Yiannoula/Joanna only found her way back to her home village some fifteen years later and after overcoming all the obstacles of what turned out to be a sealed-records adoption. Thus *The Girl from the Tower* thematizes loss, both literal and figurative (as in the loss of the village's name, which prevented Joanna from finding it on a map): the book covers the author's grief over the loss of a loving birth family, explores deflated rescue fantasies, and expresses regret over missed time and opportunity. Even finding is never the simple finding of what was lost. The promised land of chocolate did not deliver a wonderful family life (whether within the adoptive family or through marriage) or the select educational and professional options that Joanna and her mother had hoped for.

Giangardella's account has the truth factor of a memoir, but also the fiction-making quality of the adoptee's prolonged search, and even the fairytale-generating capacity of the disappointed adoptee. The author hypothesizes about what might really have happened and casts aspersions on individuals and institutions prominent in the domain of 1950s child welfare (from Joice NanKivell Loch, the Australian writer, journalist, and humanitarian worker who settled with her Scottish husband in Ouranoupoli, to UNICEF and a "special UN adoption program supported by Queen Frederica" mentioned on the book's back cover, alternating with the ISS and its unnamed caseworkers).[47] This picture may be countered by the findings of Winslow: through the 1950s, some Greek families welcomed international adoption as a means to "mitigate extreme poverty" and thus to make a "dis-

---

46. Giangardella (2011: 19–21, 151).
47. Giangardella (2011: 6, 25–28, 96, 151–52, 155–56, 161–62), confirmed via Skype communication of 28 February 2016. Susanna de Vries has written an extensive biography of NanKivell Loch, in which her life and work in Greece figure prominently (2000). This study is based on a variety of sources that extend well beyond NanKivell Loch's autobiography of 1968. According to de Vries, the international adoption of children (of Irish infants, in particular) had been on Loch's mind (2000: 73, 84, 295). Also, by the late 1950s, Loch had established closer connections to the Queen's Fund (de Vries 2000: 324).

tant stab at social mobility."[48] Some Greek parents understood US-bound adoption to be a temporary as well as an enticing solution, which promised to expand, rather than restrict, kinship relations. After all, the Greek adoption law of 1946 protected natural parents from losing their basic rights as long as the court granted a "simple" act of adoption pertaining to their child. Certain attorneys who arranged "full" US adoptions, however, still confirmed Greek parents in their belief that their legal parental rights (and their children's social and moral duties) would not be terminated, thus turning a set of conditions unfamiliar to Greek villagers to their own advantage.[49]

In a private bill of mid-1957, a prospective American mother of Greek extraction argued on behalf of a one-year-old Greek girl and distant relative, whom she and her husband wished to adopt:

> Her parents, being in poor circumstance, asked [name of the adoptive mother's aunt], who was visiting in Greece, if we might take her last child, a girl, and bring it up as our own, in the trust that we could give it a decent upbringing. The sooner the child comes to the United States, the better, as is self-evident.

The girl in question was not an orphan. Nonetheless, her pending placement in the States, by a couple that had only heard of her and might not have considered adoption otherwise, is presented as a "self-evident" better situation for the child. Understandably, widowed parents of conflicted or dislocated families felt the socioeconomic pressures even more. Demetra Mihevic, herself a (nearly) nine-year-old child at the center of such a cross-border transfer between Greek families, published a children's book about her experience. *Where a White Dog Smiles* (1991) strikes a brave and conciliatory tone but also acknowledges a profound sense of loneliness and disruption: Demetra lost out on her Greek childhood years and became suspended between two countries and two families, who grew further and further apart.[50]

By 1955, the story of two (fictitious) orphaned Greek siblings who, after being displaced by a disastrous earthquake, find loving families first in the Netherlands and then in France, had passed into (prize-winning) children's literature. The children's book, *Les Orphelins de Simitra* (1955), written by Paul-Jacques Bonzon, was translated in English as *The Orphans of Simitra* in

---

48. Winslow (2012a: 131, 132; 2017: 67).
49. See Fehrenbach (2010: 7–8, 17n24) and Winslow (2012a: 132–33; 2017: 67–68).
50. Based on Mihevic, telephone communication of 1 April 2017.

1957, saw its first American edition in 1962, and remained popular for many years. Again, Greek mediators paint the receiving country as a wonderland:

> [T]he matron broke the news to them. They were going to a distant land that was always green, where everyone was rich, and every child happy. This country had a curious name—it was called Holland. They would travel thousands of miles to get there. A family of peasant folk, like their own, was expecting them, and they would be given every care.[51]

A children's book of 1956, *Welcome, Santza*, by British author Constance Savery, situates the loving family that takes in no less than four Greek orphans in England.

Unlike the early children's books, the more extensive memoirs published by Greek-to-American adoptees are a phenomenon of the second decade of the twenty-first century, with its wide access to social media resources and self-publishing networks. They are also the creative products of the endeavors of mature adults in their fifties or sixties. A few authors who are currently drafting their memoirs pointed out that, crucially, their adoptive parents had been encouraging their research and writing—or that they had passed on. This holds true also for the first book-length Greek-to-Dutch adoption and reunification narrative: *Grieks Bloed*, or *Greek Blood* (2014), written by R. Bastiaan Touwen, one of the many infants sent to the Netherlands by the Babies' Center Metera. The same applies to Sonia Rijnsdorp, author of *Een kist met geheimen* (2017), or *A Coffin Full of Secrets* (2018). Metera is featured extensively in film footage collected by André van der Toorn, a Dutch producer and Greek-born adoptee, in his 2017 autobiographical documentary entitled *Mijn naam was Kostas*, or *My Name Was Kostas*.[52] Significantly, the Dutch adoptive mother was introduced to twenty-three babies to "choose from." Only after she and her husband had settled on André (Kostas) as "number 1" did the institution start seeking the birth mother's consent. Such practices (and pressures) would be considered unethical today.

The burden of divulging the details of private stories has fallen on the most innocent of all parties involved, that is, on the adoptees, who have also been driving the quest for knowledge about their roots. Why have none of the other parties initiated a similar writing endeavor (with the exception

---

51. Bonzon (1962: 54).
52. The documentary (in Dutch, Greek, and English) was coproduced with Wendy Hesp and is available online at http://www.kro-ncrv.nl/mijnnaamwaskostas/seizoenen/seizoen-2017/mijn-naam-was-Kostas.

of the short accounts by Clarke and Moessinger)?[53] The probable answer lies in the fact that none of the adult parties involved was entirely innocent and certainly had nothing to gain from any disclosures. Author Kostas Vaxevanis responds to this very question in his 2005 novel *The Lost Gene*. As his work progresses, Vaxevanis proves himself more of an investigative journalist than a novelist by nature, and his work delivers a chilling indictment. The author tackles the issue of the blatant and prolonged lack of any serious investigation by explaining what each side stood to gain—and lose. Sustained concealment served the interests of far too many people:

> "Why, for so many years, did nobody even scratch the surface of this affair?"
> "Who would have done so, my boy? The parents who took the children? It wasn't in their interest to do so. They didn't want anyone to learn anything. The leaders of the diaspora Greek communities were connected to the judge, or they were involved themselves, or they feared becoming entangled. Only Greece could have looked into this matter, but the power there was in the hands of those who organized it. The palace, some Greek Rasputins who gave their blessing to the crime, lawyers who organized it, and doctors who dirtied not only their hands but the entire medical profession."
> "And the families that lost their children?"
> "From what it looks like, most of them did not know. They thought that their children were dead. During wartime, what's more normal than that? Those who had any suspicions would not have known where to look and what for. You who are looking, have you found anything? No. How then would they have found anything amidst the havoc?"[54]

The Vicarious Experience of Adoption: Same Fears and Fantasies

> "Stories aren't made up, they're inherited."
> —Edgardo Cozarinsky, *The Moldavian Pimp*. Trans. Nick Caistor,
> 2006: 3

Efthalia's story related above illustrates that adoption affects many more people than merely those of the "adoption triad" of birth parent, adopted child, and prospective parent. The story of Charalambos Ebert, now deceased but born in 1950 and adopted out at age five to a family living in New Jersey, points once more to the Patras Orphanage as a common source. His experi-

---

53. Clarke (1958) and Moessinger (2003).
54. Vaxevanis (2005: 191).

ence further links adoption to postmemory and to postadoption: Charam-
lambos initiated the search for his birth mother, but after his sudden death,
his son saw it through and made the story known.[55] Thus, in the context
of adoption, postmemory may again be defined as a deeply felt experience
that addresses place, belonging, and identity in diverse and complex ways. It
affirms identity by rehabilitating the family past across generations.

Many adoptees whose experiences with their new families were negative, however, have voiced their fears of passing on their own traumas to
their children. They have done what they could to stave off the effects of
postmemory, thereby sometimes reifying those very effects. Carol, a Greek-
born child adopted out to California in 1956, expresses her anxiety and also
her desire to "break the circle":

> For me, the past is not at all a done deal: it's part of my daily struggles. My
> adoption history keeps rearing its nasty head in all I do. Most of all, it keeps
> affecting my relationships with people and with my children, especially. I am
> afraid that I may be transmitting my anxieties to them, or that I have already
> done so. But my past keeps haunting me. I do everything I can, though, on a
> daily basis, to break away from it.[56]

The testimony of Harry Diavatis, son of Father Spyridon Diavatis, the
independent "adoption agent" from San Antonio, Texas, bespeaks the links
between the adoptions of Greek-born children, historical and personal
memories, and individual quests for proper documentation. It shows how
the flow of Greek adoptions also affected the next generation of the agent's
family, which encountered criticism as well as praise. Father Diavatis tended
to reject any blame by invoking a sense of moral and patriotic duty in addition to the rhetoric of child salvation. His son imbibed this rhetoric. He
prides himself in his family's multigenerational legacy by way of other people's adopted lives, when he recalls,

> I was only about 12 years old . . . , but I remember those days quite well. My
> father was all over the news every time KLM airlines (who donated the flights)
> would bring another baby over to meet their new parents. I also remember
> that my father was harshly criticized by a few self-righteous Greeks because
> he was bringing over infants to be adopted by non-Greeks and the children
> would not be raised as Greek Orthodox. My father's response to the criti-

---

55. Michael Ebert to Dimitri Soultogiannis, *National Herald*, 4 March 2006.
56. Carol, testimony of 13 January 2016.

cism? "How many Greek orphans are you willing to adopt and give a new life to?" That usually shut up the critics.

I'm not certain how many babies my father helped place, maybe 30–40 or more. But I'm certain that they are all grateful for having been given the opportunity to be raised by loving families in this great country. They and their future generations will provide a lasting legacy towards the memory of my father.[57]

Dubinsky has introduced the notion of the "missing baby" in the context of the more recent mass international adoptions from Guatemala.[58] Like many postcolonial and rapidly modernizing countries of the mid-twentieth century, Greece went through the Civil War phase of the nation defining itself through the bodies of its youngest generation, that is, the phase of the "national baby."[59] Greece of the mid-1950s through early 1960s, however, saw a shift to its sad version of the phenomenon of the "missing baby," that is, of the large number of adoptees who should have had a chance to grow up in Greece (in a Greece with, at the very least, better-quality and more democratic social services), but whom various self-interested parties preferred to ship abroad, often under suspect circumstances. At least half of the "Diavatis babies" went missing from the son's account. So did Greek names, dossiers, and accurate remembrances.[60]

Postmemory at Work, an "Investigated" and "Imaginative" Form of Memory

> ἆρ' οἶσθ' ἀφ' ὧν εἶ;
> Do you know from what stock you come?
>
> —Sophocles, *Oedipus Tyrannus* 415. Trans. Hugh Lloyd-Jones, 1997: 364–65

The Argyriadis girls fell into the categories of "national children" and of "missing children," at least as far as the Greek dimensions of their history and memory were concerned (see part 1 of this book). However, the

---

57. H. Diavatis (2012: 2–3). For more accurate data on the Diavatis and POGO adoptions, see above, pp. 176–79.
58. Dubinsky (2010: 10–12).
59. Dubinsky (2010: 6) and above, p. 55.
60. For one, the adoptive parents actually paid for their children's airfare. Also, one of the Greek lawyers with whom Diavatis and POGO collaborated was not known for his integrity. See above, p. 177 (on Bouras).

American lives of Ioanna and Olympia Argyriadi (now Alevras), as of their descendants, may illustrate the dense layers of postmemory, which are rarely examined in detail. First, the two little sisters were politicized like no other Greek offspring, following the arrest, trial, and 1952 execution of their communist father. Also, the suicide of their mother had drawn unwanted public attention and involved the higher echelons of the Greek social services establishment. In 1955, they went "missing" after a hastily conducted adoption process: the girls' whereabouts were unknown to their Greek relatives until mid-December of 1980. For decades, Efterpi Argyriadi had no news about her half-siblings, until in 1980 she traced an address and a phone number that proved to be correct and that put her in touch with Ioanna. That call eventually re-established the family ties between Efterpi and Olympia/ Helen, but not with Ioanna/Gina, who had been living a life of fragility and trauma, leaving her unable to cope with her birth family's history. In September of 2013, Gina's adopted son Mike learned about the Argyriadis relatives who had stayed behind in Greece. By that time, his own inquisitive nature had led him to ask many questions, primarily of his aunt Helen. Mike made contacts in the States and in Greece, had important family documents translated, and looked for more traces of the unfathomable past of his older relatives, to whom he has referred as the "descendants of silver," poetically invoking the etymology of the family name.[61] Mike's quest to "re-historicize" the lives of his mother and aunt has raised perhaps as many questions as it has answered. His path of discovery has been a hazardous one, filled with surprises, few of which he has been able to share with his mother.

Touching Silences

The course of Gina's life has been uneven due to distressing personal experiences. Her physical maladies have been aggravated by mental or psychic conflicts. Whenever involuntary memories come flooding back at Gina, the painful past takes possession of her all over again. She then sinks into dull silences for long stretches of time. These reactivated memories have, for decades now, resisted recovery in words. In turn, Gina's sisters, husband, and her own son have, to this day, shielded her from information that might upset her. Her non-Greek husband, for instance, took pains to avoid the perturbing family history supposedly laid to rest in the "old country." Gina's silences, or her mute expressions of grieving, were matched also by the reticence with which her adoptive parents spoke—or, rather, did not speak—about the traumatic events that the girls had left behind in Greece. Child

---

61. Mike, 29 June 2015, online.

psychologists have posited that young victims of trauma are aided by being able to discuss their experiences with a caring parent or other adult close to them.[62] This kind of unsilencing facilitates children's understanding and memory of emotionally difficult events, and it enhances their coping capacities. But, after the brisk separation from Efterpi, Gina did not have anyone near who knew intimately what had happened in Greece and was willing to talk about it.

Gina's focus on memories of trauma has defined her way of thinking about the relationship between the past and the present, between Greece and the States. Her silences demarcate her double reality, of her own world and that of her biological parents. These realities haunt and hurt, and they have ultimately prevented Gina from living completely in the present. The silences accompany the cataclysmic "momentous events" that have returned, remained, and never fully dissipated into the past. Gina has shown the signs and symptoms of a victim of the kind of trauma that turns the past into a constant now, which she herself has been unable to transcend or "re-externalize" (using the neologism of psychiatrist Dori Laub).[63] Psychologist and psychoanalyst Philip Bromberg has vividly called a life affected by early developmental trauma as living in "the shadow of the tsunami," as per the title of his 2011 book. The events of 1951–1955 had once caused a child's sense of meaning and identity to fracture. Their persistence has marked how hard it is to verbalize traumatic experiences, that is, to integrate amorphous, disassociated, and tormenting memories into a normal consciousness.

Gina's sense of family and security was shattered again when she lost a child, but then she, too, pursued adoption and found Mike (born 1986). This second round of adoption made of Mike, both literally and metaphorically, a "witness by adoption."[64] Mike has long been searching for ways to unlock the silent solitude borne of his mother's trauma, which, he realized, was linked to silenced family secrets of the early 1950s. Gina's withdrawal, and also the quiet circumspection with which her family has treated her, mirrored and internalized, in paradoxical ways, the Greek Left's stunted public memory from the time of the Civil War, which the Right had further muzzled by imposing its own thirty-year-long silence.

Surrounded by these various forms of displaced memory and deferred communication, Mike has found ways to move beyond the pained search for identity, to break out and commune through art. His engagement with

---

62. See, for instance, Fivush and McDermott Sales (2004) and also Frierson (2015: 11).
63. Laub (1992: 69).
64. The expression expands on a phrase coined by Geoffrey Hartman (1996: 8), or on Zeitlin's "belated witness" (2001: 130, 131).

the visual arts, especially, has helped him to process the details of a Greek past broken into the pieces of incoherent family memories. Over time, his quest of memory recovery, in which his aunts have participated, has joined individual to communal trauma and has opened up new venues for dialogue and creative expression. Mike understands that his mother's story cannot be one of redemptive closure. When her unnarratable memories became even more untransmittable, he fell back on an old family tradition that had long proven to bring release and repair: he continued to paint with his mother, in a mother-son (re)mediation of traumatic experiences. "I liked the idea of our identities merging at least on the canvas," he professed.[65]

The lives of Efterpi Argyriadi and of Gina and Helen Alevras have been conditioned by what David Pillemer has defined as "memorable moments" or "momentous events," which they have frequently recalled (though not necessarily voiced) through the mechanisms of "personal event memories."[66] Based on his research on the psychology of memory, Pillemer insists that singular events or specific episodes, whose impact correlates to their suddenness, gain longevity in the subjects' personal memories and shape or even anchor lives.[67] Episodic recollections are therefore imbued with specificity and sensory-based affect, and they are attuned to a sense of reexperiencing and to the perception or assertion of truthfulness. While Efterpi and Gina have been relating to the tragic "momentous events" of their lives in very different ways, Helen's future was far less conditioned by the memories of those events: she was only two and a half years old when her father was put to death and five and a half years old when her adoption case went through. Nonetheless, Helen has been devoted to promoting cross-cultural understanding and friendship in the small Florida community where she has lived for many years.

Is there hope for Gina to heal? When a family story becomes a trauma narrative, how does it affect children—and adoptive children? Are the double layers of adoption (of growing up adopted and raising an adoptive child in a place far removed from where the horrible past took place) enough of a "distantiation process" to make healing possible? Is a vicarious experience (of the memories and emotions conveyed by parents) inevitably less meaningful than the actual skin-felt experience? Or are we—oddly and wrongly—measuring an "economy" of "authentic" suffering that is uncalled for from the perspective of postmemory?

---

65. Mike, testimony of 26 October 2014.
66. Pillemer (1998: 25, 26, and 1, respectively).
67. Pillemer (1998: 27).

Postmemory and the Destiny/ation of "Family Facts"

With some surprise, Mike has watched the seriousness of his growing pre-occupation with Greek Civil War and Cold War history. His path of re/dis-covery has challenged him to reconcile an interest in Greece that first tried to formulate personal (and lateral) responses to the early 1950s incidents with a new concern with the country's diachronic history, enriched through research and study. This research process was an arduous sequence of learning about the family past, then articulating memories and knowledge about what happened or what may have happened—and occasionally being frustrated by other people or by adverse conditions in trying to reconstruct this past. Mike set out on a path of active (re)collection and return soon after he discovered, in September 2013, that some of his maternal relatives were still living in Greece. He was fascinated to learn of the existence of an older half-sister to his mother and aunt. He established preliminary contact and scheduled a first trip to Greece for July of 2014. By April 2015, Mike had made two exploratory trips and nearly planned a third. By late summer of 2015 and after a three-month living experience as an artist-in-residence in Athens, Mike had developed a deep personal and nuanced connection to the events of the past in Greece, despite their distance in time and space. Propelled by the need to reenact distant times and make meaning of remote places, Mike also found out, however, that temporal and geographical boundaries can be crossed more easily than psychological and ideological ones.

Meanwhile, Mike has continued to build a "personal archive" from the fragments of his mother's past, which, he admits, can never be pieced together to deliver a complete and gratifying biography. This personal archive has grown into an "alternative archive" for documenting and presenting "known" historical facts differently (distinctly different from the Communist Party's archive or from any other political record). Hirsch invokes what Diana Taylor has called "the repertoire" of embodied knowledge that did not enter into the historical archive.[68] Mike's aspiration to capture historical moments and cultural peculiarities through art has inspired many imaginative plans and projects, which he has undertaken from a position that cuts across the native-versus-foreign gap and the divide between insider and outsider. He has not been writing, but has been making art "in the middle voice," rediscovering a medium that he studied and knew well as a better fit for the personal message. A family tale of recurring adoptions has become a story of repeated and proven adaptability, but also of a

---

68. Hirsch (2008: 105) and Taylor (2003).

sense of rootlessness driving a (post)modern concern with individuation. The pain of exile (to another country, to—the witnessing of—the crisis of mental trauma) has been alleviated by a (symbolic as well as physical) return to Greece. Family trauma does not easily lead to coherent conceptual meaning or merely understanding. Hopefully, however, a next generation may discover new causal relationships of national to personal and family history and may find relief and resolve in empowering itself through postmemory.

In the early stages of researching his family history, Mike was preoccupied with the question of "what actually happened?" Ironically, the Greek family, too, had been left for decades with similar questions of "what actually happened?" on the American side of the family. But Mike soon moved beyond this interpretive framework, even when some relatives did not follow him down that path. Over the past years, he has come to attach intrinsic value to the differences in narration and emphasis that have emerged: "the facts" have proven to be only partially verifiable; tales and images of what the relevant parties believed had happened, or wished had happened, have moved into the foreground. Instead of seeking to establish "the facts" in their consequential order, Mike has been walking the thin line between the objective details of past history and the subjective strands of memoir. He has been observing what relatives in Greece and in the States have been stating, recently and over time, what they choose not to mention, how they express themselves differently in private vis-à-vis in public, and so on. He has been paying attention also to what more distant relatives on both sides of the Atlantic have added to an otherwise incomplete puzzle, and to what that sharing has meant for them.

The Greek American scholar and writer Irene Kacandes has traced a similar development in her family memoir, *Daddy's War: Greek American Stories* (2009), which is conditioned by children's shock, fragmented memory, and the second generation's postmemory process. Kacandes describes how she refocused her research and writing, abandoning the quest for "the facts" and the causal relations between them. Rather, "[h]ow telling and being told is negotiated between survivors and their children would be [her] central concern."[69] Mike, too, recalls a state of elliptical half-memory or nonmemory until "the walls came tumbling down," when a cousin started a conversation with the characteristic "but don't you know . . . ?"[70] Of course, Mike's state of deferred memory presses the following questions: How much did he want to know at any

---

69. Kacandes (2009: 32).
70. Mike, testimony of 26 October 2014.

given time, and in his youth especially? How did he feel about knowing or not knowing, or about being cut off from further knowledge once he had decided to pursue "the facts"? In that light, Mike's July 2014 travel to Greece was first intended to be a data-gathering trip, then it became a "family-gathering" mission (in multiple senses of the words), until it transformed into a kind of retrospective journey, reaching far beyond the basic level of acquainting himself with Greece and with his relatives still living there. This exploratory shift from the aimed-for discovery of "objective" meanings to the appreciation of implied and negotiated meanings has been a pivotal one. It may offer up a model to other searching Greek-born adoptees and their descendants, and to those who write with and about them. Admittedly, Mike has had a more difficult time processing subjective meanings through travel and art than I did through research and writing. I have felt more "comfortable" in the role of the historiographer of another family's trauma, of another people's history, jogging memories through questions, draft versions, and timelines of the historical and political events. While Mike has remained passionate about the exactitude of the script with which this writing project has gone forward, his own artwork has concentrated on depicting absence of meaning, or the emptiness of facts that defy language.

Art as Postmemory's Medium

[T]he art becomes an external presence, like an imaginary companion.

—Richman 2014: 92

A mild degree of disappointment was inevitably part of Mike's probing relationship into the unknown past and family, which engendered confusion when more distant relatives asserted agency by claiming Greek ownership of "the story." Of course, it would be wrong to assume that there is only one story and not multiple plots, diverging subject positions, or even inscrutable questions. Mike's endeavor had been to reintegrate confounding collective and family memory into the history and biography of his self. When language and correspondence foundered, however, he sought refuge again in art—his long-time mainstay. Mike's current creative process is a life-affirming one, incorporating cognitive as well as affective strands. Thus, representational strategies have become coping mechanisms beyond communicative techniques, and these nonverbal exchanges have yielded insights and reflections captured nowhere else. Mike characteristically wrote, in an email of 17 April 2015:

I am reassessing what I am after. At first, I needed to search as a family member. I then thought that historical research was important to me. But, now, I am back to being an artist. My research uses history as material, but doesn't strive to produce history—if that makes sense.

Mike's second-generation project or postmemorial work has wanted to *"reactivate* and *reembody* more distant social/national and archival/ cultural memorial structures by reinvesting them with resonant individual and familial forms of mediation and aesthetic expression," in the apt words of Hirsch.[71] Via his email communications and online postings, Mike has allowed us to track his subjective engagement with the investigative and also the artistic process. He has found permanent solace in art to make the events of the past intelligible to himself and to his immediate circles. Because they are less easily understood than the written word, Mike's chosen media have often instigated further questions from casual observers; hence the varied attempts at contextualization. Mike's photographs, especially, have offered profound examples of memory's echo across generations and cultures—of the loud resonance of silence. Some of them illustrate how art may inscribe newly acquired memories (even if that is a contradiction in terms). They tell about ineffable memories and feelings, which reduced children to a state of in-fancy (in its original Latin meaning of the infant's condition of being unable to speak yet). They also hold out hope, however, of superseding unspeakability and the limits of representation. In words that *mutatis mutandis* apply here, Stephen Feinstein has made the following telling claim about the second generation of Holocaust survivors:

> art . . . provides a means of coping with and comprehending the trauma of parents' survival, and it focuses particularly on the question of "absence" and the impact of that absence on their own lives. It therefore often becomes a vehicle for the discovery of self.[72]

Mike's self-exploration continued in his latest role of caretaker of his mother, of extending her survival often at the expense of his own needs. He was also keenly aware of a new kind of identity-extending or identity-swapping that then took place between him and his dependent mother, between caregiver and care-receiver. He even found new artistic expres-

---

71. Hirsch (2008: 111; italics hers).
72. Feinstein (1998: 202).

sions to capture those most recent developments. Without knowing the circumstances, Hirsch concurs and adds an element of crucial import to the child of the second round of adoptions:

> Second generation fiction, art, memoir, and testimony are shaped by the attempt to represent the long-term effects of living in close proximity to the pain, depression, and dissociation of persons who have witnessed and survived massive historical trauma. They are shaped by the child's confusion and responsibility, by the desire to repair, and by the consciousness that the child's own existence may well be a form of compensation for unspeakable loss.[73]

Mike's images and our readings of them force the issue of the aesthetic value of this kind of artwork: Is the central question of whether this is good art still valid or even applicable? Is this art's accessibility to a wider public still a significant criterion? Does the artist want broader audiences to comprehend the very personal issues at stake, as they would if these issues had been communicated through an explicit written text? Mike's reconstruction of his family's past addresses, in the first place, a need to respond to the dictates of the present questioning of self-identity. Artistic outlets are often private, restorative ways of coping, not centered on formal or official forms of remembrance. While Mike's artwork functions in an intimate sphere to symbolize family trauma, his work, nonetheless, memorializes this trauma: it becomes a memorial to what was lost and what is still at risk of being lost. Thus Mike's self-(re)definition as an artist has been fashioned by encounters that have re-imbedded the affective in the political and the public. The content and enigmatic form of Mike's artwork disorientate us as viewers but do elicit reflection on the traumatic experiences of his mother, binding us in a collective exploration of the family's trauma, the descendant's posttrauma, and a people's painful recent history. The artist's recall of repressed thoughts and stories that interface with residues of the Greek past has taken on a performative dimension, in which creative ability has (re)enacted memory mediations and has uncovered therapeutic relief. It is this kind of relief, whether achieved through study, writing, or artistic expression, that may become a source of solace and strength for other survivors and postsurvivors, adoptees and postadoptees.

The above section, which revisited the Argyriadis family in later life, has attempted to recover some of the more intimate voices of postmemory, beyond the silences of memory. It also analyzed the research trajectory

---

73. Hirsch (2008: 112).

underlying this recovery process. Mike and I have been attentive recipients of the scattered family biography (in multiple meanings of the words). He has assumed the lead role in soliciting his Greek aunt's life narrative and has thus been serving as the quintessential "private" detective. I for my part have prioritized scholarly writing as a vector of transmission and dissemination. The primacy of the Greek language (for him an obstacle, for me adding to the project's appeal) has played a critical part, too, in our different but very compatible choices. Superseding feelings of linguistic inadequacy (which he has tried to overcome by pursuing Greek lessons), Mike has found in his art the most suitable mode of telling and retelling, while generously sharing his doubts and misgivings with me, his academic partner in this joint quest for knowledge. Mike also wanted to "go live," "perform," or dramatize our act of receiving, not for self-aggrandizing reasons but as a mode of personal "processing." Some scholars have spoken of the postsurvivors' sense of identification, even overidentification, which seeks expression in venues of reperformance or "modes of reenactment."[74] Lately, however, a self-reflexive type of concern about how to write or at least communicate his family history beyond (re)producing the inherited story has been worrying Mike. Confronted with the challenges of narrating history in the middle voice, he has now embraced the only-partly-known, which opens up times and spaces in which to perform postmemory creatively. Hirsch helps us read this active exercise of the postadoptee and its link to the research quest, when she claims that postmemory's "connection to its object or source is mediated not through recollection but through an imaginative investment and creation."[75]

Passing on the DNA of Adoption (Stories)

> In sixth grade, we had to do our family tree. Mine was a twig in a box.
>
> —Kim Kruse, September 2015[76]

---

74. Zeitlin (2001: 130).

75. Hirsch (1997: 22); also Hirsch (1996: 662 and 2012: 5). When Mike found the following, longer quotation from Hirsch (2008: 106–7), he joked that it had been written "especially for a second-generation searcher like him":

> Postmemory describes the relationship that the generation after those who witnessed cultural or collective trauma bears to the experiences of those who came before, experiences that they "remember" only by means of the stories, images, and behaviors among which they grew up. But these experiences were transmitted to them so deeply and affectively as to *seem* to constitute memories in their own right. Postmemory's connection to the past is thus not actually mediated by recall but by imaginative investment, projection, and creation.

76. Kruse is quoted by Dave DeLand, *St. Cloud Times*, 13 and 14 September 2015. In July of

The adoption odyssey of the Argyriadis siblings, itself deserving of a book (a book written by the family itself), has dictated our quest for a bigger and more nuanced picture, for adoption narratives of a more diverse nature, which have reinforced, in varying degrees, the political underpinnings—and expediencies—of Greece's Cold War adoption movement. Also, these additional accounts redefine the meaning of the story of the Argyriadis girls and their postadoptee generation, to whom this study has come around in full circle. As an academic writer, I have faced the complex challenge of having to discern which narratives and artistic expressions from memory are most significant for the history of twentieth-century Greece. Given that historical significance and subjective meaning do not necessarily correlate, I have felt uncomfortable at having to decide on a selection that inevitably relegates other narratives and expressions to the category of the "less important" ones. Vaxevanis, too, rightly pointed to the many players involved in adoption scenarios. It is important to hear from different players, different subjects and victims. I have sought them out by way of soliciting interviews and other accounts from Greek-born adoptees who have grown up and are currently living in the United States (with a few exceptions). But more work remains to be done on and with those who grew up or chose to live in other countries, and who may define Cold War history otherwise.

The adoption stories recounted above have more than a personal resonance; they become vignettes of intimacy in kinship and kinning relations. Even a modest collection of such stories may add important nuances to the political accounts, the reports on policymaking and policy vacuums, state and institutional projects, domestic and international casework, and so on.[77] Also, adoption tales are not narrated in an abstract or static time or space; they are, rather, performed in specific histories and topographies, contexts and at times contests. The answers through stories take us farther afield than one might imagine, beyond essentializing the idea of the biological family, or beyond romanticizing the homogeneous family. As a complex signifier of design and therefore difference, adoption raises issues inherent in nongenetic parenthood and in the "constructedness" of the adoptive family, nuclear-family-style. The personal narratives further focalize the ways in which childhood memory is transmitted into language, storytelling, or other performative expressions. At the same time, however, this collection of intimate testimonies reinforces the causal relationship of national

---

1962, Kruse was adopted from Thessaloniki's Saint Stylianos Foundling Home, which declared her a foundling.

77. The most recent book by Margaret Homans (2013) is devoted to the power and potential of (writing) adoption narratives. See also Honig (2005); Irr (2014); and Novy (2005 and 2012).

to individual and family history, and thus provides a valuable lens through which Greece's Cold War history may be observed, albeit from overseas and decades after the facts.

The intercountry adoption of very young children was at stake. These children have grown into conscious adults (and very adept users of social media). Therefore, this oral history component of our study is no longer a personal matter nor an internal Greek affair, nor is it exclusive to the past. The clusters of trajectories and experiences emerging from Greek-born adoptees' storytelling is, rather, transnational, intergenerational, and, as symptomatic of oft-abused practices, of truly global concern. Many other stories are still "out there," and every extended Greek or Greek American family seems to have one. They add to the issues that have come into view via the above analysis of a mere few samples: adoption commerce; abuse in child placement; wrongful removal of children and adoptee deportation; forced adoption and uninformed or coerced consent; an unsound and loosely policed adoption circuit, itself the outcrop of an underfunded and poorly regulated family and child welfare system; and so on.

The presentation of the biographical information on Greek-born adoptees allows us to better understand their life stories, not as the disparate experiences of lone individuals, but as collective endeavors that subvert the idea of oneself and one's family as isolated or self-contained. This presentation also lets us grasp authorship, of the written and the oral accounts alike, as authority over hybrid experiences with vast resonances, across borders and generations. It may further inspire (since it has already inspired) a more collective subjectivity among Greek adoptees or any other adoptees. Significantly, too, it may expand networks of solidarity beyond monolithic definitions of what it means to be Greek, Greek American, European, white, refugee or immigrant, parent, child, or young adult.

CONCLUSION

Greek and Greece, Where Home and History Rhyme

> It is this dissolution of any teleology of history—the disappearance of a history whose end is known—that creates today's urgent "duty to remember," a sense more mechanical and heritage-based than moral, and linked, not to the idea of "debt" but to "loss" . . .
>
> —Pierre Nora, 21 June 2001

The questions of a "postsurvivor" in the role of "searcher" (as adoption lingo has it) initiated and then propelled my investigation into the story of the Argyriadis family. This search, which found me somewhat by coincidence, drew me into my own quest for more information about the person of Elias Argyriadis, his family and descendants, their experiences through inter-country adoption, and the postwar Greek adoption circuit at large. I have reconstructed this quest, which parallels the quest of other Greek adoptees and their children into their unknown family history, via a diachronic narra-tive and analysis, integrating personal and psychological as well as cognitive and scholarly strands. Therefore, this book has also been about recollection and the collection of evidence, about painfully probing and painstakingly proving. Part 1 offered a person-centered Greek history and analyzed an even more actor-centered genealogy of push factors toward intercountry adoption. Moving beyond the microhistorical realm of part 1, part 2 decon-structed Greek-to-American adoption exports, focusing on pull factors and on the competing practices of the Ahepa and the ISS, which, in pursuit of "volume," reached beyond the PIKPA or Metera adoption platforms or the channels used by private lawyers. Part 3 added (fictitious) names to the faces of the dispersed Greek-born adoptees and their descendants—the last unknown Greek "diaspora."

The 1950s era of Greece's notorious "parastate" and "paraconstitution," byproducts of the nation's Cold War alliance with the United States, gave rise to the parafamily, the "parallel family" of secretive origins, another index of political and socioeconomic vulnerabilities. Domestically, postwar Greece invested far too little in family and child welfare for all, and it let leftist families especially fend for themselves, unsupported if not actively disrupted. Left-wingers were deemed to be on the wrong side of history as well as of ongoing reconstruction, and they did not benefit from the massive amount of American aid sent to Greece. The adult parties of adoptive families in the States, on the other hand, knew that the sought-after adoptions of the Greek-born children that they had "selected" often rested on personal or political connections, even if they could not fathom the shadowy transactions of a paraeconomy trading in children. By the time the youngsters from Greece reached adulthood in America, most parafamilies had grown into loving, supportive, and supported families; their irregular beginnings were either long forgotten or were never communicated. In contrast, the large majority of Greek families only started to enjoy full freedom and prosperity in the mid-1970s, when normalization finally ensued. Their standard of living has now been shaken by the country's prolonged economic crisis, which has again been harsh on children and young mothers in particular. Perhaps a study of what "roots" and "uprooting," especially, have come to mean to the hundreds of Greece's *xenitia*-bound adoptees of a prior crisis-stricken era may function as a timely reminder of the long-lasting effects of a lost family-scape, while the nation continues to ponder its values, its own roots, and "radicalism" (in all literal and other meanings of the word).

The US-bound adoption movement may function as a metaphor for Greece's Cold War history, a history rooted in unprincipled politics and crude capitalist priorities. The Cold War predicament matched strong American pronatalist tendencies to dire conditions in Greece, where social welfare was chronically underfunded and single ("illegitimate") motherhood remained taboo. The children's "exchange" opened up an alternative venue for conducting Cold War (Real)politics. It places a fitting prism on American as well as Greek foreign policies, security concerns, refugee provisions, and other external affairs, which were integral parts of the Cold War project. The mass adopting-out of Greek children to America proves to be a most concrete, embodied example of the politics of dependence on the United States: it helped to define not only US foreign policy but also US foreign aid. The vehicle of these unilateral adoptions symbolically (and no less physically) marked the transition to a new political and ideological status quo that sought to balance the democratic, pluralist West against the communist and totalitarian East. On the US side, orphan admissions became an anti-Soviet statement while broadcasting the West's "altruism" and promoting lofty assumptions about American identity in particular. Most Americans remember the baby lifts by plane from Korea and Vietnam. Many have heard of the orphan trains of prior decades. Few, however, still recall the "orphan planes" coming in from Greece in the 1950s. Therefore, the history of the Greek-born adoptees is also a history and cultural study of some of the defining aspects of the twentieth-century American experience.

International adoptions shake up cultural and political geographies as well as individual identities, and not only because they operate at the interstices of the politics of migration and mobility. They challenge us to see the signs of postcolonial bonds and of (neo)liberal market economies dealing in children. They map the neocolonial relationship between America and the client state. They expose a transnationalism that is at once admired and extremely fragile, by way of the vulnerable bodies of minors, themselves symbolic of any nation's future. The Greek adoption circuit may animate the modes in which the memories and postmemories of loss, separation, and susceptibility have intertwined with the transnational realms of kinship, real and imagined alike. Along with the imagined community of Greek-born adoptees, we continue to grapple with the fact that time and distance, as constitutive elements and even technologies of the Cold War Greek adoptions, are what made irregular placements possible in the first place. The lack of social healing and of political recognition has caused these transnational adoptions to be virtually forgotten since.

Evidence of a broad spectrum of illegalities can be traced back to the very moments and the Greek locales of the "sourcing" and the "transacting" of children earmarked for adoption abroad. Anomalies affected the logistical details but also engendered a spirit of secrecy and cover-up. The 1950s Greek government itself could have done far more to establish proper oversight, to distribute resources evenly, to direct the income from fundraising campaigns to all deserving institutions, to develop dignified models of symbolic adoption and child sponsorship from afar, and to reform the dominant climate of oppression that disproportionally hurt poor women and their babies. The Greek monarchy should have left the adoptions of its most defenseless subjects in the hands of qualified agencies (beyond Lina Tsaldari, antileftist politics, PIKPA, and publicity). Instead, it all too eagerly responded to the seemingly insatiable demand from abroad for Greek babies—a demand it kept cultivating.

Unable to handle real need and notoriety, the Ahepa, the very association that vouched for the Greeks' internationalization, served as a go-between, brokering coarse to corrupt adoption matches. The Ahepa was among the first to match a supply of Greek children to the American demand, but also a Greek need for money to American largesse. Other intermediaries, too, sensed correctly that the convergence of the new Cold War and the old social constraints would allow the market for Greek adoptees to thrive (and would make it look like a win-win situation). Ahepa presidents, more

specifically, put a transnational infrastructure in place that stretched policies, programs, resources—and internal goodwill. To their credit, Ahepa's
regular members were willing to commit to deliberation, introspection, and
inside investigation. Nonetheless, the basic recognition that unprofessional
practices violated children's human rights is long overdue. Along with the
adoptees, I hope that individuals and organizations will achieve the necessary political and ideological autonomy from the Greek state as well as from
the(ir) glorified past to grant such an acknowledgment.

The voices of many Greek adoptees have added nuance, shade, or a tinge
of joy and pain to my examination of the Cold War construction of (adoptee) childhood and of the legal to illicit realms of the biopolitics of the Greek
adoption export. I hope that the details and patterns emerging from these
individual histories will provide answers and also some form of closure to
those whose story has not yet been told. Adoptions will remain at the heart
of personal histories, domestic memories, and especially, the challenges
of growth. In her February 2013 TED talk, therapist Esther Perel spoke of
two types of Holocaust survivors: those who did not die and those who
came back to life. Mike's mother and aunts and a host of other Greek-born
orphans fall under a similar complex specter of the political and ideological
history of children (and grandchildren). But, on the constructive side, Mike
and many adoptees recognize that the crushing family history that fate has
dealt them represents a substantial slice of an expanding Greek national
history. The Greek adoptees' (shaken) identities have become part of the
lived experiences of their descendants, and they coexist, in multiple ways,
with American and European transnational identities; they also (eloquently
but painfully) prove that the personal and the political stories of postwar
global history intersect. Political history without a social dimension, however, might not have taken our analysis far enough, for underestimating
critical interactions between state and society. With the focus on multiple
young and precarious individuals, mid-twentieth-century personal politics
has challenged not only Greece's grand narratives but also its finer-grained
social history. Beyond government social policy, beyond the sociological
and demographic data, this social history becomes the family history of the
poor and the most vulnerable, it assesses the value of children and young
mothers to Greek society, and it discloses family moralities and survival
strategies of parents and institutions alike.

Adoptions have become an international research focus calling for
the exchange of scholarly insights and conclusions, in which the adoption
export from Greece has yet to be fully integrated. Adoptions also lend themselves to the writing of a most intimate history "from below," which, because

of its openness to memory and postmemory, may add the colorations and accretions of a psychological and sensory history to (the nuances of) a political and factual history. Adoption movements are not limited, however, to the private or familial domain; they extend to national and global spheres. I hope to have shown that, far from being a peripheral concern, the study of international adoption of the Cold War era is central to the experience and constitution of the American and the Greek sociopolitical realm, and it therefore deserves scholarly and also public attention. Furthermore, the Greek case becomes emblematic of the mistakes that were inevitably made when the intercountry adoption movement was still in its infancy. A study of the case of Greece at large may help us to avoid similar mistakes in the future. Many adoptees and postadoptees have a story . . . and many more think it's just a personal tale. I have only made a start proving otherwise, and I certainly encourage more fact-finding expeditions as well as open communications about them.

My research and writing project has placed in the foreground the reciprocal dialectics of private persons, and especially of children, in the political landscape of Greece and the United States; it has also assessed how individuals' identities were subsumed by the biopolitics of the underexplored period of 1950–1962 in particular. Thus the personal stories stemming from the trauma of the deep Civil War and the ensuing socioeconomic havoc culminate in a critique of Western expediencies of the postwar decades. The Argyriadis children were not central to Greece's history of the 1950s through early 1960s, and neither was any specific Greek-born adoptee. However, the web of their "peripheral" but inherently connected stories reveals the global reach of the displacement and hardship caused by the Greek establishment's drive to adopt out to the States, by the American demand or pull, and by the greed and lust for power of well-placed middlemen. Greek children became pawns in unrelenting games of exercising and displaying power, domestically and in global contexts. Greece's role as a transnational player, however, remained inextricably linked to some of the most distressing experiences of private or family life. Meanwhile, individual searches for identity and belonging continue, long after the papers were signed, and they foreshadow the futures of countless others displaced by conflict and crisis today.

ΛCKNOWLEDGMENTS

This study has gained tremendously from the keen insights and encouraging feedback generously offered by Aigli Brouskou (extensive email communication from the spring of 2014 onward through the present). Aigli went far beyond the call of duty to steer an unknown colleague in the direction of pertinent references, local resources, and further contacts (including some delicate ones). She added depth to this book and saved me from embarrassing errors. Mary Theodoropoulou, herself committed for life to Greek adoption research and searches through the Roots Research Center, took the time to share her thoughts and experiences with me. So did Mary Selekou, current president of SEASYP, the Research Association for the Disclosure of Information on Adopted Children: she frankly divulged her own life story and search experience with the unknown foreign interviewer.

My conversations with the following scholars and friends in modern Greek studies have been enormously beneficial, and I thank them wholeheartedly: Yiorgos Anagnostou, Eliza-Anna Delveroudi, Rosemary Donnelly, Dan Georgakas, Vicky Kaisidou, Michaela Karambini-Iatrou, Alexander Kazamias, Alexander Kitroeff, Kostis Kourelis, Vassilis Lambropoulos, Angeliki Lefkaditou, Artemis Leontis, Anastasia Marinopoulou, S. Victor Papacosma, Eirini Papadaki, Elaine Thomopoulos, Riki Van Boeschoten, and Tasoula Vervenioti. I extend my appreciation to the members and boards of the Modern Greek Studies Association of North America, who surrounded me with intellectual stimulation, collegiality, and support. I am further indebted to valued colleagues and friends at King's College London and at the University of Florida, and to Eleni Bozia, especially. I have also profited greatly from the acute intelligence of David Christenson and his deep, continuing commitment to students and colleagues. I owe additional debts to the anonymous referees of my manuscript, and to Karen Balcom, for helping me think through the material on US immigration policy, the private bill system, and the postwar adoption movement, and for many incisive comments and suggestions along the way. Two friends in different fields let me tap into their lifelong expertise and lent their critical eye to an earlier draft of the manuscript: John O. Iatrides, the doyen of the study of the Greek Civil War, and Peter Van der Naillen, retired attorney. They took the time to read my work and to offer perceptive feedback. I benefited from the legal expertise of Nicholas Zales as well. I also thank senior executive editor LeAnn Fields and Anna Pohlod, her assistant, Marcia LaBrenz, and Daniel Otis for their enthusiastic and always professional engagement with this project, which they steered toward efficient completion. I must accept full responsibility for this book's shortcomings: its faults are mine, but all of the above contributors have made them fewer in number.

I am deeply grateful also to the highly skilled University of Florida librarians Melanie Davis, David Schwieder, and Todd Venie; to Rebecka Lindau, head of the John Miller Burnam Classics Library at the University of Cincinnati; to Gail F. Whittemore, reference and special collections librarian, and also to Alyson Carney, at the Pace Law Library; to special collections librarians Adam Burkhart of San Diego State University and archivist Nathan Gerth of the Carl Albert Center at the University of Oklahoma; to researcher Dana Dorman at the Historical Society of Pennsylvania; to archivists Giannis Gklavinas, Anna Koulikourdi, and Amalia Pappa at the General State Archives in Athens; to Angeliki Nikolaou, Annita Prassa, and Alkistis Sanida at the General State Archives in Volos; to Andriani Melista at the General State Archives in Patras; to Christos Anastasiou at the Konstantinos G. Karamanlis Foundation in Athens; and to collection specialist Job Schouten of the Dutch Persmuseum in Amsterdam. Basil N. Mossaidis, executive director of the Ahepa, kindly granted me access to the Ahepa archives at the association's headquarters in Washington, DC. Director Nestor Bamidis and archivist Areti Makri made my experience at the Historical Archive of Macedonia in Thessaloniki one of the most memorable of my research career in Greece. Marcia Haddad-Ikonomopoulos, museum director at the Kedila Kedosha Janina Synagogue and Museum in New York, came to the rescue when my quest for one category of adoptees had reached a dead end. Diana Synadinos, archivist and historian at the Annunciation Greek Orthodox Cathedral in Columbus, Ohio, provided invaluable assistance by steering me toward several Greek-born and supposedly orphaned adoptees, and also to the reunion story of Dena (Polites) Poulias. Eleni Barboudaki, Maria Boletsi, E. Wayne Carp, Artemis Kliafa, Petros Koutoulas, Maria Heckinger, Ioannis Limnios Sekeris, George Paganelis, Apostolis Papageorgiou, Rabbi Robert Scheinberg, Fevronia Soumakis, and Lina Venturas helped me locate some elusive bibliographical and archival sources. Constantine Buhayer generously shared with me the unique research materials that he collected at the height of the mid-1990s public outcry in Greece. His work of 1995–1996 was commissioned by a Japanese television station, which, upon gathering the research results, did not proceed to actual filming. Merrill Jenkins kindly guided me through the intricacies of ancestry search resources and passenger manifests. A selfless collaborator in my research, he also became a trusted friend who was as keen as I was for me to get it right. Linda Carol Forrest Trotter redefined for me what it means to avail oneself of personal contacts in remote places in Greece. Ronit Kertsner and Shalom Rufeisen made me *look* anew at people and places through the trained eyes of documentary filmmakers.

Linnea Anderson, archivist at the Social Welfare History Archives of the Elmer L. Andersen Library at the University of Minnesota, was most helpful in locating relevant items in the files on Greece held by the International Social Service American Branch. Dr. Felicity Sackville Northcott, director of external partnerships and international services at the ISS-USA in Baltimore, took my follow-up questions to heart with utter professionalism and profound scholarly interest. I received an equally positive response from Chris(oula) Kontogianni, director of the ISS Hellenic Branch. Hester Storsbergen warmly responded to my queries on Greek-born adoptees in the Netherlands and forwarded copies of her dissertation and subsequent publications to me. Adoption studies expert René Hoksbergen kindly answered my questions about the Dutch collaboration with the Greek Babies' Center Metera. Ellen Giepmans and Hans van Hooff from the ISS Netherlands facilitated my research in the Dutch archives at the Nationaal Archief in the Hague. Georgette M. Constantinou graciously recounted her experiences as an intern at Metera in 1968.

Princeton University's Firestone Library and its Seeger Center for Hellenic Studies provided me with vibrant shared spaces to discuss and work on this project. Special thanks go to librarian David Jenkins and to Dimitris Gondicas, director of the Seeger Center. The Center for Hellenic Studies in Washington, too, has created an environment conducive to thinking and writing, which I experienced through a 2016 CHS Visiting Scholar Grant. My research and writing on this subject were further supported by the Cassas Professorship Fund through the Center for Greek Studies and by a research fellowship from the Department of Classics Rothman Family Endowment, both at the University of Florida.

Animated audiences in the United States and in Greece, especially, pushed my project further along with their pertinent comments and questions. I thank Vangelis Karamanolakis, Kostis Karpozilos, and Spyros Kakouriotis, who invited me to present at the Contemporary Social History

Archives in Athens in June of 2016. My gratitude goes also to the attendees who participated in my prior and shorter presentation at the Third International Conference of the Greek Oral History Association in Thessaloniki (2016). The Oral History Group of Volos and also the Department of History, Archaeology and Social Anthropology of the University of Thessaly invited me to speak in May of 2017, as did Anna Mavroleon on behalf of the Popular University of Elefsina (Eleusis). I was fortunate to be able to present also at the 2017 Conference on Roots Research Experiences and Alternative Forms of Care for Vulnerable Children in Marathon, which opened new windows on many other related issues. All of these forums, but especially my talk at the Athens Centre, Greece, made for very lively discussions and lasting contacts, for which I remain grateful. Lectures doubled as networking opportunities as well: I was graciously welcomed at the British School at Athens, the National Hellenic Research Foundation, the University of Birmingham, the University of Illinois at Chicago, at Stony Brook University, by the Anglo-Hellenic League in London and the Hellenic Community of Greater Montreal, and at the Tarpon Springs Heritage Museum. I am indebted to the hosts who made these lectures happen: Rosemary Donnelly and John Zervos, John Bennet, Maria Christina Chatziioannou, Dimitris Tziovas, Paris Papamichos Chronakis, Nikos Panou, John Kittmer, Tassos Anastassiadis, and Tina Bucuvalas.

"Mike" gave very insightful and detailed feedback, and he also granted me permission to quote from his emails. This study was improved immeasurably by his efforts. I am grateful also to numerous (named and unnamed) Greek-born adoptees for their open and giving participation. I wish that I had come to know them better and sooner. Heartfelt thanks go to Amalia Balch, Andrea, Christina, Dean, Eftychia, Ellen, Joseph, Kathy, Maria, Demetra Mihevic, Mitsos, Myrto, Pam, Rich, Robyn, and to Petros in particular. I have valued the many personal exchanges that led to discoveries, big and small. My engagement with these adoptees has left me with a sense of privilege, for being given a look into their world. As a small token of my gratitude, I have aimed to make their experiences more real to the readers. The value of Greg Terzian's contributions cannot be expressed easily in words: his wisdom and wit sustain and inspire me. Only he and I know how central he was to the writing of this book. This book honors the memory of Leonidas Polopolus (1933–2015), whose always intelligent and empathic presence I miss tremendously. To him, too, I owe gratitude beyond measure.

APPENDIX 1: CHRONOLOGY

28 Oct. 1940   The Greek-Italian War breaks out.

6 April 1941   The Nazi Germans invade Greece. World War II is raging. The Germans, Italians, and Bulgarians occupy Greece, which has joined the side of the Allies. Under the tripartite Occupation, the Greeks suffer extreme violence and deprivation.

27 Sept. 1941   The communist-led Greek National Liberation Front (EAM, Εθνικό Απελευθερωτικό Μέτωπο) forms. It puts up fierce resistance against the Germans through its military arm, the Greek Popular Liberation Army (ELAS, Ελληνικός Λαϊκός Απελευθερωτικός Στρατός).

Oct. 1944   The defeated Nazi German troops withdraw from Greece. Even though the Occupation has ended, British army troops remain in Greece after the liberation, following the "Percentages Agreement" between Churchill and Stalin that leaves Greece in the British sphere of influence.

3 Dec. 1944   Dekemvriana: Greek police shootings target left-wing resistance forces demonstrating in Athens and usher in a sharp polarization between EAM-ELAS (the National Liberation Front and its military arm) and the conservative, British-backed Greek government. The "December events" become the catalyst for a communist insurgency after the Left's initial defeat.

12 Feb. 1945   The Varkiza Agreement promises amnesty and political inclusion of the Greek communist forces but demands that they lay down their arms. This agreement seals the communists' defeat in the Dekemvriana; their insurgency abates only temporarily. Months of the so-called "White Terror" ensue (1945–1946): the reactionary Greek gendarmerie, security forces, and paramilitary gangs continue to assault leftists, and their actions go unchecked by the right-wing interim governments.

April 1945   Greece starts receiving aid from UNRRA, the United Nations Relief and Rehabilitation Administration (through December 1946).

Late April 1945   ✤ Ioanna Argyriadi is born in a village near Larisa.[1]

23 Feb. 1946   Greece issues the "new" Civil Code of 1946. Its articles concerning adoption (1568–1588) stipulate that adoptive parents have to be childless and at least fifty years of age. In practice, the adoptive parents also have to be politically conservative, Greek Orthodox Christians of some means.

5 March 1946   Churchill demarcates East versus West with his "iron curtain" statement.

31 March 1946   Greece holds its first postwar general election, with the aim of re-establishing parliamentary government after the regency of Archbishop Damaskinos of Athens, who has been appointing service or interim governments. Many leftist and communist Greeks decide to abstain—a watershed decision instigated by Nikos Zachariadis, general secretary of the Communist Party of Greece (KKE, Κομμουνιστικό Κόμμα Ελλάδας, founded in 1918). Zachariadis has secured the expulsion of the inveterate communist *kapetanios* Aris Velouchiotis (nom de guerre of Athanasios Klaras). The 1946 election and the abstentions hand a victory to the monarchists, who form a government that is far more conservative than the majority of the Greek people. Of the 7.5 million Greek people, about 1.9 million males are eligible to vote. Greek women do not yet vote in general elections.

1 Sept. 1946   A referendum held under British supervision decides on the restoration of the Greek monarchy. King George II returns to Greece but dies suddenly on 1 April 1947.

Oct. 1946   The Greek communist leaders form the Democratic Army of Greece. The Greek Civil War breaks out.[2]

1 April 1947   King Paul ascends to the Greek throne, succeeding his brother George II. King Paul's wife Frederica becomes Queen of the Hellenes.

Late spring 1947–
summer 1948   Dwight P. Griswold, chief of the American Mission for Aid to Greece (AMAG), oversees a year-long program of US military and economic aid. Among the topics of concern is the fate of the endangered children of Greece. Discussions with Greek govern-

---

1. Chronological items pertaining to the Argyriadis, Dallas, and Alevras families have been marked by a symbol (✤), so that they may be more easily recognized among the facts of global and bilateral history.

2. The starting date of the Civil War remains contested among historians of modern Greece. Some scholars see the armed conflict begin as early as 1943 and then posit "three rounds" to the Civil War (1943, Dekemvriana of 1944, 1946–1949). The body of literature on this heated debate continues to grow, while studies of the dark era of 1949–1962 remain sorely lacking.

	ment representatives raise the possible solution of the mass institutionalization of Greek children, but also the potential search for in-country foster arrangements.
22 May 1947	Guided by the Truman Doctrine and the "containment" policy, the United States approves a massive foreign aid program to Greece, to be followed by additional economic and military assistance given to the right-wing Greek government. By summer 1948, the American Mission for Aid to Greece becomes a formal part of the Marshall Plan and thus of a more comprehensive economic and military aid program (officially the European Recovery Program, to assist in Europe's recovery from World War II). These interventions mark the passing of Greece from the British into the American sphere of influence.
18 Sept. 1947	US President Truman forms the Central Intelligence Agency (CIA).
24–27 Dec. 1947	The Provisional Democratic Government establishes itself in Northern Greece. It is controlled by the Greek Communist Party. The Americans suspect the KKE of taking its directives from Moscow, but it is receiving only grudging assistance from Stalin (through Soviet satellite states). The conservative government in Athens does not recognize the competing new government and outlaws the Communist Party, which remains active underground. The Party is only legalized again in 1974.
May 1948	The international outcry about the Greek government's executions of communists reaches its height, especially in Britain.
25 June 1948	The United States issues the Displaced Persons Act (DPA or Public Law 774). This landmark act endeavors to speed Europe's postwar reconstruction and admits a general total of about 400,000 refugees over the course of four years. The Displaced Persons Act helps to bring over children born in Germany and Austria with American fathers. In general, however, Greek orphans do not qualify for special dispensations until 1950, when the DPA is extended and amended: Public Law 555 of 16 June 1950 accelerates the relief of war orphans from additional countries.
4 April 1949	The NATO alliance is being formed.
10 July 1949	Marshal Tito's speech signals the closure of the Greek-Yugoslav border: this closure delivers a major setback to the Greek Democratic Army, which sees its logistical support dwindle.
August 1949	The US-backed Greek National Army engages in its final and victorious operations against the communist-led Democratic Army, in the battles of Grammos and Vitsi. The Greek Civil War comes to an unofficial end. The exiled leadership of the Democratic Army long insists that its forces are only temporarily "grounding their arms."

30 Sept. 1949   Leniency legislation brings a temporary halt to executions of communists in Greece.

5 March 1950   The heavily contested Greek national election (and subsequent political wrangling) marks the rise of the more liberal General Nikolaos Plastiras and his National Progressive Center Union (ΕΡΕΚ, Εθνική Προοδευτική Ένωση Κέντρου).

7 June 1950   Nikos Beloyannis arrives in Greece clandestinely.

16 June 1950   US Public Law 555 accelerates the relief of war orphans from Greece, first for one year, then through June of 1952. Given the necessary processing time, Greek DPA-sponsored orphans arrive in the United States from 1951 through mid-1952. The total number of these children and teenagers is 1,246, and most of them go to Greek American families or sponsors. The United States Committee for the Care of European Children (USCOM), a private nonprofit organization commissioned by the State Department, officially approves the AHEPA, the American Hellenic Educational Progressive Association, and grants its Displaced Persons Committee a license to place Greek orphans for adoption in American homes through the DPA as amended. Despite a record of problems, the Ahepa continues to operate through the mid-1950s, albeit as a refugee service organization functioning separately from USCOM.

Late spring–
summer 1950   Most of Queen Frederica's "child-towns" or *paidopoleis* close. PIKPA, the Greek Patriotic Institution for Social Welfare and Awareness (Πατριωτικό Ίδρυμα Κοινωνικής Προνοίας και Αντίληψης), strengthens its childcare and adoption services. This organization is overseen by its right-wing president, Lina Tsaldari, and by the queen. Founded in 1914, it has been involved in (domestic) adoptions since 1933.

25 June 1950   North Korea invades South Korea, commencing the Korean War. This invasion places the United States on an even higher alert against the communist threat.

20 Dec. 1950   Beloyannis is arrested by the Greek Security Police. More arrests of members of underground Greek communist cells follow.

9 Sept. 1951   After a heavily contested Greek election, Plastiras reemerges as prime minister of a coalition government of "reconciliation and national-mindedness," only to be sidelined. This development marks a near-repeat scenario of the March 1950 election and its aftermath. The royalist Sofoklis Venizelos gains the upper hand and influences the most important government decisions from late October 1951 through mid-October 1952 (i.e., during the months most critical for the communists arrested and put on trial).

19 Oct.– 16 Nov. 1951	The first trial of Beloyannis and many of his associates lasts about one month.
14 Nov. 1951	✼ The Greek Security Police discover the wireless set operated by Elias Argyriadis in Glyfada and arrest him.
27 Nov. 1951	✼ Katerina Dalla, Argyriadis's second wife (common-law wife) and mother of Ioanna and Olympia Argyriadi, commits suicide at home, after having been interrogated for about ten days at the Athens headquarters of the Security Police.
30 Nov. 1951	✼ Shortly after Dalla's suicide and while the imprisoned Elias Argyriadis is awaiting trial, the Greek newspaper *Ta Nea* publishes a biased statement in which Lina Tsaldari asks for formal intervention in the family situation of the Argyriadis girls.
27 Nov.– 7 Dec. 1951	✼ While her father remains imprisoned, Efterpi Argyriadi takes care of her two younger half-sisters at home in Glyfada.
7 Dec. 1951	✼ A social worker accompanied by agents of the Glyfada gendarmerie takes the younger siblings away from Efterpi. For days, Efterpi's urgent requests for information as to where the children have been taken go unanswered. Efterpi subsequently learns that her half-sisters have been entered into the PIKPA welfare system, which has been expanding its operations under Tsaldari, its royalist and right-wing president. Through April 1955, PIKPA steers the official and legal decisions pertaining to the two Argyriadis girls, arranging for their long-term residential care and their adoption overseas.
25 Dec. 1951	✼ Efterpi Argyriadi is allowed to see her father for the first time since his mid-November arrest.
1 Jan. 1952	A new Greek constitution goes into effect. A separate law gives the right to vote to Greek women.
15 Feb. 1952	✼ Efterpi sees her father in person for the last time at the police headquarters.
15 Feb.– 1 March 1952	The second trial of Beloyannis and his comrades, which includes Elias and Vasilis Argyriadis, lasts for about two weeks. Charging espionage, the Permanent Military Court delivers the death penalty verdict to Beloyannis, Elias Argyriadis, and some of their other close associates. An international campaign commences aiming to save the accused and to put a permanent halt to the executions of Greek communists.
18 Feb. 1952	Greece officially becomes a member state of NATO.
12 March 1952	Nikos Ploumbidis issues a public letter in which he claims responsibility for the underground communist operation in Greece in order to absolve Beloyannis of the gravest charges laid against him.

30 March 1952	❦ Beloyannis, Elias Argyriadis, Nikos Kaloumenos, and Dimitris Batsis are executed early on a Sunday morning. Efterpi Argyriadi has now lost her father. Ioanna and Olympia lose a second parent.
1 April 1952	The Greek government proclaims "pacification measures" (Law 2058), which transform nearly all death sentences into sentences to life in prison.
27 June 1952	The restrictionist 1952 US Immigration and Nationality Act, or the McCarran-Walter Act, passes. It bars communist "subversives" and "fellow travelers" from entering the United States.
16 Nov. 1952	The right-wing hard-liner General Alexandros Papagos and his Greek Rally party (ES, Ελληνικός Συναγερμός) win the decisive November election. Papagos serves as prime minister from 1952 until his death in 1955. While the United States and its new ambassador, John Peurifoy (in office from 26 September 1950 through early August 1953), do not endorse renewed punitive measures targeting Greek communists, they do welcome the stability of a one-party majority government with the prospect of holding on to power for at least several years (the "Papagos solution").
Jan. 1953– Jan. 1961	Dwight D. Eisenhower holds the US presidency for two consecutive terms.
5 March 1953	Stalin dies. The presidency of Truman, the other architect of the Cold War, has ended some six weeks earlier. Nikita Khrushchev emerges victorious from the power struggle that ensues in the Soviet Union.
9 April 1953	Long-awaited monetary reforms must halt Greece's rapid inflation. The Papagos government devalues the Greek currency by 50 percent and introduces the "new" drachma (as equal to 1,000 "old" drachmas). Greece keeps to an equivalency of 30 drachmas to the US dollar.
7 May 1953	The Greek Central Intelligence Service (ΚΥΠ, Κεντρική Υπηρεσία Πληροφοριών) is being formed.
7 August 1953	President Eisenhower signs into law the Refugee Relief Act. This Relief Act or "Orphan Program" is set to expire on 31 December 1956. The RRA marks the growing trend to distinguish adoptable children from other refugees, and thus to consolidate intercountry adoption as nonrelative and confidential adoption (with sealed records). More than 500 Greek adoptees enter the United States under this Act; among them are the Argyriadis girls.
Late Oct.– Dec. 1953	King Paul and Queen Frederica visit the United States.
27 Jan. 1954	The US State Department formally recognizes the Ahepa Refugee Relief Committee, which, under Supreme President Leo Lamber-

son, prepares to place many Greek children through adoption in US homes. Lamberson further expands the Ahepa's participation in the 1953 Refugee Relief Act by prioritizing Greek children's predeparture adoptions by proxy. Other high-placed Ahepa officers and influential Greeks and Greek Americans follow in his footsteps and launch a lucrative black market in Greek adoptees that gains "clients" from all across the United States but flourishes especially on the East Coast.

14 Aug. 1954   Nikos Ploumbidis is executed.

31 March 1955   ⚘ George and Betty Alevras file their petition with the Athens Court of First Instance, officially asking to adopt Ioanna and Olympia Argyriadi.

5 April 1955   ⚘ During the court hearing in Athens, at which the Alevrases and their lawyer are present, the girls' adoption case is reviewed.

12 April 1955   ⚘ Unbeknown to Efterpi Argyriadi, the Greek court finalizes the adoption case of Ioanna and Olympia, assigning them as children to the Alevrases. The American Embassy in Athens then issues the girls' entry visas to the United States.

1 May 1955   ⚘ Ioanna and Olympia are formally admitted to enter the United States as orphans adopted from (and in) Greece.

14 May 1955   The military alliance of the Warsaw Pact, led by the Soviet Union, is being formed. This Pact constitutes the communist counterpart to NATO.

11 Aug. 1955   A special act passed by the US Congress accelerates the adoption of six Korean war orphans by Harry and Bertha Holt, an evangelical couple from rural Oregon. This cross-border and interracial adoption speaks to the imagination of patriotic and faith communities across the United States and shines too bright a light on independent or proxy initiative in the placement of foreign-born children. Repeated mass "airlifts" of Korean orphans arranged by the Holts attract nationwide attention.

5 Oct. 1955   The first larger group of about a dozen Greek adoptees sponsored by the ISS fly from Athens to New York via Frankfurt. The Flying Tigers charter flight's arrival predates by some nine months the more visible orphan planes scheduled by the Ahepa. More ISS arrivals soon follow, typically with a smaller number of Greek children for adoption.

1 Nov. 1955   The Vietnam War starts and lasts until 30 April 1975. The first major hostilities occur, however, in September of 1959.

19 Feb. 1956   The conservative National Radical Union (ERE, Εθνική Ριζοσπαστική Ένωσις) of Konstantinos Karamanlis wins the first Greek general election in which women participate on equal terms with men. Lina Tsaldari becomes minister of social welfare.

25 Feb. 1956   Following the 20th Congress of the Communist Party of the

Soviet Union, held from 14 through 25 February 1956, a process of destalinization, led by Khrushchev, commences and affects communist parties worldwide.

Late spring 1956   After about two years of making preparations and collecting applications from Greek American and American adoptive parents, the Ahepa Refugee Relief Committee is ready to embark Greek-born adoptees on planes headed for New York.[3]

22 June 1956   At least six Ahepa-sponsored Greek adoptees arrive at New York's Idlewild Airport (JFK Airport). Some adoptees continue their journey to the West Coast of the United States.

12 July 1956   As chair of the Ahepa Refugee Relief Committee, Lamberson poses for the cameras on the arrival of his "airlift" of twelve Greek orphans at Idlewild Airport. Seven of them continue their journey via Chicago to destinations in the Midwest and on the West Coast.

Mid-Aug. 1956   The Ahepa terminates the work of Lamberson's Refugee Relief Committee, after problematic placements are alleged to have been cases of abuse of power and trust.

11 Dec. 1956   Arrival of the first "Diavatis baby," bound for San Antonio, Texas. Father Diavatis of the St. Sophia Greek Orthodox Church in San Antonio and later the organization called Parents of Greek Orphans (POGO) bring over approximately ninety Greek children (through 1962).

11 Sept. 1957   The successor act to the 1953 Refugee Relief Act (and its extension) goes in effect. The Act of 1957 (Public Law 85–316, the Refugee-Escapee Act) ups the age limit for orphans to fourteen years old and allows another 1,360 Greek-born children to enter the United States. The act is set to expire on 30 June 1959 but is extended through the period ending 30 June 1961.

4 Oct. 1957   The Soviet Union launches Sputnik into orbit, accelerating the Cold War space race.

17 Oct. 1957   Invoking the 11 September 1957 Act (but contravening the Ahepa's decision to halt the work of its Refugee Relief Committee), Ahepa Supreme President Constantine Verinis reappoints Michael Tsaparis, Lamberson's collaborator in Athens, asking him to go out and find eligible orphans in Greek orphanages, institutions, or private homes.

11 May 1958   The United Democratic Left (EDA, Ενιαία Δημοκρατική Αριστερά) emerges from the Greek election as the leading

---

3.   This important temporal fact contradicts generalizations and outright misinformation about the Ahepa's Greek Orphans Program, whose starting date and scale some sources overstate (pushing the program back to an earlier date and exaggerating the numbers of predeparture adoptions).

opposition party to Karamanlis's National Radical Union. This party grows more vocal on matters of political reform and social welfare.

Mid-Aug. 1958   New York newsman and Ahepan George Douris presents a first damning report of Lamberson's abuses at the Ahepa's Boston convention. The report falls on deaf ears, but Douris persists. Signs of friction show in the highest echelons of the Ahepa leadership. Meanwhile, a formal investigation is underway: it is spearheaded by the vocal Ernest A. Mitler, New York County assistant district attorney, who does not belong to the Ahepa ranks.

27 April 1959   Karamanlis announces his ambitious Preliminary Five-year Program for Economic Development (1960–1964).

5 May 1959   The arrest of prominent Ahepan and New York City magistrate Stephen S. Scopas, charged with selling Greek babies, makes front-page news in the *New York Times*. The article, by Jack Roth, is informed by Mitler's investigation, and it is among the first to break the scandal in the United States. News of the scandal travels back to Greece. Greek American finger-pointing but also introspection result from follow-up publications, such as Mitler's bold report in the English-language Sunday edition of the Greek American newspaper *Atlantis* (in six installments, from 1 November through 6 December 1959).

May–June 1959   The court case of the People v. Scopas is being held in New York. Scopas has been placing Greek infants with New York couples for some two years, and he has been receiving payment for these allegedly unauthorized placements. Scopas is soon released. His case does not go to trial. He petitions for the charges to be dismissed one year later, by June 1960, upon which the New York State prosecutor appeals the case on questions of law. In March 1962, the Appeals Court upholds the earlier dismissal of the charges.

20 Nov. 1959   The United Nations adopts the Declaration of the Rights of the Child.

12 May 1960   The court case of the People v. Issachar is being held in New York. Maurice and Rebecca Issachar have been placing Greek infants with New York Jewish couples for some three years. The charges are formally dismissed.

9 July 1961   At the instigation of Karamanlis, Greece signs a Treaty of Association with the European Economic Community (EEC).

August 1961   Construction starts on the Berlin Wall, which divides East and West Berlin until November 1989.

26 Sept. 1961   The US Congress closes the loophole of proxy adoptions and makes permanent provisions for the immigration of foreign-born

children for adoption, through the Immigration and Nationality Act of 1961 (Public Law 87–301 of 26 September 1961).

Fall 1961–
spring 1962   Adoptions and even proxy adoptions of Greek-born children by US parents continue (through the Issachars), but they plummet by the mid-1960s.

29 Oct. 1961   Karamanlis is reelected amid allegations of corruption and criticisms of his autocratic leadership style.

Oct. 1962   The Cuban Missile Crisis intensifies the Cold War standoff between the United States and the Soviet Union.

Dec. 1962   News of the discovery of child trafficking at the Saint Stylianos Foundling Home in Thessaloniki remains somewhat contained, even though the trade began in the postwar era and probably lasted for a full fifteen years.

11 June 1963   Karamanlis resigns and subsequently goes into self-imposed exile in Paris.

6 March 1964   Crown Prince Constantine ascends to the Greek throne on the death of his father, King Paul.

Mid-June 1964   The director and eight employees or affiliates of Thessaloniki's Saint Stylianos Foundling Home appear before a Thessaloniki court, which charges them with falsifying documents and profiteering from selling babies for adoption. Despite the confessions of wrongdoing, they receive very light or no sentences.

2 July 1964   The US Civil Rights Act goes into effect.

3 Oct. 1965   US President Lyndon Johnson signs into law the Immigration and Nationality Act of 1965, the Hart-Cellar Act. This Act bolsters ethnic pluralism by abolishing the national origins quota system, the linchpin of the Immigration Act of 1924 (the Johnson-Reed Act), which favored immigrants of certain ethnonational backgrounds and prohibited most Asian immigration.

17 Aug. 1966   Greek Legislative Decree 4532 lowers the minimum age requirement of Greek adoptive parents from fifty to thirty-five years of age. It reiterates the official Greek preference for adoptive parents of Greek descent in case of international adoptions, and for such adoptions to be carried out by certified agencies or organizations (without naming them).

11 Dec. 1970   Greek Royal Decree 795 (signed by Regent Georgios Zoïtakis) actually specifies the authorized agencies, organizations, and institutions through which any subsequent international adoptions of Greek children will have to take place. These agencies and institutions are the ISS, PIKPA, the Babies' Center Metera, and the Municipal Orphanages of Athens, Patras, and Thessaloniki.

July 1974	The collapse of the Greek military dictatorship of 1967–1974 and the ascent of the socialist party PASOK (Panhellenic Socialist Movement, Πανελλήνιο Σοσιαλιστικό Κίνημα) open up a new era in which it becomes possible to question the past of former communists and their families, their charges, and their trials. PASOK consolidates its hold on government in 1981 and remains in power through the 1980s.

❦ Efterpi Argyriadi uses this newfound freedom to make further inquiries about the whereabouts of her lost half-siblings.

8 Dec. 1974 The Greek monarchy is abolished by way of a plebiscite that records an overwhelming vote against the kingship and in favor of a Greek parliamentary republic.

Nov. 1980 *The Man with the Carnation*, a Greek film version of the Beloyannis affair produced by Nikos Tzimas, is first released. The movie generates renewed interest in the trial and execution of Beloyannis and his comrades, as seen in a sequence of articles and interviews published by Oikonomeas et al. in the Greek newspaper *Eleftherotypia*, which begins on 6 December 1980 and ends on 16 January 1981.

6 Dec. 1980 ❦ Efterpi Argyriadi gives an interview to *Eleftherotypia* in which she relates the events of 1951–1952. She emphasizes that, despite her best efforts, she has never been properly informed of the whereabouts of her two younger half-siblings. This interview is published in the paper's 7 December issue and entitled "Δεν τάμαθες; Σκότωσαν τον πατέρα σου!," "Haven't You Heard? They Killed Your Father!," with reference to the disturbing way in which an acquaintance broke the news to Efterpi on the day of Elias's execution.

9 Dec. 1980 ❦ *Eleftherotypia* publishes a formal request issued by MP Konstantinos Alavanos and addressed to the minister of social welfare, asking for more information about the fate of the children of Elias Argyriadis and Katerina Dalla.

16 Dec. 1980 ❦ *Eleftherotypia* reporters Oikonomeas and Oikonomidis publish news on the whereabouts of Ioanna and Olympia Argyriadi and also quote extensively from the legal act that finalized the girls' adoption case. The news makes the paper's front page. Not only Efterpi but all interested Greeks thus learn that the girls were assigned as adopted children to a Greek American couple in April of 1955. The newspaper schedules a transatlantic phone call from Efterpi to Ioanna/Gina on 16 December, on which it promises to report extensively in its next issue.

17 Dec. 1980 ❦ The surprise phone call from Efterpi to Ioanna/Gina is disap-

	pointing, especially after the media hype raised by *Eleftherotypia* (report by Oikonomeas and Oikonomidis).
20 Sept. 1982	The Greek government officially recognizes the (communist-led) Greek National Resistance against the occupying forces of World War II (Decree 1285). Formal recognition of the Greek Civil War as a civil war follows in 1989.
18 Feb. 1983	The new Greek Family Law (Law 1329) expresses a new vision of parenthood and partnership within the Greek household. The law proves key in halting the country's practice of adopting out overseas: it abolishes discrimination against "illegitimate" children and prepares to legalize abortion (finalized in 1986).
Nov. 1989	The demolition of the Berlin Wall marks the approaching end of the Cold War.
Dec. 1991	The Soviet Union collapses.
May 1995	The discovery of postwar child trafficking at the Saint Stylianos Foundling Home in Thessaloniki prompts a public outcry, even though the first discoveries were made in 1962. On this occasion, and unlike with the revelations of May 1959, the scandal breaks in Greece and reverberates back to the United States.
16 Sept. 2013	❧ Mike learns about the Argyriadis family members left behind in Greece.
July 2014	❧ Mike travels to Greece to meet Efterpi and to hear her testimony. Some of the Argyriadis relatives enjoy a first family reunion after more than sixty years.

APPENDIX 2

Practical Information for Greek-Born Adoptees—Pathways and Paperwork

> I was "born" in a filing cabinet . . . I disappeared. After that, even the filing cabinet disappeared.
>
> —Greek-born adoptee who wishes to remain anonymous

Greek adoptees and their descendants have wanted to understand their position in Greek and US history for many long decades. They remind us that transnational adoption affects not only the adoptees themselves but also their children and grandchildren. The queries of the Greek-born adoptees, with or without papers related to their cases and often without any memories of Greece, continue to be the queries of subsequent generations. These modern generations deem the lack of proper documentation resulting in missing or unfounded memories to be painfully unacceptable. Adoption is still the descendant's adoption, too. This second appendix may help to guide the Greek-born adoptees and their family circles through the patchwork of postwar practices that moved Greek children across national borders.

The following paragraphs present some basic facts and search guidelines, meant to cover the most common adoption scenarios from Greece to the United States, the Netherlands, and Sweden. In the latter two areas, especially, this analysis is necessarily provisional and incomplete. It does not cover the praxis and the geography of domestic Greek adoptions, either. However, until Greek orphanages and other institutions, the adoption mediators, and agency officials grant to researchers access to the case files, the data presented here may be the best available. The US-bound scenarios range from placements with relatives and politically driven adoptions that targeted certain individuals to the mass adoptions that were economically and socially charged. To avoid polemics, these scenarios require the kind of careful parsing that parts 1 and 2 of this book aim to deliver, while part 3 illustrates various trajectories by drawing on personal testimonies and interviewees' experiences and memories.

The Greek-to-American adoptions tend to fall into eight major categories during the critical years of 1950 to 1962, and they delivered a total of about 3,200 Greek-born children to the United States. This approximate total of 3,200 Greek-to-American adoptees is derived from the baseline count of 3,116 US visas issued. Of these, 1,246 Greek children arrived in 1950 through mid-1952; another 506 to 510 joined them by the end of 1956, and another 1,360 children had come over by late 1962. Two additions must be made to the baseline count of 3,116 US visas issued: (1) 54 cases of Greek-to-American adoptions stemming from 1953 legislation that benefited American military and government personnel stationed abroad; (2) approximately 30 to 40 Greek-born children who were adopted by US citizens under the private law system, which resolved US immigration and naturalization issues caused by unusual hardship or extraordinary circumstances, and most often on behalf of (teenage) adoptees sponsored by Greek American relatives.[1] The Greek-to-Dutch adoptions, on the other hand, cover a total of nearly 600 cases from 1956 through 1980, and they follow one key pattern, to be described below. The Greek-to-Swedish adoptions totaled 40 children from the postwar years through 1966, and they follow a pattern similar to that of the Dutch adoptions. Some trends here overlap with the domestic Greek adoptions. The reader may also want to consult the links and references in "Information and Reunification Sites for Greek-Born Adoptees," below pp. 275–76. This book's index may serve as a guide to further analysis and data on the various categories and the agents and institutions involved.

Greek-to-American Adoptees

1. A watershed date in the Greek-to-American adoption movement was the passage of the US Refugee Relief Act in the summer of 1953. Before this date, a total of 1,246 Greek-born children had migrated to the United States on assurances of adoption by relatives or sponsors. Their migration was made possible through the 1948 Displaced Persons Act, as amended in June 1950. The large majority of these refugee and orphaned children traveled overseas during the summer of 1951 and through the summer of 1952. They traveled by ship (on the SS *Nea Hellas*, the SS *Atlantic*, and the SS *Homeland*, for instance). The migration of these Greek minors "for adoption" (but often "for sponsorship") was facilitated through the (loosely combined) efforts of the US Displaced Persons Commission and its caseworkers on site in Ath-

---

1.   The postwar US private law system, which involved several Greek cases, is the subject of an ongoing study by Karen Balcom, who has kindly shared her preliminary conclusions and estimates with me (email communication of 4 April 2017). See also Weil (1984: 279, 280, his table 1) and above, pp. 77–78 and pp. 103–4, n. 109.

ens, various philanthropic organizations, PIKPA (the Greek Patriotic Institution for Social Welfare and Awareness, Πατριωτικό Ίδρυμα Κοινωνικής Προνοίας και Αντίληψης), and some lawyer-negotiated arrangements. The Ahepa, the American Hellenic Educational Progressive Association, took credit for up to one-third of the total of 1,246 cases of 1950–1952, as part of its pre-1953 refugee relief work. Many of the organization's members helped newcomers from Greece settle and adjust to urban life, especially in New York and Chicago.[2]

Most of these Greek children or "war orphans" traveled to join family members, more distant relatives, or acquaintances. The teenage boys by far outnumbered the girls and smaller children. Many traveled in sibling groups of two to four. For all these reasons, this early 1950s phenomenon of the mass relocation of Greek (male) minors is better defined as family or kin migration than as child adoption. In essence, scores of these "adoptees" were "named" and sponsored teenagers, specified by name in their new parents' applications for adoption. They viewed themselves as young refugees and immigrants rather than as adoptees. Also, they tend to not search for their roots, because the knowledge of their family origins was not lost to them. Many, too, had left traumatic circumstances behind in Greece, which they preferred not to revisit. The archival information about their individual cases, travel arrangements, and sponsorship or adoption procedures is scant.

2. After the passing of the US Refugee Relief Act of 1953 and by the end of 1956, some 500 more Greek-born children migrated to the United States either as adoptees or adoptees-to-be. They started landing on American shores from the late spring of 1954 onward, and arrivals peaked in 1956. While adoptions by Greek American family members and sponsors continued, Greek "orphans" (as they kept being called) were now also, for the first time, widely perceived as white, adoptable, and adaptable children, whom desperate prospective parents might hope to receive sooner than if they were to go through US domestic agencies or other channels. The group of "named" children now decreased compared to the category of the "unnamed" children, who were designated as available for "stranger" adoption given their status as orphans, foundlings, or relinquished "illegitimate" children. A fair number of the 1953–1956 placements still occurred within Greek American circles, but as nonrelative adoptions, they differed from the prior wave of kin migration. The many nonrelative "matches" of the mid-

---

2.   See above, pp. 95–102, or the section "From Aiding Displaced Persons to Placing Adoptable Orphans: The Ahepa, Early 1950s."

1950s helped to shape the definition of transnational adoption as subsequent generations came to understand it: they relied on finite, closed-records procedures and placed children who, prior to these procedures, were unknown "strangers" to their adopters (and vice versa).

Many US-bound adoptions continued to be handled through PIKPA and the Greek Ministry of Social Welfare, which built on their 1940s wartime legacy and on Queen Frederica's politicized philanthropy. Often they also involved charitable organizations or independent agents and lawyers, who represented the adoptive parents. By 1953, PIKPA ran modest support services for children and their families to help with daunting structural and logistical challenges. Crucially, too, PIKPA extended a model of institutionalized childcare vested in the Greek queen's *paidopoleis*, the state-sponsored "child-towns" of the Civil War and its immediate aftermath. It oversaw individual foster homes for orphaned children, in addition to its residential care facilities, which accommodated children with special needs (such as the larger facilities on the Penteli mountain slopes, northeast of Athens, and on the coast in Voula). Overseas adoptions through PIKPA, which were most commonly adoptions by proxy vetted by courts in Greece, continued to operate under the auspices of the Greek queen through the late 1950s. From 1958 on, such predeparture adoptions could proceed also under the supervision of the newly founded Welfare Department of the Greek Orthodox Archdiocese of North and South America. PIKPA pursued coreligious placements, which meant cocultural placements as well. The institution also prided itself on training and engaging social workers.

The "named" children of 1953 through 1956 again have fewer questions concerning their birth family's histories, because their origins were rarely obscured. However, the group of children more broadly available for adoption cannot hope to find much in the PIKPA archives, where the personal case files, especially, have been notoriously elusive. Adoptees may glean most of the available information from documents that their adoptive parents may have preserved: paperwork with the PIKPA logo, the formal act of adoption from the Court of First Instance (of any major Greek city), the name(s) of the intermediaries or attorney(s) involved, etc. The division of the General State Archives (GAK) in Athens holds the bulk of the adoption acts that were passed by the Athens Court of First Instance, which processed most predeparture adoption cases from the Patras Orphanage as well as from institutions in Athens (for PIKPA but also for other mediators). Key to a search in the records of the Athens Court of First Instance is the protocol number of the adoption act, which was often written in the adoptee's Greek passport. The GAK Athens is located on Dafnis 61, 15452 Psychiko, Athens. The email address is archives@gak.gr.

3. While PIKPA was seeking to adopt out, the initiative to take in a Greek-born child most often originated with the adoptive parents in the United States. After 1953, many hopeful American couples directly approached PIKPA and Greek orphanages, in particular; others appointed a Greek attorney to submit an application on their behalf. Some prospective parents traveled to Greece to "select" their child and to continue to work with the orphanage and the lawyer there. Others delegated the "choice" of the child to an attorney, friend, or acquaintance. The institution's board of directors reviewed every serious application, and if the right (basic) conditions were fulfilled, it granted the adoption, which was finalized in a Greek Court of First Instance.

These private adoption cases, as they are called, require that the searching adoptees accurately identify the originating institution or orphanage based on any existing paperwork. Was it the Municipal Orphanage of Athens, of Patras, of Thessaloniki (the Saint Stylianos Foundling Home), or the Geronymakeio Orphanage in Irakleio, Crete? These are just a few of the more familiar orphanages of origin, which some English translations call "children's asylums." The adoptee can then approach the institution or orphanage with a request for personal information from its ledgers or logbooks. If the adoptee was a foundling, as was very common, he or she cannot hope to find much. But there may be a foundling record (filed by the local police) and a brief mention of the address where the baby was discovered and by whom. Sometimes the foundling was discovered at a private address and taken to the nearest police station, to be transferred from there to the closest orphanage. On many occasions, however, the foundling was delivered directly to the orphanage by way of the infamous (and anonymizing) baby hatch. An adoptee from the Athens Orphanage can request an "Application from the Historical Archive" (a form entitled "Aitisi istorikou archeiou," Αίτηση ιστορικού αρχείου) via email address dimvrefa@otenet.gr or dimvrefa@cosmotemail.gr. He or she then fills out the one-page form, attaches proper identification, and returns scans of these documents to the same email address, requesting confirmation of receipt. It helps if the adoptee can also send along a copy of the Greek act of adoption showing the ledger number (*arithmos mitroou* or A.M.) assigned to him or her by the orphanage. Adoptees born in the 1950s who spent time at the Athens Orphanage carry a five-digit ledger number that begins with 43, 44, or 45. Ledger numbers for those born in the 1950s who passed through the Patras Orphanage range from just below 10,000 through more than 11,000. Requests via regular mail may be addressed to Dimotiko Vrefokomeio Athinon, Grafeio Istorikou Archeiou, Rodou Street 181, 10443 Sepolia, Athens,

Greece. An adoptee from the Patras Orphanage can compose a similar request and send it to vrefokopatras@hotmail.com, or via regular mail to Dimotiko Vrefokomeio Patron, Anazitisi Rizon, Sotiriadi 6, 26225 Patras, Greece. The adoptee can proceed this way independently or may choose to assign power of attorney to a Greek lawyer or search specialist.

4. Several hundred Greek-born adoptees were sponsored by the International Social Service, that is, the ISS Hellenic Branch in collaboration with the ISS-USA. These children, ranging from infants up to age ten, traveled to the United States starting in 1955 and through the early 1960s. They traveled on visas issued under the 1953 Refugee Relief Act, which expired by the end of 1956 but was later repeatedly renewed (and the age limit was raised to fourteen). The ISS Hellenic Branch, directed by Maria King-Tsileni and located on 1 Sofokleous Street in central Athens, operated with a small local staff that included caseworker Georgia Choras, who handled most of the Greek-to-American adoption cases in close collaboration with Dorothy H. Sills, case consultant on the US side. Many of the ISS-sponsored adoptees of 1955–1956 came from the Patras Orphanage. In 1956, too, a small number of slightly older children came from the Saint Stylianos Foundling Home in Thessaloniki. Through the early 1960s, the ISS Hellenic Branch sourced infants from the Babies' Center Metera in Athens (for Metera's mailing address, see below, p. 273). Several placements were negotiated between the ISS Hellenic Branch and birth families in distress, especially in central and northern Greece, where some regional social services centers stepped in to facilitate the contacts. Many children were adopted out as sibling groups that were kept together. Most of the ISS-sponsored adoptees traveled by plane on Flying Tiger Line (aka Flying Tigers) and arrived at New York's Idlewild Airport (later renamed JFK), where the adoptive parents were asked to come and meet them. Many of the ISS flights were paid for by the Intergovernmental Committee for European Migration (ICEM, founded in 1951; currently the International Organization for Migration, IOM), which helped resettle refugees and displaced persons in the aftermath of the war. The offices of Easy Travel based in Kolonaki, Athens, assisted with the travel arrangements.

On the American side, the applicant-parents worked with the ISS-USA and with local social services agencies. They filled out and signed an assurance form that had to be endorsed by such a local agency, which agreed to conduct the home studies and to forward the follow-up reports as well. This DSR-5 form, "Assurance of Adoption and Proper Care for Orphan," committed the prospective parents to financially sponsoring an orphan known to them. Form DSR-6 was required for a child that the ISS (or another designated agency) would match with the adoptive parents. From 1963 on, form I-600, a "Petition to Classify Alien as an Eligible Orphan," served similar purposes of filing the assurances of professional social workers on behalf of an adoptee specified by name, to clear the child's legal entrance into the United States and its subsequent path to citizenship. The waiting parents also paid a bond of $1,000 (in the mid-1950s) to cover any additional expenses in case the adoption plan did not work out and the ISS incurred the cost of accommodating and rehoming the foreign child in the States. The ISS returned this bond money to the new parents when the adoption process was legally completed in the child's US home state. Over the course of some two years, the legal guardianship of foundlings or of children otherwise available for adoption was transferred from the president of the orphanage's board of directors, who consented to the children's emigration, to the ISS, and then to the American parents, following the formal US adoption procedure.

Adoptees who passed through the ISS can expect to find a bulky file, which they can request from the American or from the Greek branch (the latter's current address is Derigny Street 24, 10343 Athens, Greece; email: issgr@otenet.gr). The ISS-USA office in Baltimore, Maryland, can request a copy of the file on the adoptee's behalf either from the ISS archives in Minneapolis or from the Greek branch (for a modest fee). The mailing address is ISS-USA, 1120 N Charles Street, Suite 300, Baltimore, MD 21201, USA; email: question@iss-usa.org). Often the adoptee's file exists in both countries and contains largely the same materials. ISS-sponsored adoptees received Greek and English-language migration paperwork for the purpose of an anticipated adoption, which was expected to be finalized in the United States following a mandatory waiting period (according to state as well as federal laws and with input from the state's bureau of child welfare and from local social services, including child-focused "adjustment reports"). Therefore, the adoptee-to-be traveled to the States under his or her Greek name (whether it was a genuine Greek name or the fictitious name assigned by a Greek orphanage to a foundling). This Greek name was typically dropped when the adoption was concluded in court in the US home state. Unless ISS-sponsored adoptees took their Greek name back in later life, their original names have been replaced by their American adoptive names. Most of the ISS adoptions were stranger or nonrelative placements with families that were not Greek Orthodox. It is therefore critical that the ISS adoptee first find out about his or her Greek name (allowing for various conventions in spelling and transliteration and even for inevitable spelling mistakes), to then start looking for members of his or her birth family, a birth certificate or foundling record, visa documents, airplane arrival passenger lists, etc.

5. Greek-born adoptees sponsored by the Order of AHEPA, the American Hellenic Educational Progressive Association, started arriving in the United States in the late spring of 1956 and kept coming through the late 1950s. The first groups of these children, too, had their visas issued under the 1953 Refugee Relief Act, and they traveled by plane as well, typically via a route leading through Switzerland. The first arrivals were organized by the Ahepa Refugee Relief Committee, a nonprofessionalized channel that brought many children over in the summer of 1956—that is, by the end of its two and a half years of service. On the American side, Leo Lamberson and Stephen Scopas were most closely involved. On the Greek side, attorney Michael Tsaparis passed the adoptions by proxy through the Greek Court of First Instance (which meant that the adoptive parents did not need to be present). The travel agency Acropole Express of N. J. Cassavetes, with offices in New York and Athens, issued the children's visas and took care of the flight arrangements. In mid-August 1956, the Ahepa terminated the work of its Refugee Relief Committee, but that did not stop Lamberson, Scopas, Tsaparis, and a few others from continuing to build an adoption business, often abusing the Ahepa name to cement relations of trust in Greece. Scopas's adoptions, especially, led to a scandal and investigations in May of 1959, after which his operation declined. Lamberson, however, kept bringing over Greek children, but at a slower pace. After September 1957, various renewals and extensions of the Refugee Relief Act could again grant US visas to Greek adoptees. Thus the Ahepa-sponsored children also constituted a good number of the total of 1,360 Greek adoptees who arrived in the States between 1957 and 1962. The second major section of this post-1956 count was formed by ISS-sponsored adoptees.[3]

In practice, most Ahepa-*sponsoring* adoptees arrived between 1956 and May 1959, and most can trace their roots back to the Patras Orphanage. Since Patras did not have its own Court of First Instance, Tsaparis was typically the one to see their cases through the court in Athens. Many of these children went to (unrelated) Greek American families. A good number, too, went to all-American families that had managed to make contact with an Ahepa member, a sponsor, or with Lamberson or Scopas directly. Because the adoptions were finalized in Greece by Tsaparis, the children next traveled under their new adoptive names (as the relevant visa documents, passports, and airplane arrival passenger lists show). In this transition process, traces of the children's birth names routinely disappeared.

---

3.   See above, pp. 103–7, starting with the section "From Placing to Gathering Eligible Alien Orphans: The Ahepa, Mid-1950s."

The Ahepa headquarters did not preserve any of the adoption files, which were never comprehensive to begin with (and certainly lacked proper casework). Lamberson and Scopas never turned in their logistical records to the association, either. Tsaparis could not be pressed into submitting the case files, because he remained at his home base in Greece. His widow tossed out any adoption-related paperwork many years ago. Ahepa adoptees and "Scopas babies" can only hope that their adoptive parents have kept their paperwork and have passed it on. To state it unambiguously: there is not a single piece of documentation on individual adoption cases—or on hundreds of seemingly ephemeral but life-altering decisions—to be found in the Ahepa's central archives. If such documentation exists in the private hands of Ahepa members or their descendants, please help to make it available, whether it reflects well or ill on the association. A correction to this deplorable situation, which weighs heavily on the adoptees, is long overdue!

6. Father Spyridon Diavatis was one of several independent agents involved in placing Greek-born children for adoption in the United States in the mid-1950s through early 1960s. Diavatis served as the parish priest of the St. Sophia Greek Orthodox Church in San Antonio, and he responded to requests from hopeful adoptive parents across southern Texas. His adoptions by proxy of Greek children covered especially the geographical areas of San Antonio, Austin, and Houston. Through the spring of 1959, Diavatis received his first adoptees from the Athens Orphanage. These proxy adoptions were passed through the Athens Court of First Instance by lawyer Fotios Bouras. From 1958 on and with demand on the rise, Diavatis started procuring adoptees also from Thessaloniki's Saint Stylianos Foundling Home. There, Diavatis found a willing collaborator in lawyer Dimitrios Kazakis, who processed numerous adoptees in 1959 alone, all destined for prospective parents living in Texas.[4] These parents, who received their children between late 1956 and 1962, founded a regional association named Parents of Greek Orphans (POGO). POGO handled the adoption flow even after Diavatis had moved out of Texas. Adoption files no longer exist on the US side, but adoptees can try approaching the Athens Orphanage (dimvrefa@otenet.gr or dimvrefa@cosmotemail.gr) or the Saint Stylianos Foundling Home (http://www.agios-stylianos.gr/for-kid/search-root or agstyl1@otenet.gr) with a request for personal information from their ledgers. Adoptees do well trying to locate their ledger number or "A.M" number, which is likely to show on their act of adoption from the Greek court (the Court of First Instance in

---

4.   See further Van Steen (2016) and also above, pp. 176–79.

Thessaloniki). Adoptees who were born in the 1950s and spent time at the Saint Stylianos Foundling Home carry a four-digit ledger number that starts with either 7 or 8. The regular mailing address of the Athens Orphanage is listed above, p. 267. The mailing address of the Saint Stylianos Foundling Home is Vrefokomeio Thessalonikis O Agios Stylianos, Anazitisi Rizon, 28th October Street 99, 54642 Thessaloniki, Greece.

7. Greek-born adoptees who came to the United States through the operations of the brother-and-sister pair Maurice and Rebecca Issachar were typically infants whose adoptions were finalized in Greece, again through the proxy adoption system. Between 1957 and 1962, the Issachars sourced the children directly from the Patras Orphanage, from maternity clinics in and around Athens, and from desperate birth mothers. They placed many, putatively orphaned Greek children with (unknowing) Jewish families on the East Coast and in New York, especially.[5]

The dossiers of the more than 220 "Issachar babies" no longer exist beyond what the adoptive parents may have preserved. A few of these adoptees have had some luck turning to Greek television programs that specialize in family reunifications. Some birth mothers have come forward in response to emotional calls, but they are broadcast on sensationalized shows that resemble reality TV episodes. A small group of Issachar and other babies is currently the focus of a documentary film-making project undertaken by Ronit Kertsner.

8. Adoptions arranged privately between couples or individuals and biological mothers are legal in Greece to this day, and they cover all sorts of scenarios, including shady and unlawful practices. Advocates of privately arranged adoptions claim that they leave the birth mother with the power to select the adopters herself, and to see the adoption through in a shorter amount of time while facing fewer bureaucratic hurdles. In reality, however, such arrangements exploit the fact that the average birth mother has hardly any choices. Adoptees in such cases depend on the willingness of their adoptive parents to share with them any details about their biological mothers or families—or to reveal to them that they have been adopted in the first place. Official Greek acts of adoption protect the privately arranged adoptions and do not reveal much additional information.

---

5.   See above, p. 134 and pp. 155–60, starting with the section "Home Sweet Home: The Issachars in Action, 1957–1962."

Greek-to-Dutch Adoptees

The overwhelming majority of Dutch adoptive parents received their Greek children from the Babies' Center Metera in Athens, which maintained branches in Iraklcio, Crete, and also on the island of Corfu (Kerkyra).[6] Metera became operational only in September of 1955, and its links to the regional branches were consolidated thereafter. By the early 1960s, Metera also collaborated with the orphanage of Kalamata and with regional child services centers. Throughout its first decade, Metera functioned under the auspices of Queen Frederica.

Most Greek adoptees from Metera arrived in the Netherlands between 1956 and 1970. The ISS Netherlands (founded in 1955) and also the Dutch Association for Foster Families (NVP, Nederlandse Vereniging voor Pleeg-gezinnen) served as mediating agencies in most of these cross-border cases, and they provided better-quality oversight than their (earlier) US counter-parts. Some Dutch adopters, however, acted on their own initiative and responded to announcements published in print media or to promotional materials issued by Metera.[7] Nearly all of the Greek-to-Dutch adoptions were stranger or nonrelative placements with families who were not Greek Orthodox.

Because both Metera and the ISS Netherlands adhered to relatively strict methods and compiled their archives, Greek-to-Dutch adoptees today can turn to Metera and to the ISS Netherlands (if applicable) and request their dossiers. Social workers at Metera are aware of their legal and moral obliga-tions to assist with root searches and provide further information to adult adoptees and also to birth mothers or birth siblings (following strict pro-tocols): http://kvmhtera.gr/index.php?detail_id=25. The mailing address is: Kentro "I Metera," Programma Anazitisis Rizon, Leoforos Dimokratias 65, 13122 Ilion, Athens, Greece.

Greek-to-Swedish Adoptees

Swedish adoptive parents received their Greek-born children from the Babies' Center Metera in Athens (or from its branches in the provinces).[8] From 1965 on, these adoptions were guided by a formal agreement between

---

6.   See above, pp. 61–62 and note 137, especially.
7.   See also various pictures and postings on Ta Pedia, the Facebook site of the close-knit group of Greek adoptees in the Netherlands, https://www.facebook.com/ta.pedia.7.
8.   See above, p. 64 and note 150, especially.

the Swedish National Social Welfare Board and Metera, which stipulated that the Swedish adopters had to appear in person to facilitate the "matching." The numbers of Greek placements in Sweden remained relatively small. Adoptees who are searching may want to follow the same instructions as those mentioned above for the Greek-to-Dutch adoptees.

INFORMATION AND REUNIFICATION SITES FOR
GREEK-BORN ADOPTEES

General Information

All adoptees and searching birth families may be helped by uploading their DNA test results to sites such as GEDmatch, Tools for DNA and Genealogy Research (www.gedmatch.com). US-based Greek adoptees may also want to collect their travel and immigration information through www.ancestry.com or www.familysearch.org. Enter your name, allow for variants, and try to find your name on the passenger lists and among the US naturalization records. Some of these documents contain additional names, dates, places of origin, and other information.

Sometimes the immigration records of Greek-to-American adoptees reveal information that was known during the visa issuance process but that has since been lost or forgotten. Adoptees may file a "Freedom of Information Act/Privacy Act Request" with Form G-639 for free online, via the website of the U.S. Citizenship and Immigration Services, www.uscis.gov: https://www.uscis.gov/g-639. Instructions (seven pages) on how to fill out and file the four-page Form G-639 are available online as well. These FOIA/PA requests enter a queue, and the wait may be up to five months. Applicants can follow the progress of their request online until the day that the CD-ROM arrives in the mail. The regular mailing address and email address are National Records Center (NRC), FOIA/PA Office, P.O. Box 648010, Lee's Summit, MO 64064–8010. Email: uscis.foia@uscis.dhs.gov.

Reunification Sites in Alphabetical Order
(all last accessed 15 September 2018)

- Adoption.com (including Adoption Registry Connect)
  https://registry.adoption.com/
  https://www.adopted.com/adoptee-connect.html
- The Eftychia Project: Helping Greek Adoptees Find Their Roots
  https://www.facebook.com/TheEftychiaProject/?notif_
    id=1554657914434047&notif_t=page_fan
  mynameiseftychia@gmail.com or theeftychiaproject@gmail.com

- ΕΙΚΟΝΙΚΕΣ ΓΕΝΝΕΣ-ΠΑΡΑΝΟΜΕΣ ΥΙΟΘΕΣΙΕΣ-ΕΛΛΑΔΑ-ΕΞΩΤΕΡΙΚΟ
  (Virtual Births-Illegal Adoptions-Greece-Abroad)
  https://www.facebook.com/groups/265712270638455/
- Greek Adoptees in Search of Their Birth Family
  https://www.facebook.com/groups/903363209695520/
- Greek Adoptions, S.E.A.S.Y.P., Athens, Greece, and Greek Reunion Registry
  (current president Mary Selekou) (literally: Σύλλογος Έρευνας κι Αποκάλυψης
  Στοιχείων Υιοθετημένων Παιδιών, Research Association for the Disclosure of
  Information on Adopted Children)
  https://greekadoptions.gr/
  seasyp@hol.gr
  info@greekadoptions.gr
- Greek Orphans Seeking Answers (GOSA) (Facebook group founded by Ioannis
  Kalos)
  https://www.facebook.com/groups/225165427849789/
- Hellenic Genealogy Geek, Facebook group (search "adopted," "adoption")
  https://www.facebook.com/groups/118224528189671/
- Hellenic Red Cross, Directorate for Searches
  http://www.ifrc.org/en/what-we-do/where-we-work/europe/hellenic-red-cross/
  http://www.redcross.gr/
  tracingstaff@redcross.gr
- *Light in the Tunnel, Games of Life*—Search (weekly Greek TV show of Angeliki
  Nikolouli)
  http://anikolouli.gr/en/
  http://www.anikolouli.gr/index.php?pathID=1_118
- ΜΙΑ ΖΩΗ ΣΕ ΨΑΧΝΩ (I Have Been Looking for You All My Life)
  https://www.facebook.com/ΜΙΑ-ΖΩΗ-ΣΕ-ΨΑΧΝΩ-356133544570988
- ΜΗ ΝΟΜΙΜΕΣ ΥΙΟΘΕΣΙΕΣ ΣΤΗ ΕΛΛΑΔΑ (Illegal Adoptions in Greece)
  https://www.facebook.com/groups/231951560218680/
- ΜΗΠΩΣ ΕΙΣΑΙ ΥΙΟΘΕΤΗΜΕΝΟΣ ? (Are You Perhaps Adopted?)
  https://www.facebook.com/groups/50477198069/
- Missing Greeks—Illegal Greek Adoptions
  http://illegalgreekadoptions.blogspot.com/
- My Greek Adoption (partly in Greek)
  https://www.youtube.com/watch?v=ySr_iG5YOOg
- *Pame Paketo* (*The Package*) (Greek TV show of Vicky Chatzivasileiou)
  http://www.alphatv.gr/shows/entertainment/pamepaketo/webtv
- Roots Research Center (NGO cofounder Mary Theodoropoulou)
  http://www.roots-research-center.gr/en/home/
- Ta Pedia, Facebook group for Greek-to-Dutch adoptees
  https://www.facebook.com/ta.pedia.7
- *Υιοθεσιες παιδιων* (Adoptions of Children)
  https://www.facebook.com/groups/661360793957548/about/

REFERENCES

Primary Sources

Major Archival Collections, Records, and Papers

Greece

Archive of P.I.K.P.A. (1945–1995), the Patriotic Institution for Social Welfare and Awareness, General State Archives (GAK). Athens.

Archive of the Child's Asylum of Volos, Archives of the Prefecture of Magnesia, General State Archives. Volos.

Archive of the Municipality of Volos, Itemized Decisions of the Municipal Councils of the City of Volos, Municipal Center for Historical Research and Documentation of Volos. Volos.

Archive of the Municipal Orphanage of Athens, General State Archives. Athens.

Archive of the National Council for Child Protection, unclassified Archive of the Ministry of Health (and Social Welfare), General State Archives. Athens.

"The Babies' Center Metera," Archive of the Former Royal Palace (1861–1971), General State Archives. Athens.

"Chief Court Mistress [Mary C. Carolou]," Archive of the Former Royal Palace (1861–1971), General State Archives. Athens.

Contemporary Social History Archives (ASKI). Athens.

"Donations," Archive of the Former Royal Palace (1861–1971), General State Archives. Athens.

Greek Literary and Historical Archive (ELIA). Athens.

Lina Tsaldari Archive, Konstantinos G. Karamanlis Foundation. Athens.

Records of the Court Case of the Saint Stylianos Foundling Home, Historical Archive of Macedonia. Thessaloniki.

The Netherlands

International Social Service (ISS), ISS Netherlands Branch Papers. Nationaal Archief. The Hague, the Netherlands.

United States of America

American Hellenic Educational Progressive Association (AHEPA). Archives (including *The Ahepan*, minutes of the Supreme Lodge meetings, proceedings of the annual Supreme [National] Conventions, year books, etc.). Washington, DC.

Atlantis, National Daily Greek Newspaper Records, Historical Society of Pennsylvania (HSP). Philadelphia, PA.

CARE Records, Manuscripts and Archives Division, New York Public Library. New York.

Child Welfare League of America Records. Social Welfare History Archives (SWHA), University of Minnesota Libraries. Minneapolis, MN.

Department of State Records, National Archives and Records Administration (NARA). College Park, MD.

Dwight D. Eisenhower Presidential Library, Museum, and Boyhood Home, DDE's Records as President. Abilene, KS.

Immigrants' Protective League Records, Special Collections and University Archives, University of Illinois at Chicago. Chicago, IL.

International Social Service (ISS), American Branch Papers. Social Welfare History Archives, University of Minnesota Libraries. Minneapolis, MN.

Library of Congress, Prints & Photographs Division. Washington, DC.

New York Arrival Records, 1820–1957, National Archives at New York City (New York Passenger Lists on Ancestry.com).

Personal archives, papers, and photograph collections (with permission).

Records of the Children's Bureau, National Archives and Records Administration. College Park, MD.

Records of the Displaced Persons Commission, 1948–1952, National Archives and Records Administration. College Park, MD.

Records of US Foreign Assistance Agencies, 1942–1963, National Archives and Records Administration. College Park, MD.

Robert Carlton Wilson Papers, 1953–1980. Special Collections and University Archives, San Diego State University. San Diego, CA.

Robert S. Kerr Collection, 1871–1970. Carl Albert Center Archives, University of Oklahoma. Norman, OK.

Primary-Source Newspapers, Magazines, Newsletters, and Journals

Serial Publications

The Ahepan (1926–present). Washington, DC: Order of Ahepa.

I and N Reporter. Newsletter published by the United States Immigration and Naturalization Service (INS).

ISS World News. Newsletter published by the American Branch of the International Social Service. New York.

Skyliner, Trans World Airlines Weekly Employee Publication. Magazine issues from 1929 to 2002 held at the State Historical Society of Missouri (online) [last accessed 15 September 2018].

Online Access to Newspapers (all last accessed 15 September 2018)

Digital Library of Newspapers and Periodical Press, National Library of Greece, online at efimeris.nlg.gr.

Newspaper archive, Hellenic Parliament Library. Athens, Greece. Catalogs online at http://catalog.parliament.gr/hipres/help/null/horizon/microfilms.htm.

Newspapers.com.

Individual Articles (anonymous articles are listed in chronological order)

Ahepa Refugee Relief Committee (October–December 1954). "Ahepans! Have You Joined the 'Crusade for Sponsors'?" *The Ahepan* 28, no. 4: 9.

Alavanos, Konstantinos (9 December 1980). "Βουλή· Τί έγιναν τα 2 παιδιά του Αργυριάδη;" "Parliament: What Became of the Two Children of [Elias] Argyriadis?" *Eleftherotypia*, 1, 15.

Anonymous (September–October 1946). "Greek War Relief in Action." *The Ahepan* 20, no. 4: 14–17.

Anonymous (March 1947). "Orphan Greece: Shall Uncle Sam Adopt This Problem Child?" *Senior Scholastic* 50: 5–6.

Anonymous (15 March 1948). "As the Twig Is Bent." *Time Magazine*, 37.

Anonymous (11 January 1950). "Τα ορφανά πολέμου· Μια στατιστική του Υπουργείου Προνοίας." "The War Orphans: Statistics from the Ministry of Social Welfare." *I Thessalia*, 3.

Anonymous (21 January 1950). "Μεταβατικός σταθμός προς τον θάνατον ήτο η 'Βρεφική Στέγη.'" "The 'Baby Shelter (of Piraeus)' Has Been a Transit Station to Death." *Tachydromos* (Volos).

Anonymous (January–March 1950). "Ahepa in Forefront in Arousing Public Opinion for Liberation of the 28,000 Abducted Greek Children: Mass Meetings, Demonstrations, Proclamations, Sponsored by Ahepa Chapters; Ahepan Phelps Phelps, Chairman of American Committee, Spearheading Drive." *The Ahepan* 24, no. 1: 5.

Anonymous (23 February 1950). "Adopted Daughter." *The Hi-Po*, 8 [student newspaper of High Point College (now University) in North Carolina].

Anonymous (8 May 1950). "42 Nations to Join in Making Choice of Year's Mothers." *The Cincinnati Enquirer*, 12.

Anonymous (21 July 1950). "Crippled Greek Orphan Starts Home." *New York Times*, 21.

Anonymous (18 November 1951). "Ο Η. Αργυριάδης αποκαλύπτει· Λεπτομερή στοιχεία της οργανώσεως του δικτύου κατασκοπείας και διαβιβάσεως πληροφοριών." "Elias Argyriadis Discloses: Detailed Information about the Organization of the Espionage Network and of the Transmission of Intelligence." *Eleftheria*, 1, 6.

Anonymous (20 November 1951). "Νέαι σοβαραί αποκαλύψεις διά τους ασυρμάτους." "New [and] Serious Revelations about the Wireless Stations." *Neologos Patron*, 1, 4.

Anonymous (28 November 1951). "Αυτοκτόνησε χθες δι' άγνωστους λόγους η ερωμένη του κομμουνιστού κατασκόπου της Γλυφάδας Ηλ. Αργυριάδη." "Yesterday, the Lover of Elias Argyriadis, the Communist Spy of Glyfada, Committed Suicide for Unknown Reasons." *Akropolis*, 1, 4.

Anonymous (28 November 1951). "R. E. [Religious Education] Club Will Send Gifts to Vassiliki Douna." *The Hi-Po*, 1 [student newspaper of High Point College (now University) in North Carolina].

Anonymous (30 January 1952). "Children's Return Held Dim in Greece: Those Taken to Red Satellites Will Soon Be 'Neither Greeks Nor Children,' U. N. Is Told." *New York Times*, 9.

Anonymous (2 March 1952). "Εξεδόθη η απόφασις δια την κομμουνιστικήν κατασκοπίαν." "The Verdict on the Communist Espionage Plot Has Been Delivered." *Akropolis*, 1, 6.

Anonymous (30 March 1952). "Έκτακτος έκδοσις· Εξετελέσθησαν την πρωίαν 4 κομμουνισταί κατάσκοποι." "Special Edition: 4 Communist Spies Were Executed Early Morning." *Akropolis*, 1, 6.

Anonymous (31 March 1952). "Πώς κρίνουν τας εκτελέσεις οι εδώ συμμαχικοί κύκλοι και αι ξέναι εφημερίδες;" "How Do the Allied Circles Here and the Foreign Newspapers Judge the Executions?" *Athinaïki*, 6.

Anonymous (1 April 1952). "Το φωτογραφικόν ρεπορτάζ της *Ακροπόλεως* από την εκτέλεσιν των 4 κομμουνιστών." "The Photo Reportage of the *Akropolis* from the Execution of the Four Communists." *Akropolis*, 1, 3.

Anonymous (15 June 1952). "Adopted War Orphan Flies in from Greece." *New York Times*, 18.

Anonymous (April–June 1953). [Picture caption]. *The Ahepan* 27, no. 2: 27.

Anonymous (26 October 1953). "Greece: The King's Wife." *Time Magazine*, 35–40 and front cover.

Anonymous (16 November 1953). "Royal Greeks Meet Governors—and Greeks: They Make a Real Try at Seeing the U.S. the Hard Way." *Life Magazine*, 56–60, photo reportage and front cover.

Anonymous (January–March 1954). "Ahepa Refugee Relief Committee Recognized by State Department." *The Ahepan* 28, no. 1: 6.

Anonymous (4 May 1954). "War Orphan Adopted by Trojans." *Troy Record* (Troy, New York), 14.

Anonymous (October–December 1954). "Chairman Lamberson Reports on Ahepa Refugee Program." *The Ahepan* 28, no. 4: 12.

Anonymous (13 November 1954). "Shy Greek Girl Finds Loving Parents Here." *Chicago Daily Tribune*, 1.

Anonymous (13 May 1955). "Ομογενείς θα υιοθετήσουν 126 παιδιά του Βρεφοκομείου." "Greek Americans Will Adopt 126 Children from the Orphanage." *Neologos Patron*, 4.

Anonymous (July–August 1955). "The Ahepa on Capitol Hill." *The Ahepan* 29, no. 4: 4–6.

Anonymous (19 October 1955). "Αφανίζουν την Ελλάδα." "They Are Obliterating Greece." *I Avgi*, 3.

Anonymous (8 January 1956). "Greek War Orphans to Sample U. S. Life." *New York Times*, 19.

Anonymous (2 February 1956). "Ανέρχονται μέχρι τούδε εις 34.700 οι άποροι Α' κατηγορίας Μαγνησίας." "Thus Far Magnesia's Number of Destitute of the First Category Amounts to 34,700 People." *I Thessalia*, 1.

Anonymous (23 June 1956). "Αμερικανική οργάνωσις διεξάγει εμπόριο βρεφών στην Θεσσαλονίκη." "An American Organization Is Carrying out a Baby Trade in Thessaloniki." *I Avgi*, 1.

Anonymous (24 June 1956). "Εμπόριο βρεφών." "Baby Trade." *I Avgi*, 5.

Anonymous (13 July 1956). "12 Greek Orphans Fly in to Begin Life as Americans in 9 States." *New York Times*, 3.

Anonymous (23 August 1956). "TWA Photo Parade." *Skyliner, Trans World Airlines Weekly Employee Publication*, 4.

Anonymous (24 December 1956). "Een kind zoekt zijn toekomst: Alleen zijn naam is nog van hem." "A [Male] Child Searches for His Future: Only His Name Is Still His." *Nieuwe Leidsche Courant*, 16.

Anonymous (31 March 1957). "Film Premiere to Aid Greece." *New York Times*, 91.

Anonymous (May–July 1957). "Official Summary of the 30th National Convention Minutes, Order of AHEPA, Waldorf-Astoria Hotel, New York, N.Y., August 12 through 19, 1956." *The Ahepan* 31, no. 2: supplement I–XXIV.

Anonymous (February 1958). "ISS Featured on CBS Network Show; 'Circle Theater' Explores Adoptions." *ISS World News*, 2.

Anonymous (28 February 1959). "Orphan Inquiry on: Magistrate May Face Queries on Greek War Children." *New York Times*, 22.

Anonymous (March 1959). "Constance Verinis." *The Ahepan* 33, no. 3: 10.

Anonymous (5 May 1959). "Ελληνοαμερικανός δικαστής κατηγορείται ως ενεχόμενος εις 'μαύρην αγοράν' βρεφών." "Greek American Judge Stands Accused of Being Involved in a 'Black Market' of Babies." *To Vima*, 1.

Anonymous (5 May 1959). "Ένας Ελληνοαμερικανός ειρηνοδίκης συνελήφθη χθες δια τας υιοθεσίας ορφανών παιδιών από την Ελλάδα." "A Greek American Magistrate Was Arrested Yesterday for the Adoptions of Orphan Children from Greece." *I Kathimerini*, 1.

Anonymous (6 May 1959). "NY Judge, 3 Others Nabbed for Selling Black Market Babies." *The Panama American*, 3.

Anonymous (7 May 1959). "Μητέρες ζητούν να μάθουν για την τύχη 'υιοθετηθέντων' από Αμερικανούς παιδιών τους." "Mothers Ask to Learn about the Fate of Their Children 'Adopted' by Americans." *I Avgi*, 1, 6.

Anonymous (8 May 1959). "270 παιδιά απέστειλε στην Αμερική ο κ. Τσαπάρης για λογαριασμό του Σκόπα." "Mr Tsaparis Sent 270 Children to America on Scopas's Account." *I Avgi*, 5.

Anonymous (8 May 1959). "Η μαύρη αγορά των βρεφών εις την Αμερικήν." "The Black Market in Babies [Sent] to America." *Makedonia*, 1. Cartoon held also in the *Atlantis*, National Daily Greek Newspaper Records, MSS 43, box 31, folder 4, "Scopas #2," Historical Society of Pennsylvania. Philadelphia, PA.

Anonymous (9 May 1959). "Εματαιώθη η αποστολή εις Ηνωμένας Πολιτείας προς υιοθεσίαν δέκα βρεφών από το Δημοτικόν Βρεφοκομείον Ηρακλείου Κρήτης." "The Plan to Send 10 Babies for Adoption from the Municipal Orphanage of Irakleio, Crete, to the United States Has Been Canceled." *To Vima*.

Anonymous (9 May 1959). "Θα δημοσιευθή η έκθεσις του Υπουργείου Προνοίας για το εμπόριο των βρεφών." "The Report of the Ministry of Social Welfare about the Baby Trade Will Be Published." *I Avgi*, 5.

Anonymous (10 May 1959). "Ομογενής είχε καταγγείλει πέρυσι στην Κυβέρνησιν την μαύρη αγορά βρεφών." "A Greek American Had Last Year Reported the Baby Black Market to the Government." *I Avgi*, 1, 5.

Anonymous (10 May 1959). "Σταυροφορίαν κατά του βρεφεμπορίου αναλαμβάνει συντόμως η Ιερά Σύνοδος. Αβελτηρίαν επέδειξεν η Κυβέρνησις." "The Holy Synod Will Shortly Undertake a Crusade against the Baby Trade. The Government Has Shown Itself Inept." *Makedonia*, 8.

Anonymous (20 May 1959). "Κανένα βρέφος από το Βρεφοκομείο Θεσσαλονίκης δεν υιοθετήθη κατά ύποπτο τρόπο στην Αμερική." "No Baby from the Foundling Home of Thessaloniki Was Given out for Adoption in America in a Suspect Manner." *I Avgi*, 5.

Anonymous (25 May 1959). "The Market in Orphans." *Newsweek*, 57.

Anonymous (27 May 1959). "Ο Υπουργός Προνοίας δεν δίδει στην δημοσιότητα την έκθεσιν για το θέμα της υιοθεσίας." "The Minister of Social Welfare Does Not Make Public the Report on the Topic of Adoption." *I Avgi*.

Anonymous (June–July 1959). "Ahepa's Projects at St. Basil's a Reality." *The Ahepan* 33, no. 5: 9–11.

Anonymous (1 July 1959). "Greeks Probe Procedures of Adoption: 'Hear Black Market Reports from U.S.'" *Chicago Daily Tribune* [based on Reuters news reporting of 30 June 1959].

Anonymous (12 July 1959). "Greece Is Revising Her Adoption Laws." *New York Times*, 6.

Anonymous (11 May 1962). "First Lady's Gift Rattle Ends White House Bawl." *New York Times*, 14.

Anonymous (12 May 1962). "Greek Orphan Arrives as Mother's Day Gift." *Pacific Stars and Stripes*, 2.

Anonymous (15 September 1966). "Δεν εβασανίζετο ο 7ετής εις Πάτρας." "The Seven-Year-Old in Patras Was Not Tortured." *Eleftheria*, 8.

Anonymous (17 January 2002). "Adoption Trial." *I Kathimerini*.

Argyriadi, Efterpi (7 December 1980). "Δεν τάμαθες; Σκότωσαν τον πατέρα σου!" "Haven't You Heard? They Killed Your Father!" Interview by Giorgos Oikonomeas. *Eleftherotypia*, 13.

Argyriadi, Efterpi (9 April 2017). "Ήταν η εκτέλεση των τεσσάρων, όχι μόνο του Μπελογιάννη." "It Was the Execution of the Four, Not Just of Beloyannis." Interview by Lambros Stavropoulos. *To Vima*, A16–A17. Also online at http://www.tovima.gr/politics/article/?aid=872972 [last accessed 15 September 2018].

Athanasiou, Areti (11 January 2003). "Βρήκε την αδελφή του 52 χρόνια μετά." "He Found His Sister 52 Years Later." *Ta Nea*.

Bigart, Homer (6 January 1959). "New York Is Cited as a Baby Market: Joint Committee Here Hears the Sources Are Chicago, Miami and Greece." *New York Times*.

Bogiopoulos, Nikos (21 April 1996). "Το 'παιδομάζωμα', η Φρειδερίκη και το δουλεμπόριο της εθνικοφροσύνης." "The 'Child-Gathering,' Frederica, and the Human Trafficking of the *Ethnikofrosyni* ['National Conviction']." *Rizospastis*, 6. Republished in the online Greek newspaper *Imerodromos* of 9 September 2016, accessible at http://www.imerodromos.gr/paidomazwma-freiderikh-douleborio-ethnikofrosynhs/ [last accessed 15 September 2018].

Bonner, Raymond (13 April 1996). "Tales of Stolen Babies and Lost Identities: A Greek Scandal Echoes in New York." *New York Times*.

Chatzianastasiou, A. (28 November 1951). "Νέον δραματικόν στοιχείον εις την υπόθεσιν της κατασκοπείας." "New Dramatic Element in the Espionage Affair." *Ethnikos Kiryx*, 1, 3.

Clarke, Philip (3 May 1958). "The Lad and I Came Through." *Saturday Evening Post*, 32–33, 72–74.

DeLand, Dave (13 and 14 September 2015). "The Baby in the Box Digs for Her Greek Roots: Kim Kruse Hopes Finding Her Original Family Will Fill a Void in Her Troubled Life." *St. Cloud Times*, Minnesota. Online at http://www.sctimes.

com/story/news/local/2015/09/04/baby-box-digs-greek-roots/71710560/ [last accessed 15 September 2018].

Diavatis, Harry (30 January 2012). "Monday Update." Weekly online newsletter of the Vallejo High School in Vallejo, California. Pdf document of 47 pages, online at http://vhs62.com/vhs/newsletter/2012/120130.pdf [last accessed 15 September 2018].

Doughty, Clayton B. (April 1964). "Adoption and Immigration of Alien Orphans." *I and N Reporter* 12, no. 4: 50–52.

Ducker, Ruth W. (1958). "Little Greek Girl Becomes American." Unidentified and undated newspaper clipping.

The Editors [of *The Ahepan*] (July–August 56). "Ahepa on the March: The Fateful Years 1954–1956." *The Ahepan* 30, no. 4: 4–6.

Endt, Friso (21 September 1963). "In Griekenland zijn kinderen te koop!" "There Are Babies for Sale in Greece." *Margriet*, 136–40.

Fields-Meyer, Thomas (28 October 1996). "A Sense of Belonging." *People Magazine*, 98–101.

Garantzioti, N. (17 April 1996). "Παιδομάζωμα με τα δρομολόγια του 'Φρειδερίκη.'" "Child-Gathering with the Itineraries of the [SS *Queen*] *Frederica*." *Ethnos*, 14–15.

Germanos, Freddy (18 January 1959). "Οι 'έμποροι βρεφών' δρουν στην Ελλάδα· 1." "The 'Baby Traders' Are Active in Greece: 1." *Eleftheria*, 9, 10.

Germanos, Freddy (20 January 1959). "Οι 'έμποροι βρεφών' δρουν στην Ελλάδα· 2." "The 'Baby Traders' Are Active in Greece: 2." *Eleftheria*, 3, 4.

Germanos, Freddy (21 January 1959). "Οι 'έμποροι βρεφών' δρουν στην Ελλάδα· 3." "The 'Baby Traders' Are Active in Greece: 3." *Eleftheria*, 3.

Grapsas, Marinos (16 April 1996). "Άνθρωποι από το πουθενά βρήκαν τις ρίζες τους." "People Out of Nowhere Have Found Their Roots." *Eleftherotypia*.

Greek Jubilee: The Newsletter of Adoptees in Motion 1, no. 1 (May 1997). Edited by Amalia Balch.

Grigoris, S. (13 May 1955). "Αυτά πρέπει να λέγονται." "These Things Must Be Said." *I Avgi*, 2.

Hoover, Felix (22 December 2000). "Adoptee Gets Finest Gift: Her History. Woman Brings Birth Parents from Greece for Christmas." *Columbus Dispatch*, E1.

Hudson, Edward (3 June 1956). "Flights Bringing Refugees Here Reach Peak." *New York Times*, 214.

International Social Service (November 1957). *ISS World News*. Newsletter published by the American Branch of the International Social Service. New York.

International Social Service (February 1958). *ISS World News*. Newsletter published by the American Branch of the International Social Service. New York.

International Social Service (June 1958). *ISS World News*. Newsletter published by the American Branch of the International Social Service. New York.

Kalmoukos, Theodoros (25–26 September 1993). "Δύο αδέλφια ξαναβρέθηκαν έπειτα από τριάντα πέντε χρόνια." "Two Siblings Find Each Other Again after Thirty-Five Years." *Ethnikos Kiryx*, 1, 5.

Kambylis, Takis (9 March 2008). "The Tragedy of the Children of the Civil War Years." *I Kathimerini*.

Kerr, Adelaide (10 May 1952). "No Child Is Lost." *Pacific Stars and Stripes*.

Knights of Thermopylae Committee (October–December 1952). "Knights of Thermopylae." *The Ahepan* 26, no. 4: 20–22.

Konstandaras, Nikos (22 September 1996). "Greece's Black-Market Babies Come Home—Stolen Children Demand to Know Their Histories." *Seattle Times*.

Konstandaras, Nikos (29 September 1996). "Greek Americans Fear They May Have Been Black-Market Babies." *Los Angeles Times*.

Konstandaras, Nikos (8 November 1996). "'Stolen' Babies back in Greece. Lost Children Coming Home. Voices from a Dark Past Speak Out." *Athens News* 1, 15.

Krichefsky, Gertrude D. (October 1958). "Immigrant Orphans." *I and N Reporter* 7, no. 2: 19–21, 28.

Krichefsky, Gertrude D. (April 1961). "Alien Orphans." *I and N Reporter* 9, no. 4: 43–46, 51.

Lamberson, Leo J. (March–April 1955). "A Challenge to the Ahepa family." *The Ahepan* 29, no. 2: 31.

Lamberson, Leo J. (November–December 1955). "Leo J. Lamberson, Refugee Committee Chairman." *The Ahepan* 29, no. 6: 15.

Le Varn, Carol (7 October 1957). "Jane Russell Works to Bring Europe's Orphans to America." *Victoria Advocate*, 3. Victoria, TX.

Manta, John L. (February–April 1957). "Ahepa: 'The Ark of Hellenism in America.' Essence of Manta's Message." *The Ahepan* 31, no. 1: 3–12.

Mantzoros, Peter N. (15 May 1959). "Scopas Arrested in 'Sale of Babies.'" *Chicago Pnyx*, 1–2.

Mathioudaki, Kat. (17 April 1996). "Λίστα με 'επίσημες' παράνομες υιοθεσίες." "List with 'Official' Illegal Adoptions." *Eleftheros Typos*, 27.

McWhorter, John M. (April 1960). "The Orphan Program." *I and N Reporter* 8, no. 4: 47–48.

Mitler, Ernest A. (1 November 1959). "Testimony on Black Market Adoptions: Verbatim Facts Presented before Congressional Committee Revealed: Part I." *Atlantis* (English-language Sunday edition).

Mitler, Ernest A. (8 November 1959). "Testimony on Black Market Adoptions: Verbatim Facts Presented before Congressional Committee Revealed. Analysis of Proxy Adoptions Procedure: Part II." *Atlantis*.

Mitler, Ernest A. (15 November 1959). "Testimony on Black Market Adoptions: Verbatim Facts Presented before Congressional Committee Revealed. Analysis of Proxy Adoptions Procedure: Part III." *Atlantis*.

Mitler, Ernest A. (22 November 1959). "Testimony on Black Market Adoptions: Verbatim Facts Presented before Congressional Committee Revealed. Analysis of Proxy Adoptions Procedure: Part IV." *Atlantis*.

Mitler, Ernest A. (29 November 1959). "Mitler Report on Black Market Adoptions: Adoption Operations in Greece Reviewed. Conditions in Orphanages 'Deplorable': Part V." *Atlantis*.

Mitler, Ernest A. (6 December 1959). "Mitler Report on Black Market Adoptions: Steps Proposed to Prevent Exploitation. Senator Keating's Interest Cited: Part VI." *Atlantis*.

Mitler, Ernest A., and Bill Slocum (28 December 1954). "Babies: Our One Remaining Black Market." *Look Magazine*, 90–94.

Nikolopoulos, Christos (13 May 1959). "Το εμπόριο βρεφών διευθύνεται από τον υπόκοσμο της Αμερικής." "The Baby Trade Is Being Directed by the Underworld of America." *I Avgi*, 1, 5.

Oikonomeas, Giorgos, and F. Oikonomidis (16 December 1980). "Η 'Ε' βρήκε τα 2 παιδιά του Αργυριάδη· Βρίσκονται στην Αμερική υιοθετημένα από ομογενή." *"Eleftherotypia* Has Found the Two Children of [Elias] Argyriadis: They Are in America, Adopted by a Greek American." *Eleftherotypia*, 1, 15.

Oikonomeas, Giorgos, and F. Oikonomidis (17 December 1980). "Η δραματική συνομιλία των αδελφών Αργυριάδη." "The Dramatic Conversation of the Argyriadis Sisters." *Eleftherotypia*, 1, 9.

Oikonomeas, Giorgos, F. Oikonomidis, Potis Paraskevopoulos, and Nikos Pigadas (6 December 1980–16 January 1981). "Υπόθεση Μπελογιάννη· 28 χρόνια μετά . . ." "The Beloyannis Affair: 28 Years Later . . ." *Eleftherotypia*.

Onisenko, Costas (12 March 2008). "Looking for Birth Parents." *I Kathimerini*.

Papadopoulos, Lefteris (11 November 1984). "Οι πάνες με τα αργύρια." "The Diapers with the Silver Coins." *Ta Nea*, 13.

Petritsi, Loukia (10 February 1952). "Μία αξιέπαινος προσπάθεια· Χιλιάδες ορφανά που ξαναζούν στην θαλπωρή της οικογένειας." "A Worthwhile Effort: Thousands of Orphans Who Are Again Living in the Warmth of a Family." *Embros*, 3–4.

Polos, George A. (January–March 1952). "Ahepa Displaced Persons Committee Reports." *The Ahepan* 26, no. 1: 10–11, 35.

Prodromidis, Paul (January 1959). "An Acropolis on the Hudson: St. Basil's Academy." *The Ahepan* 33, no. 1: 5–7.

Psathas, Dimitris (28 December 1956). "Απώλεια σκύλου." "Loss of a Dog." *Ta Nea*, 1.

Reuter, Richard W. (August–September 1959). "'CARE' in Greece." *The Ahepan* 33, no. 6: 13.

Roth, Jack (5 May 1959). "Scopas Arrested in Sale of Babies: Ex-Magistrate and Lawyer Accused of Black Market in Greek Children Here." *New York Times*, 1, 24.

Rusk, Howard A. (11 June 1950). "Foster Parents Plan Helping Young Sufferers Live Anew: Greek Boy Recently Brought Here Only One of Many Thousands Receiving Aid." *New York Times*, 78.

Silverman, Milton (19 March 1960). "The Happy Orphans of Metera: This Greek Institution Provides a New Kind of Care for the Babies of Unwed Mothers, with Remarkable Benefits for the Children." *Saturday Evening Post*, 26–27, 101–6.

Sroiter, Antonis (16 April 1996). "Υιοθέτησαν παράνομα 2.000 Ελληνόπουλα." "They [the Americans] Illegally Adopted 2,000 Greek Children." *Apogevmatini*, 10.

Synadinos, Diana (November 2000). "And I Always Thought I Was from Sparta!" *The Charioteer* [in-house newsletter distributed to the parishioners of the Annunciation Greek Orthodox Cathedral in Columbus, Ohio], 13–15.

Thayer, Mary V. R. (17 November 1958). "Queen Frederika Bests Helen of Troy." *Washington Post and Times Herald*, B5.

Thomopoulos, E. (19 November 1951). "Η συμμετοχή των γυναικών στο δίκτυο κατασκοπείας του ΚΚΕ." "The Participation of Women in the Espionage Network of the KKE." *Athinaïki*, 1, 5.

Thompson, Margaret (May–June 1947). "So Little Can Do So Much." *The Ahepan* 21, no. 3: 19–21.

Thomson, Helen (21 August 2015). "Study of Holocaust Survivors Finds Trauma Passed on to Children's Genes." *The Guardian*.

Tsaldari, Lina P. (30 November 1951). "Τα παιδιά της Δάλα." "The Children of Dala." *Ta Nea*, 1.

Voultepsis, I. (6 May 1959). "Οι πρωταγωνισταί του σκανδάλου της 'μαύρης αγοράς' των βρεφών." "The Protagonists of the Scandal of the 'Black Market' of Babies." *I Avgi*, 1, 5.

West, Jean (3 August 2015). "Holocaust Survivors' Grandchildren Call for Action Over Inherited Trauma." *The Guardian*.

Whittemore, Allen (1 February 2012). "Manalapan: One Centenarian's Secret to One Long Life: Spicy Greek Food." *Coastal Star*.

Zotos, Stefanos (6 May 1959). "Αναμένονται και νέαι συλλήψεις δια την 'μαύρην αγοράν' βρεφών." "Further Arrests to Be Expected in the 'Black Market' of Babies." *To Vima*, 1.

Typescript and Printed Primary Sources

Anonymous [based on Ernest A. Mitler] (1 May 1959). "Survey of Greek-U.S. Proxy Adoptions" (based on a study made by the New York State Joint Legislative Committee on Matrimonial and Family Laws and prepared by Ernest A. Mitler, special consultant to the committee). Typescript, 15 pages, held in the archives of the International Social Service, American Branch Papers, box 31, folder 2: "Greece: ISS Greek Branch Adoptions, 1959–1964," Social Welfare History Archives, University of Minnesota Libraries. Minneapolis, MN.

Athinogenis, A., and F. Papathanasiou (10 April 1959). "Έρευνα επί καταγγελιών του ημερησίου τύπου περί εμπορίας βρεφών." "Study on the Accusations of the Daily Press about Baby Trade." Typescript, 58 pages, held in folder 469, Archive of PIKPA (1945–1995), General State Archives. Athens, Greece.

Chebithes, Victor I. (1959). [Speech] (untitled subsection of "Discussion"). In *Order of Ahepa, Proceedings 37th Supreme Convention, Hollywood, CA*, edited by the Order of Ahepa. Vol. 2, 474–84. Washington, DC: Order of Ahepa.

Chirekos, Nicholas (16 August 1961). "Minutes Supreme Lodge Meeting, Wednesday, Aug. 16, 1961, Deauville Hotel." Typescript, 1 page. In *Ahepa Supreme Lodge Minutes, 1951–1964*, edited by the Order of Ahepa (collection of many separately numbered typescript sets of minutes). Washington, DC: Order of Ahepa.

Cochran, Lena E., and Helen McKay (24 August 1951). Letter to "Mr. Robert J. Corkery, European Coordinator U.S. Displaced Persons Commission, Frankfurt A/M, Germany." Typescript, 4 pages, held in the Records of the Displaced Persons Commission, 1948–1952, box 58, folder "Orphan Procedures—Public Law 555," National Archives and Records Administration. College Park, MD.

Congressional Record (1953), 83 Cong. Rec. Accessed via heinonline.org [last accessed 15 September 2018].

Congressional Record (1959), 105 Cong. Rec. Accessed via heinonline.org [last accessed 15 September 2018].

Constantelos, Demetrios J., editor (1976). *Encyclicals and Documents of the Greek Orthodox Archdiocese of North and South America, Relating to Its Thought and Activity the First Fifty Years (1922–1972)* (in English and Greek). Thessaloniki: Patriarchal Institute for Patristic Studies and the Greek Orthodox Archdiocese of North and South America.

Critzas, Constantine J. (1957). "Report of Ahepa Refugee Relief Committee in Liquidation." In *Order of Ahepa Year Books: 1957 Year Book*, edited by the Order of Ahepa, part 1, 101–13. Washington, DC: Order of Ahepa.

Daravinga, Kaiti (9 January 1963). "Πόρισμα ενόρκου διοικητικής ανακρίσεως." "Findings of the Administrative Interrogation under Oath." Typescript report, 10 pages, held in the Historical Archive of Macedonia, Records of the court case of the Saint Stylianos Foundling Home (GRGSA-IAM JUS 008.02). Thessaloniki, Greece.

Doukas, Kimon A. (16 May 1959). "Minutes—Supreme Lodge Emergency Meeting. May 16th—Henry Hudson Hotel, New York City." Typescript, 5 pages. In *Ahepa Supreme Lodge Minutes, 1951–1964*, edited by the Order of Ahepa (collection of many separately numbered typescript sets of minutes). Washington, DC: Order of Ahepa.

Douris, George ([August] 1958). "Report of the Investigating Committee: Ahepa Refugee Relief Committee." [Report presented to the Ahepa Convention in Boston, MA]. Typescript, 5 pages, held in the *Atlantis*, National Daily Greek Newspaper Records, MSS 43, box 31, folder 4, "Scopas #2," Historical Society of Pennsylvania. Philadelphia, PA. See also the verbatim proceedings of Douris's delivery of this report: "Report of Ahepa Refugee Relief Committee by the Chairman, George Douris." In *Order of Ahepa, Proceedings 32nd Supreme Convention, Boston, Mass.*, edited by the Order of Ahepa. Vol. 2, 950–65. Washington, DC: Order of Ahepa, 1958.

Douris, George ([August] 1959). [Report presented to the Ahepa Convention in Hollywood, CA] (untitled in the original draft). Typescript, 11 pages, held in the *Atlantis*, National Daily Greek Newspaper Records, MSS 43, box 31, folder 5, "Scopas #3," Historical Society of Pennsylvania. Philadelphia, PA. See also the verbatim proceedings of Douris's delivery of this report: "Report on Refugee Relief Committee. George Douris, Chairman." In *Order of Ahepa, Proceedings 37th Supreme Convention, Hollywood, CA*, edited by the Order of Ahepa. Vol. 2, 446–60. Washington, DC: Order of Ahepa, 1959.

Doxiadis, Spyros (10 November 1960). Letter to Mary Carolou. Typescript, 1 page, held in "Chief Court Mistress," folder 1119, Archive of the Former Royal Palace (1861–1971), General State Archives. Athens, Greece.

Eisenhower, Dwight D. (8 February 1956). "Message from the President of the United States Transmitting Recommendations Relative to Our Immigration and Nationality Laws." Copy, 6 pages, held in the Robert S. Kerr Collection, 1871–1970, series 3: Legislative, 1935–1962, box 11, folder 6: "Immigration, 1956–1959," Carl Albert Center Archives, University of Oklahoma. Norman, OK.

Foster Parents' Plan for War Children (1957). *Foster Parents' Plan: Report, 1937–1957*. New York: Foster Parents' Plan for War Children.

Gonzales, Valdemar (27 July 1960). "A Report on The Association of Parents of Greek Orphans." Typescript, 6 pages, held in the archives of the International Social Service, American Branch Papers, box 10, folder 18: "Independent Adoption Schemes: Diavitis [sic], Reverend Spyrus 1960," Social Welfare History Archives, University of Minnesota Libraries. Minneapolis, MN.

Government Gazette of the Kingdom of Greece, Efimeris tis Kyverniseos tou Vasileiou tis Ellados (17 August 1966 and 11 December 1970).

Government Gazette of the Greek Republic, Efimeris tis Kyverniseos tis Ellinikis Dimokratias (30 December 1996).

Hagerty, James C. (31 May 1956). "Immediate [Press] Release: The White House." Typescript, 4 pages, held in the Dwight D. Eisenhower Presidential Library, Museum, and Boyhood Home, DDE's Records as President, Official File, Box 764, OF 325 People-to-People Program (2); NAID #12649394. Abilene, KS. Online at https://www.eisenhower.archives.gov/research/online_documents/people_to_people/BinderV.pdf [last accessed 15 September 2018].

Hellenic Parliament, Official Minutes. Athens, Greece.

Howard, Harry N. (April 1950). "The Greek Question in the Fourth General Assembly of the United States." Reprinted from the *Department of State Bulletin* of February 27 and March 6, 1950. Washington, DC: Department of State, Division of Publications, Office of Public Affairs.

Hyde, Laurin, and Virginia P. Hyde (June 1958). "A Study of Proxy Adoptions." Typescript, 31 pages, based on a survey conducted for the Child Welfare League of America in collaboration with the ISS. Held in the archives of the International Social Service, American Branch Papers, box 11, folder 14: "Proxy Adoption study 1959," Social Welfare History Archives, University of Minnesota Libraries. Minneapolis, MN.

Intergovernmental Committee for European Migration (Spring 1957). "Intergovernmental Committee for European Migration." *International Organization* 11, no. 2: 404–6.

International Social Service (ca. 1955). "Simple Phonetic Greek/English Vocabulary." Typescript, 4 pages, held in the personal archive of Mitsos.

King-Tsileni, Maria (11 May 1957). "Report on Activities of ISS Greek Branch: October 1956–May 1957. Prepared for the International Council Meeting, Geneva, 31 May–1 June 1957." Typescript, 2 pages, held in the International Social Service (ISS), ISS Netherlands Branch Papers, folder 8: "ISS—Afdelingen 1956–1957 (en correspondenten), l. Griekenland," Nationaal Archief. The Hague, the Netherlands.

Kirk, William T., and Susan T. Pe[t]tiss (30 June 1955). Letter to "ISS, Greek Branch, Athens. Re: Inter-country adoptions. Eligible orphans under section 5a of RRA for 'Matching.'" Letter, 2 pages, held in the personal archive of Mitsos.

Koutsoumaris, Aristotelis (31 August 1957). "Προς· Το Υπουργείον Κοινωνικής Προνοίας." Letter "To the Ministry of Social Welfare." Typescript, 4 pages, held in the Lina Tsaldari Archive, folder 8, subfolder 4, item 14: "Adoptions 1957–1958," Konstantinos G. Karamanlis Foundation. Athens, Greece.

Koutsoumaris, Aristotelis (13 June 1958). Letter to William T. Kirk. Letter, 6 pages, held in the archives of the International Social Service, American Branch Papers, box 10, folder 37: "Proxy Adoptions 1954–1956," Social Welfare History Archives, University of Minnesota Libraries. Minneapolis, MN.

Lamberson, Leo J. (10 May 1954). "Πρός τήν Α. Ε. τόν Ὑπουργόν τῶν Ἐσωτερικῶν Κύριον Ἰωάννην Νικολίτσαν." "To His Excellency, the Minister of Internal Affairs, Mr Ioannis Nikolitsas." Typescript, 1 page, held in the Archive of the Child's Asylum of Volos, folder 2125, "Documents of the Ministry of Social Welfare and Other Ministries, 1954–1956," Archives of the Prefecture of Magnesia, General State Archives. Volos, Greece.

Lamberson, Leo J. (31 July 1955). "Report of the Ahepa Refugee Relief Committee." In *Order of Ahepa Year Books: 1955 Year Book*, edited by the Order of Ahepa, part 1, 46–49. Washington, DC: Order of Ahepa.

Lamberson, Leo J. (1956a). "Committee Report, Refugee Relief Committee." In *Order of Ahepa, Proceedings 30th National Convention, New York, NY*, edited by the Order of Ahepa. Vol. 2, 671–90. Washington, DC: Order of Ahepa.

Lamberson, Leo J. (1956b). "Refugee Relief Act—Greek Phase: Recommendations." In *Amendments to Refugee Relief Act of 1953. Hearing before the Subcommittee of the Committee on the Judiciary, United States Senate, Eighty-fourth Congress, Second Session, May 3, 1956*, 95–96. Washington, DC: US Government Printing Office. Accessed via heinonline.org [last accessed 15 September 2018].

Lamberson, Leo J. (1958). "Remarks of Leo J. Lamberson re Above Report [i.e., Report of Ahepa Refugee Relief Committee by the Chairman, George Douris]." In *Order of Ahepa, Proceedings 32nd Supreme Convention, Boston, Mass.*, edited by the Order of Ahepa. Vol. 2, 967–98. Washington, DC: Order of Ahepa.

Lamberson, Leo J. (June 1959). "My Dear Congressman: [blank]." Original letter held in the *Atlantis*, National Daily Greek Newspaper Records, MSS 43, box 31, folder 4, "Scopas #2," Historical Society of Pennsylvania. Philadelphia, PA.

LaRocca, Joseph M. (1948). *A.M.A.G. Study of the Greek Ministry of Social Welfare*. N.p.

Mela, Alexandra (n.d.). *Χρονικόν της Βασιλικής Προνοίας. Chronicle of the Royal Welfare Fund*. Athens: Greek Literary and Historical Archive (E.L.I.A.). Unpublished, book-length typescript.

Ministry of Social Welfare of Sweden (1967). *Adoption av utländska barn: Betänkande avgivet av tillkallade utredningsmän. Adoption of Foreign Children: Report Delivered by Commissioned Researchers*. Government's Official Research Series 1967: 57. Stockholm: Victor Pettersons Bokindustri.

Minouvides, George (4 November 1959). First letter in Greek to the Greek American newspaper *Atlantis*, New York. Received 10 December 1959 and translated by *Atlantis* office staff. Original Greek letter and English translation held in the *Atlantis*, National Daily Greek Newspaper Records, MSS 43, box 31, folder 4, "Scopas #2," Historical Society of Pennsylvania. Philadelphia, PA.

Minouvides, George (8 January 1960). Second letter in Greek to the Greek American newspaper *Atlantis*, New York (no date of receipt given and left untranslated). Original Greek letter held in the *Atlantis*, National Daily Greek Newspaper Records, MSS 43, box 31, folder 4, "Scopas #2," Historical Society of Pennsylvania. Philadelphia, PA.

"Minutes of the 43rd Meeting of the [Greek National] Council for Child Protection" (25 January 1966). "Πρακτικὰ 43ης Συνεδρίας τοῦ Συμβουλίου Παιδικῆς Προστασίας." Typescript, 5 pages, held in the Archive of the National Council for Child Protection, "Minutes of the Years 1960–1968," box 299, folder D2, unclassified Archive of the Ministry of Health (and Social Welfare), General State Archives. Athens, Greece.

National Archives and Records Administration, *Foreign Relations of the United States, 1951, The Near East and Africa*. Vol. V. Available online at http://images.library.wisc.edu/FRUS/EFacs2/1951v05/reference/frus.frus1951v05.i0010.pdf [last accessed 15 September 2018].

National Archives and Records Administration, *Foreign Relations of the United States 1952–1954. Vol. VIII, Eastern Europe; Soviet Union; Eastern Mediterranean.* Available online at https://history.state.gov/historicaldocuments/frus1952–54v08 [last accessed 15 September 2018].

National Welfare Organization (Εθνικός Οργανισμός Προνοίας, Ε.Ο.Π.) (1977). *Σύντομη αναφορά στην ίδρυση και τις δραστηριότητες του Εθνικού Οργανισμού Προνοίας (κατά την πρώτη τριακονταετία της λειτουργίας του [1947–1977]). Brief Report on the Foundation and the Activities of the National Welfare Organization (during the First Thirty Years of Its Operations [1947–1977]).* Athens: National Welfare Organization, EOP.

Papakonstantinou, Konstantinos (5 December 1957). "Εγκύκλιος 126899/84." "Circular Order 126899/84." Typescript, 2 pages, held in the Lina Tsaldari Archive, folder 8, subfolder 4, item 17: "Adoptions 1957–1958," Konstantinos G. Karamanlis Foundation. Athens, Greece.

Papa-oikonomou, Aik[aterini] (ca. 1962). "Κέντρον Βρεφών 'Η Μητέρα'· Έκθεσις πεπραγμένων έτους 1961." "Babies' Center Metera: Report on Activities of the Year 1961." Typescript, 8 pages, held in "The Babies' Center Metera," folder 1260, Archive of the Former Royal Palace (1861–1971), General State Archives. Athens, Greece.

Paris, C. G. (1953). "Report of the Displaced Persons Committee." In *Order of Ahepa Year Books: 1953 Year Book,* edited by the Order of Ahepa, part 3, 1–7 and financial report, 8–16. Washington, DC: Order of Ahepa.

People v. Issachar (Maurice and Rebecca Issachar) (12 May 1960). People v. Issachar, 24 Misc.2d 826, 203 N.Y.S.2d 667 (Ct. Gen. Sess., N.Y. Cnty. 1960). Online case brief at www.leagle.com [last accessed 15 September 2018].

People v. Scopas (June 1959, June 1960, and March 1962, on appeal). People v. Scopas, 11 N.Y.2d 120, 181 N.E.2d 754 (1962). Appeal record at the Pace Law Library, White Plains, NY. Online case briefs at www.leagle.com [last accessed 15 September 2018].

Pettiss, Susan T. (8 February 1957). Letter to Rosalind Giles. Letter held in the archives of the International Social Service, American Branch Papers, box 10, folder 3: "Adoption 1955–1958," Social Welfare History Archives, University of Minnesota Libraries. Minneapolis, MN.

Pettiss, Susan T. (11 February 1959). Letter to ISS Greece—Mrs. King. Letter held in the archives of the International Social Service, American Branch Papers, box 31, folder 13: "Greece: Legal Procedures 1957–1962," Social Welfare History Archives, University of Minnesota Libraries. Minneapolis, MN.

Peurifoy, John (28 March 1952). Telegram from Athens to Secretary of State (no. 4281). Telegram, 2 pages, held in Department of State Records 781.00/3–2852, National Archives and Records Administration. College Park, MD.

Politis, Athanasios G. (16 November 1950). "ΠΡΟΣ Τό B. Ὑπουργεῖον τῶν Ἐξωτερικῶν." "To the Ministry of Foreign Affairs." Letter, 3 pages, held in the unclassified Archive of the Ministry of Health (and Social Welfare), box 5, General State Archives. Athens, Greece.

Polos, George A. (1952). "Report of the Ahepa Displaced Persons Committee." In *Order of Ahepa Year Books: 1952 Year Book,* edited by the Order of Ahepa, part 1, 75–83. Washington, DC: Order of Ahepa.

"Proceedings and Decision of the Thessaloniki Court of Appeals Judges" (6 February 1965). "Πρακτικὰ καὶ ἀπόφασις τοῦ Δικαστηρίου τῶν ἐν Θεσσαλονίκῃ Ἐφετῶν." Typescript, 62 pages, held in the Historical Archive of Macedonia, Records of the court case of the Saint Stylianos Foundling Home (GRGSA-IAM JUS 008.02). Thessaloniki, Greece.

Roots Research Center, editor (2002a). Οδηγός Έρευνας για ενήλικα υιοθετημένα άτομα. Search Guide for Adult Adoptees. Athens: Roots Research Center.

Roots Research Center, editor (2002b). Πρακτικά 1ου Ευρωπαϊκού Σεμιναρίου Υιοθεσία και Εύρεση Ριζών. Proceedings of the First European Seminar on Adoption and Roots Research. Athens: Roots Research Center.

Royal Welfare Fund (Βασιλική Πρόνοια) (1957a). Απολογισμός δεκαετίας 1947–1957. Report on the Decade of 1947–1957. Athens: Vasiliki Pronoia.

Royal Welfare Fund (Βασιλική Πρόνοια) (1957b). Μετά μίαν δεκαετίαν 1947–1957. One Decade Later (1947–1957). Athens: Vasiliki Pronoia.

Royal Welfare Fund (1963). "Vassiliki Pronia": 17 Years' Activities, 1947–1963 (in English and French). Athens: Vasiliki Pronoia.

Scopas, Stephen S. (1955). "Statement of Stephen S. Scopas, President, Order of Ahepa, Accompanied by Andrew D. Vozeolas." In Amendments to Refugee Relief Act of 1953. Hearings before the Subcommittee of the Committee on the Judiciary, United States Senate, Eighty-fourth Congress, First Session, on S. 1794, S. 2113, and S. 2149, Bills to Amend the Refugee Relief Act of 1953, so as to Relax Certain Requirements for Qualifying under Such Act, June 8, 9, 14, 16, and 21, 1955, 140–47. Washington, DC: US Government Printing Office. Accessed via heinonline. org [last accessed 15 September 2018].

Scopas, Stephen S. (1956). "Statement of Stephen S. Scopas, National President, Order of Ahepa." In Amendments to Refugee Relief Act of 1953. Hearing before the Subcommittee of the Committee on the Judiciary, United States Senate, Eighty-fourth Congress, Second Session, May 3, 1956, 94–95. Washington, DC: US Government Printing Office. Accessed via heinonline.org [last accessed 15 September 2018].

Solomonidis, Ch. (27 September 1954). Circular letter with protocol no. 5912. Typescript, 1 page, held in the Archive of the Child's Asylum of Volos, folder 2125, "Documents of the Ministry of Social Welfare and Other Ministries, 1954–1956," Archives of the Prefecture of Magnesia, General State Archives. Volos, Greece.

Sophocles (1997). Ajax, Electra, Oedipus Tyrannus. Edited and translated by Hugh Lloyd-Jones. Cambridge, MA: Harvard University Press.

Soultogiannis, Dimitri (4 March 2006). "Son Finds Father's Birth Mother." National Herald.

State of New York (1962). Report of Joint Legislative Committee on Matrimonial and Family Laws.

Truman, Harry A. (12 March 1947). "Truman Doctrine: President Harry S. Truman's Address before a Joint Session of Congress, March 12, 1947." Accessible online at http:// avalon.law.yale.edu/20th_century/trudoc.asp [last accessed 15 September 2018].

Tsaparis, Michael G. (21 August 1954). "Πρός τό Σεβαστόν Υπουργεῖον Κοινωνικῆς Προνοίας." "To the Venerable Ministry of Social Welfare." Typescript, 2 pages, held in the Archive of the Child's Asylum of Volos, folder 2125, "Documents of the Ministry of Social Welfare and Other Ministries, 1954–1956," Archives of the Prefecture of Magnesia, General State Archives. Volos, Greece.

Tsitidis, N. (31 December 1964). "Πρός τόν κ. Πρόεδρον ΠΙΚΠΑ." "To Mr President of PIKPA." Typescript, 13 pages, held in folder 469, Archive of PIKPA (1945–1995), General State Archives. Athens, Greece.

United Nations (1948–1962). *Demographic Yearbook*. Accessible online at http://unstats.un.org/unsd/demographic/products/dyb/dyb2.htm [last accessed 15 September 2018].

United States Committee on the Judiciary (1958). *Refugee Relief Act of 1953, as Amended: Final Report of the Administrator of the Refugee Relief Act of 1953, as Amended*. Washington, DC: US Government Printing Office.

United States Department of State (4 October 1951). "Memorandum of Conversation. Subject: Meeting with Miss Olsen re U.S. Committee for Care of European Children and Ahepa DP Committee." Typescript, 1 page, held in the Records of US Foreign Assistance Agencies, 1942–1963, box 9, folder "Displaced Persons Committee (Orphans Program) Order of AHEPA: Correspondence," National Archives and Records Administration. College Park, MD.

United States Displaced Persons Commission (1952). *Memo to America: The DP Story. The Final Report of the United States Displaced Persons Commission*. Washington, DC: US Government Printing Office.

United States Statutes at Large 69 (1955). Private Law 475 of 11 August 1955: "An Act for the Relief of Certain Korean War Orphans." Accessible online at http://digital.library.unt.edu/ark:/67531/metadc86502/m1/929/?q=harry [last accessed 15 September 2018].

Verinis, Constantine P. (17 October 1957). Appointment letter to Michael Tsaparis. Original letter in English held in the *Atlantis*, National Daily Greek Newspaper Records, MSS 43, box 31, folder 4, "Scopas #2," Historical Society of Pennsylvania. Philadelphia, PA.

Verinis, Constantine P. (5 May 1959). "Ahepagram to All Officers and Members of the Order of Ahepa." Telegram-style letter reproduced on the front page of the *Chicago Pnyx* of 15 May 1959; copy held in the *Atlantis*, National Daily Greek Newspaper Records, MSS 43, box 31, folder 4, "Scopas #2," Historical Society of Pennsylvania. Philadelphia, PA.

Verinis, Constantine P. (2 June 1959). "Ahepagram to All Officers and Members." Original telegram-style letter held in the *Atlantis*, National Daily Greek Newspaper Records, MSS 43, box 31, folder 4, "Scopas #2," Historical Society of Pennsylvania. Philadelphia, PA.

World Bank Databank. "Population, Total, 1960." http://databank.worldbank.org/data/views/reports/tableview.aspx?isshared=true [last accessed 15 September 2018].

X., Michael, "Mike" (28 August 2013–7 October 2015). Extensive email communications.

Secondary Sources

Adorno, Theodor W. (1998). "The Meaning of Working Through the Past." In *Theodor W. Adorno, Critical Models: Interventions and Catchwords*. Translated and with a Preface by Henry W. Pickford, 89–103. New York: Columbia University Press.

Agapitou, Maria (January–March 1958). "Κοινωνικές υπηρεσίες στην Ελλάδα· Κέντρον Βρεφών 'Η Μητέρα.'" "Social Services in Greece: Babies' Center Metera." *Koinoniki Pronoia: Theoria kai praxis* 2, no. 8: 283–98.

AHEPA, American Hellenic Educational Progressive Association. Mission statement online at www.ahepa.org [last accessed 15 September 2018].

Alexander, Jeffrey C., Ron Eyerman, Bernhard Giesen, Neil J. Smelser, and Piotr Sztompka (2004). *Cultural Trauma and Collective Identity*. Berkeley: University of California Press.

Alivizatos, Nikos K. [Nicos C.] (1981). "The 'Emergency Regime' and Civil Liberties, 1946–1949." In *Greece in the 1940s: A Nation in Crisis*, edited by John O. Iatrides, 220–28. Hanover, NH: University Press of New England.

Alivizatos, Nikos K. (1995) [1st ed. 1983]. *Οι πολιτικοί θεσμοί σε κρίση (1922–1974)· Όψεις της Ελληνικής εμπειρίας. Political Institutions in Crisis (1922–1974): Aspects of the Greek Experience*. Translated from the French by Venetia Stavropoulou. 3rd ed. Athens: Themelio.

Alivizatos, Nikos K. (2008). "Η αδύνατη μεταρρύθμιση· Σύνταγμα και παρασύνταγμα στη δεκαετία του ΄60." "[The Era of] Weak Reform: Constitution and Paraconstitution in the Decade of the 1960s." In *Η "σύντομη" δεκαετία του ΄60· Θεσμικό πλαίσιο, κομματικές στρατηγικές, κοινωνικές συγκρούσεις, πολιτισμικές διεργασίες. The "Short" Decade of the 1960s: Institutional Framework, Political Party Strategies, Social Clashes, and the Workings of Culture*, edited by Alkis Rigos, Serafeim I. Seferiadis, and Evanthis Chatzivasileiou, 49–56. Athens: Kastaniotis.

Alivizatos, Nikos K. (2011). *Το Σύνταγμα και οι εχθροί του στη Νεοελληνική ιστορία, 1800–2010. The Constitution and Its Enemies in Modern Greek History, 1800–2010*. Athens: Polis.

Altstein, Howard, and Rita J. Simon (1991). "Introduction." In *Intercountry Adoption: A Multinational Perspective*, edited by Howard Altstein and Rita J. Simon, 1–20. New York: Praeger.

Amera, Anna (2012). "Litsa (Chariklia) Alexandraki (1918–1984)." *Social Work and Society: International Online Journal* 10, no. 1. Online at http://www.socwork.net/sws/article/view/315/661 [last accessed 15 September 2018].

Anagnostou, Yiorgos (2009). *Contours of White Ethnicity: Popular Ethnography and the Making of Usable Pasts in Greek America*. Athens, OH: Ohio University Press.

Anastasiadis, Athanasios (2012). "Transgenerational Communication of Traumatic Experiences: Narrating the Past from a Postmemorial Position." *Journal of Literary Theory* 6, no. 1: 1–24.

Anonymous (spring 1964). "The Immigration and Nationality Act of 1952 as Amended through 1961." *International Migration Digest* 1, no. 1: 34–46.

Anonymous (15 February 1965). "Εμπόριον βρεφών!" "Baby Trade!" *Ekklisia: Episimon Deltion tis Ekklisias tis Ellados* 42, no. 4: 123–24.

Anonymous (1989). *Οι δίκες για κατασκοπεία την άνοιξη του 1960. The Espionage Trials of the Spring of 1960*. Athens: Synchroni Epochi.

Anonymous (2014–2015). "Ηλίας Αργυριάδης." "Elias Argyriadis." Online Wikipedia entry composed by various authors [last accessed 15 September 2018].

Antze, Paul, and Michael Lambek, editors (1996). *Tense Past: Cultural Essays in Trauma and Memory*. New York: Routledge.

Apostolidou, Venetia (2010). *Τραύμα και μνήμη· Η πεζογραφία των πολιτικών προσφύγων. Trauma and Memory: The Prose Writing of the Political Refugees.* Athens: Polis.

ArcheioTaxio 16 (2014): 4–171. Special section: "Η Ακροδεξιά στο φως της ιστορίας." "The Extreme Right in the Light of History."

ArcheioTaxio 18 (2016): 3–117. Special section: "1956· Ο κόσμος όλος έγινε άνω κάτω." "1956: The Whole World Turned Upside Down."

Armitage, David (2017). *Civil Wars: A History in Ideas.* New York: Alfred A. Knopf.

Askounes Ashford, Nicholas, and Robert Askounes Ashford (2000). "Venette Askounes Ashford (1906–1994)." In *Greek-American Pioneer Women of Illinois,* edited by Elaine Thomopoulos, 91–112. Chicago: Arcadia.

Atzakas, Giannis (2007). *Διπλωμένα φτερά. Folded Wings.* Athens: Agra.

Atzakas, Giannis (2008). *Θολός βυθός. Muddy Bottom.* Athens: Agra.

Atzakas, Giannis (2013). *Φώς της Φονιάς. Light of Fonia.* Athens: Agra.

Avdela, Efi (2002). *"Διά λόγους τιμής"· Βία, συναισθήματα και αξίες στη μετεμφυλιακή Ελλάδα. "For Reasons of Honor": Violence, Emotions, and Values in Post–Civil War Greece.* Athens: Nefeli.

Avdela, Efi, Thomas Gallant, Nikolaos Papadogiannis, Leda Papastefanaki, and Polymeris Voglis (2018). "The Social History of Modern Greece: A Roundtable." *Social History* 43, no. 1: 105–25.

Aymond, Laura (2000). "Vision of Family Unity Sparks Greek Genealogy Web Site." Online at https://groups.google.com/forum/#!topic/soc.culture.greek/FI_VNRI3uxg [last accessed 15 September 2018].

The Baby Scoop Era Research Initiative: Research and Inquiry into Adoption Practice, 1945–1972. Online at http://babyscoopera.com/ [last accessed 15 September 2018].

Bada, Konstantina, and Pothiti Hantzaroula (2017). "Family Strategies, Work, and Welfare Policies toward Waged Domestic Labor in Twentieth-Century Greece." *Journal of Modern Greek Studies* 35, no. 1, Special section: "Unveiling Domestic Work in Times of Crisis," 17–41.

Baerentzen, Lars (1987). "The 'Paidomazoma' and the Queen's Camps." In *Studies in the History of the Greek Civil War, 1945–1949,* edited by Lars Baerentzen, John O. Iatrides, and Ole L. Smith, 127–57. Copenhagen: Museum Tusculanum Press.

Balcom, Karen A. (2011). *The Traffic in Babies: Cross-Border Adoption and Baby-Selling between the United States and Canada, 1930–1972.* Toronto: University of Toronto Press.

Balcom, Karen A. (2012). "The Back Door In: Private Immigration Bills and Transnational Adoption to the United States in the 1940s and 1950s." Paper delivered at the Fourth International Conference of the Alliance for the Study of Adoption and Culture, Claremont College.

Baltsiotis, Lambros (2004). "Η ιθαγένεια στον Ψυχρό Πόλεμο." "Citizenship in the Cold War." In *Τα δικαιώματα στην Ελλάδα 1953–2003· Από το τέλος του Εμφυλίου στο τέλος της Μεταπολίτευσης. Civil Rights in Greece, 1953–2003: From the End of the Civil War to the End of the Metapolitefsi* [post-1974 redemocratization], edited by Michalis Tsapogas and Dimitris Christopoulos, 81–98. Athens: Kastaniotis.

Barboudaki, Eleni (2015). *Οι "Σεισμοί του Βόλου". Πολιτικές, κοινωνικές-*

οικονομικές και βιωματικές διαστάσεις. The "Earthquakes of Volos": Political, Socioeconomic, and Experiential Dimensions. MA thesis, University of Thessaly, Volos, Greece.

Baughan, Emily (2018). "International Adoption and Anglo-American Internationalism, c. 1918–1925." *Past and Present* 239: 181–217.

Beloyannis, Nikos (1980). "Η απολογία του Νίκου Μπελογιάννη." "The Defense Speech of Nikos Beloyannis." In *Ο άνθρωπος με το γαρύφαλο. The Man with the Carnation,* edited by Potis Paraskevopoulos, 146–59. Athens: Kaktos.

Beloyannis, Nikos (1981). "Η απολογία του Νίκου Μπελογιάννη." "The Defense Speech of Nikos Beloyannis." In *Ποιοί και γιατί σκότωσαν το Νίκο Μπελογιάννη και τους συντρόφους του; Who and Why Did They Kill Nikos Beloyannis and His Comrades?,* edited by Tasos Vournas, 115–29. Athens: Tolidis.

Bon Tempo, Carl J. (2008). *Americans at the Gate: The United States and Refugees during the Cold War.* Princeton, NJ: Princeton University Press.

Bonzon, Paul-Jacques (1955). *Les Orphelins de Simitra.* Paris: Hachette.

Bonzon, Paul-Jacques (1962). *Les Orphelins de Simitra.* Translated as *The Orphans of Simitra* by Thelma Niklaus. New York: Criterion Books.

Botsiou, Konstantina E. (2007). "Anti-Americanism in Greece." In *Anti-Americanism: History, Causes, and Themes,* edited by Brendon O'Connor. Vol. 3, 213–34. Westport, CT: Greenwood.

Botsiou, Konstantina E. (2010). "The Origins of Greece's European Policy." In *The Constantinos Karamanlis Institute for Democracy Yearbook 2010,* edited by Constantine Arvanitopoulos and Konstantina E. Botsiou, 93–108. Berlin: Springer.

Botsiou, Konstantina E., and Giannis Sakkas, editors (2015). *Η Ελλάδα, η Δύση και η Μεσόγειος, 1945–62· Νέες ερευνητικές προσεγγίσεις. Greece, the West, and the Mediterranean, 1945–62.* Thessaloniki: University of Macedonia.

Boutos, Vasilis (2000). *Τα δάκρυα της Βασίλισσας· Μυθιστόρημα. The Queen's Tears: A Novel.* Athens: Nefeli.

Brian, Kristi (2012). *Reframing Transracial Adoption: Adopted Koreans, White Parents, and the Politics of Kinship.* Philadelphia: Temple University Press.

Briggs, Laura (2012). *Somebody's Children: The Politics of Transracial and Transnational Adoption.* Durham, NC: Duke University Press.

Briggs, Laura, and Diana Marre (2009). "Introduction: The Circulation of Children." In *International Adoption: Global Inequalities and the Circulation of Children,* edited by Diana Marre and Laura Briggs, 1–28. New York: New York University Press.

Bromberg, Philip M. (2011). *The Shadow of the Tsunami and the Growth of the Relational Mind.* New York: Routledge.

Brouskou, Aigli (2015). *"Λόγω της κρίσεως σας χαρίζω το παιδί μου"· Η διακίνηση των παιδιών στην Ελληνική κοινωνία του 20ού αιώνα. Το παράδειγμα του Δημοτικού Βρεφοκομείου Θεσσαλονίκης "Άγιος Στυλιανός." "Because of the crisis, I give you my child": The Circulation of Children in Greek Society of the Twentieth Century. The Case Study of the Municipal Foundling Home of Thessaloniki, "Saint Stylianos."* Thessaloniki: Symepe.

Buchanan, Andrew (2014). *American Grand Strategy in the Mediterranean during World War II.* New York: Cambridge University Press.

Cameron, Frank (1964). *Hungry Tiger: The Story of the Flying Tiger Line.* New York: McGraw-Hill Book Company.

Campbell, John K. (1964). *Honour, Family and Patronage: A Study of Institutions and Moral Values in a Greek Mountain Community.* Oxford, UK: Oxford University Press.

Carabott, Philip, and Thanasis D. Sfikas, editors (2004). *The Greek Civil War: Essays on a Conflict of Exceptionalism and Silences.* Aldershot, UK: Ashgate.

CARE International. Online at http://www.care-international.org [last accessed 15 September 2018].

Carp, E. Wayne (1998). *Family Matters: Secrecy and Disclosure in the History of Adoption.* Cambridge, MA: Harvard University Press.

Carp, E. Wayne (2002). "Introduction: A Historical Overview of American Adoption." In *Adoption in America: Historical Perspectives,* edited by E. Wayne Carp, 1–26. Ann Arbor: University of Michigan Press.

Carp, E. Wayne (2014a). "The History of the Law of Adoption in the United States." *Adoption & Culture* 4: 32–42.

Carp, E. Wayne (2014b). "The History of Orphans and Orphanages in the United States." *Adoption & Culture* 4: 43–51.

Carp, E. Wayne, and Anna Leon-Guerrero (2002). "When in Doubt, Count: World War II as a Watershed in the History of Adoption." In *Adoption in America: Historical Perspectives,* edited by E. Wayne Carp, 181–217. Ann Arbor: University of Michigan Press.

Carro, Jorge L. (1994). "Regulation of Intercountry Adoption: Can the Abuses Come to an End?" *Hastings International and Comparative Law Review* 18, no. 1: 121–55.

Carsten, Janet (2004). *After Kinship.* Cambridge, UK: Cambridge University Press.

Caruth, Cathy, editor (1995). *Trauma: Explorations in Memory.* Baltimore, MD: Johns Hopkins University Press.

Caruth, Cathy (1996). *Unclaimed Experience: Trauma, Narrative, and History.* Baltimore: Johns Hopkins University Press.

Chantzaroula, Pothiti (2012). *Σμιλεύοντας την υποταγή· Οι έμμισθες οικιακές εργάτριες στην Ελλάδα το πρώτο μισό του εικοστού αιώνα. Crafting Subordination: Female Salaried Domestic Workers in Greece of the First Half of the Twentieth Century.* Athens: Papazisis.

Chin, Art (1993). *Anything, Anytime, Anywhere: The Legacy of the Flying Tiger Line, 1945–89.* Seattle, WA: Tassels & Wings.

Chourchoulis, Dionysios (2015). *The Southern Flank of NATO, 1951–1959: Military Strategy or Political Stabilization.* Lanham, MD: Lexington Books.

Choy, Catherine Ceniza (2013). *Global Families: A History of Asian International Adoption in America.* New York: New York University Press.

Christopoulos, Dimitris (2012). *Ποιός είναι Έλληνας πολίτης; Το καθεστώς ιθαγένειας από την ίδρυση του ελληνικού κράτους ως τις αρχές του 21ου αιώνα. Who Is a Greek Citizen? The Establishment of Citizenship from the Foundation of the Greek State until the Beginnings of the Twenty-First Century.* Athens: Vivliorama.

Clogg, Richard, editor (1999). *The Greek Diaspora in the Twentieth Century.* Houndmills, UK: MacMillan Press, and New York: St. Martin's Press.

Clogg, Richard, editor (2008). *Bearing Gifts to Greeks: Humanitarian Aid to Greece in the 1940s.* Houndmills, UK: Palgrave MacMillan.

Clogg, Richard (2013). *A Concise History of Greece*. 3rd ed. Cambridge, UK: Cambridge University Press.

Close, David H. (2002). *Greece Since 1945: Politics, Economy and Society*. London: Longman.

Close, David H. (2004). "The Road to Reconciliation? The Greek Civil War and the Politics of Memory in the 1980s." In *The Greek Civil War: Essays on a Conflict of Exceptionalism and Silences*, edited by Philip Carabott and Thanasis D. Sfikas, 257–78. Aldershot, UK: Ashgate.

Close, Kathryn (1953). *Transplanted Children: A History*. New York: The United States Committee for the Care of European Children.

Cohen, Gerard Daniel (2012). *In War's Wake: Europe's Displaced Persons in the Postwar Order*. New York: Oxford University Press.

Conn, Peter (1996). *Pearl S. Buck: A Cultural Biography*. Cambridge, UK: Cambridge University Press.

Coumantaros, Stella (1984). "'Philoptochos' Major Achievements: The Greek Orthodox Ladies Philoptochos Society Had Extraordinary Success in 1959–1984." In *History of the Greek Orthodox Church in America*, edited by Rev. Miltiades B. Efthimiou and George A. Christopoulos, 271–92. New York: Greek Orthodox Archdiocese of North and South America.

Cowan, Jane K. (1990). *Dance and the Body Politic in Northern Greece*. Princeton, NJ: Princeton University Press.

Cozarinsky, Edgardo (2006). *The Moldavian Pimp*. Translated from the Spanish by Nick Caistor. London: Harvill Secker.

Crandall, Russell (2014). *America's Dirty Wars: Irregular Warfare from 1776 to the War on Terror*. New York: Cambridge University Press.

Dalianis-Karambatzakis, Mando A. (1994). *Children in Turmoil during the Greek Civil War 1946–49: Today's Adults. A Longitudinal Study on Children Confined with Their Mothers in Prison*. Stockholm: Karolinska Institutet.

Dalianis-Karambatzakis, Mando A. (2009). *Παιδιά στη δίνη του ελληνικού εμφυλίου πολέμου 1946–1949, σημερινοί ενήλικες. Διαχρονική μελέτη για τα παιδιά που έμειναν στη φυλακή με τις κρατούμενες μητέρες τους*. Translated from the English by Kostas A. Zervos. Edited by I. Tsiantis and D. Ploumbidis. Athens: Benaki Museum.

Dalianis, Mando, and Mark Mazower (2000). "Children in Turmoil during the Civil War: Today's Adults." In *After the War Was Over: Reconstructing the Family, Nation, and State in Greece, 1943–1960*, edited by Mark Mazower, 91–104. Princeton, NJ: Princeton University Press.

Damousi, Joy (2012). "The Greek Civil War and Child Migration to Australia: Aileen Fitzpatrick and the Australian Council of International Social Service." *Social History* 37, no. 3: 297–313.

Damousi, Joy (2015). *Memory and Migration in the Shadow of War: Australia's Greek Immigrants after World War II and the Greek Civil War*. Cambridge, UK: Cambridge University Press.

Damousi, Joy (2017). "Mothers in War: 'Responsible Mothering,' Children, and the Prevention of Violence in Twentieth-Century War." *History and Theory, Theme Issue* 55: 119–34.

Danforth, Loring M., and Riki Van Boeschoten (2012). *Children of the Greek Civil War: Refugees and the Politics of Memory*. Chicago: University of Chicago Press.

Davvetas, Nikos (2009). *Η Εβραία νύφη· Μυθιστόρημα. The Jewish Bride: A Novel.* Athens: Kedros.

Davvetas, Nikos (2013). *Ο ζωγράφος του Μπελογιάννη· Πολιτικό νουαρ μυθιστόρημα. The Painter of Beloyannis: Political Mystery Novel.* Athens: Metaichmio.

Dedousi, Amalianna (2012). *Υιοθετημένες αναμνήσεις. Adopted Memories.* Athens: Gavriilidis.

De Grazia, Victoria (2005). *Irresistible Empire: America's Advance through Twentieth-Century Europe.* Cambridge, MA: Belknap Press of Harvard University Press.

Delveroudi, Eliza-Anna (2004). *Οι νέοι στις κωμωδίες του ελληνικού κινηματογράφου, 1948–1974. Young People in the Comedies of the Greek Cinema, 1948–1974.* Athens: Kentro Neoellinikon Erevnon.

Demertzis, Nicolas [Nikos] (2011). "The Drama of the Greek Civil War Trauma." In *Narrating Trauma: On the Impact of Collective Suffering,* edited by Ron Eyerman, Jeffrey C. Alexander, and Elizabeth Butler Breese, 133–61. Boulder, CO: Paradigm Publishers.

Demertzis, Nikos, Eleni Paschaloudi, and Giorgos Antoniou, editors (2013). *Εμφύλιος· Πολιτισμικό τραύμα. Civil War: Cultural Trauma.* Athens: Alexandreia.

De Pauw, Anniek, René A. C. Hoksbergen, and Gilbert Van Aelst, editors (1998). *Interculturele adoptie in de kijker: Evaluatie en toekomst. Intercultural Adoption in the Spotlight: Evaluation and Future.* Leuven (Louvain), Belgium, and Apeldoorn, the Netherlands: Garant.

De Vries, Susanna (2000). *Blue Ribbons Bitter Bread: The Life of Joice NanKivell Loch.* Alexandria, NSW, Australia: Hale & Iremonger.

Dijsselbloem, Han, Justin Fugle, and Uwe Gneiting (2014). "Child Sponsorship and Rights-Based Interventions at Plan: Tensions and Synergies." In *Child Sponsorship: Exploring Pathways to a Brighter Future,* edited by Brad Watson and Matthew Clarke, 113–38. Houndmills, UK: Palgrave MacMillan.

Dionou, C. Dionysios (2011). *Twentieth-Century Janissary: An Orphan's Search for Freedom, Family, and Heritage.* Bloomington, IN: Xlibris.

DiVirgilio, Letitia (November 1956). "Adjustment of Foreign Children in Their Adoptive Homes." *Child Welfare* 35: 15–21.

Dos Guimarães Sá, Isabel (1991). "The 'Casa da Roda do Porto': Reception and Restitution of Foundlings during the Eighteenth Century." In *Enfance Abandonnée et Société en Europe XIVe–XXe Siècle,* edited by École française de Rome, 539–72. Rome: École française de Rome.

Doxiadis, Evdoxios (2011). *The Shackles of Modernity: Women, Property, and the Transition from the Ottoman Empire to the Greek State (1750–1850).* Cambridge, MA: Harvard University Press.

Dubinsky, Karen (2010). *Babies without Borders: Adoption and Migration across the Americas.* New York: New York University Press.

Dubisch, Jill, editor (1986). *Gender and Power in Rural Greece.* Princeton, NJ: Princeton University Press.

Du Boulay, Juliet (1974). *Portrait of a Greek Mountain Village.* Oxford, UK: Oxford University Press.

Eichengreen, Barry, editor (1995). *Europe's Post-war Recovery.* Cambridge, UK: Cambridge University Press.

Engerman, David C. (2010). "Ideology and the Origins of the Cold War, 1917–1962." In *The Cambridge History of the Cold War*. Vol. 1, *Origins*, edited by Melvyn P. Leffler and Odd Arne Westad, 20–43. Cambridge, UK: Cambridge University Press.

Epstein, Helen (1979). *Children of the Holocaust: Conversations with Sons and Daughters of Survivors*. New York: G.P. Putnam's Sons.

Evans Grubbs, Judith (2013). "Infant Exposure and Infanticide." In *The Oxford Handbook of Childhood and Education in the Classical World*, edited by Judith Evans Grubbs and Tim Parkin, 83–107. New York: Oxford University Press.

Evans Grubbs, Judith, and Tim Parkin, editors (2013). *The Oxford Handbook of Childhood and Education in the Classical World*. New York: Oxford University Press.

Fehrenbach, Heide (2010). "How to Handle a Birth Parent: From Local Practice to International Policy in Early Intercountry Adoption, 1948–1960." Paper, 19 pages, delivered at the conference titled "Adoption: Secret Histories, Public Policies." Massachusetts Institute of Technology, Cambridge, MA, 1 May 2010.

Fehrenbach, Heide (2015). "Children and Other Civilians: Photography and the Politics of Humanitarian Image-Making." In *Humanitarian Photography: A History*, edited by Heide Fehrenbach and Davide Rodogno, 165–99. New York: Cambridge University Press.

Fehrenbach, Heide (2016). "From Aid to Intimacy: The Humanitarian Origins and Media Culture of International Adoption." In *Dilemmas of Humanitarian Aid in the Twentieth Century*, edited by Johannes Paulmann, 207–33. Oxford, UK: Oxford University Press.

Feinstein, Stephen C. (1998). "Mediums of Memory: Artistic Responses of the Second Generation." In *Breaking Crystal: Writing and Memory after Auschwitz*, edited by Efraim Sicher, 201–51. Urbana: University of Illinois Press.

Felman, Shoshana, and Dori Laub, editors (1992). *Testimony: Crises of Witnessing in Literature, Psychoanalysis, and History*. New York: Routledge.

Fessler, Ann (2006). *The Girls Who Went Away: The Hidden History of Women Who Surrendered Children for Adoption in the Decades before Roe v. Wade*. New York: Penguin Press.

Fieldston, Sara (2015). *Raising the World: Child Welfare in the American Century*. Cambridge, MA: Harvard University Press.

Fivush, Robyn, and Jessica McDermott Sales (2004). "Children's Memories of Emotional Events." In *Memory and Emotion*, edited by Daniel Reisberg and Paula Hertel, 242–71. Oxford, UK: Oxford University Press.

Flountzis, Antonis I. (1977). *Στρατόπεδα Λάρισας-Τρικάλων 1941–1944· Η γέννηση του Ανταρτικού στη Θεσσαλία. The Detention Camps of Larisa and Trikala, 1941–1944: The Birth of the Resistance Struggle in Thessaly*. Athens: Papazisis.

Fong, Rowena, Ruth G. McRoy, and Hollee McGinnis (2016). "Overview of Intercountry Adoptions." In *Transracial and Intercountry Adoptions: Cultural Guidance for Professionals*, edited by Rowena Fong and Ruth McRoy, 19–37. New York: Columbia University Press.

Forbes, Susan S., and Patricia Weiss Fagen (1984). *Unaccompanied Refugee Children: The Evolution of U.S. Policies—1939 to 1984*. Washington, DC: Refugee Policy Group.

Fountedaki, Katerina (2010). *Υιοθεσία· Ο Ν. 2447/1996, οι τροποποιήσεις και η εφαρμογή του. Adoption: Law 2447/1996, Its Modifications and Its Application.* Athens: Sakkoula.

Fournier, Suzanne, and Ernie Crey (1997). *Stolen from Our Embrace: The Abduction of First Nations Children and the Restoration of Aboriginal Communities.* Vancouver, Can.: Douglas & McIntyre.

Frederica, Queen of the Hellenes (1971). *A Measure of Understanding.* New York: St. Martin's Press.

Friedl, Ernestine (1962). *Vasilika: A Village in Modern Greece.* New York: Holt, Rinehart and Winston.

Friedlander, Saul (1992). "Trauma, Transference and 'Working through' in Writing the History of the *Shoah.*" *History and Memory* 4, no. 1: 39–59.

Frierson, Cathy A. (2015). "Introduction: I Survived. I Speak." In *Silence Was Salvation: Child Survivors of Stalin's Terror and World War II in the Soviet Union,* edited by Cathy A. Frierson, 1–23. New Haven, CT: Yale University Press.

Gage, Sue-Je Lee (2007). "The Amerasian Problem: Blood, Duty, and Race." *International Relations* 21, no. 1: 86–102.

Gailey, Christine Ward (2010). *Blue-Ribbon Babies and Labors of Love: Race, Class, and Gender in U.S. Adoption Practice.* Austin: University of Texas Press.

Gallant, Thomas W. (1991). "Agency, Structure, and Explanation in Social History: The Case of the Foundling Home on Kephallenia, Greece, during the 1830s." *Social Science History* 15, no. 4: 479–508.

Gallant, Thomas W. (2016). *Modern Greece: From the War of Independence to the Present.* 2nd ed. London: Bloomsbury.

Gangi, Sarah, Alessandra Talamo, and Stefano Ferracuti (2009). "The Long-Term Effects of Extreme War-Related Trauma on the Second Generation of Holocaust Survivors." *Violence and Victims* 24, no. 5: 687–700.

Gardika, Katerina, Anna Maria Droumbouki, Vangelis Karamanolakis, and Kostas Raptis, editors (2015). *Η μακρά σκιά της δεκαετίας του '40· Πόλεμος—Κατοχή—Αντίσταση—Εμφύλιος. The Long Shadow of the Decade of the 1940s: War—Occupation—Resistance—Civil War.* Athens: Alexandreia.

Georges, Eugenia (2008). *Bodies of Knowledge: The Medicalization of Reproduction in Greece.* Nashville, TN: Vanderbilt University Press.

Gerolymatos, André (2004). *Red Acropolis, Black Terror: The Greek Civil War and the Origins of Soviet-American Rivalry, 1943–1949.* New York: Basic Books.

Gerolymatos, André (2016). *An International Civil War: Greece, 1943–1949.* New Haven, CT: Yale University Press.

Giangardella, Joanna S. (2011). *The Girl from the Tower: A Journey of Lies.* Lexington, KY: CreateSpace Independent Publishing Platform.

Giannoulaki, Eleni (2018). *Η δίκη του Αγίου Στυλιανού, μελανό σημείο στην ιστορία του Ιδρύματος. The Trial of Saint Stylianos, a Black Spot in the History of the Institution.* MA thesis, University of Macedonia, Thessaloniki, Greece.

Golden, Mark (2015) [1st ed. 1990]. *Children and Childhood in Classical Athens.* Baltimore, MD: Johns Hopkins University Press.

Graff, E. J. (November–December 2008). "The Lie We Love." *Foreign Policy,* 58–66.

Grigoratos, Dionysis, director (2015). *Fils de Grèce: Τα παιδιά του Εμφυλίου. Sons of Greece: The Children of the Civil War.* Film. Athens, Greece.

Hague Convention on Protection of Children and Co-operation in Respect of Inter-

country Adoption (29 May 1993), online at http://www.hcch.net/upload/conventions/txt33en.pdf [last accessed 15 September 2018].

Halkias, Alexandra (2004). *The Empty Cradle of Democracy: Sex, Abortion, and Nationalism in Modern Greece*. Durham, NC: Duke University Press.

Handman, Marie-Élisabeth (1983). *La violence et la ruse: Hommes et femmes dans un village grec*. Aix-en-Provence, France: Édisud.

Handman, Marie-Élisabeth (1993). "Ο παραδοσιακός τρόπος υιοθεσίας στην Αρναία Χαλκιδικής." "Traditional Adoption in Arnaia, Chalkidiki." Translated into Greek by Foteini Tsimbiridou. In *Ανθρωπολογία και παρελθόν· Συμβολές στην κοινωνική ιστορία της νεότερης Ελλάδας. Anthropology and the Past: Contributions to the Social History of Modern Greece*, edited by Efthymios Papataxiarchis and Theodoros Paradellis, 193–212. Athens: Alexandreia.

Hartman, Geoffrey H. (1996). *The Longest Shadow: In the Aftermath of the Holocaust*. Bloomington: Indiana University Press.

Hassiotis [Chasiotis], Loukianos I. (2009). "Εθνικοφροσύνη και αντικομμουνισμός στο νεανικό τύπο· Η περίπτωση του περιοδικού *Παιδόπολις*, 1950–51." "*Ethnikofrosyni* ["National Conviction"] and Anticommunism in the Juvenile Press: The Case of the Magazine *Paidopolis*, 1950–51." *Istor* 15: 277–305.

Hassiotis [Chasiotis], Loukianos I. (2011). "Relocating Children during the Greek Civil War, 1946–49: State Strategies and Propaganda." In *The Disentanglement of Populations: Migration, Expulsion and Displacement in Post-War Europe, 1944–9*, edited by Jessica Reinisch and Elizabeth White, 271–88. New York: Palgrave MacMillan.

Hassiotis [Chasiotis], Loukianos I. (2013a). *Τα παιδιά του Εμφυλίου· Από την "Κοινωνική Πρόνοια" του Φράνκο στον "Έρανο" της Φρειδερίκης (1936–1950). The Children of the Civil War: From the "Social Welfare" of Franco to the "Fund" of Frederica (1936–1950)*. Athens: Estia-Kollaros.

Hassiotis [Chasiotis], Loukianos I. (2013b). "Raising the 'Future of the Nation': Child Welfare in Spain and Greece during the Civil Wars (1936–39, 1946–49)." In *Children and War: Past and Present*, edited by Helga Embacher, Grazia Prontera, Albert Lichtblau, Johannes-Dieter Steinert, Wolfgang Aschauer, Darek Galasinski, and John Buckley, 213–33. West Midlands, UK: Helion.

Hassiotis [Chasiotis], Loukianos I. (2014). "Εμφύλιος πόλεμος και δημόσια ιστορία· Η περίπτωση του 'Εράνου' της Βασίλισσας." "Civil War and Public History: The Case of the 'Queen's Fund.'" *Ta Istorika* 60: 107–24.

Hatzivassiliou [Chatzivasileiou], Evanthis (2001). *Η άνοδος του Κωνσταντίνου Καραμανλή στην εξουσία, 1954–1956. The Rise to Power of Konstantinos Karamanlis, 1954–1956*. Athens: Patakis.

Hatzivassiliou, Evanthis (2006). *Greece and the Cold War: Frontline State, 1952–1967*. London: Routledge.

Hatzivassiliou, Evanthis (2014). "Shallow Waves and Deeper Currents: The U.S. Experience of Greece, 1947–1961. Policies, Historicity, and the Cultural Dimension." *Diplomatic History* 38, no. 1: 83–110.

Herman, Ellen (2008). *Kinship by Design: A History of Adoption in the Modern United States*. Chicago: University of Chicago Press.

Herman, Ellen (2009). "Numbers as Narratives: Quantification and the Growth of the Adoption Research Industry in the United States." *Adoption & Culture* 2: 123–39.

Herzfeld, Michael (1980). "Honour and Shame: Problems in the Comparative Analysis of Moral Systems." *Man* n.s. 15, no. 2: 339–51.

Herzfeld, Michael (1983). "Semantic Slippage and Moral Fall: The Rhetoric of Chastity in Rural Greek Society." *Journal of Modern Greek Studies* 1, no. 1: 161–72.

Herzfeld, Michael (1992). *The Social Production of Indifference: Exploring the Symbolic Roots of Western Bureaucracy*. New York: Berg.

Hibbs, Euthymia D., editor (1988). *Children and Families: Studies in Prevention and Intervention*. Madison, CT: International Universities Press.

Hibbs, Euthymia D., editor (1991). *Adoption: International Perspectives*. Madison, CT: International Universities Press.

Hirsch, Marianne (1996). "Past Lives: Postmemories in Exile." *Poetics Today* 17, no. 4: 659–86.

Hirsch, Marianne (1997). *Family Frames: Photography, Narrative, and Postmemory*. Cambridge, MA: Harvard University Press.

Hirsch, Marianne (2008). "The Generation of Postmemory." *Poetics Today* 29, no. 1: 103–28.

Hirsch, Marianne (2012). *The Generation of Postmemory: Writing and Visual Culture after the Holocaust*. New York: Columbia University Press.

Hirschon, Renée, editor (1984). *Women and Property—Women as Property*. London: Croom Helm, and New York: St. Martin's Press.

Hitchcock, William I. (2010). "The Marshall Plan and the Creation of the West." In *The Cambridge History of the Cold War*. Vol. 1, *Origins*, edited by Melvyn P. Leffler and Odd Arne Westad, 154–74. Cambridge, UK: Cambridge University Press.

Hochfield, Eugenie (October 1963). "Across National Boundaries: Problems in the Handling of International Adoptions, Dependency and Custody Cases." *Juvenile Court Judges Journal* 14, no. 3: 3–7.

Hoksbergen, René A. C. (2002). *Vijftig jaar adoptie in Nederland: Een historisch-statistische beschouwing. Fifty Years of Adoptions in the Netherlands: Historical and Statistical Reflections*. Utrecht, the Netherlands: Utrecht University, Afdeling Adoptie.

Hoksbergen, René A. C., editor (2006). *Vertraagde start: Geadopteerden aan het woord. Delayed Start: Adoptees Speaking*. Soesterberg, the Netherlands: Aspekt.

Hoksbergen, René A. C. (2011). *Kinderen die niet konden blijven: Zestig jaar adoptie in beeld. Children Who Could Not Stay: Sixty Years of Adoptions Brought within View*. Soesterberg, the Netherlands: Aspekt.

Hoksbergen, René A. C., Hester E. Storsbergen, and C. Brouwer-van Dalen (1995). *Het begon in Griekenland: Een verkenning van de achtergrond van in Griekenland geboren, geadopteerde jongvolwassenen en de betekenis van de adoptiestatus. It Began in Greece: An Exploration of the Background of Greek-born and Adopted Young Adults and the Significance of the Adoption Status*. Utrecht, the Netherlands: Utrecht University, Adoptie Centrum, ISOR.

Hoksbergen, René A. C., and Hans Walenkamp, editors (2000). *Adoptie: Een levenslang dilemma. Adoption: A Lifelong Dilemma*. Houten, the Netherlands: Bohn Stafleu van Loghum.

Holt, Bertha, with David Wisner (1956). *The Seed from the East*. Los Angeles: Oxford Press.

Homans, Margaret (2013). *The Imprint of Another Life: Adoption Narratives and Human Possibility*. Ann Arbor: University of Michigan Press.

Honig, Elizabeth Alice (2005). "Phantom Lives, Narratives of Possibility." In *Cultures of Transnational Adoption*, edited by Toby Alice Volkman, 213–22. Durham, NC: Duke University Press.

Howell, Signe (2006). *The Kinning of Foreigners: Transnational Adoption in a Global Perspective*. New York: Berghahn Books.

Hübinette, Tobias (2006). *Comforting an Orphaned Nation: Representations of International Adoption and Adopted Koreans in Korean Popular Culture*. Seoul, Korea: Jimoondang.

Huebner, Sabine R. (2013). "Adoption and Fosterage in the Ancient Eastern Mediterranean." In *The Oxford Handbook of Childhood and Education in the Classical World*, edited by Judith Evans Grubbs and Tim Parkin, 510–31. New York: Oxford University Press.

Iatrides, John O. (2005). "Revolution or Self-Defense? Communist Goals, Strategy, and Tactics in the Greek Civil War." *Journal of Cold War Studies* 7, no. 3: 3–33.

Iatrides, John O. (2018). "Αμερικανικές παρεμβάσεις στην Ελλάδα του πρώιμου Ψυχρού Πολέμου· Η αναζήτηση του 'ισχυρού ανδρός' και η 'λύση Παπάγου.'" "American Interventions in Greece of the Early Cold War: The Search for a 'Strongman' [Government] and the 'Papagos Solution.'" In *Η Ελλάδα και ο Ψυχρός Πόλεμος· Επεκτείνοντας τις ερμηνείες. Greece and the Cold War: Extending the Interpretations*, edited by Nikos Marantzidis, Iakovos Michailidis, and Evanthis Hatzivassiliou [Chatzivasileiou], 19–48. Thessaloniki: Epikentro.

Iatrides, John O., and Linda Wrigley, editors (1995). *Greece at the Crossroads: The Civil War and Its Legacy*. University Park: Pennsylvania State University Press.

Immerman, Richard H., and Petra Goedde, editors (2013). *The Oxford Handbook of the Cold War*. Oxford, UK: Oxford University Press.

Ioakimidis, Vasilios (2011). "Expanding Imperialism, Exporting Expertise: International Social Work and the Greek Project, 1946–74." *International Social Work*, published online at http://isw.sagepub.com/content/early/2011/01/27/0020872 810385832 [last accessed 15 September 2018].

Irr, Caren (2014). "Literature and Adoption: Themes, Theses, Questions." *American Literary History* 26, no. 2: 385–95.

Jeffery, Judith S. (2000). *Ambiguous Commitments and Uncertain Policies: The Truman Doctrine in Greece, 1947–1952*. Lanham, MD: Lexington Books.

Johnson, Deborah (2003). "Addendum by Deborah Johnson." In *Welcome Home! An International and Nontraditional Adoption Reader*, edited by Lita Linzer Schwartz and Florence W. Kaslow, 50–54. Binghamton, NY: Haworth Clinical Practice Press.

Jones, Howard (1985). "The Diplomacy of Restraint: The United States' Efforts to Repatriate Greek Children Evacuated during the Civil War of 1946–49." *Journal of Modern Greek Studies* 3, no. 1: 65–85.

Jonet, Ahilemah (1990). "Legal Measures to Eliminate Transnational Trading of Infants for Adoption: An Analysis of Anti-Infant Trading Statutes in the United States." *Loyola of Los Angeles International and Comparative Law Review* 13, nos. 2–3: 305–30.

Journal of Modern Greek Studies 1, no. 1 (1983). Special issue: "Women and Men in Greece: A Society in Transition," edited by A. Lily Macrakis and Peter S. Allen.

Journal of Modern Greek Studies 27, no. 2 (2009). Special issue on the Marshall Plan in Greece.

Kacandes, Irene (2009). *Daddy's War: Greek American Stories.* Lincoln, NE: University of Nebraska Press.

Kairofylas, Giannis (1993). *Η Αθήνα στη δεκαετία του '50. Athens in the Decade of the 1950s.* Athens: Filippotis.

Kaisidou, Vassiliki (2019). "To Remember and Forgive: The Afterlives of Queen Frederica's Childtowns in Contemporary Greek Fiction." In *Retelling the Past in Contemporary Greek Literature, Film, and Popular Culture,* edited by Trine Stauning Willert and Gerasimus Katsan, 85–101. Lanham, MD: Lexington Books.

Kalamaro, Lilian (1981). *Βαρύτατο τίμημα 1941–1952. The Heaviest Possible Price, 1941–1952.* 2nd ed. Athens: Dodoni.

Kalliga, Eleni (1990). *Η πρόνοια για το παιδί στην Ελλάδα του 19ου αιώνα. Child Welfare in Greece of the 19th Century.* Athens: Dodoni.

Kaloutsi-Tavlaridou, Aspasia (1970). *Συμβολή στην κατανόηση προβλημάτων υιοθεσίας· Η διαταραχή της ταυτότητος στην υιοθεσία. A Contribution to the Understanding of Problems in Adoption Cases: The Disturbance of Identity through Adoption.* Athens: Koultoura.

Kalyvas, Stathis N. (2000). "Red Terror: Leftist Violence during the Occupation." In *After the War Was Over: Reconstructing the Family, Nation, and State in Greece, 1943–1960,* edited by Mark Mazower, 142–83. Princeton, NJ: Princeton University Press.

Kalyvas, Stathis N. (2006). *The Logic of Violence in Civil War.* Cambridge, UK: Cambridge University Press.

Kalyvas, Stathis N., and Nikos Marantzidis (2015). *Εμφύλια πάθη· 23 ερωτήσεις και απαντήσεις για τον Εμφύλιο. Civil War Passions: 23 Questions and Answers on the Civil War.* Athens: Metaichmio.

Kantsa, Venetia, editor (2013). *Η μητρότητα στο προσκήνιο· Σύγχρονες έρευνες στην ελληνική εθνογραφία. Motherhood in the Forefront: Contemporary Investigations in Greek Ethnography.* Athens: Alexandreia.

Karagiannis, Giorgos, Vangelis Tzoukas, Vasiliki Lazou, Michalis P. Lymberatos, Takis Lazaridis, and Giannis Skalidakis (2011). *Η δίκη του Μπελογιάννη. The Trial of Beloyannis.* Athens: *Eleftherotypia* [supplement to Sunday edition of 6 March 2011].

Karamanolakis, Vangelis (2019). *Ανεπιθύμητο παρελθόν· Οι φάκελοι κοινωνικών φρονημάτων στον 20ό αι. και η καταστροφή τους. Undesirable Past: The Dossiers of 'National Convictions' in the Twentieth Century and Their Destruction.* Athens: Themelio.

Karankitsou, Electra, and Pantelis Simos Karankitsos (2013). *Τα παιδιά της ξενιτιάς· Η μνήμη της δικής μου αλήθειας. Αυτοβιογραφία ενός κομμουνιστή. The Children of Foreign Lands: The Memory of My Truth* [by E. K.]. *Autobiography of a Communist* [by P. S. K.]. Athens: Museum of Political Exiles of Aï Stratis.

Kardamitsi Adami, Maro (1993). "Το Ορφανοτροφείο της Αίγινας." "The Orphanage of Aegina." *O Mentor* 26: 97–112.

Kazamias, Alexander (unpublished ms.). *Greece and the Cold War: Diplomacy and Colonialism after the Civil Conflict*. London: I. B. Tauris.

Kédros, André (1990). *L'homme à l'œillet*. Paris: Robert Laffont.

Kelmis, Maria (2012). *Golden Strangers: An Adoption Memoir*. Bloomington, IN: AuthorHouse.

Kim, Eleana J. (2010). *Adopted Territory: Transnational Korean Adoptees and the Politics of Belonging*. Durham, NC: Duke University Press.

Kitroeff, Alexander (1 February 2002). "Law and Disorder: 1952 and Other Unconstitutional Conventions." Online at http://www.greekworks.com/content/index. php/weblog/extended/law_and_disorder_1952_and_other_unconstitutional_ conventions/ [last accessed 15 September 2018].

Kitroeff, Alexander (1 April 2002). "The Communist with the Carnation." Online at http://www.greekworks.com/content/index.php/weblog/extended/the_communist_with_the_carnation/ [last accessed 15 September 2018].

Klein, Christina (2003). *Cold War Orientalism: Asia in the Middlebrow Imagination, 1945–1961*. Berkeley: University of California Press.

Kliafa, Artemis (2016). *Η παιδική προστασία τη δεκαετία του '50 και η κριτική της ΕΔΑ. Child Protection during the 1950s Decade and Its Critique by the United Democratic Left*. MA thesis, Panteion University of Social and Political Sciences, Athens, Greece.

Kofas, Jon V. (1989). *Intervention and Underdevelopment: Greece during the Cold War*. University Park, PA: Pennsylvania State University Press.

Koras[s]idou, Maria (1995). *Οι άθλιοι των Αθηνών και οι θεραπευτές τους· Φτώχεια και φιλανθρωπία στην ελληνική πρωτεύουσα τον 19° αιώνα. Les Misérables d'Athènes et leurs thérapeutes: Pauvreté et philanthropie dans la capitale grecque au XIXe siècle* [her translation]. Athens: Kentro Neoellinikon Erevnon.

Korma, Lena (2017). "The Historiography of the Greek Diaspora and Migration in the Twentieth Century." *Historein: A Review of the Past and Other Stories* 16, nos. 1–2: 47–73.

Kornetis, Kostis (2014). "Public History and the Issue of Torture under the Colonels' Regime in Greece." *Ricerche Storiche* 44, no. 1: 81–100.

Kostis, Kostas (2018). *History's Spoiled Children: The Story of Modern Greece*. Translated by Jacob Moe. New York: Oxford University Press.

Koulouris, Nikos A. (2000). *Ελληνική βιβλιογραφία του Εμφυλίου Πολέμου 1945–1949· Αυτοτελή δημοσιεύματα 1945–1999. Greek Bibliography on the Civil War, 1945–1949: Stand-alone Publications, 1945–1999*. Athens: Filistor.

Kourkouvelas, Lykourgos (2011). *Η Ελλάδα και το ζήτημα των πυρηνικών όπλων, 1957–1963. Greece and the Issue of Nuclear Weapons, 1957–1963*. Athens: Patakis.

Kousidou, Dounia A., and Stavros G. Stavropoulos (ca. 1998). *Η υπόθεση Νίκου Πλουμπίδη και ο Ν. Ζαχαριάδης. Σύγκρουση δύο πολιτικών· Ιστορία—αρχεία—καταθέσεις. The Nikos Ploumbidis Affair and N[ikos] Zachariadis. Clash of Two Politicians: History—Archives—Depositions*. Athens: Diogenis.

Kous[s]idou, Tas[s]oula, editor (2000). *Υιοθεσία· Τάσεις, πολιτική, πρακτική. Adoption: Trends, Policy, Practice*. Athens: National Organization for Social Care, Babies' Center "Metera," and Grigoris.

Koussidou, Tassoula, and Billy Maganiotou (1991). "Adoption and the Metera Babies

Center." In *Adoption: International Perspectives*, edited by Euthymia D. Hibbs, 167–81. Madison, CT: International Universities Press.

Kovras, Iosif (2014). *Truth Recovery and Transitional Justice: Deferring Human Rights Issues*. London: Routledge.

Kyrou, Alexandros K. (2008). "The Greek-American Community and the Famine in Axis-occupied Greece." In *Bearing Gifts to Greeks: Humanitarian Aid to Greece in the 1940s*, edited by Richard Clogg, 58–84. Houndmills, UK: Palgrave Mac-Millan.

Lagani, Eirini, and Maria Bontila, editors (2012). *"Παιδομάζωμα" ή "Παιδοσώσιμο"; Παιδιά του Εμφυλίου στην Ανατολική και Κεντρική Ευρώπη*. "Gathering the Children" or "Saving the Children"? Children of the Civil War in Eastern and Central Europe. Thessaloniki: Epikentro.

Laliotou, Ioanna (2004). *Transatlantic Subjects: Acts of Migration and Cultures of Trans-nationalism between Greece and America*. Chicago: University of Chicago Press.

Lapatsanis, P. D., S. Nakou, S. Pantelakis, and T. Valaes (1994). "Spyros Doxiadis: 1917–1991. A Pioneer of Social Pediatrics in Greece." *Acta Paediatrica: Supplement* 83, s394: 1–2.

Lapidot-Firilla, Anat (2009). "'Subway Women' and the American Near East Relief in Anatolia, 1919–1924." In *Gendering Religion and Politics: Untangling Modernities*, edited by Hanna Herzog and Ann Braude, 153–71. New York: Palgrave MacMillan.

Larned, Ruth (1956). *International Social Service: A History, 1924–1955*. Typescript "Prepared for International Social Service," held in the New York School of Social Work Library.

Larned, Ruth (1960). *A Digest of the History of the International Social Service*. Geneva, Switzerland: American Branch of the International Social Service.

Laub, Dori (1992). "Bearing Witness or the Vicissitudes of Listening." In *Testimony: Crises of Witnessing in Literature, Psychoanalysis, and History*, edited by Shoshana Felman and Dori Laub, 57–74. New York: Routledge.

Lazaridis, Takis (1998). *Απλά μαθήματα ιστορίας. Simple Lessons of History*. Athens: Papazisis.

Lazou, Vasiliki (2012). "Οι 'εσωτερικοί πρόσφυγες' του εμφυλίου πολέμου. Ζητήματα χαρακτηρισμού και πρόνοιας." "The 'Internal Refugees' of the Civil War. Questions of Definition and Welfare." In *Η εποχή των ρήξεων· Η Ελληνική κοινωνία στη δεκαετία του 1940. The Era of Ruptures: Greek Society in the Decade of 1940*, edited by Polymeris Voglis, Flora Tsilaga, Iasonas Chandrinos, and Menelaos Charalambidis, 111–37. Thessaloniki: Epikentro.

Leber, George J. (1972). *The History of the Order of AHEPA (The American Hellenic Educational Progressive Association) 1922–1972, Including the Greeks in the New World, and Immigration to the United States*. Washington, DC: Order of Ahepa.

Lederer, William J., and Eugene Burdick (1958). *The Ugly American*. New York: Norton.

Lee, Shawyn ChoHee (2016). *Mother America: Cold War Maternalism and the Institutionalization of Intercountry Adoption from Postwar South Korea, 1953–1961*. PhD dissertation, School of Social Work, University of Minnesota, St. Paul.

Leinaweaver, Jessaca (2015). "Geographies of Generation: Age Restrictions in International Adoption." *Social & Cultural Geography* 16, no. 5: 508–21.

Leinaweaver, Jessaca, and Sonja van Wichelen, editors (2015). "The Geography of Transnational Adoption." Special issue of *Social & Cultural Geography* 16, no. 5.

Leinaweaver, Jessaca, and Sonja van Wichelen (2015). "The Geography of Transnational Adoption: Kin and Place in Globalization." *Social & Cultural Geography* 16, no. 5: 499–507.

Leonard, Henry B. (1973). "The Immigrants' Protective League of Chicago, 1908–1921." *Journal of the Illinois State Historical Society* 64, no. 3: 271–84.

Leontis, Artemis (1995). *Topographies of Hellenism.* Ithaca, NY: Cornell University Press.

Lialiouti, Zinovia (2010). "Challenging Americanism: The Public Debate about the 'American Way of Life' in Cold-War and Post-Cold-War Greece." In *The United States and the World: From Imitation to Challenge,* edited by Andrzej Mania and Lukasz Wordliczek, 115–36. Krakow: Jagiellonian University Press.

Lialiouti, Zinovia (2015). "Greek Cold War Anti-Americanism in Perspective, 1947–1989." *Journal of Transatlantic Studies* 13, no. 1: 40–55.

Lialiouti, Zinovia (2016a). *Ο Αντιαμερικανισμός στην Ελλάδα (1947–1989). Anti-Americanism in Greece (1947–1989).* Athens: Asini.

Lialiouti, Zinovia (2016b). "Contesting the Anti-totalitarian Consensus: The Concept of National Independence, the Memory of the Second World War and the Ideological Cleavages in Post-war Greece." *National Identities* 18, no. 2: 105–23.

Lifton, Betty Jean (2009) [1st ed. 1979]. *Lost & Found: The Adoption Experience.* 3rd ed. Ann Arbor: University of Michigan Press.

Loch, Joice NanKivell (1968). *A Fringe of Blue: An Autobiography.* London: John Murray.

Loizos, Peter, and Evthymios Papataxiarchis, editors (1991). *Contested Identities: Gender and Kinship in Modern Greece.* Princeton, NJ: Princeton University Press.

Lovelock, Kirsten (2000). "Intercountry Adoption as a Migratory Practice: A Comparative Analysis of Intercountry Adoption and Immigration Policy and Practice in the United States, Canada and New Zealand in the Post W.W. II Period." *International Migration Review* 34, no. 3: 907–49.

Lymberatos, Michalis P. (2015). *Μετά τον Εμφύλιο· Πολιτικές διαδικασίες και κοινωνική πόλωση στις απαρχές της προδικτατορικής περιόδου. After the Civil War: Political Procedures and Social Polarization at the Onset of the Pre-Dictatorship Period.* Athens: Notios Anemos.

Maganiotou, Billy, and Tassoula Koussidou (1988). "A General Assessment of Adoptive Parents' Experience of Adoption." In *Children and Families: Studies in Prevention and Intervention,* edited by Euthymia D. Hibbs, 385–97. Madison, CT: International Universities Press.

Maglinis, Elias (2013). *Η ανάκριση.* Translated as *The Interrogation* by Patricia Felisa Barbeito. Birmingham, UK: University of Birmingham.

Maguire, Bernadette (1997). *Immigration: Public Legislation and Private Bills.* Lanham, MD: University Press of America.

Marantzidis, Nikos (2010). *Δημοκρατικός Στρατός Ελλάδας (ΔΣΕ) 1946–1949. The Democratic Army of Greece, 1946–1949.* Athens: Alexandreia.

Maratou-Alipranti, Laura (2004). "Childbearing." In *Recent Social Trends in Greece 1960–2000,* edited by Dimitris Charalambis, Laura Maratou-Alipranti, and Andromachi Hadjiyanni, 120–27. Montreal: McGill–Queen's University Press.

Margaritis, Giorgos (2000–2001). *Ιστορία του Ελληνικού Εμφυλίου Πολέμου 1946–1949. History of the Greek Civil War, 1946–1949.* 2 vols. Athens: Vivliorama.

Marketou, Pelagia (1999). *Προνοιακές πολιτικές για τα έκθετα βρέφη· Το Δημοτικό Βρεφοκομείο Αθηνών, Αθήνα 19^ος αι. Welfare Policies for Infant Foundlings: The Municipal Orphanage of Athens, Athens, Nineteenth Century.* MA thesis, University of Athens, Greece.

Marre, Diana, and Laura Briggs, editors (2009). *International Adoption: Global Inequalities and the Circulation of Children.* New York: New York University Press.

Marshall, Dominique (2013). "International Child Saving." In *The Routledge History of Childhood in the Western World,* edited by Paula S. Fass, 469–90. London: Routledge.

Marshall Plan Filmography (2010). www.marshallfilms.org/mpf.asp [last accessed 15 September 2018].

Martin, Susan F. (2014). *International Migration: Evolving Trends from the Early Twentieth Century to the Present.* New York: Cambridge University Press.

Mastrogiannis, Ioannis D. (1962). *Η υιοθεσία ως κοινωνικός θεσμός. Adoption as a Social Institution.* Athens: n.p.

Matthews, Robert C. (1987*). The Littlest Immigrants: The Immigration and Adoption of Foreign Orphans.* PhD dissertation, Center for Public Administration and Policy, Virginia Polytechnic Institute and State University, Blacksburg, VA.

May, Elaine T. (2008) [1st ed. 1988]. *Homeward Bound: American Families in the Cold War Era.* New York: Basic Books.

Mazower, Mark, editor (2000). *After the War Was Over: Reconstructing the Family, Nation, and State in Greece, 1943–1960.* Princeton, NJ: Princeton University Press.

McKee, Kimberly D. (2019). *Disrupting Kinship: Transnational Politics of Korean Adoption in the United States.* Urbana, IL: University of Illinois Press.

McKnight, Joseph W. (2001). "The Shifting Focus of Adoption." In *Critical Studies in Ancient Law, Comparative Law and Legal History,* edited by John W. Cairns and Olivia F. Robinson, 297–331. Oxford, UK: Hart Publishing.

McNeill, William Hardy (1957). *Greece: American Aid in Action, 1947–1956.* New York: Twentieth Century Fund.

Melosh, Barbara (2002). *Strangers and Kin: The American Way of Adoption.* Cambridge, MA: Harvard University Press.

Mignot, Jean-François (2019). "Child Adoption in Western Europe, 1900–2015." In *Cliometrics of the Family,* edited by Claude Diebolt, Auke Rijpma, Sarah Carmichael, Selin Dilli, and Charlotte Störmer, 333–66. Switzerland: Springer.

Mihevic, Demetra (1997) [1st ed. 1991]. *Where a White Dog Smiles.* 4th ed. Unionville, NY: Royal Fireworks Press.

Miller, James E. (2009). *The United States and the Making of Modern Greece: History and Power, 1950–1974.* Chapel Hill: University of North Carolina Press.

Mitsopoulou, Anastasia I. (2014). *Ο ελληνικός αντικομμουνισμός στον "σύντομο 20ό αιώνα"· Όψεις του δημόσιου λόγου στην πολιτική, στην εκπαίδευση και στη λογοτεχνία. Greek Anticommunism in the "Short Twentieth Century": Views of the Public Discourse in Politics, Education, and Literature.* Thessaloniki: Epikentro.

Moessinger, Naomi (2003). "From Couple to Family." In *Welcome Home! An International and Nontraditional Adoption Reader*, edited by Lita Linzer Schwartz and Florence W. Kaslow, 35–50. Binghamton, NY: Haworth Clinical Practice Press.

Molumphy, Henry D. (1984). *For Common Decency: The History of Foster Parents Plan, 1937–1983*. Warwick, RI: Foster Parents Plan International.

Moschos, Sassa E. (1981–1982). "The Rights of the Child in Greece." *Columbia Human Rights Law Review* 13: 347–409.

Moskos, Peter C., and Charles C. Moskos (2014). *Greek Americans: Struggle and Success*. 3rd ed. New Brunswick, NJ: Transaction Publishers.

Mouzelis, Nicos, and George Pagoulatos (2005). "Civil Society and Citizenship in Post-war Greece." In *Citizenship and the Nation-State in Greece and Turkey*, edited by Faruk Birtek and Thalia Dragonas, 87–103. London: Routledge.

Nachmani, Amikam (1990). *International Intervention in the Greek Civil War: The United Nations Special Committee on the Balkans, 1947–1952*. New York: Praeger.

Nackenoff, Carol (2014). "The Private Roots of American Political Development: The Immigrants' Protective League's 'Friendly and Sympathetic Touch', 1908–1924." *Studies in American Political Development* 28, no. 2: 129–60.

Nanou, Katerina (2011). "The Social Acceptance of Illegal Practices in the Greek Domestic Adoption System." *Adoption & Fostering* 35, no. 3: 60–67.

Nash, Catherine (2005). "Geographies of Relatedness." *Transactions of the Institute of British Geographers* 30, no. 4: 449–62.

Nikolaïdou, Sophia (2012). *Χορεύουν οι ελέφαντες· Μυθιστόρημα. The Elephants Are Dancing: A Novel*. Athens: Metaichmio.

Nikolaïdou, Sophia (2015). *Χορεύουν οι ελέφαντες· Μυθιστόρημα. The Elephants Are Dancing: A Novel*. Translated as *The Scapegoat* by Karen Emmerich. New York: Melville House.

Nikolakopoulos, Elias (2001). *Η καχεκτική δημοκρατία· Κόμματα και εκλογές, 1946–1967. The Stunted Democracy: Political Parties and Elections, 1946–1967*. Athens: Patakis.

Nikoloutsos, Konstantinos P. (2013). "Reviving the Past: Cinematic History and Popular Memory in *The 300 Spartans* (1962)." *Classical World* 106, no. 2: 261–83.

Nora, Pierre (1989). "Between Memory and History: *Les Lieux de Mémoire*." *Representations* 26: 7–24.

Nora, Pierre (21 June 2001). "The Tidal Wave of Memory." *Project Syndicate*, online at http://www.project-syndicate.org/commentary/the-tidal-wave-of-memory#0KDHvESxq2oZxxwI.99 [last accessed 15 September 2018]. Revised in "Reasons for the current upsurge in memory." *Eurozine* (19 April 2002), online at http://www.eurozine.com/articles/2002-04-19-nora-en.html [last accessed 15 September 2018].

Novy, Marianne (2005). *Reading Adoption: Family and Difference in Fiction and Drama*. Ann Arbor: University of Michigan Press.

Novy, Marianne (2012). "New Territory: Memoirs of Meeting Original Family by Seven Adopted American Women." *Adoption & Culture* 3: 124–40.

Odzak, Lazar (2006). *"Demetrios is now Jimmy": Greek Immigrants in the Southern United States, 1895–1965*. Durham, NC: Monograph Publishers.

Ogden, Daniel (1996). *Greek Bastardy in the Classical and Hellenistic Periods*. Oxford, UK: Oxford University Press.

Oh, Arissa H. (2015). *To Save the Children of Korea: The Cold War Origins of International Adoption*. Stanford, CA: Stanford University Press.

O'Reilly, Alison (2018). *My Name Is Bridget: The Untold Story of Bridget Dolan and the Tuam Mother and Baby Home*. Dublin: Gill and Macmillan.

Palmieri, Daniel, and Irène Herrmann (2016). "Two Crosses for the Same Aim? Swiss and Swedish Charitable Activities in Greece during the Second World War." In *Dilemmas of Humanitarian Aid in the Twentieth Century*, edited by Johannes Paulmann, 171–83. Oxford, UK: Oxford University Press.

Palmos, Panos (1988). "Deprivation of a Normal Family Environment in Infancy: The Contribution of the Metera Babies' Center." In *Children and Families: Studies in Prevention and Intervention*, edited by Euthymia D. Hibbs, 381–84. Madison, CT: International Universities Press.

Panera, Elpetha (1991). "Private and Independent Adoptions in Greece through the Agency of Social Welfare." In *Adoption: International Perspectives*, edited by Euthymia D. Hibbs, 145–52. Madison, CT: International Universities Press.

Panourgia, Neni (2009). *Dangerous Citizens: The Greek Left and the Terror of the State*. New York: Fordham University Press [also https://dangerouscitizens. columbia.edu/, last accessed 15 September 2018].

Papachristou, Dimosthenis A., editor (1997). *Νίκος Πλουμπίδης Ντοκουμέντα· Γράμματα από τη φυλακή 1953–1954. Nikos Ploumbidis Documents: Letters from Prison, 1953–1954*. Athens: Delfini.

Papadaki, Eirini (2013). "Διεκδικώντας τη μητρότητα στον κόσμο της υιοθεσίας· Η περίπτωση ενός διαδικτυακού τόπου." "Asserting Motherhood in the Adoption World: The Case of an Internet Forum." In *Η μητρότητα στο προσκήνιο· Σύγχρονες έρευνες στην ελληνική εθνογραφία. Motherhood in the Forefront: Contemporary Investigations in Greek Ethnography*, edited by Venetia Kantsa, 171–97. Athens: Alexandreia.

Papadaki, Eirini (2015). *Πολιτικές εκσυγγένευσης· Υιοθεσία και η ηθική οικονομία της αναπαραγωγής στην σύγχρονη Ελλάδα. Policies of Kinning: Adoption and the Ethical Economy of Reproduction in Contemporary Greece*. PhD dissertation, School of Social Sciences, University of the Aegean, Mytilene, Lesvos, Greece.

Papadaki, Eirini (2018). "Undoing Kinship: Producing Citizenship in a Public Maternity Hospital in Athens, Greece." In *Reconnecting State and Kinship*, edited by Tatjana Thelen and Erdmute Alber, 178–99. Philadelphia: University of Pennsylvania Press.

Papadimitriou, Despoina I. (2006). *Από τον λαό των νομιμοφρόνων στο έθνος των εθνικοφρόνων· Η συντηρητική σκέψη στην Ελλάδα 1922–1967. From the Loyalist People to the Nation of the National-Minded: Conservative Thought in Greece, 1922–1967*. Athens: Savvalas.

Papadopoulos, Yannis, and Nikos Kourachanis (2015). "Overall European Overseas Outflows and Internationally Assisted Movements (1945–1960): Who Was Helped to Move? Where to?" In *International "Migration Management" in the Early Cold War: The Intergovernmental Committee for European Migration*, edited by Lina Venturas, 143–88. Corinth, Greece: University of the Peloponnese, School of Social and Political Sciences.

Papailias, Penelope (2005). *Genres of Recollection: Archival Poetics and Modern Greece*. Houndmills, UK: Palgrave MacMillan.

Papaioannou, Voula (ca. 1999). *Λεύκωμα ζωής· Φωτογραφικές αναμνήσεις από το Δημοτικό Βρεφοκομείο Αθηνών 1947–1950*. *Value of Life: Photo Memories from the Municipal Foundling House of Athens 1947–1950* (in English and Greek). Kaisariani, Athens: Roots Research Center and Entos Publications.

Paraskevopoulos, Potis (1980). *Ο άνθρωπος με το γαρύφαλο. The Man with the Carnation*. Athens: Kaktos.

Park Nelson, Kim (2016). *Invisible Asians: Korean American Adoptees, Asian American Experiences, and Racial Exceptionalism*. New Brunswick, NJ: Rutgers University Press.

Parmenas, Timon (September 1949). "Τὰ ὀρφανεμένα Ἑλληνόπουλα." "The Orphaned Greek Children." *Aktines: Organon tis "Christianikis Enoseos Epistimonon"* 12, no. 96: 401–15.

Parry-Giles, Shawn J. (2000). "Militarizing America's Propaganda Program, 1945–55." In *Critical Reflections on the Cold War: Linking Rhetoric and History*, edited by Martin J. Medhurst and H. W. Brands, 95–133. College Station, TX: Texas A&M University Press.

Parry-Giles, Shawn J. (2002). *The Rhetorical Presidency, Propaganda, and the Cold War, 1945–1955*. Westport, CT: Praeger.

Paschaloudi, Eleni (2010). *Ένας πόλεμος χωρίς τέλος· Η δεκαετία του 1940 στον πολιτικό λόγο 1950–1967. A War without End: The Decade of 1940 in the Political Speech of 1950–1967*. Thessaloniki: Epikentro.

Paschaloudi, Eleni (2013). "Τα γεγονότα πριν από τον μύθο." "The Events Prior to the Myth." In *Ο ζωγράφος του Μπελογιάννη· Πολιτικό νουάρ μυθιστόρημα. The Painter of Beloyannis: Political Mystery Novel*, by Nikos Davvetas, 209–15. Athens: Metaichmio.

Paschaloudis, Kostas (2013). *Από δω και πέρα θα είσαι ο Νίκος. From Now On, You'll Be Nikos*. Thessaloniki: Epikentro.

Pate, SooJin (2014). *From Orphan to Adoptee: U.S. Empire and Genealogies of Korean Adoption*. Minneapolis: University of Minnesota Press.

Paxson, Heather (2004). *Making Modern Mothers: Ethics and Family Planning in Urban Greece*. Berkeley: University of California Press.

Peña, Rosemarie (2014). "Intercountry/Interracial Adoption: A Bibliography." *Adoption & Culture* 4: 184–89.

Perel, Esther (February 2013). "The Secret to Desire in a Long-term Relationship." Online at http://www.ted.com/speakers/esther_perel [last accessed 15 September 2018].

Peristiany, John G., editor (1966). *Honour and Shame: The Values of Mediterranean Society*. London: Weidenfeld and Nicolson.

Petropoulos, Giorgos, and Nikos Chatzidimitrakos (2015a). "Εισαγωγή· Η δολοφονία του Ν. Μπελογιάννη." "Introduction: The Murder of N. Beloyannis." In *Υπόθεση Νίκου Μπελογιάννη· Η προανακριτική έκθεση της Ασφάλειας για την πρώτη δίκη. The Nikos Beloyannis Affair: The Prehearing Exposé of the Security Police for the First Trial*, edited by Giorgos Petropoulos and Nikos Chatzidimitrakos, 15–42. Athens: Kastaniotis.

Petropoulos, Giorgos, and Nikos Chatzidimitrakos, editors (2015b). *Υπόθεση Νίκου Μπελογιάννη· Η προανακριτική έκθεση της Ασφάλειας για την πρώτη δίκη. The Nikos Beloyannis Affair: The Prehearing Exposé of the Security Police for the First*

Trial. Athens: Kastaniotis. With auxiliary website at http://beloyannis.kastaniotis.com [last accessed 15 September 2018].

Petropoulos, Giorgos, Nikolas Zirganos, and Nikos Chatzidimitrakos, editors (2016). *Απόρρητος φάκελος 26029/Α. Νίκος Ζαχαριάδης· Οι ποινικές διώξεις. Classified Dossier 26029/A. Nikos Zachariadis: The Criminal Prosecutions.* Athens: Kastaniotis.

Petroula, Dimitra Sotiri (1986). *"Πού 'ναι η μάνα σου, μωρή;" "Where Is Your Mother, You?"* 7th ed. Athens: Kedros.

Pettiss, Susan T. (October 1955). "A Board Member Speaks: Adoption by Proxy." *Child Welfare: Journal of the Child Welfare League of America* 34, no. 7: 20–21.

Pettiss, Susan T. (October 1962). "Cultural Factors in Adoption of Immigrant Children." *Social Work* 7, no. 4: 22–25.

Pettiss, Susan T., and Lynne Taylor (2004). *After the Shooting Stopped: The Story of an UNRRA Welfare Worker in Germany, 1945–1947.* Victoria, BC: Trafford Publishing.

Pillemer, David B. (1998). *Momentous Events, Vivid Memories.* Cambridge, MA: Harvard University Press.

Plakoudas, Spyridon (2017). *The Greek Civil War: Strategy, Counterinsurgency and the Monarchy.* London: I. B. Tauris.

Ploumbidis, Dimitris N. (1997). "Ο Δημήτρης Πλουμπίδης για τον πατέρα του." "Dimitris Ploumbidis on His Father." In *Νίκος Πλουμπίδης Ντοκουμέντα· Γράμματα από τη φυλακή 1953–1954. Nikos Ploumbidis Documents: Letters from Prison, 1953–1954,* written and edited by Dimosthenis A. Papachristou, 9–16. Athens: Delfini.

Ploumbidis, Nikos (1981). "Η απολογία του Νίκου Πλουμπίδη." "The Defense Speech of Nikos Ploumbidis." In *Ποιοί και γιατί σκότωσαν το Νίκο Μπελογιάννη και τους συντρόφους του; Who and Why Did They Kill Nikos Beloyannis and His Comrades?,* edited by Tasos Vournas, 131–81. Athens: Tolidis.

Politakou, Eva N. (July–August–September 1958). "Γύρω από την υιοθεσία." "Concerning Adoption." *Aktines: Organon tis "Christianikis Enoseos Epistimonon"* 21, no. 193: 313–17.

Potamitis, N. Y. (2008). "Antagonism and Genre: Resistance, the Costume Romance and the Ghost of Greek Communism." In *Discourse Theory and Cultural Analysis: Media, Arts and Literature,* edited by Nico Carpentier and Erik Spinoy, 119–37. Cresskill, NJ: Hampton Press.

Quartly, Marian, Shurlee Swain, and Denise Cuthbert, with Kay Dreyfus and Margaret Taft (2013). *The Market in Babies: Stories of Australian Adoption.* Clayton, Victoria, Australia: Monash University Publishing.

Read, Peter (2010). *The Stolen Generations: The Removal of Aboriginal Children in New South Wales, 1883 to 1969.* 8th ed. Surry Hills, New South Wales, Australia: New South Wales Department of Aboriginal Affairs.

Redmond, Paul J. (2018). *The Adoption Machine: The Dark History of Ireland's Mother and Baby Homes and the Inside Story of How Tuam 800 Became a Global Scandal.* Kildare, Ireland: Merrion Press/Irish Academic Press.

Rentetzi, Maria (2009). "Gender, Science and Politics: Queen Frederika and Nuclear Research in Post-war Greece." *Centaurus* 51: 63–87.

Richman, Sophia (2014). *Mended by the Muse: Creative Transformations of Trauma.* New York: Routledge.

Richter, Heinz A. (2013). *Griechenland 1950–1974: Zwischen Demokratie und Diktatur*. Mainz, Germany: Franz Philipp Rutzen.

Rijnsdorp, Sonia (2017). *Een kist met geheimen*. Zoetermeer, the Netherlands: Lecturium.

Rijnsdorp, Sonia (2018). *A Coffin Full of Secrets*. English translation in pdf distributed by the author.

Rogers, Kim Lacy, Selma Leydesdorff, and Graham Dawson, editors (1999). *Trauma and Life Stories: International Perspectives*. London: Routledge.

Rossini, Gill (2014). *A History of Adoption in England and Wales, 1850–1961*. Barnsley, South Yorkshire, UK: Pen and Sword Books.

Rousopoulou, Agni (February 1957). "Υιοθεσία Ελληνοπαίδων παρ' αλλοδαπών." "The Adoption of Greek Children by Foreigners." *Nomikon Vima* 5, no. 4 [offprint pp. 1–16].

Russell, Jane (1985). *Jane Russell: My Path & My Detours. An Autobiography*. New York: Franklin Watts.

Sakellaropoulos, Spyros, editor, and Grigoris Sakellaropoulos, researcher (2016). *Έτσι αγαπάμε εμείς την Ελλάδα· Πλήρη πρακτικά και ιστορικό των δικών Μπελογιάννη—Τα σήματα Βαβούδη*. *This Is How We Love Greece: Complete Proceedings and Historical Chronology of the Trials of Beloyannis—The Messages of Vavoudis*. Athens: Topos.

Sakis Karagiorgas Foundation, editor (1994–1995). *Η Ελληνική κοινωνία κατά την πρώτη μεταπολεμική περίοδο (1945–1967). 4° Επιστημονικό Συνέδριο, Πάντειον Πανεπιστήμιο, 24–27 Νοεμβρίου 1993*. *Greek Society during the First Postwar Period (1945–1967). Fourth Scientific Conference, Panteion University, 24–27 November 1993*. 2 vols. Athens: Sakis Karagiorgas Foundation.

Sakkas, Dimitris N. (2010). *Ο Κωνσταντίνος Καραμανλής και το κράτος του της περιόδου 1955–63· Χωρίς εξιδανίκευση*. *Konstantinos Karamanlis and His State of the Period 1955–1963: Without Idealization*. Athens: Gutenberg.

Sakkas, John (2013). *Britain and the Greek Civil War, 1944–1949: British Imperialism, Public Opinion and the Coming of the Cold War*. Mainz, Germany: Franz Philipp Rutzen.

Saloutos, Theodore (1964). *The Greeks in the United States*. Cambridge, MA: Harvard University Press.

Samatas, Minas (2014). "A Brief History of the Anticommunist Surveillance in Greece and Its Lasting Impact." In *Histories of State Surveillance in Europe and Beyond*, edited by Kees Boersma, Rosamunde Van Brakel, Chiara Fonio, and Pieter Wagenaar, 49–64. London: Routledge.

Sant Cassia, Paul, with Constantina Bada (1992). *The Making of the Modern Greek Family: Marriage and Exchange in Nineteenth-Century Athens*. Cambridge, UK: Cambridge University Press.

Savery, Constance (1956). *Welcome, Santza*. New York: Longmans, Green and Co.

Schwartz, Lita Linzer, and Florence W. Kaslow, editors (2003). *Welcome Home! An International and Nontraditional Adoption Reader*. Binghamton, NY: Haworth Clinical Practice Press.

Seymore, Malinda L. (2004). "International Adoption & International Comity: When Is Adoption Repugnant [?]" *Texas Wesleyan Law Review* 10: 381–401.

Sfikas, Thanasis D. (2007). *Το "χωλό άλογο"· Οι διεθνείς συνθήκες της ελληνικής* κρίσης, 1941–1949. The "Lame Horse": The International Conditions of the Greek Crisis, 1941–1949. Athens: Vivliorama.

Sfikas, Thanasis D., editor (2011). Το Σχέδιο Μάρσαλ· Ανασυγκρότηση και διαίρεση της Ευρώπης. The Marshall Plan: Reconstruction and Division of Europe. Athens: Patakis.

Sfikas, Thanasis D., and Anna Mahera (2011). "Does the Iliad Need an Agamemnon Version? History, Politics and the Greek 1940s." Historein: A Review of the Past and Other Stories 11: 80–98.

Sicher, Efraim, editor (1998). Breaking Crystal: Writing and Memory after Auschwitz. Urbana: University of Illinois Press.

Simon, Rita J., and Howard Altstein (2000). Adoption across Borders: Serving the Children in Transracial and Intercountry Adoptions. Lanham, MD: Rowman & Littlefield.

Skiadas, Eleftherios G. (1999). Δημοτικό Βρεφοκομείο Αθηνών, 1859–1999. Municipal Orphanage of Athens, 1859–1999. Athens: O Mikros Romios.

Skiadas, Eleftherios G. (2005). Ληξιαρχείον Αθηνών (1836–2006)· Ιστορικά στοιχεία και σωζόμενα αρχεία. The Office of Vital Statistics of Athens (1836–2006): Historical Data and Preserved Archives. Athens: Development Association, Municipality of Athens.

Skouras, Spyros P. (2013). Memoirs (1893–1953). Compiled and edited by Ilias Chrissochoidis. Stanford, CA: Brave World.

Skroumbelos, Thanasis (2005). Bella Ciao· Μυθιστόρημα. Bella Ciao: A Novel. Athens: Ellinika Grammata.

Smith, James M. (2007). Ireland's Magdalen Laundries and the Nation's Architecture of Containment. Notre Dame, IN: University of Notre Dame Press.

Solinger, Rickie (2000) [1st ed. 1992]. Wake Up Little Susie: Single Pregnancy and Race before Roe v. Wade. New York: Routledge.

Solinger, Rickie (2001). Beggars and Choosers: How the Politics of Choice Shapes Adoption, Abortion, and Welfare in the United States. New York: Hill and Wang.

Sotiriou, Dido (1976). Εντολή. Command. Athens: Kedros.

Soumakis, Fevronia K. (2015). A Sacred Paideia: The Greek Orthodox Archdiocese, Immigration, and Education in New York City, 1959–1979. PhD dissertation, Teachers College, Columbia University, New York.

Stathakis, Giorgos (2004). Το Δόγμα Τρούμαν και το Σχέδιο Μάρσαλ· Η ιστορία της αμερικανικής βοήθειας στην Ελλάδα. The Truman Doctrine and the Marshall Plan: The History of American Aid to Greece. Athens: Vivliorama.

Stathopoulos, Petros A. (2005). Κοινωνική πρόνοια· Ιστορική εξέλιξη—Νέες κατευθύνσεις. Social Welfare: Historical Evolution—New Directions. Athens: Papazisis.

Stefanidis, Ioannis D. (2007). Stirring the Greek Nation: Political Culture, Irredentism and Anti-Americanism in Post-War Greece, 1945–1967. Aldershot, UK: Ashgate.

Stefatos, Katherine [Stefatou, Katerina] (2011). Engendering the Nation: Women, State Oppression and Political Violence in Post-war Greece (1946–1974). PhD dissertation, Goldsmiths, University of London.

Stefatos, Katherine [Stefatou, Katerina] (2013). "Επίμετρο για Τα παιδιά της ξενιτιάς." "Afterword to The Children of Foreign Lands." In Τα παιδιά της ξενιτιάς· Η μνήμη *της δικής μου αλήθειας. Αυτοβιογραφία ενός κομμουνιστή.* The Children of Foreign Lands: The Memory of My Truth [by E. K.]. *Autobiography of a Communist* [by P. S. K.], by Electra Karankitsou and Pantelis Simos Karankitsos, 249–58. Athens: Museum of Political Exiles of Aï Stratis.

Steil, Benn (2018). *The Marshall Plan: Dawn of the Cold War.* New York: Simon & Schuster.

Storsbergen, Hester E. (2004). *Psychische gezondheid en welbevinden van volwassen Grieks geadopteerden in Nederland: De invloed van het geadopteerd zijn. Mental Health and Well-being of Greek Adopted Adults in the Netherlands: The Influence of Being Adopted.* PhD dissertation, Utrecht University, Utrecht, the Netherlands.

Storsbergen, Hester E., Femmie Juffer, Maarten J. M. van Son, and Harm 't Hart (2010). "Internationally Adopted Adults Who Did Not Suffer Severe Early Deprivation: The Role of Appraisal of Adoption." *Child and Youth Services Review* 32, no. 2: 191–97.

Stratakis, Antonis (2003). *Κοινωνική Πολιτική στην Ελλάδα κατά την δεκαετία του 1940· Η Κοινωνική Πρόνοια και το Υπουργείο Εθνικής/Κοινωνικής Πρόνοιας. Social Policy in Greece during the Decade of 1940: Social Welfare and the Ministry of National/Social Welfare.* PhD dissertation, School of Philosophy, University of Crete.

Svolopoulos, Konstantinos (2011). *Καραμανλής 1907–1998· Μια πολιτική βιογραφία. Karamanlis, 1907–1998: A Political Biography.* Athens: Ikaros.

Svolopoulos, Konstantinos (1992–2001). *Η ελληνική εξωτερική πολιτική.* Τόμ. 1, *1900–1945.* Τόμ. 2, *1945–1981. The Greek Foreign Policy.* Vol. 1, *1900–1945.* Vol. 2, *1945–1981.* Athens: Estia-Kollaros.

Svolopoulos, Konstantinos, editor (1992–1997). *Κωνσταντίνος Καραμανλής Αρχείο· Γεγονότα & Κείμενα. Konstantinos Karamanlis Archive: Facts and Texts.* 12 vols. Athens: Konstantinos G. Karamanlis Foundation, Ekdotiki Athinon.

Tatsopoulos, Petros (2006). *Η καλοσύνη των ξένων· Μια αληθινή ιστορία. The Kindness of Strangers: A True Story.* Athens: Metaichmio.

Taylor, Diana (2003). *The Archive and the Repertoire: Performing Cultural Memory in the Americas.* Durham, NC: Duke University Press.

Theodoropoulou, Mary (2006). *Μαρία 43668. Maria 43668.* Athens: Nikas Books, Elliniki Paideia.

Theodoropoulou, Mary (unpublished ms.). *Maria 43668.* Revised ed. in English. Athens.

Theodorou, Vas[s]iliki (2015). "Μεταβαλλόμενα πλαίσια συνάφειας μεταξύ εθελοντών, ειδικών και κράτους· Το παράδειγμα του Πατριωτικού Ιδρύματος Προστασίας του Παιδιού." "Changing Frames of Affinity between Volunteers, Experts, and the State: The Case of the Patriotic Foundation for the Protection of the Child." In *Μορφές δημόσιας κοινωνικότητας στην Ελλάδα του εικοστού αιώνα. Forms of Public Sociality in Twentieth-Century Greece,* edited by Efi Avdela, Charis Exertzoglou, and Christos Lyrintzis, 82–100. Rethymno, Crete: University of Crete.

Theologis, Thomas (2006). *Φρειδερίκη και παιδοπόλεις χωρίς φόβο και πάθος. Frederica and the Children's Villages, without Fear or Passion.* Athens: Pelasgos.

Tilly, Louise A., Rachel G. Fuchs, David I. Kertzer, and David L. Ransel (1992). "Child

Abandonment in European History: A Symposium." *Journal of Family History* 17, no. 1: 1–23.

Tomka, Béla (2013). *A Social History of Twentieth-Century Europe*. London: Routledge.

Tourgeli, Giota, and Lina Venturas (2015). "Guiding the Migration Apparatus in Peripheral States of the 'Free World.'" In *International "Migration Management" in the Early Cold War: The Intergovernmental Committee for European Migration*, edited by Lina Venturas, 217–91. Corinth, Greece: University of the Peloponnese, School of Social and Political Sciences.

Touwen, R. Bastiaan (2014). *Grieks bloed. Greek Blood.* The Netherlands: n.p.

Tsaldari, Lina P. (1967). *Εθνικαί κοινωνικαί πολιτικαί προσπάθειαι. National, Social, and Political Efforts.* 2 vols. Athens: n.p.

Tsekou, Katerina (2013). *Έλληνες πολιτικοί πρόσφυγες στην Ανατολική Ευρώπη 1945–1989. Greek Political Refugees in Eastern Europe, 1945–1989.* Athens: Alexandreia.

Tzavaras, Athanase, Dimitris Ploumbidis, and Ariella Asser (2007–2008). "Greek Psychiatric Patients during World War II and the Greek Civil War, 1940–1949." *International Journal of Mental Health* 36, no. 4: 57–66.

Tzimas, Nikos, producer (2010) [1st release, 1980]. *Ο άνθρωπος με το γαρύφαλλο. The Man with the Carnation.* DVD. Athens: Audio Visual Entertainment.

Tziovas, Dimitris, editor (2009). *Greek Diaspora and Migration since 1700: Society, Politics and Culture.* Farnham, UK: Ashgate.

Van Boeschoten, Riki (2015). "Enemies of the Nation—A Nation of Enemies: The Long Greek Civil War." In *After Civil War: Division, Reconstruction, and Reconciliation in Contemporary Europe*, edited by Bill Kissane, 93–120. Philadelphia: University of Pennsylvania Press.

Van Boeschoten, Riki, Tasoula Vervenioti, Eftychia Voutyra, Vasilis Dalkavoukis, and Konstantina Bada, editors (2008). *Μνήμες και λήθη του Ελληνικού Εμφυλίου Πολέμου. Memories and Oblivion of the Greek Civil War.* Thessaloniki: Epikentro.

Van Dongen, Marina, editor (2013a). *De adoptiemonologen. The Adoption Monologues.* Schiedam, the Netherlands: Scriptum.

Van Dongen, Marina (2013b). "Geadopteerd, en dan?" "Adopted. And Then What?" In *De adoptiemonologen. The Adoption Monologues*, edited by Marina van Dongen, 11–12. Schiedam, the Netherlands: Scriptum.

Van Haren, Marten (2006). "Een vreemde eend in de bijt." "Odd Man Out." In *Vertraagde start: Geadopteerden aan het woord. Delayed Start: Adoptees Speaking*, edited by René A. C. Hoksbergen, 247–63. Soesterberg, the Netherlands: Aspekt.

Van Steen, Gonda (2003). "Margarita Papandreou: Bearing Gifts to the Greeks?" *Journal of Modern Greek Studies* 21, no. 2: 245–82.

Van Steen, Gonda (2011). *Theatre of the Condemned: Classical Tragedy on Greek Prison Islands.* Oxford, UK: Oxford University Press.

Van Steen, Gonda (2015). *Stage of Emergency: Theater and Public Performance under the Greek Military Dictatorship of 1967–1974.* Oxford, UK: Oxford University Press.

Van Steen, Gonda (2016). "Μητρώα και ψέματα· 'Βρέθηκαν' στη Θεσσαλονίκη, 'χάθηκαν' στο Τέξας." "Of Ledgers and Lies: 'Found' in Thessaloniki, 'Lost' in Texas." Translated into Greek by Spyros Kakouriotis. *ArcheioTaxio* 18: 192–200.

Vasiloudi, Vasiliki [Vassiloudi, Vassiliki] (2014). "Re-imagining Homeland in the Aftermath of the Greek Civil War (1946–1949): Children's Magazines." *Journal of Modern Greek Studies* 32, no. 1: 165–86.

Vassiloudi, Vassiliki, and Vassiliki Theodorou (2012). "Childhood in the Maelstrom of Political Unrest: The Childtowns (Παιδοπόλεις/Paidopoleis) and the Experience of Displacement in Thrace during the Greek Civil War (1946–1949)." *Journal of the History of Childhood and Youth* 5, no. 1: 118–49.

Vaxevanis, Kostas (2005). *Το χαμένο γονίδιο. The Lost Gene.* Athens: Ellinika Grammata.

Venieris, Dimitris, and Christos Papatheodorou, editors (2003). *Η κοινωνική πολιτική στην Ελλάδα· Προκλήσεις και προοπτικές. Social Policy in Greece: Challenges and Prospects.* Athens: Ellinika Grammata.

Venturas, Lina, editor (2015). *International "Migration Management" in the Early Cold War: The Intergovernmental Committee for European Migration.* Corinth, Greece: University of the Peloponnese, School of Social and Political Sciences.

Verrier, Nancy Newton (2012) [1st ed. 1993]. *The Primal Wound: Understanding the Adopted Child.* Baltimore, MD: Gateway Press.

Vervenioti, Tasoula (2002). "Charity and Nationalism: The Greek Civil War and the Entrance of Right-Wing Women into Politics." In *Right-Wing Women: From Conservatives to Extremists around the World*, edited by Paola Bacchetta and Margaret Power, 115–26. New York: Routledge.

Vervenioti, Tasoula (2009). "Παιδομάζωμα ή/και παιδοφύλαγμα." "Gathering the Children and/or Saving the Children." In *Ιστορία της Ελλάδας του 20ού αιώνα. Τόμ. Δ´.2, Ανασυγκρότηση—Εμφύλιος—παλινόρθωση 1945–1952. History of Greece in the Twentieth Century.* Vol. 4.2, *Reconstruction—Civil War—Restoration, 1945–1952*, edited by Christos Chatziiosif, 82–107. Athens: Vivliorama.

Vinyes, Ricard (2005). *Els nens perduts del franquisme. The Lost Children of Francoism.* Barcelona: Televisió de Catalunya [print and documentary].

Vogli, Elpida (2011). "The Making of Greece Abroad: Continuity and Change in the Modern Diaspora Politics of a 'Historical' Irredentist Homeland." *Nationalism and Ethnic Politics* 17: 14–33.

Voglis, Polymeris (2002). *Becoming a Subject: Political Prisoners during the Greek Civil War.* New York: Berghahn Books.

Voglis, Polymeris (2013). "Επίμετρο· Η υποκειμενικότητα ενός κομμουνιστή." "Afterword: The Subjectivity of a Communist." In *Από δω και πέρα θα είσαι ο Νίκος. From Now On, You'll Be Nikos*, by Kostas Paschaloudis, 191–98. Thessaloniki: Epikentro.

Voglis, Polymeris (2014). *Η αδύνατη επανάσταση· Η κοινωνική δυναμική του εμφυλίου πολέμου. The Weak Revolution: The Social Dynamics of the [Greek] Civil War.* Athens: Alexandreia.

Volbert, Alexander, and George D. Demopoulos (1989). *Stabilization Policies in Greece in the Context of Modern Macroeconomic Theory.* Berlin: Duncker and Humblot.

Vorria, Panayiota, Maria Ntouma, Maria Vairami, and Michael Rutter (2015). "Attachment Relationships of Adolescents Who Spent Their Infancy in Residential Group Care: The Greek Metera Study." *Attachment & Human Development* 17, no. 3: 257–71.

Vournas, Tasos (1981). *Ποιοί και γιατί σκότωσαν το Νίκο Μπελογιάννη και τους* συντρόφους του; *Who and Why Did They Kill Nikos Beloyannis and His Comrades?* Athens: Tolidis.

Voutira, Eftihia [Voutyra, Eftychia], and Aigli Brouskou (2000). "'Borrowed Children' in the Greek Civil War." In *Abandoned Children,* edited by Catherine Panter-Brick and Malcolm T. Smith, 92–110. Cambridge, UK: Cambridge University Press.

Vrachniaris, Christos (1983). *Τα χρόνια της λαϊκής εποποιίας· Πόλεμος—Κατοχή—Αντίσταση. The Years of the People's Epic Struggle: War—Occupation—Resistance.* Athens: Panorama.

Weil, Richard H. (1984). "International Adoptions: The Quiet Migration." *International Migration Review* 18, no. 2: 276–93.

White, Hayden (1999). "Historical Emplotment and the Problem of Truth in Historical Representation." In *Figural Realism: Studies in the Mimesis Effect,* 27–42. Baltimore, MD: Johns Hopkins University Press.

White, Hayden (2010). "Writing in the Middle Voice." In *The Fiction of Narrative: Essays on History, Literature, and Theory, 1957–2007,* edited by Robert Doran, 255–62. Baltimore, MD: Johns Hopkins University Press.

Winslow, Rachel E. (2012a). *Colorblind Empire: International Adoption, Social Policy, and the American Family, 1945–1976.* PhD dissertation, Department of History, University of California, Santa Barbara, CA.

Winslow, Rachel E. (2012b). "Immigration Law and Improvised Policy in the Making of International Adoption, 1948–1961." *Journal of Policy History* 24, no. 2: 319–49.

Winslow, Rachel R. (2015). "Thinking Historically about International Adoption." In *The Intercountry Adoption Debate: Dialogues across Disciplines,* edited by Robert L. Ballard, Naomi H. Goodno, Robert F. Cochran, and Jay A. Milbrandt, 331–47. Newcastle upon Tyne, UK: Cambridge Scholars Publishing.

Winslow, Rachel R. (2017). *The Best Possible Immigrants: International Adoption and the American Family.* Philadelphia: University of Pennsylvania Press.

Wittner, Lawrence S. (1982). *American Intervention in Greece, 1943–1949.* New York: Columbia University Press.

Woo, Susie (2015). "Imagining Kin: Cold War Sentimentalism and the Korean Children's Choir." *American Quarterly* 67, no. 1: 25–53.

Wood-Ritsatakis, Anne (1970). *An Analysis of the Health and Welfare Services in Greece.* Athens: Center of Planning and Economic Research.

Yalouri, Eleana (2001). *The Acropolis: Global Fame, Local Claim.* Oxford, UK: Berg.

Yngvesson, Barbara (2002). "Placing the 'Gift Child' in Transnational Adoption." *Law and Society Review* 36, no. 2. Special issue on nonbiological parenting, 227–56.

Yngvesson, Barbara (2010). *Belonging in an Adopted World: Race, Identity, and Transnational Adoption.* Chicago: University of Chicago Press.

Zahra, Tara (2011). *The Lost Children: Reconstructing Europe's Families After World War II.* Cambridge, MA: Harvard University Press.

Zeitlin, Froma I. (2001). "The Vicarious Witness: Belated Memory and Authorial Presence in Recent Holocaust Literature." In *Shaping Losses: Cultural Memory and the Holocaust,* edited by Julia Epstein and Lori Hope Lefkovitz, 128–60. Urbana: University of Illinois Press.

Zelizer, Viviana A. (1985). *Pricing the Priceless Child: The Changing Social Value of Children*. New York: Basic Books.

Zervakis, Peter A. (1997). "The Greek Lobby and the Reemergence of Anti-Communism in the United States after World War II." In *Enemy Images in American History*, edited by Ragnhild Fiebig-von Hase and Ursula Lehmkuhl, 301–36. Providence, RI: Berghahn Books.

Zouvas, Panagis D. (1956). *Η Βασίλισσα Φρειδερίκη εις την Υπηρεσίαν του Έθνους. Queen Frederica in the Service of the Nation*. Athens: n.p.

SUGGESTIONS FOR FURTHER READING
AND VIEWING

Greek-to-American Adoption Narratives
(mostly book-length publications)

Dionou, C. Dionysios (2011). *Twentieth-Century Janissary: An Orphan's Search for Freedom, Family, and Heritage.* Bloomington, IN: Xlibris.

Giangardella, Joanna S. (2011). *The Girl from the Tower: A Journey of Lies.* Lexington, KY: CreateSpace Independent Publishing Platform.

Heckinger, Maria (2019). *Beyond the Third Door. Based on a True Story.* Vancouver, WA: n.p.

Johnson, Deborah (2003). "Addendum by Deborah Johnson." In *Welcome Home! An International and Nontraditional Adoption Reader,* edited by Lita Linzer Schwartz and Florence W. Kaslow, 50–54. Binghamton, NY: Haworth Clinical Practice Press.

Kelmis, Maria (2012). *Golden Strangers: An Adoption Memoir.* Bloomington, IN: AuthorHouse.

Moessinger, Naomi (2003). "From Couple to Family." In *Welcome Home! An International and Nontraditional Adoption Reader,* edited by Lita Linzer Schwartz and Florence W. Kaslow, 35–50. Binghamton, NY: Haworth Clinical Practice Press.

Greek-to-Dutch Adoption Narratives

De Boer, Antoinette (2019). *De vondeling van Kreta. The Foundling from Crete.* Overveen, the Netherlands: n.p.

Rijnsdorp, Sonia (2017). *Een kist met geheimen.* Zoetermeer, the Netherlands: Lecturium.

Rijnsdorp, Sonia (2018). *A Coffin Full of Secrets.* English translation in pdf distributed by the author.

Touwen, R. Bastiaan (2014). *Grieks bloed. Greek Blood.* The Netherlands: n.p.

Movies and Documentaries

Borshay Liem, Deann, director (2000). *First Person Plural.*

Borshay Liem, Deann, director (2010). *In the Matter of Cha Jung Hee.*

Borshay Liem, Deann, director (2016). *Geographies of Kinship: The Korean Adoption Story.*

Dolgin, Gail, and Vicente Franco, directors (2002). *Daughter from Danang.*

Frears, Stephen, director (2013). *Philomena.*

Grigoratos, Dionysis, director (2015). *Fils de Grèce: Τα παιδιά του Εμφυλίου. Sons of Greece: The Children of the Civil War.*

Loach, Jim, director (2010). *Oranges and Sunshine.*

McBrearty, Don, director (1995). *Butterbox Babies.*

Papaioannou, Sofia, director (2019). *Τα χαμένα παιδιά της Ελλάδας του Ψυχρού Πολέμου. The Lost Children of Greece of the Cold War.* Broadcast of 18 April 2019 of *360 Moires, 360 Degrees.* Available online at http://www.alphatv.gr/show/360/ekpobes_360/?vtype=play-er&vid=37568&showId=823&year=2019/ [last accessed 7 June 201 https://www.youtube.com/watch?v=0hIxbgAYz_c&t=9s [with English subtitles].]. https://www.facebook.com/TheEftychiaProject/videos/361153664748271/ [with English subtitles].

Papanikola, Anna, director (2009–2010). *Τα παιδιά του "Μητέρα." The Children of "Metera."* Mega TV, *Protagonistes, Archive of Stavros Theodorakis.* Documentary on the Greek-to-Dutch adoptees. Available online at http://www.alphatv.gr/show/360/ekpobes_360/?vtype=play-er&vid=37568&showId=823&year=2019/ https://www.youtube.com/watch?v=0hIxbgAYz_c&t=9s https://www.facebook.com/TheEftychiaProject/videos/361153664748271/ [the latter two with English subtitles; all last accessed 12 September 2019].

Tzimas, Nikos, producer (2010) [1st release, 1980]. *Ο άνθρωπος με το γαρύφαλλο. The Man with the Carnation.* DVD. Athens: Audio Visual Entertainment.

Van der Toorn, André, and Wendy Hesp, producers (2017). *Mijn naam was Kostas. My Name Was Kostas.* The Netherlands: Wasp Media and KRO/NCRV. Available online at http://www.kro-ncrv.nl/mijnnaamwaskostas/seizoenen/seizoen-2017/mijn-naam-was-Kostas [last accessed 15 Sept. 2018].

Vinyes, Ricard (2005). *Els nens perduts del franquisme. The Lost Children of Franco-ism.* Barcelona: Televisió de Catalunya [print and documentary].

INDEX

Locators containing *"f"* indicate a figure. Locators containing "n" indicate a note.